MY DANCING WHITE HORSES

My Dancing
WHITE HORSES

ALOIS PODHAJSKY

AUTHOR OF

The White Stallions of Vienna

Translated by

FRANCES HOGARTH-GAUTE

HOLT, RINEHART AND WINSTON

New York   Chicago   San Francisco

ACKNOWLEDGMENTS

The illustrations are reproduced by permission of the following:
Werner Menzendorf, Berlin (Nos. 10, 11); Hildegard Zeuner, Munich (Nos. 17, 18); Gustav J. Essinger, Frankfurt (Nos. 24, 25); Tony Armstrong-Jones, London, Agentur Schweitzer-Hecht, Munich (Nos. 41, 48); Fritz Kern, Vienna (Nos. 51, 52); Charles J. Belden, St Petersburg, Florida (No. 16); Canada Pictures, Toronto (Nos. 30, 31); Conrad Horster, Cologne (No. 37); Carl Pospesch, Salzburg (Nos. 46, 47); Heereslichtbildstelle, Vienna (No. 6); Bruno Kerschner, Salzburg (No. 13); Erwin Horninger, Wels (No. 19); Lothar Rübelt, Vienna (No. 20); Publifoto, Rome (No. 21); Wilhelm Karl Sturm, Salzburg (No. 22); Irish Times, Dublin (No. 23); Deutsche Presse-Agentur (No. 27); Budd, New York (No. 28); Associated Press (No. 29); Heinrich von der Becke, Berlin (No. 32); Dierks, Basle (No. 33); Theodor Janssen, Kaltzum b. Düsseldorf (No. 35); Guido Wedding, Essen (No. 38); Barratt's Photo Press, London (No. 39); Hans Hammarskiöld, Stockholm (No. 40); Mateo, Barcelona (No. 43); Carretero, Madrid (No. 45); Herbert Kofler, Vienna (No. 49); Gustav Schikola, Vienna (No. 53); Poll, Vienna (No. 54); Podhajsky (Nos. 1, 2, 3, 4, 5, 7, 8, 9, 12, 14, 15, 26, 34, 36, 42, 44, 50).

PREFACE

IN the following pages I shall attempt to describe the unique success and world-wide triumph of the Spanish Riding School and the white animal artists in my care. This is in response to the demands of many friends and the requests of countless fans and followers of the Spanish Riding School all over the world. This book will serve as a memorial, presented by their riders, to the superb grace and magnificent artistry of the Lipizzaner horses.

It is frightening to think how quickly a rider's achievement is forgotten! The painstaking labour of a sculptor is still admired after thousands of years, while pictures and musical compositions continue for centuries to excite those who appreciate art. Yet the rider's creative work ends with the relatively short life of his horse; of the perfect harmony and grace of their enchanting movements, which bring so much pleasure to all lovers of beauty, only a faint memory remains after a few years, and even this fades and is soon obliterated by the merciless pressure of the present. Riders and horses who once had the power to stir the emotions of thousands are completely forgotten.

Perhaps this book may succeed in keeping alive for a little longer the memory of the triumphs of the Lipizzaner, the animal members of an ancient riding-school. Their world-wide successes have brought them praise and acclamation, thus making them the best possible ambassadors for Austria.

When I was entrusted in the spring of 1939 with the directorship of the Spanish Riding School in Vienna I had no inkling that this was to be the hardest task of my life. It must have been difficult enough to be director of such an institution after 1918, when its traditional setting was lost after the disintegration of the defeated capital of the Habsburg empire, and the motorization and mechanization of everyday life drove out many habits that were dear to us. But the Second World War with its totality, and the demands of new ideologies allowing only certain traditions to be preserved, brought problems that seemed insoluble and seriously threatened the continued existence of the oldest riding-school in Austria—indeed, in the world.

Now as I look back I marvel that I managed to survive so many crises and lead the Spanish Riding School out of the chaos into a happier future. Count Ferdinand Arco-Valley, in the disturbed days of 1945, gave his own explanation: the Spanish Riding School was saved only because I looked upon it as my personal property, and nursed it and protected it as such, fighting for its survival with all the passion that only such circumstances can arouse.

There is a great deal of truth in this, for from the first moment I took over the Spanish Riding School I did not consider it as a pleasant change in my long military career, but as a definite vocation. For me caring for the Lipizzaner horses was the realization of my life's ambition, for I am bound to admit that I have always been what is commonly called 'horse-mad.' Nevertheless, enthusiasm, growing in the course of time into deep love, would obviously not by itself have been enough to bring success. I shall be eternally grateful that I was lucky enough to have the necessary ability to accomplish my great mission.

The result of my efforts has been that my name is inseparably linked with the Spanish Riding School, as I have been told countless times; so it seems right—indeed, my duty—to describe my own career in some detail, giving an account of the path I had to tread to become what used to be called in the Austro-Hungarian Army a *Reitkaiser*. At the same time I take the opportunity to proffer to all my riders and helpers the thanks that is their due, and to pay tribute to the tremendous spiritual strength we have drawn from our mutual affection, faith, and loyalty.

I belong to the generation destined to live at the meeting-point of two eras, and will begin by looking back to a long-vanished age, so often described as 'the good old days.'

CONTENTS

ILLUSTRATIONS

CHAPTER 1

Youth

My father was a serving soldier in the great Austro-Hungarian Army, and the varied and colourful Danube empire was the vast homeland of my earliest years. The romantic mountain scenery of Bosnia and Hercegovina, the unending plains of Hungary and Croatia, the broad, storm-tossed territories of Galicia and Bukovina, all these countries were just as much my home as Vienna, where my mother was born, or the beloved countryside of what is now the Republic of Austria, which, perhaps because of my mother's homesickness, always features in nostalgic dreams of my childhood.

Yet in all that vast fatherland there was not a single strip of ground that was really home, in the sense of being an essential part of my youthful memories. My upbringing was a succession of farewells inevitable with constant changes of garrison. So many upsets are not normally without drawbacks, and a new posting in the Austro-Hungarian Empire usually meant also a change of language. We went from Serbian to Polish, then back to Croatian, Hungarian, Bohemian, and many other tongues. The effect on me was that everywhere I went I had to make myself understood to my newly found playmates in yet another language, and as soon as I had got into the way of it I was once more the ugly duckling of another strange farmyard. The peoples among whom we had to live showed every possible variation of character from crazy hot temper to the deepest melancholy.

It is not surprising, therefore, that with the constant change of cities and countries I never had a particularly strong feeling for home, and my childhood was fraught with difficulty. But, whether I was in the savage north or the hot south of the great empire, one thing remained constant and unshaken: my passionate devotion to the magnificent horsemanship of Austria-Hungary, a passion that was to have a decisive influence on my youth.

17

I was born on February 24, 1898, in the garrison of Mostar, a northern town in the province of Hercegovina, which had recently become a part of the Austro-Hungarian Empire. When the Army chaplain lifted me out of the font my first reaction was to grab at his war medals, and this he interpreted as a sign that I should become a soldier.

But I had no chance of closer acquaintance with the town of my birth, for after barely a year I was wrapped up in a warm shawl because of the strong bora, the dreaded cold wind that swept across this southern landscape, and taken over mountain roads in a post-chaise on a journey lasting several hours, with many unwelcome halts, to the second camp of my life— at Travnik, in Bosnia. From there we soon moved to Esseg, in Croatia, where for the first time the seriousness of life impinged on the carefree days of my childhood. I had to go to a school where I was forced to speak a foreign language—Croatian.

But the most vivid memories of this period are the hours when I managed to steal away—often to the annoyance of my parents—and with thumping heart and shining eyes admire the drill and exercises of the squadrons and regiments of the Austro-Hungarian cavalry, rich in experience, the traditions of horsemanship and knightly combat. Even as a very small boy I could identify them all: the Hussars, with their rich frogged braid; the resplendent Uhlans; the Dragoons, who looked so elegant because of the very simplicity of their tunics. And I could name accurately the regiments that had joined Wallenstein in decisive battles, those that had been led to victory by Prince Eugène and under Father Radetzky added new laurels to those already won. So it was understandable that one deep desire governed all my thoughts and actions; to be allowed in due course to wear the uniform of one of these illustrious regiments. But for the time being I had to be satisfied with merely watching them, for my father insisted that I should pass my school examinations before any decision was taken about my career, and so my entry into the Cavalry Cadet School remained a dream that was never to be realized.

My interest in the cavalry was combined with an intense love of horses, and I seized every opportunity to get near them, offering them stolen titbits, or, often for hours on end, watching their work in the riding-school instead of playing with companions of my own age. I was as thrilled and delighted by the beautiful and exciting manœuvres of the riders as I was deeply shocked by the rough handling they often gave their mounts.

It had been my dearest wish as long as I could remember to have a horse of my own, a wish that was in one sense fulfilled about my third birthday when I was given a magnificent grey—unfortunately, only a rocking-horse. But on my wooden charger I tried to imitate the drill of the soldiers, executing all the movements with as much care and attention as I saw being taken in the riding-school. Even though I enjoyed these early rides, my thoughts darted way beyond my trusty steed, building up a picture of a real horse, still the object of my dreams. I sometimes managed to persuade our servants to let me sit on one of my father's horses and make a round of the barrack square perched high on its back. Then my joy knew no bounds and I thought I was a king. Later I took clandestine riding lessons with some of the grooms who were fond of me. It was often terribly difficult to conceal the damage to my clothes and myself that resulted from these escapades, for my stern father would have none of his son's passion for riding, and my surreptitious excursions had to be kept from him.

It was years later before I had my first serious riding lessons, but these stolen pleasures of my childhood were not to be spoiled by the succession of postings to Lemberg, Tarnopol, Sadogura, Czernowitz, Vienna, and Wels, although these changes always brought their own difficulties: other schools, new playmates, foreign languages and customs—how hard it was to keep having to adjust myself.

The constant change of schools brought, as well as the many language problems, some grotesque experiences. In Tarnopol, for instance, there was no German school, and because I must go to a Croatian and not a Polish one my parents found a tutor for me. He taught me German, but often got tied up over the grammar. To avoid gross errors my mother attended these classes, always ready to deal immediately with any howlers. Once during a dictation, when their combined efforts proved fruitless, my father had to be called in to help. He began patiently enough to straighten out the confusion, but when the excited teacher obstinately stood his ground the classes were discontinued and I never again saw this champion of the German language.

At last, when I was twelve years old, I was allowed to take my first riding lessons with a dragoon sergeant-major, proud possessor of a magnificent moustache. The appearance of this warrior was so terrifying, and his teaching so harsh, that I soon realized that riding was not intended merely for pleasure. Indeed, I often clenched my teeth with pain as I sat on the back of this noblest of all animals, and when I dismounted my grey riding-breeches were often tinged with red. In other ways, too, my instructor's methods were completely barbaric. He asked me a few days after I started, while I was still riding without stirrups, whether I would like to jump one of the hurdles in the riding-school. I did not think I was ready to meet such a challenge, not yet having mastered the difficulties of balance and a good seat, and answered unhesitatingly and frankly—for I always had a habit of voicing my thoughts and showing my feelings, which was to lead me into a good deal of unpleasantness in later life—"No." So the sergeant-major drove me over the hurdle, but I could not stay in the saddle and fell off. I was made to remount and repeat the jump, once more with the same lack of success. This went on until, at the eighth attempt, I managed to keep my seat, but it was not really a triumph, for it spoiled all my pleasure in jumping for a very long time. However, it did not stop me from enduring still greater suffering day after day, for I hoped that one day I might be considered a worthy candidate for admission to the illustrious Austro-Hungarian cavalry.

Later, when I became a riding-master myself, I was able to use the experience I had gained from my first teacher to help my pupils. One should increase the demands made on the young rider by degrees, so that his skill is not too painfully acquired, thus perhaps ruining any possible enjoyment right at the start, and I always took a great deal of trouble to make my pupils enjoy riding instead of hating it. It was to the moustachioed tyrant of my youth that I owed this piece of wisdom.

At the outset of my riding career, therefore, I learned two important maxims of the greatest significance for any kind of success: that self-discipline and self-control are essential, and that in life even what appears bad can be turned to good use. The way to the heights, whether in art, sport, or ordinary life, is long, thorny, and thickly beset with obstacles. It will lead us to our goal only if we have conquered ourselves sufficiently to overcome all the difficulties we meet. But self-control is the most important virtue for anyone who hopes to lead other living creatures or be their master. This quality is just as important for a statesman as for a rider, a fact more widely appreciated in the old days, when it was considered good form for all people in high places to take an interest in riding. On horseback they had the opportunity of practising self-control and cultivating a virtue that would stand them in good stead in the fulfilment of the duties that were their destiny. The human qualities that we nowadays include under the heading 'chivalrous' are qualities that were at one time expected of any rider—then called a 'cavalier' (both words from the French *cheval*)—so it seems that the value of riding in the upbringing of children has been recognized for many hundreds of years. Self-discipline and self-control, however, develop only with stern training, and I am particularly grateful to my parents, who by giving me a strict upbringing laid the best possible foundations for my further development.

A great many things that I did not understand as a child, and perhaps thought pointless, have helped me in later life to endure with greater fortitude unrealized expectations, renunciations, and disappointments. I am absolutely convinced of the importance of a systematic and uncompromising upbringing for children. In less happy situations and moments where self-sacrifice is called for—and they come to all of us—we should be grateful to those who brought us up for the self-discipline they tried to instil, often with great difficulty, to make life easier for us.

After the outbreak of the First World War my youthful ambition was at last realized. In May 1916 I enlisted in the 4th Kaiser Ferdinand Dragoons.

How different it all was from my dreams and expectations! Modern war had taken over with brutal might, and destroyed almost all the romance of belonging to the cavalry. Instead of making a dashing charge, naked blade in hand, on the back of that noblest and truest of comrades, the horse, and meeting the foe face to face, we now always had to attack the enemy on foot from a trench, without even seeing him properly. Only very seldom did the opportunity arise for us to gallop against the enemy in small patrols, brandishing our flashing sabres. But, during our long stretches of months at a time in the trenches, we had one consolation: we could now and again visit our four-legged friends, look into their faithful, loyal eyes, and, as we rested our cheeks against their soft necks, dream of heavenly rides upon their backs.

In 1917, alas! we were forced to take final leave of our horses, which were withdrawn for the artillery and taken off to other duties. This was the most serious blow in my life, and it became more and more obvious that for me this was a real crisis. Besides, the transition from a careful home, where there were high standards of morals and manners, and ideals were lovingly nurtured, to the dull realities of my new life was altogether too abrupt, and it unquestionably had a shattering effect on a sheltered sensitive boy of eighteen. But there was no time for such sentimental thoughts, particularly during those war-riven years, even though they did weigh on the individual.

Life mercilessly demands its tribute, and the long war against a world of enemies took its toll of all the participants. Our rousing successes of the first year were followed by a stalemate, with many reverses, and the noisy patriotic rejoicings had long subsided into a dumb resignation as the tramp of the marching soldiers became ever more weary. Where was the romance of the cavalry now? Riders without horses, and horses starved to veritable skeletons! The war became for man and beast an unending martyrdom, and the ideals of a stormy youth, so stirred by stories of knightly combat, were lost for ever in the muddy trenches of Flanders, and all that remained was a sense of duty. Men under a similar obligation were bound together by an abiding sense of comradeship, and this bond, unsullied by selfish ambition, helped us to endure even the blackest hours, so that we often preferred the Front to our homeland with all its troubles and worries. Of course, we did not dream, or at least refused to believe, that a centuries-old empire lay on its deathbed.

And I too offered to this dying Colossus, this holy alliance of the peoples of Central Europe, my blood sacrifice, and in October 1917 made my sad journey home with a severe wound in the neck. And then came the fearful end of the Danube monarchy. The mighty empire was divided into several small states, the great transformation was complete, and a world in which I had grown up, and in which I steadfastly believed, had suddenly disappeared. Everything that I held sacred and inviolable had been trampled in the mire, every heroic deed was looked upon as arrogant madness, and the mob ruled in the streets, cursing and attacking the brave soldiers who for years on end had risked their lives for their country. All these ugly demonstrations bore the honoured name of Revolution. Owing to my upbringing, and my unshakable belief in tradition, the word 'revolution' had always had a dread sound for me; the events of November 1918 gave me no reason to modify my opinion.

In any case the revolution was not the usual uprising of a downtrodden people, but the complete collapse of a world empire. Peoples who, in spite of differences of language, had lent their strength to one of the mightiest powers in Europe because of their long-standing alliance, and had fought and died together for the same causes on countless fields of battle, now opposed each other in self-destructive hatred. A noble conception was robbed of its splendour and trampled underfoot by the raging masses. Only later were these peoples to recognize that they had utterly destroyed the safety and security of their own homes in the troubled days of 1918.

For me almost all the playgrounds of my childhood had suddenly become foreign lands. The majority of the officers of the old imperial army streamed back into the little area of German Austria that remained. I myself, having lost my voice as a result of my wound, battled like a bird with a broken wing against the merciless storms of life. Grim years followed, and I was fleetingly happy if, without being seen, I could offer a crust of bread to some resigned, dispirited nag pulling a cart, or even pat its neck. So ended the dream of my youth, and left behind it only unbroken sadness, a sadness that I felt again many years later when I was asked during the Third Reich why it was that so many of the ex-officers of the Austro-Hungarian Army were so melancholy. My reply came from the bottom of my heart. They were in deep mourning for a lost empire, an empire that had been not only great, but also very beautiful.

CHAPTER 2

—◆◆◆—

Learning to be a Rider

Years went by before a gleam of light lit up my dreary existence. My voice came back—against all the prognoses of the doctors—and in 1922 I was able to exchange my office stool for the regimental service I loved. How happy I was to be allowed to work with living things instead of dusty documents! If my activities as officers' instructor and dispatch-rider to an infantry regiment, as well as responsible guardian of all its horses, hardly lived up to the dashing ideas I had held as a youth, I was none the less delighted with this new sphere of activity after the bitterness of the past few years.

My knowledge of riding, which I had begun to acquire in very early youth, was greatly increased by my first riding-master in the Officers' School, Rittmeister Count Teleki, who singled me out from the rest and took me under his wing. I was one of his favourite pupils, and I considered him my ideal of what a rider should be, and because of his manly qualities he influenced us all strongly.

He often demanded more of me than of the others, but I quickly saw the good intentions behind his severity. At this time I was a very self-satisfied rider, and when I managed to gain some mastery over a difficult horse, and did not fall off at stiff jumps, I considered myself very clever. With more practice I grew less arrogant and more proficient, for I now realized how rarely we humans reach perfection. It was enirely owing to my grounding in the Officers' School that I was able to train my pupils of the 5th Infantry Regiment to such a pitch that in a short time they could beat crack cavalry regiments.

Besides teaching I had the chance to improve the available material, for the horses were very mediocre. Of all the animals in my charge a big chestnut called Napoleon, who was harnessed to a field kitchen, interested me most. His name seemed ill-suited to his prosaic occupation, and so I tried to ride him, hoping to discover his possibilities as a jumper. The chestnut soon proved worthy of his name, for in 1925 we managed to attract general attention in an open competition. Everybody was full of admiration for my Napoleon, and absolutely astounded at the infantry officer who had routed so many stylish cavalry men. Thereafter the jumping events in the various competitions in Vienna became my concern, until I was ordered one day by my commanding officer to enter for dressage as well. I did not find it at all easy to give this temperamental horse the special training needed, and so as not to risk hampering his hard-won progress I gave up jumping almost completely during these months.

At last I was able to display my winter's work in an Elementary dressage event before critical judges, and was quite well placed. But when I went into the ring for the jumping I noticed immediately, to my great delight, how much Napoleon's form had improved, and realized for the first time the importance of giving show jumpers training in dressage.

In post-War Austria there was a fixed idea that there was no connexion at all between dressage and jumping, so it was only too easily understandable that I, accepting the views held in leading riding circles, should have come up against initial difficulties in training Napoleon purely as a jumper. As soon as I realized that through his dressage schooling he was able to conquer his other difficulties much better the scales fell from my eyes. This experience enriched my modest knowledge of horsemanship and enabled me later to turn apparently hopeless hunters into successful jumpers.

After this dressage interlude I had several successes with Napoleon and Erna, a cavalry reject whom I had also begun to ride, and often beat all my fellow-competitors, including many who had been to the Militär-Reit- und Fahrlehrerinstitut, as well as cavalry officers. As a result the Inspector of Cavalry insisted on my returning to my troop, and in the summer of 1927 I had to take leave of my gallant Napoleon, who had been chosen as a mount for my erstwhile C.O. I hated saying goodbye, for Napoleon had given me many happy hours and taught me so much during our successful competitions. But Fate at least allowed our partnership to end in a fitting manner: on my last public appearance riding Napoleon I won the final jumping event at the International Horse Show in Vienna against a host of famous riders. So I parted in a glorious moment from my faithful partner in the first triumphs of my riding career.

After my return to the cavalry I took a two-year course at the Militär-Reit- und Fahrlehrerinstitut at Schlosshof, where, in addition to jumping, I tried to delve into the mysteries of the finer points of dressage. For a long time I tried to take an equal interest in both, but jumping remained my chief interest. Now for the first time I really understood the fundamental difference between these two branches of the sport: in jumping training should be gradually stepped up and reach its peak with the competition, while dressage involves uninterrupted schooling and polishing of the horse's behaviour, the best way to achieve this often being, in fact, to enter for competitions. Thus good dressage training never ceases, and the rider finds his real satisfaction not so much in public success as in the ever-widening range of his pupil's capabilities, until with growing understanding the highest goal is ultimately reached: the fusion of two living beings moving as one. More than in any other branch of the sport the rider becomes proficient not only in physical skill, but in understanding the strength and weakness of his partner and grasping what is in his mind. A horse untrained in dressage is like a mosaic as yet unassembled, and it is for the rider to put each of the many pieces carefully into its correct place. I began to find great pleasure in this peaceful, patient task.

My knowledge and skill were tremendously enriched by my posting to the Austrian Militär-Reit- und Fahrlehrerinstitut. Good, hand-picked horses were at my disposal, and the best riding instructors were chosen to teach me. I was able to store up some important though not always positive impressions at this time, and make use of them later in both teaching and riding. For instance, I became convinced through my daily observations in the school that a good riding teacher's prime duty is to awaken and instil into his pupil a love of horses and to guard against any sort of aversion or fear. It did not add to the pleasure of riding when pupils had to be dragged out of the way because the remounts, most of them stud horses being tried out, responded to these less exciting duties by bucking crazily and delightedly tossing up their depressing riders in a mighty arc. The toll of broken bones and injuries sustained by fallen riders in this way often reached disturbing proportions, so naturally the pupils' confidence sank accordingly, and the horses became alarmingly wild. For many of my companions riding horses like these became utter misery, and their stay at the Institute a complete hell, while their joy in riding, which had barely begun to blossom, was turned into definite hatred of the sport. I was able to judge for myself how important self-confidence is for the rider, for Juro, a notoriously difficult horse, gave me an effective lesson.

I can still recall the daily performance in the second-year remount section. As soon as we were mounted and ready to move off the slightest noise would be a signal for wild bucking, and after a few minutes the riderless horses would gallop away, while their companions, still more or less under control, strained to follow them. Juro, always the ringleader, expressed his views particularly strongly, and the rider he had unseated usually had to be dragged unconscious out of the school. Then began a search by the teacher for a new victim for this uncontrollable beast, and in due course the choice fell on me. In the first few lessons I managed to keep my seat in spite of Juro's bucking, and my self-confidence was so strengthened by this that I began to believe I should ultimately master this ill-disposed animal. This faith helped me along in the ensuing days to counter all the attacks of my companion and to become familiar with his plan of action: he would swerve sharply to the left without warning and, lowering his head and neck, buck vigorously until he had thrown his unbalanced rider out of the saddle.

After I realized what to expect from him when I urged him forward I once forced him across a large field at a flat gallop. I took the precaution of having a companion on either side, thinking that the tremendous pace would prevent the usual wicked dart to the left. I was wrong! At top speed, practically knocking over the horse beside him, Juro went into his usual act and dumped me on the grass with such force that I was literally unable to see or hear. But, much worse, I now lost all my confidence and increased Juro's sense of power. From then on I frequently and most unwillingly kissed the dust, and was very satisfied if I could come out of these involuntary dismountings more or less in one piece. But gradually I succeeded in forestalling the intentions of my bucking horse, and Juro lost his tendency to swerve, until at last I really mastered him, and as long as I rode him he never made any attempt to disobey me. Even when, after months, he was given another rider he remained well-mannered, until he managed to surprise the newcomer, who promptly fell off. From that moment he once more became the rider's dread.

Later in my teaching days I always did my utmost to prevent young riders falling off, taking a great deal of trouble to boost their self-confidence. I tried equally to prevent young horses from getting rid of their riders, and so cultivating ideas of their own power and superiority. By this method, which I later followed in building up the Spanish Riding School, my pupils enjoyed their riding more, and perhaps I was able to bring at least one or two of them to the greatest of all earthly pleasures, to be found nowhere but on horseback.

I had my own views, too, on the correct training for hunting. Riding to hounds is undoubtedly one of the happiest experiences a rider can have if he is competent. There is certainly nothing more delightful than galloping rhythmically behind the hounds and enjoying the glorious tints of the autumn countryside. But to be able to taste this pleasure a rider needs a horse that does not have to be constantly watched and is willing to co-operate. Good hunters, however, will be available only if they are carefully and properly trained. Unfortunately, this was not at all the way things were done. Young horses, barely broken in to riding, were plunged straight into the hunting field, and the instructors hardly bothered to find out how their pupils were faring with these novice horses.

From an academic point of view this method of training was absolutely wrong for both man and horse. The rider might perhaps gain some worth-while experience, but the young horses that had scarcely had a chance to make the adjustment from their old existence—part of which had been spent out at grass—were so terrified when they were sent out hunting, without any preparation, that they started to tremble as soon as they saw the hounds, and bolted off as soon as the field began to move. This was not out of instinctive eagerness for the hunt, but the direct result of the unreasonable demands put upon them. Much the same thing happens to men who have overtrained.

Thus the riders tasted none of the joy of riding to hounds, and it was no unfamiliar sight to see them struggling with their bolting horses, trying not to make a nuisance of themselves in the hunting field. The riding instructor did not fully appreciate the devastating results of his teaching, for he himself was riding a well-broken horse. Thus I soon realized that the teacher, who must always set an example to his pupils, must also be very careful not to demand the impossible. If only this rule had been followed the allocation of horses for hunting would have been made quite differently.

What, then, was the outcome of these wild exhibitions in the hunting field? Unwilling, even angry riders, with no taste at all for the sport, giving it up prematurely, and, worse still, ruined horses in a lamentable condition after a single season— altogether a costly experiment which a civilian would never have been able to afford. One wit made an apt remark: "Our poor horses will go on chasing the hounds until there is nothing left of them but their shoes!" Thus hunting not only lost its value as a sport, but was robbed of its enchantment. However, I was able to turn to good use later even this instance of thoroughly bad training.

While I was taking this course at the Militär-Reit- und Fahrlehrerinstitut I managed also to improve my own riding by plenty of practice, and I came to realize more and more how important it is for the teacher to be able to impart his knowledge to his pupils—both two- and four-legged— and to achieve this with the greatest possible integrity.

Times without number I was shown just how things ought not to be done. One such instance concerned a magnificent fiend of a jumper called Götz, who always let his rider down in competitions. The result was that the Institute kept switching riders, and in due course it was my turn. I spent the winter months giving Götz a thorough schooling in dressage, and was delighted to find that he was improving steadily at weekly jumping practices, easily clearing obstacles that grew ever higher, too high for many of the good jumpers. At this point I began to realize that my riding instructor intended to take Götz from me the very first time he refused and give the horse to one of his pet pupils. So I was absolutely determined not to give him any excuse for making such a change, and, to do him justice, Götz never missed a single jump. But all the same he was taken away from me just before the competition, and the praise I was given for all my work did nothing to soften this injustice, and I was very bitter about it.

I had a quite different experience with Broomhill, a beautiful Irish horse, imported by a business tycoon who, finding the chestnut difficult to ride, gave him to the Institute to be reschooled. He was drafted to the jumping section because of his great possibilities, with the certainty of being one of those chosen for the Salzburg Horse Show in 1930. But during the very last practice he threw his rider, so I inherited him as a 'consolation' for losing Götz. The difficulty with Broomhill was that he would stop dead when he was going very fast, give a kind of hop, and refuse to budge. Such disobedience is usually because a horse loses his impetus and needs more help from the rider to spur him on. Broomhill's fits of obstinacy were widely known, so as soon as I came into the ring at Salzburg everybody was waiting for him to stop. Although I had ridden him only a few times before the competition I managed to catch him at the right moment and urge him forward sharply. In riding, as in life, it is easier to correct a mistake at the beginning than when it has become a deeply ingrained habit. I not only had a clear round with Broomhill, but we took first and second place in the two jumping events. This interesting success strengthened my opinion that a good rider must be in perfect sympathy with his horse and awaken and sustain in him the urge to go forward without hesitation. The whole value of riding lies in keeping going.

I include here as a curiosity a saying of one of my riding-masters that the Chief of Staff served the Emperor with his head, while the cavalryman, particularly the riding instructor, served him with his seat! It seemed a harmless little proverb at first sight, but I have since repeatedly proved how utterly false it was, for the rider will succeed in bringing his horse to the peak of perfection only if he has thoroughly worked out beforehand every detail of its training. And only an intelligent rider will ultimately be entitled to be called an artist, while the thoughtless ones will never be better than mediocre, and all their lives remain merely craftsmen.

These episodes from my training are typical of my whole riding career, showing that my life too has been spiced with irritation and disappointment; and that every success has been, to some extent, the result of a lengthy struggle. Lasting success falls into nobody's lap; it demands considerable effort, as young riders should never forget. Then perhaps they would face up more easily to the setbacks that occur, and develop the patience they need.

My training took a remarkable turn when I took a severe toss jumping a young thoroughbred mare. She kicked me in the back after throwing me, and I lay like a shot animal and had to be taken to hospital. The doctor's laconic report read: "Fracture of the fourth lumbar vertebra," and I was tied to my bed for months. Luckily, after painful and wearisome treatment, my legs, which had been affected by the injury, gradually improved, but for a long time I could not bend or move the upper part of my body when I was jumping, so I had to give it up, but every day I got some one to lift me on to the horse allotted to me, and at this time my whole attention turned to the finer points of training.

None the less, it was a bitter disappointment to me when after two years of my course I was sent back to the troop instead of completing a third year at the Institute, because, according to my not very friendly riding instructor, I was "finished," and there could be "no question of further training." This sudden return to the troop was a terrible blow, for I had to leave behind all the horses I had been schooling in dressage and jumping, and now stood empty-handed, all my hopes in ruins at my feet. In post-war Austria we officers could not own our horses, so I was like a sportsman whose equipment had been taken away from him. However, I was determined to make a new start, and searched among the remounts of the squadron for a likely-looking horse. This was not at all easy, for most of them were too small for me. At last I settled for Nora, a not particularly beautiful mare but with plenty of dash, who richly repaid my labour by her willingness and loyalty.

Because my collaboration with Nora marked an important chapter in my career as a horseman I will linger a little longer over her. This inelegant mare, whom many considered downright ugly, was handed over to me with alacrity by the not very knowledgeable riders of the top dressage group.

After intensive training throughout that winter Nora was good enough for an intermediate dressage trial, and I made up my mind to enter the following spring for a national dressage event. Permission to do this had to be obtained from a military commission headed by the Inspector of Cavalry, and I was dreadfully disappointed when the president announced after some preliminaries that Nora had certainly been very well ridden, but had not the necessary qualities for a dressage horse, and so permission to enter could not be granted. This crushing decision ended with the laconic remark: "The horse is a reject, not a suitable dressage mount for a captain."

After a sleepless night I decided to keep faith with poor old Nora, who had always given me such good service, and to continue training her undaunted. A year of exhausting work followed, and then I appeared in public with her at the great 1933 International Horse Show in Vienna. But the prejudice against this horse was so strong that in the national Intermediate dressage class I was placed only third, behind two competitors who came last and next to last in the international dressage events that followed. In these, by a unanimous decision of judges from other countries, I won both the Intermediate and Advanced classes against very strong opposition. The ice was now broken, and it was a wonderful feeling as I stood before the daïs during the playing of the Austrian national anthem. It was the first time our flag had been hoisted for a win in an international dressage competition, and my salute expressed my gratitude to my dear Nora. As I stood there the thought came unbidden into my mind that loyalty is, after all, worth while.

When later the president of that earlier military commission asked about the magnificent horse I had just ridden to victory I saluted and replied, "It was the reject, General!" And it was only a year later in 1934 that I made my debut in a foreign competition on Nora and her stable companion Nero, of whom more later, at the Concours de Dressage in Thun, Switzerland. But it is part of my life's pattern that everything fresh I undertake is fraught with difficulties. And so it proved on this occasion; Nora hurt herself and could not be worked for a long time, and Nero was suffering from hoof trouble, and he too went lame.

Nero, son of Dark Ronald out of Seehausen, bred in Klein-Eichholz by Mr W. Welp, began his career as a thoroughbred race horse under the name of Sinbad, and was bought by Count Seilern for 10,000 marks to race at Freudenau, in Vienna. But he did not distinguish himself by his speed on grass, and his disappointed owner sold him to the Austrian Army. Posted to the Militär-Reit- und Fahrlehrerinstitut, the poor creature had a bad time. He had neither the energy nor the urge for jumping, and for dressage he showed little aptitude, so the commandant of the Institute ordered him to be handed over to the troop. But Nero had an ally in the Inspector of Army Remounts, who was unwilling to let the son of Dark Ronald be lost in the troop, and he asked me if I would take him on as an additional sporting mount. I was only too delighted, for the allotment of horses in the Army was at that time very restricted.

In the morning I rode in the Spanish Riding School, and in the afternoon I exercised my two horses Nora and Otto in the Prater, and now Nero accompanied them. My new 'attraction' made a most disappointing impression. I was asked by jeering Viennese riders where I had got hold of this "sausage," and behind my back they laughed openly at both of us.

I gritted my teeth and refused to be deflected from the work I had begun, with the result that at the end of a mere six months we were ready to enter for a dressage competition, and not only catch the eye of the experts, but also silence the mocking laughter for ever. The six-year-old Nero secured fifth place out of seventeen at the Concours Hippique in Vienna in an international Advanced class.

This first appearance with Nero occurred in the same year that I achieved the first international success for Austria with Nora, and an article appeared in the Vienna daily, the *Wiener Journal*, on October 2, 1933:

> But the greatest surprise was Captain Podhajsky's achievement. Here is a rider who, by his elegant appearance and the fine performance he gave on Nora and Nero, seems destined to carry on the highest equestrian traditions of the old imperial Austria.

During the final judging of the international Advanced class I caught a fleeting glimpse of my friend Professor Ludwig Koch among the spectators. In honour of this fine portrayer of Austrian horsemanship I took Nora, on a simple curb with only one hand on the reins, through all the prescribed exercises, including the *pirouette, piaffe,* and changes of leg. Koch was so delighted that he came up and put his arm round me as I dismounted saying that he wanted to paint me on Nora. Unfortunately, this was not to be, for he fell ill shortly afterwards and never recovered. A week before his death he sent a message to tell me that the glorious picture Nora and I had inspired had been constantly before his eyes during his illness, and his first task when he was better must be to paint us both in brilliant colours. But Fate had other ideas!

After training throughout the winter of 1933–34 I did very well in the spring competitions in Vienna with Nora and Nero, who took the first two places in all the dressage events. After that I was chosen for the Concours de Dressage at Thun, and thus was given my first opportunity to ride outside my own country.

I duly arrived there, but at first I could not work my horses because of their lameness, and this was very worrying, for I knew the tremendous interest being taken at home in my performance. It was not until the very day of the competition that I was able to ride Nora, after an interval of four weeks. Now I should discover how the long and conscientious training would pay off. The gallant mare moved with such precision that she secured third place in the Grand Prix de Dressage against stiff opposition. So I succeeded with Nora, this long-suffering mare from Burgenland, in upholding once again the great tradition of Austrian horsemanship that had been triumphantly celebrated at Turin in 1902, for the few trips abroad by Austrian riders since 1918 had so far brought very few successes.

In this crisis Nero too rose to the occasion, and went rhythmically in the big dressage competition as if his training had not been interrupted at all. His efforts were well rewarded, and he took seventh place out of seventeen, against the leading riders from Germany, France, and Switzerland.

My companion on my first foreign tour was Major-General Arthur von Pongràcz, former adjutant to Emperor Franz Josef. I had known General Pongràcz for many years, for he had stabled his horses for a long time with my squadron, but on this trip we grew even better acquainted and became good friends. I have seldom known such a wonderful riding companion, whose judgment was always absolutely fair.

For me, as a rider of the younger generation, the General provided a magnificent model. He was at home in any saddle, and had won countless show-jumping and dressage events. In 1908 he established a jumping record by clearing an obstacle of well over six feet. To those endless critics and grumblers who claimed that in their day standards of horsemanship were incomparably higher General Pongràcz would always reply in his firm, deep, and emphatic voice, "I rode in the old days and I still ride to-day, and so I am best qualified to give my opinion that since the First World War the standard is much higher both in show jumping and dressage."

He was not only the embodiment of the dapper, dashing Austro-Hungarian cavalry officer, but one of those individualists who very occasionally emerged in the Danube empire. His comments and advice were inexhaustible, and, however peculiar they might sound at times, they were always full of common sense and wisdom. He might say, "When I left riding-school one of my companions switched over to publishing articles about riding and he became famous ten years before I did, though I had devoted myself completely to the sport." Or he would advise me, "Don't forget that the worse your horse goes, the wider your smile must be; then the judges will think you are pleased with your horse and will give you better marks in spite of themselves." I can still see him schooling his Georgina and letting his groom give the commands for the various movements. Once they just would not go right, and he asked quite suddenly, "Novotny, do I at least look cheerful?"

His originality came out also in sporting matters. I once saw him, at the age of nearly sixty, jumping his horse Turidu. For this he chose the thickest and heaviest pole he could find, and had it put up to three feet. At the first attempt the horse knocked it off, so he had it put up four inches. At the next jump the same thing happened, and the height went up another four; and then another four. This time the horse behaved so disastrously that the heavy log crashed down, only just missing the General, supine on the ground. He got up and said with an oath, "That nearly killed me, Novotny. Put it up another inch."

He got back into the saddle and sailed over, while I looked on, my hair standing on end with anxiety for the ageing General.

Once he asked if he might ride my Nora, and when he dismounted said enthusiastically, "I have never ridden such a remarkable horse. When she goes into a fast trot her action is as smooth as if she were on wheels and running along rails!" And he kept on telling his friends this, even though I was his constant rival.

I was friendly with him for many years, and our relationship was never ruffled by any unpleasantness, unfortunately a rare occurrence among competitive riders.

Faithful Nora had repaid my devotion many times over, not only by her countless successes in both national and international competitions, but also because it was such a pleasure to ride her. And she also confirmed my contention, which some captious critics dispute, that a good dressage horse must also be a competent hunter. I rode Nora for the first time to hounds in the Schloss-park and around Laxenburg, and was completely satisfied—even delighted—with her performance. She was eager to go,

1. Lieutenant in the 4th Dragoons

2. The First Big Dressage Success on Nora, 1933

3. A Particularly Difficult Horse: Otto, 1936

easy to control out in front or in the middle of the field, or even behind, and I had plenty of opportunity of observing a good many riders sawing at the bit. They did not exactly give the impression that they were savouring the greatest of earthly joys upon their horses!

But Fate is not always kind, and Nora accidentally trod in a rabbit-hole, straining her fetlock so badly that she never completely recovered. Ever after she tended to show a little lameness after working in the riding-school. So I had to pay for showing off the correct training of my dressage horse with the loss of many years of careful work, for every rider knows the immense patience needed to teach a horse the *piaffe, passage, pirouette*, and changes of leg, and how sad to have the results thrown away in a single instant.

This experience made me resolve in future to be much more careful with my horses and not expose them to such risks. Most dressage riders would agree with this—but it should never be said that a dressage horse is not suitable for hunting.

With Nora's uneven action there was no longer any question of using her for dressage; later, during my period as instructor in the Institute, I employed her as a mount for my pupils, and she very soon got into the way of it, and became the best school horse we had. When I was posted back to the troop I had to leave Nora behind, as all my requests to be allowed to buy her were curtly refused, so I was most upset to learn a year later, quite by chance, from one of my fellow-competitors at the International Horse Show in Aachen that she had been sold to a Viennese butcher. This treatment put the final touch to the whole picture of the envy my success had aroused: the riding instructors could not bear to have their pupils pick out as the best schooled in the Institute a horse that I had trained. I can still recall how the news of Nora's fate, which I had learned during a lively party at Aachen, took all the pleasure out of this happy occasion, and I felt sick at heart and went sadly away.

Later I often saw the mare in the Prater bearing her new owner and executing the *passage* and *piaffe*, and my heart always missed a beat, for she had to carry a rider of nearly sixteen stone. I tried hard to get her back, but could make no headway with her contented owner.

My collaboration with Nora was a definite milestone and a turning-point in my career. I had begun by concentrating on show jumping, considering the great demands of dressage beyond me and only to be admired from a distance. Later I tried for a time to excel in both, but it was not until Nora came into my life that I began to concentrate on dressage.

Working with horses, I have come to realize that very few riders indeed can cultivate both these branches of the sport simultaneously to a high standard, because they differ so widely at the top. Show jumping can be far more easily and conclusively judged by counting points for faults and time penalties than dressage can possibly be, for here there is often a wide divergence of opinion on the best method of deciding the winner, and the views of the various judges are almost irreconcilable, as I discovered frequently to my cost.

The fundamental difference between these two equestrian arts is best demonstrated by considering the collaboration of the two creatures involved. When I felt in good form I could usually ride my horse to victory in a jumping competition, and the enthusiastic cheers of the public always had a good effect on us both, but in dressage riding these superficial conditions were not enough. I noticed that I often mounted my horse full of energy and optimism, and was very disappointed to find I could not accomplish the difficult exercises, whereas another time, when I started off much less pleased with myself, all the movements, even the most complicated, flowed smoothly. Excited applause does not help in the least; what is needed is perfect sympathy and harmony with one's partner.

My wide riding and training experience gave me a clear general picture of judging in the various branches of equestrian sport, and particularly of the correct division of responsibility between horse and rider.

Thus I found that in racing success depends primarily on the quality of the horse, and only to a lesser extent on the rider's skill. A dogged and determined rider, all other things being equal, can win because of his greater riding skill. But the best jockey in the world cannot win the race unless his horse has the necessary speed.

In jumping, on the contrary, responsibility rests almost equally on horse and rider. The best show jumper will give of his best only if his rider not merely does not hinder him, but actively assists him, though, of course, a poor rider can get a good jumper over small obstacles. In dressage the success rests largely on the skill of the rider, and the ability of the horse is only secondary. The best-ridden dressage horse will not be able to show what he has been taught unless his rider has achieved the necessary proficiency through equally careful training. But a good rider often may achieve brilliant success with a not very promising horse, which has been systematically trained, as was the case, for instance, with Nora.

In all three branches the rider must possess much greater knowledge to work with an unbroken horse than with one that has already had some schooling. In order of difficulty, first comes racing, then jumping, and lastly dressage, which makes the greatest demands of all.

The beauty of controlled power in a jumper can be compared at its best to that of the acrobat. The formal beauty of dressage, on the other hand, has its counterpart in ballet, and the art of horsemanship is even depicted in prehistoric drawings.

Any rider can become moderately competent with practice in both jumping and dressage, which are fundamentally the same, but high achievement in dressage demands subtleties of co-operation not really called for in jumping—and, in fact, sometimes even a disadvantage. This is one of the reasons why the training for open military intermediate competitions is done in separate sections.

In dressage the rider sets himself a fascinating task, for to learn the character of his horse thoroughly he must study it in detail and turn himself into an animal psychologist. Success will come only to the dressage rider who wins the friendship of his four-legged partner and turns him into an ally. But even then there is still much more to be done than with a jumper.

Because of my success with Nora my superiors considered me suitable to be transferred to the Spanish Riding School. Thus one of my dearest ambitions was realized; to me as a rider the hallowed riding-hall in the Josefsplatz in Vienna meant much the same as a shrine means to the faithful. As I entered this *alma mater* of riders I felt like a man emerging from darkness into light; I was blinded by the brilliant spectacle of great ability and quite intoxicated with the perfection of the noblest equestrian skill. I refused to let this feeling of ecstatic happiness be damped when, after a long time, my eyes had grown accustomed to this excellence and I detected even here subtle errors of execution. I noted particularly that the teachers of the Spanish Riding School were not really expounding anything but exact obedience to the basic traditional precepts of riding.

It was here that I learned the tremendous importance of handling a horse with understanding—as a living creature—and also the enormous value of correct academic training. The instructors taught me through their Lipizzaner the right attitude of mind, giving me practical demonstrations of control, two essentials for anyone schooling horses to the highest demands of dressage. Thanks to my two riding-masters—man and horse—I improved vastly in both skill and knowledge.

The most remarkable teacher I had at the Spanish Riding School was Oberbereiter (Senior Rider) Polak, who towered above the rest and was a real artist, which could not be said of every one belonging to this renowned school, many only meriting the title of craftsmen. I admired and trusted this great man, allowing nobody to shake my faith in him and fiercely countering any attacks made on him, though it was an open secret that the running of the Spanish Riding School would have been quite unthinkable without Polak. So there sprang up between pupil and teacher a relationship of mutual trust that later brought rich rewards. It could even be called perfect co-operation, and I advise young riders to submit without reservation to the directions of their teachers, exercising complete self-discipline. If they trust their instructor and show him proper respect they are bound to succeed. But the teachers must prove themselves worthy of this trust, and be a good example to their pupils, as any teacher always must.

The great value of the Spanish Riding School lies in individual instruction. The riding-master devotes himself during the lessons, as periods of instruction are called, to one pupil only, until he can assess his physical capabilities as well as his character and latent talent, and so decide what will be the most effective method of training. Then the master chooses from among the Lipizzaner he himself schooled and knows thoroughly a horse suitable for his pupil, thus making his own task easier and enabling the pupil to attune himself to the personality of his animal teacher.

There was an intensive course of riding without stirrups to achieve a strong seat, not only desirable from an aesthetic point of view, but essential if horse and rider are to work properly together.

Since in the opinion of the head of the Spanish Riding School, Major Count van der Straten, I was the most successful of all the cavalry officers sent there, my posting was extended a further year. After this was over the Ministry of Agriculture suggested that I should remain still longer at the Spanish Riding School to be trained up to succeed the present Director in due course. But this plan met with strong opposition from the War Ministry, and that expert the Inspector of Army Remounts explained that he was not going to let me sit on a rotting branch—by which he meant the moribund Spanish Riding School—when he could give me a chance to impart my knowledge to young Army officers. It would be a much more rewarding and important task for me to hand on to the young the great legacy of Austrian riding tradition, so my stay in the last stronghold of classic horsemanship came to an end in 1934, and with it a long and very varied course of training.

Saying good-bye to the Spanish Riding School was very difficult, for it represented the close of a particularly significant period of my life. Ever after I was to think of myself with pride as a pupil of the Spanish Riding School, and to feel that it shared in every triumph I had later, and this was my way of showing my gratitude to this academy. It was here that my vision was sharpened and I learned to distinguish between good and bad and to detect even the smallest error. But above all my knowledge of physical and psychological factors was enormously widened, thus enabling me to assess correctly how much could be demanded of my pupils and to hit on the right way to win their trust and awaken in them a delight in riding.

I can remember, too, the less good instructors, for even these helped me by showing what *not* to do. And I must not forget to thank the difficult horses, who may have made my life miserable, but who were better teachers than the well-behaved school horses who raised no problems. I have always made a rule to master any horse, however difficult or obstinate, and to make it as easy to ride as possible. But the struggle was often a grim one, involving so many problems, though, of course, I acquired much valuable experience and knowledge denied to people who only ride horses that are thoroughly schooled and broken.

The older I grow the more certain I become that the Greek philosopher's view that time is needed for greatness is very true of riding, and particularly of dressage. In the rush of modern life, where every one is out for quick success, riders should never forget this maxim.

CHAPTER 3

My Career as a Rider

As the youngest instructor of the Militär-Reit- und Fahrlehrerinstitut, which provided the best training in horsemanship for the Austrian Army, I now had the opportunity of imparting to the young cavalry officers all that I had learnt. I tackled the task with youthful impetuosity, regarding my new activities as a vocation to which I could apply myself heart and soul.

In the instructional and schooling departments during the first year, and later in the dressage department for the competition horses, I began by ensuring that the young officers were properly mounted, which seemed to me essential for any successful training. It is useless to give a nervous rider a temperamental and nervous horse, because each will only upset the other. But it is just as silly to give a phlegmatic rider a lazy horse, for both of them will be bored to death. Thus the right combination of man and horse must be found if each is to support and complement the other. I used to take great pains also to see that there was no antipathy between rider and horse, knowing only too well from my own experience how little chance there can be of success when the rider is in constant conflict with his horse, and I have often noticed how horses take a definite dislike to certain riders and cause them endless trouble, but obey others contentedly and without fuss.

To create a good partnership between horse and rider one must study the temperament and character of both. I learnt to assess the riders by watching how they handled their horses. There are the knowledgeable ones, who crown their efforts with success; the weak, who are satisfied with partial success and, if no one is watching, are ready to accept even failure without complaint; the vain, who try only when they are being watched, but at all other times show little eagerness, unlike the reckless riders, who tend to allow themselves to be led into taking senseless risks, and are even guilty of rough handling. Some are brutal past masters in inventing tortures, but give in as soon as they sense the horse's resistance—and this can be dangerous for the tormentors—and lastly there are the ditherers, who are always ready to compromise because they have no real objective.

Myself a strong advocate of bold riding, I demanded dash and enthusiasm from my pupils both physically and spiritually. I used to give new commands, varying the drill in a constant effort to keep riders and horses— particularly the latter—on the *qui vive* and prevent them from anticipating the wishes of their riders. I soon saw how much the horses reacted to my voice, often executing my commands without waiting for their rider's directions. So every now and again I introduced prearranged words instead of the regular commands to force the horses to pay attention to their riders. I worked hard every day with my pupils, and so could never be taken by surprise if there was a sudden inspection. Indeed I trained my pupils to cope with the unexpected at all times, and accustomed them to quick thought and action.

This careful training bore fruit at inspections, for my departments always came out best and were held up as examples of uniformity and enthusiasm.

I had unwittingly won my pupils' hearts by cutting down criticisms and complaints to a minimum in the riding-school and giving praise for even the slightest improvement, instead of waiting for perfection. When they came to say good-bye many of my pupils told me that that little word "Good" had often given them new heart and helped them over setbacks and disappointments, convincing them that they were at least on the right track.

All this time I was stepping up my own training and that of my horses. Nora had to be kept at her peak, and this is often more difficult than reaching it, and the young horses had to be schooled. Among my novice horses was Nero, who was to be my companion for more than twenty years, carrying me with dash and spirit to a rare succession of victories over the finest riders in the world. Nero had come on splendidly in a year and a half, and a few months after Thun shared with Nora wins in the dressage events at the International Horse Show in Vienna, where the experts singled him out as a strong and reliable contender for all international competitions, including the Olympic Games. The accuracy of this forecast was proved at the 1935 Concours de Dressage in Budapest when Nero won the big dressage prize against the best contenders in Europe, including a hot favourite from Germany. This win, at that time a riding sensation, was Austria's greatest success in this field and the sweetest triumph of my life.

At the next International Horse Show in Vienna I was again undisputed winner with Nero, followed closely by Nora. One of the leading Viennese newspapers stated that after this achievement I stood alone on the heights, and in another sense too this paper was right, for the higher I climbed through my successes, and the greater my circle of fans became, the smaller grew the number of those I had supposed my friends, and I grew lonelier and lonelier. General Pongràcz was right again in saying that a man will always have a crowd of companions and friends as long as he is not too able or more skilful than they, but as soon as he starts to outstrip them only a very few remain faithful. I have suffered many disappointments that in the long run may have had a lasting effect on my character, for the ease and friendliness with which I used to greet people have turned to shyness and reserve. I was always eager and willing to use my knowledge and skill in helping other riders, to whom, incidentally, I had no obligation as a teacher. I expected no thanks for this, only to be decently treated. This was not to be; my help was not acknowledged and my work was misrepresented, to play down my part in their success.

Once, against my better judgment, I taught a friend's horse to do the *piaffe*. It had been so badly schooled in this exercise that Oberbereiter Polak, who watched me begin my task, urged me not to waste my efforts, for I should never get this "thousand-footed creature" (meaning the fidgety, uncontrolled horse) to do a *piaffe*. Actually I did after some long time, and its rider was later much praised for the excellent execution of this exercise. That he completely forgot my help would not have been so bad, but I found it very hurtful that on one occasion he objected to my being chosen as winner, on the ground that I had come in a few seconds late for the final trial. In fact the objection was overruled, because I had not been informed that the time had been changed, but I could not get rid of the bitter taste it left in my mouth.

My experience over the years has completely changed my youthful views on the ennobling effect that riding has on mankind. One can only improve qualities that exist already, and if they are absent riding will not of itself create them, and thus the educational value of riding and the actual success of the training are lessened because people will not abandon the fallacy that a man must be the embodiment of all that is noble and good just because he rides. The educational value of this sport will depend much more on the character of the person, and this will be greatly reduced if the proper attitude towards what is so often termed the noblest of all sports is affected by material considerations or moments of vanity. The idea of taking up a career with the intention of making as much money as possible out of it, and also the unhealthy quest for success for the satisfaction of personal vanity, have severely damaged the traditional value of riding as a means of developing character.

The year 1936, with the Olympic Games in Berlin, was a definite milestone in my riding career. They provided the greatest equestrian opportunities of modern times. Twenty-two nations competed—with 133 riders.

Even Austria entered a team for all three sections: military, dressage, and jumping. I was chosen for the dressage team with Nero, who, on the strength of the Budapest victory and other international dressage successes, started favourite. The "sausage" had gone a long way in barely three years.

Nero, described in the spring by the critics as a long-legged, dull thoroughbred of little charm, had become handsomer with training and was at the top of his form. Nora and he convinced me that correct and systematic training also improves a horse's appearance, just as humans can make their figures better by suitable exercises. Of course, neither competitions nor riding will make a beauty out of a naturally ugly creature, so Nero never became what one could call really handsome. But he had the power to thrill audiences and experts by his vitality and supple action as well as by his skill and absolute obedience, these qualities combining to give such a harmonious whole that any physical shortcomings were hardly noticeable. It was always more difficult, of course, for Nero to defeat more beautiful horses, and he had to execute his dressage tasks with the maximum of correctness to outstrip rivals better endowed by Nature.

And I too had a heavier burden to carry at the Olympics than when I went the previous year to Budapest, for there any win would have been a triumph, whereas in Berlin I had to strive to hold on to my high position—always more difficult and nerve-racking—and I could not forget that I had to prepare myself as well as possible for the most difficult competition of my life. And this final preparation, following years of conscientious training, served me well, for Nero gave of his best, and his brilliant programme was loudly applauded.

That Nero made a tremendous impression can best be gathered from the contemporary Press reports. These are all the more significant because half of the journalists concentrated on giving extravagant praise to the German riders.

When I finally dismounted I was surrounded by excited crowds who shook me by the hand, congratulated and hugged me, while Nero was patted and offered lumps of sugar. We were the heroes of the hour.

Suddenly a gentleman forced his way through the crowd, flung his arms wide, and shouted, "I am so proud of you. You were always my best pupil!" Looking up, I recognized my old riding-master, whom I could recall only with bitterness because of his unfairness to me and his decision that there could be "no question of [my being given] further training." The rancour I had felt so many years before suddenly surged up again, and for a moment I considered taking this wonderful opportunity of avenging myself in front of a crowd of spectators. But after a few seconds I dismissed the idea, and, better nature prevailing, I forced myself to forget spectres of the past and silently accepted his congratulations. But my delight was short-lived for after a long wait the result of the main dressage event was announced: "Kronos (Germany), first, 15 points; Absinth (Germany), second, 18; Nero (Austria), third, 19; Thersina (Sweden), fourth, 26," and so on. I also noticed all round me too a great deal of headshaking over this result, which was discussed everywhere, including the newspapers. The German judge was responsible for pushing me back into third place, because he not only put his own three countrymen first, second, and third, but placed me only seventh, unlike his four fellow judges, who had all put me somewhere in the first four. In a long article on the decision the German paper *St Georg* reckoned that I was entitled to third place even without the Austrian judge, who had placed me first.

Talking of this disappointment, it is not without interest that many years later, in 1943, the influential secretary of the German judge announced openly during a lunch at the Jockey Club in Vienna that he had deliberately marked me down in the 1936 Olympics, being determined that a German rider should win. This meant marking up his countrymen and downgrading the dangerous favourites, and his tactics cost me at least the Silver Medal, if not the Gold, in Berlin.

The outcome of the Olympic dressage event was a great disappointment to me, but another blow was to follow, for the high-ranking officers accompanying the Austrian team ignored me after the competition, out of pique that I had not won. None the less it was the greatest riding success Austria had had so far: to get an Olympic medal in an individual event, and 4627 points in the team total, because I came third, Colonel Dolleschall twelfth, and General Pongràcz sixteenth, only thirty points behind the Swedish team, who took the bronze medal.

Ten days later in Bad Aachen, where most of the Olympic riders appeared, I won all the dressage events I entered on Nero and Otto, thus giving convincing proof of my form in Berlin, since I was competing against the same people I had met there. The German Press, however, preserved a significant and almost complete silence over my sweeping victory, having been gagged after their earlier enthusiastic comments on my performance in Berlin. It prompted a good deal of discussion all the same which naturally turned on the difference between the Berlin and Aachen results.

The Reichsverband für Zucht und Prüfung deutschen Warmbluts bestowed on me later the German Riding Gold Badge, the first Austrian to receive it, "in recognition of [my] achievement at the 1936 Olympic Games in Berlin," so honour was satisfied!

A month after the Olympics the big International Horse Show took place in Vienna, and Nero emerged as undefeated champion, and my second string, Otto, was only forced into second place by his stable companion. This was a wonderful experience for me, a splendid exception to the list of disappointments for the year 1936. In the Advanced dressage class I had taken first with Nero and second with Otto on the strength of the preliminary round. But Nero's hoof was again giving so much trouble that it seemed unlikely that I should be able to ride him twice more: in the finals of this competition and in an Olympic dressage event. From completely sporting motives I decided to withdraw Nero from the finals of the Advanced dressage class and thereby give up a prize already a certainty, in order to be able to fly the Austrian flag against foreign competitors in the Olympic dressage. But something bordering on the incredible happened in the Advanced event. Instead of following the usual practice of putting Otto into first place after the withdrawal of Nero, who had beaten him before, the judges left Otto in second place and did not award the first prize—already won by me in the preliminaries on Nero! This was not only a singular decision, but a very strange way of 'honouring' the Olympic medallist on his return home!

I recall this Viennese episode without rancour, and without going farther into the probable motives behind it, to show that my riding career was not always crowned with its expected success.

In this same year there was a change in my service career: I was appointed Commandant of the Army Remount Section and took over a fine, reliable staff. This remnant of three squadrons had to school horses for the two cavalry regiments and the mounted infantry officers, thus performing a function similar to that of the Eidgenössische Pferderegieanstalt in Switzerland. Now at last I could indulge my passion to the full and devote myself to the service of the horse.

But I must not end my account of this important year without recalling the traditional Hubertusjagd. Two days beforehand I received, as a special recognition of Dr Schuschnigg's appreciation, an invitation to take part in this hunt in the Prater. There was no chance to prepare my horses for hunting in the short time I had been back from the various competitions, so I made a snap decision and chose Otto, transferring him without further preparation from the dressage ring into the hunting field. This decision, taken under pressure, proved highly successful. Otto was most agreeable to ride and easy to handle, because he was always obedient and, although temperamental, never tried to get his head, so I was also able to demonstrate that daily dressage provides a very intensive training of the horse's body and improves his wind, so that he can easily hold his own with the horses who have been given the less taxing hunting training, for Otto, unused to galloping across fields, never started to blow at all.

I had a word with Chancellor Schuschnigg, not perhaps a very confident rider, but a very spirited one. He was not an easy person to talk to, for he seemed shy and reserved. I felt I was in the presence of a very learned but somewhat unworldly leader of his people.

The year 1937 was from a riding point of view a particularly successful one, perhaps even the zenith of my sporting career. Whenever I entered my horses Nero, Otto, and Rokoko I was victorious, and very rarely took a second, still less a third. I made a longer foreign tour to Berlin, Verden, and Bad Aachen, where I again had an opportunity of measuring myself against my Olympic opponents, and succeeded in defeating the 1936 Silver Medallist several times.

I remember one particularly pleasant interlude. Quite by chance at one of the many parties in Bad Aachen, a hospitable town, the Swedish dressage judge Colonel Clas Cederström expressed a wish to ride Nero just once. In the relaxed atmosphere of the evening I happily arranged his ride to be after my last event. Then his compatriots made me regret my promise by telling me that Colonel Cederström had not ridden for years, and that in his time he had been more used to a racing than a dressage saddle. I was horrified, but kept on hoping that with all the things going on during the tournament my promise would be forgotten. But no such luck. As I got down after winning the Kür (an event where the rider chooses his own programme) Colonel Cederström came up to me in the dismounting enclosure and asked me if he could ride Nero now. At my invitation he mounted and began with simple exercises. It all went much better than I had feared, and Colonel Cederström grew more ambitious, trying *pirouettes*, changes of leg, and *piaffes* and thoroughly enjoying Nero's vigorous *passage*. The old man was enchanted, and there was no holding him. He tried out new movements until his face grew scarlet with excitement, and I began now to be as fearful for him as for Nero. When he had finished he said—for he had been one of my judges in the Kür—"You won, but all the same it was not fair of me to mark you down, thinking Nero sometimes pulled too hard. Now that I have ridden him myself I can see how wrong I was, for he is particularly light to handle."

My wonderful 1937 competition season ended with the International Autumn show in Vienna, where, although the foremost international dressage riders were competing, I finished as supreme champion in everything I entered with Nero and Rokoko.

I should have had every reason to be happy and contented. In the glow of this splendid success I could look forward to the quieter winter months; and my Remount section had been winning recognition as the months went by. But life always restores the balance lest we humans should grow too arrogant. I was not worried by the political waves rising so alarmingly in my homeland, with imminent and disastrous consequences that we could not in the least foresee, so much as by a slight pain near my heart that I occasionally felt when riding. I tried to take no notice of this dismal visitor, however, clutching at every possible explanation for it, like a drowning man at a straw; but I did confide in the veterinary surgeon serving at the time, and

felt that his opinion, that we men at a certain age always tend to be hypo-
chondriacs, fitted my case exactly. For fear of being told something different I neglected to seek the advice of a doctor, an omission that I was
later to regret bitterly. But, despite all my self-control, I could not shake
off a dull, nagging anxiety that marred the pleasure in my general success.

In 1938 my life was interrupted without warning by world events. Austria
was absorbed into the German Reich, the Army disbanded, and its officers
were taken over by the German Wehrmacht. I was suddenly faced with a
quite new situation and an unpredictable future. In any case my beloved
Army Remount section was, like so many groups in the Austrian Republic,
condemned to be disbanded.

Shortly after the German troops marched in the section was inspected by
the cavalry General von Perfall. He had previously visited the Militär-
Reit- und Fahrlehrerinstitut in Schlosshof and then the 1st Dragoons in
Stockerau. Rumour had it that the General had been very displeased
with the standard of riding there, a piece of news that was not exactly encouraging, particularly as in those days we had been forced to give up so
many of our customs and ideas.

My riding section, however, met with the General's approval. I was able
to enjoy this inspection afresh many months later during the autumn
manœuvres in Fürstenwalde when, during a pause, General von Perfall
happened to remark to the officers standing in an informal group around
him that in the early days of the occupation of Austria he had been put in
charge of her mounted divisions and had been disappointed with the
standard of riding instruction in the Austrian Army, except for one Remount
section, whose C.O. had a very difficult name to remember. He had found
lively, willing, gentle, and reliable horses, showing evidence of having been
correctly schooled. I was particularly proud to hear this since I had obviously been successful in making some contribution to Austria's reputation
for horsemanship. The General was most astonished when he saw me and
recognized me as the major whose name he had forgotten.

In April 1938 I went with my two horses to Berlin for the Grüne Woche.
I had wanted for many years to take part at this German gathering of
representative sport, but the ultimate fulfilment of my dream was, as so often
in life, a dreadful disappointment. I could not produce my best form in the
dressage events. Berlin has always been a bad place for me in sport.

At the same meeting the Spanish Riding School made an appearance after
a break of twelve years, but the performance was, unfortunately, not very
impressive, and with the best will in the world one could not claim that
Austrian horsemanship had made a triumphal entry into the new capital.

During the tournament I introduced myself to the current Inspector of
Cavalry, General von Goslar. I was very impressed when this high-ranking
officer replied, "It must be hard for you after so many years' service to

wear the uniform of another army. I sympathize with your difficulty, but, unfortunately, can do nothing to help. It is not our fault that politics have taken this turn."

In May of the same year I took part in the traditional Horse Show in Vienna with Nero, Teja, and Rokoko, and took firsts on all three horses. I had no idea at the time that this would be my farewell appearance in the competition ring in Vienna, for a few days later I was posted to the Cavalry School at Hanover, to take part with the German team in the Concours de Dressage in London. I never returned to Vienna, and so had no further chance of taking part in competitions there.

I think back to this posting with mixed feelings. I felt like a cock in a strange henhouse, being attacked from all sides for some reason or another. The trouble was partly jealousy over my achievements, and partly the fact that the Austrian mentality was completely misunderstood. Frequently our way of carrying out a task with the least possible friction and without fuss was considered weakness, and from this misapprehension arose the appellation 'slipshod Austrians.' Because I looked back with pride on Austrian tradition I was up in arms at the slightest breath of criticism of my countrymen or my country. But in the end it was just this that enabled me to come to terms in a short time with the German Wehrmacht and soon earned me the trust and respect of my new comrades. In the early days, however, I often had to clench my teeth as I adapted myself to unaccustomed situations.

Good fortune did not attend our trip to London. In the big dressage event Colonel Gerhardt, the Silver Medallist in 1936, took part on Absinth, and I on Nero. Although individual Englishmen were charming to us, we could not but be aware of the rising political feeling aroused by the Anschluss.

I myself had a remarkable meeting with the general secretary of the F.E.I., the French Commandant Hector, outside the Piccadilly Hotel. He greeted me in a friendly fashion and asked which uniform I should be wearing during the show. When I replied that I now had to wear German uniform he turned away and hurried off without another word. We were also rather roughly treated in the Grand Prix de Dressage and unfairly placed, for Nero, in spite of a magnificent performance, finished fifth, and Absinth only twelfth.

When I recall my first visit to the English capital I always think of one agreeable episode during my two weeks' stay in London. Those taking part in the Horse Show, which in those days took place at Olympia, had a very varied programme of outside engagements, including a visit to the famous Ascot race-meeting. This invitation placed us in a dilemma, for we had with us tails and dinner jackets, light and dark suits, but no morning coats and grey toppers. A visit to Ascot without these traditional clothes would have been shocking, and we were loath to resort to hiring them. So we decided to wear full dress uniform in honour of the occasion. On the course an elderly gentleman asked us if we were Yugoslav officers, and when we replied, "No, German," gazed at us as if we were some strange beings. But we had been standing in the crowded enclosure only a few moments when a very elegant gentleman, a veritable Dorian Gray, came up to us, introduced himself as a diplomat, and said, "Only in England could German officers appear at the races without anybody taking any notice of them or providing them with an escort. May I accompany you?" He looked after us most attentively, and led us during the intervals between the races into the various very exclusive clubs, where he toasted the newly established German-English friendship in champagne, a severe test for our heads, for there were a great many intervals and it was hot!

After the races he invited us to visit several estates round London. These entrancing gentlemen's houses, usually protected from the outside world by beautifully kept grounds, reminded us of fairy-tale castles. I was specially impressed by the home of a retired general, who received us most hospitably and made his granddaughter, rather like the Sleeping Beauty in this quiet estate, ask us to tea. The old man kept on repeating what an honour it was for him to be able to welcome German officers, and treated us with exceptional friendliness and kindness—in spite of the political tension. In the course of our conversation he led me by the arm into the well-kept garden, embellished with guns of various calibres from the First World War. He stopped in front of quite a large cannon, and pointed it out to me as the most precious of all the firearms that as a former divisional commander he had been able to bring back. As a token of his great pleasure at our visit he presented the gun to me. When I acknowledged this unusual gift with a smile of thanks he was almost offended, and insisted that the offer was serious. Now I was really embarrassed, for what on earth could I do with this colossal parting present, and how could I avoid hurting the feelings of my host? I repeated my thanks, begging him to look after this valuable gift for me, so that I could gloat over my new possession on my next visit. He was happy with this solution, and we parted good friends.

The great distincton between personal opinion and political trends was illustrated by a policeman who proudly showed me his medals from the First World War, won in the great tank battle at Cambrai, and said he thought it had been a gross injustice to the Germans to occupy the Rhineland in 1918 when the War ended. I was astounded when he added that it was a great pity England would have to go to war with Germany again, since she could not look on for ever while Germany occupied one country after another. And this was in June 1938.

When I recounted this to the German Military Attaché in London he begged me and the other riders to lay stress when we returned on the firm resolve of the English to take action, for all his reports along these lines had been dismissed as pessimistic, and nobody would pay attention to them.

After I returned from London my period of service at the Cavalry School in Hanover was extended, and I was also asked how I felt about my transfer to the German Wehrmacht and offered the post of instructor to the Cavalry School in Hanover. But I declined it, and left it to the personnel office in Berlin to confirm my transfer.

From Hanover I went with the Cavalry School team to take part in competitions in Verden on the Aller, Cologne, and Düsseldorf. I remember this with little pleasure, for I felt a complete stranger and was made aware of it by my companions, as my approach to competition riding was completely different from theirs. While I entered Nero in only the stiffest dressage classes, winning on him every time, my two young horses Teja and Rokoko always had to meet the top horses Absinth, Fels, and others in the easier classes, and had to be satisfied with finishing lower down. When one of the judges asked me why I did not enter Nero as well in the easier dressage classes I replied that it was against my riding principles. I had learned these in the old Austro-Hungarian Army, remained faithful to them in the Austrian Army, and had no desire to relinquish them in the German Wehrmacht, and there was no possible way round it. It was not so much how often but how well one won that mattered. The judge commented that it was a very noble attitude and one that could certainly have an excellent effect on riding in Germany.

At the big tournament in Aachen I came first before an international jury with three entries on Nero, and left my rivals from the previous competitions, including Absinth, far behind. Here in Aachen Nero became champion dressage horse of Germany.

I took up my new post with the rank of major on the staff of the 9th Cavalry Regiment in Fürstenwalde on the Spree. But first I had to part with Rokoko, with whom I had already been so successful. She was returning to my beloved Vienna, the sole member of the "Podhajsky Team."

In Fürstenwalde I found it hard going at first, for the officers of my regiment concentrated mainly on racing, showing little interest in dressage. But when I rode my dressage horses Nero or Teja to the first meets of the autumn, and galloped into the field with shortened stirrups, they began to take notice, and then grew interested in the riding lessons I had for first and second lieutenants. In the end the interest became so great that even the *Rittmeister* (captain of cavalry) begged me to form a third instruction group for them.

From then on I found there such an extraordinary appreciation of my horse's work that the C.O. of the regiment urged me, of his own accord, to use one of the squadron mounts for hunting rather than my dressage horses, even offering me his own service horse, saying it would be a shame

4. Appointment as *Rittmeister* to the Spanish Riding
School: Favory Montenegra in the *Piaffe*, 1934

5. Conversano Stornella, 1934

6. Nero on his Way to World Class, 1935

7. Nero in the *Piaffe*, 1936

if I lamed one of my horses riding to hounds, for then the long and patient schooling would be completely wasted.

These rides in Fürstenwalde were enchanting. Just outside the town one could take glorious gallops on the sandy ground, which provided excellent going for the horses. The many natural obstacles increased the pleasure of following the hounds, though perhaps they were often rather too difficult for some of the riders. On one occasion over a fairly broad stream only a few of the forty or fifty riders managed to get across, while the rest of the field either disported itself in the water or, struggling with the horses on the other bank, gazing sadly across at the hunt streaming out of sight.

The squadron horse I rode was an East Prussian and potentially a first-rate jumper, though with a reputation of being a frightful puller, but when he had tried vainly to get his head during our first ride he was soon cured of this bad habit. I had occasion once more to appreciate the enormous value of being able to sit a horse without having to hang on to the reins, even in the hunting field.

Because, following my custom, I thoroughly tested all the horses ridden by my officer pupils during classes, I came to appreciate the wonderful qualities of East Prussian horses; incidentally, I also won my pupils' trust when they saw how well their horses could go, and that I was not asking the impossible.

During my service in Fürstenwalde I had to make great sacrifices to indulge my passion for riding. Lengthy field exercises or other tactical commitments meant that I often had to fit in my riding between four and six in the morning. Just before the 1939 International Show in Berlin I had, in fact, to prepare my competition horses after these exercises, between 10 P.M. and midnight, and when I got to Berlin I was tired out already.

There, on the strength of his success, Nero was the only German horse to qualify for the Kür. Unfortunately, I had caught a bad cold during the show, and managed to keep down the fever only by vigorous dosing, in order to be able to take part on the evening of the last day. Nero executed his programme with remarkable skill and won the victor's ribbon, but I had no idea that this would be his last win in a big international competition.

I paid dearly for this Berlin victory. The medicine had certainly managed to control my temperature, but could not prevent a severe attack of influenza, which kept me in bed for quite a time. The doctor who was called in was less concerned about the flu than the condition of my heart. He diagnozed a severe weakness of the heart muscles and told me I should need lengthy treatment. This diagnosis reminded me of the first symptoms of my illness, which in 1937 I had, unfortunately, ignored.

While I lay ill I was visited one day by the Cavalry Inspector of the Supreme Command. It was remarkable enough that such a high-ranking officer should come at all from Berlin to Fürstenwalde to see me, but it turned out to be of extra interest to me when he asked me my opinion of the importance of the Spanish Riding School. As a genuine devotee and sincere admirer of this ancient academy I gave an exhaustive report of its value to horsemanship in general, and emphasized the possibility of its being of service to German sport, thinking that the Inspector had come to me for information because I was Austrian. This sort of thing was happening all the time, for the military in Berlin were anxious to understand the mentality of the newly formed 'province.' When I had finished my discourse I was astounded to be asked whether I would take over the direction of the Spanish Riding School. The Inspector had already noticed me during competitions in Aachen and Berlin, and had come to the conclusion that I should be the right man for the job. In addition, the former head of the school, Count Rudolf van der Straten-Ponthoz, had considered Richard Wätjen and myself for this post, but had preferred me, because he liked the idea of this institution's being directed in the future by an Austrian.

This appointment was a definite turning-point in my career. It represented not only the highest recognition of my riding achievements, but also the realization of a pipe dream that I had never really expected to be fulfilled. And at this significant moment of my life I had to undergo prolonged medical treatment! The weeks seemed like years, and it was only too obvious that my new sphere of duty would not provide the necessary rest and time to cure my complaint, but in this I was mistaken.

CHAPTER 4

Appointment to the Spanish Riding School

After the German troops marched into Austria in March 1938 there was (though little was known of it outside) a bitter struggle for power between Party and Wehrmacht about the Spanish Riding School, resulting in its being placed under the protection of the German Wehrmacht.

The Spanische Hofreitschule belonged, until the disintegration of the Danube empire in 1918, to the Emperor's court, and was then taken over by the Ministry of Agriculture of the new Austrian Republic. The home of a special riding culture, it was regarded in just the same light as the court theatre and similar establishments of public worth, and was spared the fate of the other court riding-school, the Campagne-Reitschule.

The end of the Campagne-Hofreitschule and of the royal stables provides the saddest chapter in the transition from empire to republic. The heart of every animal-lover, particularly horse-lovers, bled to witness the bargaining of the horse-dealers, butchers, and cabbies over the highly bred imperial horses. These carefully nurtured animals were driven, often with shouts and curses, out of the royal stables by their rough new owners to a very different and dismal future. Felix Saltens's *Florian, das Pferd des Kaisers* was inspired by the fate of these pathetic horses, which were once part of the magnificence of the imperial court and had known so much joy and splendour.

Most of the horses of the Spanish Riding School were spared this sad fate. Some of them had, indeed, to go back to Lipizza, the birthplace of their ancestors, in fulfilment of an understanding with Italy that she had a claim on the Lipizzaner.

Even the school horses of the Spanish Riding School found the period that followed quite a drastic change from their previous way of life. Gone were the crowds of admirers who had so enjoyed their dancing movements; the food ration in starving Vienna had become more than wretched for these artists as well. Worst of all, these animals, accustomed to publicity, now had to be kept out of sight so as not to rouse the uncertain temper of the people. The Emperor had gone, and everything connected with him was more or less handed over to the 'liberated' masses for their sport, so the Lipizzaner often had to remain in hiding, and for days at a time could not come out of their stables because they had to cross a street to get to the riding-hall, where they and their ancestors had worked for nearly two hundred years.

Later, when it was safe for them to be brought by degrees out of their Sleeping Beauty existence, and they were unobtrusively shown to the citizens of Vienna in public processions, an effort was made to 'modify' the school's title of Hofreitschule by omitting the word *Hof* ('court') because of its 'disturbing' effect—though the chemist's shop, the old Hofapotheke in the Stallburg, was allowed to retain its former title without 'modification.'

People had from time immemorial been allowed to watch the morning practices on certain days. The invitations for special occasions were by tradition reserved for the chosen few, and were first issued at the turn of the century to the countless international congresses held in Vienna, so that visitors from all over the world might have the opportunity to admire the white horses. After the events of 1918 the Spanish Riding School had to make its contribution by countless public performances, extending its training to be able to carry them out. These displays, which for months took place nearly every Sunday, and the necessity of putting numbers of the school horses at the disposal of many civilian pupils badly interfered with the riding programme of the school. On the other hand, the public displays of the classic art of riding and the watching of the morning workouts by all horse-lovers excited mounting interest far beyond the borders of Austria.

In the unsettled days of March 1938 the S.A., who were responsible for feeding the Reich, wanted to get their hands on the Spanish Riding School, basing their claims to it on the fact that even under the Austrian regime it had been under the Ministry of Agriculture. This intention was, however, thwarted by the German troops who had marched in, for the C.O., General von Bock, invited the head of the Spanish Riding School to tea as soon as Vienna was occupied to avoid any premature negotiations by the Party by telephone before he could obtain high-level authority from Berlin to place the Spanish Riding School under the protection of the German Wehrmacht. This proved later to be a very happy solution for the school.

At first no changes were made in the Spanish Riding School, neither in the way it was run nor in personnel, until its precise standing had been finally clarified. The Wehrmacht laid great stress on their desire to retain its traditional structure, so they were particularly anxious that the current head, Count van der Straten, should remain at his post. Numerous Army study commissions came to Vienna to decide the future rôle of the school by first-hand observation and negotiation on the spot. Finally, on January 1, 1939, the Spanish Riding School was definitely taken over by the German Wehrmacht and placed directly under the Supreme Command. At the same time it was given back its traditional title and was once more known, as it had been through the centuries since its foundation, as the Spanische Hofreitschule.

Count van der Straten for private reasons could no longer devote all his time to the Spanish Riding School, hence the changeover, with his full agreement, and my appointment to take his place.

Before I took up my new command I had to go before the Inspector of Cavalry to receive my orders. This distinguished officer told me that I knew more about the traditional structure of the ancient riding academy than he did, and so his only specific assignment would be to carry on its traditions undeterred by any pressure from local political parties. He promised me his full support for any reasonable measure and gave me a completely free hand.

And so I now entered the famous riding-hall of Fischer von Erlach for the first time not as a visitor or pupil, but as the responsible head of a unique establishment of horsemanship. I could not allow myself to be merely dazzled by the glamour of the oldest riding-school in the world, but must take a good look behind the scenes. Beneath the superficial splendour lurked many problems clamouring to be solved, and these gave me many headaches in the days that followed.

But first I abolished one monstrosity. Since March of this same year the riders had acknowledged applause by lifting their right hand in the Nazi salute. This gesture by men in historic uniform, in place of raising their cocked hats with a flourish, seemed to me utterly incongruous. My forceful arguments prevailed, and the old traditional salute, as befitted the Festsaal in the Josefplatz, was restored to favour.

For months the horses had been only very inadequately exercised, the essential renovation of the riding-hall having once more been delayed, so the first problem was to complete the work on the actual riding space so that serious training could begin. But even then only the minimum demands could be met, for anything more meant prolonged negotiation, and the sympathy of the appropriate authority in Berlin had first to be won.

After much careful thought I prepared an unvarnished report on May 6, 1939, which would give the Inspector of Cavalry a complete picture of the situation. First I dealt with the school's personnel:

When I took over there were three *Oberbereiter* [senior riders], aged 56–57, who had all belonged to the imperial Hofreitschule, four *Bereiter* [riders], aged 27–41, and one 28-year-old trainee.

From this it can be seen that the riders of the Spanish Riding School are much too old, and the question of introducing new blood was given little consideration after the War. This fact is all the more regrettable, since at the moment only the three senior riders (Zrust, Lindenbauer, and Polak) belong to the classical school of riding. Of the remaining *Bereiter* not one has given a single horse its *haute école* training without help. In future special attention will be paid to the training of younger riders, and to this end the rich experience of the senior riders will be used exclusively for training. A start must soon be made on the basic education of trainees.

The riders feel strongly that their financial position has deteriorated. They were not well paid before, but the introduction of the mark as currency at a rate of 1·50 Schillings to the mark has inevitably meant a reduction in their salaries, for in a short time the prices and cost of living in Vienna have changed. Above all there is now remarkably little difference between the salaries of the riders and the wages of the grooms. This was already becoming noticeable in Austria, but now, since the wage adjustments, the situation has become more acute. It is desirable and only fair that the question of pay should be given immediate attention.

On the horses I was obliged to report:

Of the Lipizzaner at present in the school one-third are much too old and classified as below standard in training, so replacement by younger horses is absolutely essential.

After describing the inadequacy and hygienic deficiencies of the washing- and changing-rooms of the riders and dealing with various administrative questions the report dealt last of all with the training:

The task of the Spanish Riding School consists both in cultivating the classical art of riding and in training officers. This task can be properly performed because in the ancient tradition of *haute école* the fundamentals of schooling are identical with basic dressage training. In recent years this has been somewhat neglected and conflicting methods of training for "Airs above the Ground," for it has been largely done in an attempt to meet public demand by giving a great many performances at the expense of traditional basic training. In the future great care must be taken to ensure that horses from the Remount section are once more schooled in the old way, avoiding as far as possible sacrificing thoroughness to speed in training.

Officers at the Spanish Riding School will not be given *haute école* training before they are ready for it; they might too easily stray from modern riding customs through a misapprehension. They ought to learn in Remount courses and smaller riding-schools many more of the subtleties and refinements necessary for intensive training. This is why even in the old days officers were posted to the Low School training—*Campagnekurse*, as it was called—of the Spanish Riding School. Special school horses are set aside for the training of officers to give them the right feeling and proper instruction. But picked pupils should also take part in competitions, not only to stimulate their interest, but to prove that the Spanish Riding School is not a museum, but a valuable training-place for dressage riders. The Lipizzaner horses, because of their smallness and stocky build, are quite unsuitable for present-day competition horses, and thus would come out badly in any judging against thoroughbreds; but the officers entering the Spanish Riding School could form a sort of competition stable with their own mounts.

It was not easy to carry through the necessary reforms, although they were in the main nothing more than a return to actual tradition. In a school where training is mainly evolved by word of mouth it is only too easy for convenience to be promoted to tradition, and the departure from the well-established way seemed justified. One of the senior riders, for instance, offered in all seriousness his opinion that the school horses ought not to strike off at the canter from the trot. Walking also had been badly neglected in the Spanish Riding School, both phenomena being concessions to the requirements of the many public performances.

To plan a training that would get rid of such bad habits was far from simple, and without the co-operation of the three senior riders would have been quite impossible. The 1898 directives of His Excellency von Holbein —the only written records—did give me a useful basis, but their scope is far too small for carrying out reforms.

So it was a matter of awakening the interest of the *Oberbereiter* and stirring their memories to retain the traditional paths of this old academy that had enjoyed its heyday under Weyrother and Niedermayer. I had to go very carefully and with infinite tact, for these three pillars of the Spanish Riding School, as is, unfortunately, quite common among artists as well as among riders, simply could not get on with one another, and never agreed over professional matters. Worse still, if one of them thought a suggestion had been made by a colleague he would automatically oppose it. I tried to overcome these difficulties by discussing all my rulings, naturally based on von Holbein's, with all three men together. Then I managed to make a clear distinction between the training for the Spanish Riding School and general dressage riding, which also helped me to devote my energies to making various suggestions in high places. For an institution functioning with living creatures—men and animals—cannot be run as a museum if it is not to risk losing the public interest.

On June 18, 1939, a gala performance in the renovated riding-hall in the Josefsplatz marked the ceremonial take-over of the Spanish Riding School by the Wehrmacht, a special occasion at which everybody of importance was present, including many generals and local dignitaries, headed by the Mayor of Vienna. Only the Gauleiter of Vienna was conspicuous by his absence.

The Inspector of Cavalry, Colonel von Langermann, who had come from Berlin, opened the proceedings by welcoming the guests in a long speech, in which he paid tribute to the history and the former direction of the old riding-school. He concluded with these words:

"After the Austrian Anschluss with the German Reich the Spanish Riding School came under the command of the German Wehrmacht, and a serving officer, Major Podhajsky, was put in charge of it. As the Inspector responsible for riding in the Army I greet you, Major Podhajsky, as the head of your school, expressing the Army's pleasure in being able to preserve and maintain this unique training establishment for the benefit of German horsemanship. My greetings also to the riders and all the staff. It gives me special pleasure, Major Podhajsky, that you yourself trained here, winning an Olympic medal in 1936. May the Spanish Riding School under your direction go forward to a future worthy of its great past!"

In the overcrowded hall the Lipizzaner then gave a demonstration of the classic art of riding, celebrating in this famous Festsaal, which through the centuries had witnessed many historic scenes, a recent event of great significance.

There was a great deal of public interest, and one of the leading papers published the following on June 19:

> The sight of such graceful beauty and power completely captivated the many hundreds of delighted spectators. Repeated applause broke the deep silence in the white hall with its lofty pillars. It was astounding. All eyes were on the horses, and the spectators, marvelling at their floating action, their proud bearing, the elegant play of their muscles, acclaimed them, admiring in their beauty and strength the Nature that had created them. Possibly the highest praise one can give the riders is to say that they were not particularly noticeable, seeming rather to be fused into one single being with their white Lipizzaner horses.

In spite of Germany's great isolation at that time the news of the changes in the Spanish Riding School filtered beyond the borders of the Reich, and brought me many letters from riding friends all over the world. The Commandant of the Eidgenössischen Pferderegieanstalt, Lieut.-Colonel Thommen, wrote, "I shall take every opportunity of sending officers to your school, particularly since the whole affair may perhaps become more military in future."

On the strength of my report the new establishment for the Spanish Riding School was laid down in a relatively short time. It was quite different from the existing one of one Director and seven *Bereiter*, for it consisted of one staff officer as commandant, one staff officer as instructor, two majors as *Bereiter* officers, nine *Bereiter* and four sergeants as trainees. Thus the Spanish Riding School was put in the position, from the point of view of the classic style of riding, its foundation from time immemorial, of becoming the *haute école* of German riding, where the most talented riders in the Army would be given intensive training, to be able to meet the demands of modern competitions, which had become so much greater since the First World War. They would also learn here to school their own horses, to break down a system recently becoming prevalent in Germany whereby many amateur dressage riders appear in dressage trials on horses trained by professionals.

In the old Austria it would have been impossible for an officer to take part in anything competitive on a horse that he had not schooled himself, but in Germany, unfortunately, it was generally accepted that dressage horses were ridden by professionals, and trained by them up to the very last moment, the amateur rider having only to swing into the saddle already warmed for him to be acclaimed as the final winner. This practice involves an undesirable dependence on professional riders and cannot possibly be described as sportsmanlike.

I recall the famous German riding teacher Otto Lörke greeting me at a show in Berlin, immediately after the Anschluss, with the words that he would have a horse for me for the 1940 Olympic Games that was already good enough to win the top dressage prizes. He simply could not understand my refusal of this offer and my answer that I had never entered anything in competitions except my own work. He, with his typically German mentality, could not follow my train of thought, and walked away shaking his head, probably considering my attitude excessively arrogant. There were still enough experts, however, who recognized how harmful it could be for officers to get the credit for riding horses schooled by professional trainers, and they did their utmost to utilize the Spanish Riding School, which now belonged to the Reich, for the higher training demanded by German sport, so it once more assumed its traditional importance and function. But it set me a fine task and opened a wide field of activity.

The proposed expansion could be made only by degrees, for it was essential to avoid any reduction in quality through haste. To get up to the necessary strength I was empowered to find in the course of the summer the best riders from the many mounted squadrons of the German Army.

For the summer of 1939 an extended tour was planned, to familiarize interested German riders at the important competitions at Verden-on-the-Aller, Hanover, and Insterburg with the existence of the Spanish Riding School. So, on the orders of the Oberkommando, we took this journey with five riders and twelve school horses. In Verden, in the heart of the breeding-ground of Hanoverian horses and the stronghold of competition riding, the Spanish Riding School was wildly cheered by large crowds.

As I had the opportunity of repeating my two previous successes with Nero, and to do well with Teja, our success in Verden was complete.

General von Fritsch, who had retained his love of riding even in his present high position, came on one of the days. During an interval I was ordered to his box, where he congratulated me on the school and on my personal victories. To meet this great man, who displayed such warmth despite his stern military bearing and matter-of-factness—the typical Prussian officer—was a real experience, and as I stood facing him I could understand why Army officers loved and respected him.

In the finals I had ridden Teja, who was so like Nero in colour and movements that even experts occasionally confused them, so I was impressed when the General remarked that he liked the bay I had ridden better than the one at the Olympic Games in Berlin. He had thus not only been able to distinguish one horse from another, but even remembered their peculiarities, so great was the interest of the former Commander-in-Chief and real architect of the German Army.

Our subsequent appearance in Hanover turned out rather differently, for here we had to perform before a very critical public. Even before the show began, following my orders I had talks with the teaching staff of the Cavalry School, into which we were taken, and often had great difficulty in convincing the sceptics of the connexion between the horsemanship cultivated in the Spanish Riding School and competition riding. For those doubts, which I was always encountering, the rivalry of the Hanover Cavalry School was not, of course, entirely to blame. Another reason was the not very successful display by the Spanish Riding School in 1938 at the Berlin Horse Show, and it took a long time and a great deal of special effort to put this right. Still I was always ready to listen to any sincere critic, and did all I could to eliminate our weaknesses one by one and, which was much more difficult, to convince the senior riders of the obvious faults, which were now almost traditional. My main attention was concentrated on improving the walk and the extended trot—two weaknesses of the old school —to take the wind out of our opponents' sails.

At the beginning of August I went with the Spanish Riding School team to Insterburg, in East Prussia. There an extraordinary scene was played out before us: this Eastern part of the Reich was like an Army camp, and there was talk of nothing but war, in spite of the preparations for the Tannenberg celebrations and the visit of the Lipizzaner. Both events were actually arranged purely for propaganda purposes, to disguise by peaceful activities the preparations for war now in full swing, but the inhabitants of East Prussia were not deceived and greeted us with deep dejection. Women burst into tears on the slightest pretext, and the men were gloomy and depressed. Everybody, whether civilian or soldier, showed an open dislike of being in any way involved in war, and the few fanatics could not change this attitude. Of the wild enthusiasm for war that I had felt as a youth in 1914 there was not a sign.

This depression naturally had an adverse effect on the Horse Show, for with their deep anxiety about the future the people had little heart for enjoying beautiful horses and good riding, so the performance of the Spanish Riding School faded and left no trace.

I took part on Nero and Teja in the dressage competitions and won all three events, but any joy in my success was damped by the depressing mood in Insterburg, and I became more convinced than ever that I should have to give up competitions for a long time, if not for ever.

Insterburg itself was still suffering from its experiences in the fortunes of the First World War. Thus I lived in an old-fashioned hotel room with decorations that had not been changed for decades, because here in the First World War both the German Commander, Marshal von Hindenburg, and the Russian Commander, General Rennenkampf, had stayed and set up their headquarters.

My last appearance with Nero was fraught with difficulties. After the last long journey in the stifling heat it was obvious from the first day's training that the horse was sickening for rheumatic fever, and it was only the skilful efforts of the veterinary surgeon that kept this dangerous illness in check. To get rid of the inflammation as quickly as possible I let Nero stand for several days in the swift waters of the Angerrap, and this proved so successful that I was still able to enter him for an Advanced class dressage event.

During Nero's cold-water cure a groom tied him to one of the girders, and then stood on the bridge, but the brave little horse would stay in the water only if he could see the man he trusted leaning over the balustrade. If the groom left his post even for a moment Nero began to get restless and neighed anxiously, so necessary to this horse was human contact.

It was entirely due to Nero's unshakable loyalty and reliability that we were able to win the dressage event in spite of his illness and the interruption to his training, but this final triumph was anything but agreeable for me. His back had been rubbed with embrocation, and was so tender that I had to use all my skill not to put him off balance by putting too much weight on him, and I sat as if on eggs.

The minute the show was over the horses had to be loaded on to the train, for we had to get them away as quickly as possible—that very night, in fact—through the Polish Corridor, now becoming too dangerous. As I sat once more in the westbound train there lay over East Prussia, bristling with arms, the typical calm before the storm. The pleasant if melancholy landscape seemed full of sadness, and my eyes tried to capture every detail of the strange beauty of this eastern corner of Germany, for I could not help wondering with growing apprehension if I should ever see the strangely lovely landscape again.

On August 13 I reported in Berlin to the Cavalry Inspector, Colonel von Langermann, a personal friend of General von Brauchitsch. When I asked him whether there would be a war my chief answered that General von

Brauchitsch had stated several days before in a report to the Führer on the military and political situation that Germany was certainly ready for a war with Poland, but could not face a showdown with France and England with any hope of success. Hitler's answer was that, according to the information given by his Foreign Ministers, France and England would never risk a war with Germany over Poland, to which the General replied that this time the two great Powers would not stand idly by as they had done in the case of Austria and Czechoslovakia. Hitler dismissed this as a false assessment of the situation, and waved away any suggestion of caution, but he was to learn in a very few days that the Commander-in-Chief's view of the general position was correct!

Back in Vienna I realized that, under the present dreary political sky threatening our thoughts and actions more and more, the building plans already agreed for the Spanish Riding School, from my point of view to some extent in specific form, would meet with all kinds of difficulties. Barely two weeks later the outbreak of hostilities made all our efforts worthless, and it proved an enormous task even to preserve the existing fabric of the Spanish Riding School through the difficult months that were to follow.

CHAPTER 5

———◆◆◆◆◆———

The Spanish Riding School
and the Second World War

In the middle of August 1939 after the grand tour the staff was given leave until the middle of September, so as to set about the tasks of reconstructing the school and training future *Bereiter* with renewed vigour. The political situation was, of course, very strained, and the rumours of imminent war could no longer be silenced, but we had after all lived for many years under constant strain and grown accustomed to creating from the smallest signs new hopes of a solution of the crisis. This attitude was essential in those troubled times, if all efforts to keep the peace were not to fall victim to paralysing fear of the future.

On August 25, therefore, mobilization, like the first clap of thunder in a threatening storm, shocked even the most optimistic out of their belief in Hitler's peaceful intentions. The young riders and grooms were called up, and I was ordered to form the 11th Cavalry replacement detachment in Stockerau. The Lipizzaner horses remained deserted in the Stallburg under the direction of the head groom, and were looked after by the few remaining elderly grooms. The attempt to recall my predecessor to direct the Spanish Riding School during my absence was unsuccessful, for Count van der Straten telephoned me to say that owing to pressing business on his estate he could come to Vienna only every two or three weeks, for a day or two at the most.

In this unhappy, and for the Spanish Riding School extraordinarily dangerous, situation the nearness of Stockerau shed the only ray of light, for I could attend to its affairs as well as command my cavalry detachment. But, of course, doing two jobs at once strained me almost to breaking-point, for the formation of the squadrons in Stockerau needed my full attention, especially as I had been absent from the cavalry for so long and found many innovations. It was only my unshakable devotion to the old Austrian academy that gave me the strength and endurance to carry out this almost superhuman task.

Every morning I was busy for several hours in the Spanish Riding School, averting at least the most serious disasters, before hurrying over to Stockerau, where I was fully occupied forming and commanding the cavalry detachment until late in the evening. It was a wretched existence, and, once the War had begun, looked like becoming a permanency. The most pressing need in the Spanish Riding School was to see that the horses were exercised at least once a day, so I recalled the three senior riders from leave to help the grooms who had not been called up for military service. The older school horses were led, and the young Lipizzaner worked in turn by the *Oberbereiter*.

First, however, I intended to prevent a Government department from storing grain in the riding-school, a delicate operation, because the Party members, in their enthusiasm for the War, showed little desire to have their plans upset. But the Lipizzaner training quarters at least must be saved, apart from the fact that it would have been a shame for the riding-hall, which had taken months to redecorate, to be involved in yet another change.

The Spanish Riding School was in a poor way over training. From autumn 1938 to spring 1939 the horses could not be worked at all because of the repairs to the Winter School, then the festival tour and the period of leave had once more interrupted the work, which had scarcely been resumed, and now the three old Senior Riders were responsible for thirty-three Lipizzaner. I realized fully that if training were interrupted any longer, especially in view of the great age of the *Oberbereiter*, it would mean the dissolution of the whole institution. But the Spanish Riding School, unlike similar schools in other countries, has survived to the present day because in the course of the centuries of incessant fighting and revolution during the Austro-Hungarian Empire it was never seriously endangered. Naturally enough, in the first months of the War everybody's feelings were still very confused, either by the shouts of triumph that the Polish campaign aroused or by the drastic conditions of daily life, and it was a slow business to make people realize the pressing danger that the old riding-school was facing. It took still longer for any practical action to be taken.

By unceasing efforts I finally managed to get the necessary support from both the local recruiting authorities in Vienna and the central office in Berlin, and at last all the riders and some of the grooms who had been called up came back to the Spanish Riding School, and by mid-December 1939 we managed to resume public performances, which were warmly welcomed.

In a report dated January 17, 1940, to the Cavalry Inspector in Berlin I raised once again the important question of new riders:

In my opinion the most important task of the Spanish Riding School at the moment is to concentrate on training a full complement of apprentice *Bereiter*. This can be achieved only if the old *Oberbereiter* continue to serve as teachers. This raises certain difficulties, for these men, grown old in the service, for many years had the false impression that they were the last defenders of the art of classic riding, and that this old culture would die with them. So for decades they have paid only scant attention to the training of new riders, and this is why the huge gap between their horsemanship and that of the others, some of whom have been in the school for as long as fourteen and twenty years, has grown even wider. By stating repeatedly that only through his pupils can the name of a riding-master endure have I succeeded in persuading them to give more instruction.

This report brought me the authority, in spite of the War, to enrol a certain number of sergeants as trainees, a measure of tremendous importance for the school's continuance. It should not be forgotten that in making this concession the High Command in Berlin was keeping back from active service young men who could have been fighting—in order to preserve an equestrian culture that was Austrian in origin. A more positive pointer to the value of European culture could not be imagined! Even the American General Patton, himself a rider and patron of the Spanish Riding School, later wrote in his memoirs that at the first performance by the Spanish Riding School in St Martin in May 1945 he had been amazed to meet so many fit young men whom the German Reich, even though it was fighting for its life, had released from military service, merely to foster an old culture that was no longer of any possible value to the war effort.

But there was still one more thing to be done to ensure the school's survival. The German High Command in Berlin, on its own initiative, relieved me of my command of the Cavalry detachment on February 1, 1940, so that I could devote myself to the Spanish Riding School. My orders ended with the comment that there were plenty of commanders in Germany for cavalry detachments, but only one for the Spanish Riding School.

With this alleviation of my burdens I could once more give my full attention to the other problems that cropped up in connexion with the school. I reopened my former demands for more spacious quarters and tried to acquire the rooms next to the riding-hall that until 1918 had been used by the Master of the Horse's staff. But these were now occupied by a firm producing Party publications, so my plan was fiercely opposed on the grounds that war-time was not a suitable moment for carrying through alterations. I dug in my heels, and finally the quarters were inspected by a commission of representatives of the Wehrmacht and the Government. This inspection very nearly turned out badly for us, for the occupants raised all kinds of difficulties about removing their rotogravure machines. But, since

I had never seen these on the many occasions I had walked through, I induced the local commander who was present to insist on seeing them himself. This was a lucky shot, for the editor of the *Ostmarkbriefe* had to admit that the machines were in fact in the printing offices of *Vorwärts*, whereupon the Government representative gave immediate orders for the rooms to be vacated. Now it was possible to carry out the proposed installation of decent reception- and changing-rooms and the necessary plumbing.

The completion of supplies of uniform was next on the list, as well as of saddles and tack, but this was not so much a matter of the money we had to spend as of the rationing that the War Ministry had introduced. Things that could once be bought without difficulty now involved endless running about and negotiation. But at last, in spite of the War, the redecoration was completed most successfully, and the Spanish Riding School had at last a splendid and worthy setting in every respect, and what had involved so much bother and personal effort was taken for granted.

But in the spring of 1940 there were new troubles, for I fell ill, and there was sickness among the Lipizzaner. The horses were stricken by a fever epidemic that had obviously been brought from the Front by the soldiers visiting the stables. Similar illnesses cropped up in the Stallburg nearly every year and often caused the head of the school some embarrassment, but they had never been so protracted or so severe before. Indeed, there were some deaths, and the horses had to be transferred at once for several months to Freudenau, the lovely Viennese racecourse, to break the infection and to enable the stables to be thoroughly disinfected. The practical result was that for nearly nine months all regular work had to be discontinued, and there were other unhappy things that my agitated friends and acquaintances recounted to me as I lay in bed.

The continual overstrain of many months had so undermined my health that collapse was inevitable, and, however hard I tried to ignore the symptoms becoming daily more obtrusive, I could not fend it off. One day my heart simply gave out, and this was the beginning of a long and agonizing period of physical weakness. For months I lay in hospital, first in Vienna, then in Bad Nauheim, almost in despair to see all the work wasted that I had begun with so much energy and love.

In spite of my condition, and against the wishes of the doctors who were treating me, I carried on the work of the school from my sickbed with the help of my wife, who in those difficult times was devotedly assisting the nursing staff. There were orders to dispatch to Vienna and requests to compose for Berlin, as I once more took up the fight for better pay for the riders.

In the practical organization of the Spanish Riding School during the War I found the greatest supporters in two of the departmental heads of the Army High Command, Colonel Stein and Major von Mirbach, both

8. The New Stables in the Lainz Zoo

9. In the Lipizzaner Paradise: before the Hermesvilla in Lainz

10. Young Stallions on a Morning Ride

11. Work is a Pleasure

of whom later became my friends. It was their co-operation and sympathy for the school that enabled me to carry out all my plans. Major von Mirbach was my ideal of an easy colleague, dealing so painstakingly with anything that concerned us, and even in post-War years, when he was driven out of his homeland and lay ill, he still followed our activities with undiminished interest.

The determined arguments I conducted by letter from my hospital bed in Bad Nauheim finally prevailed, and the riders, after the temporary concession of an interim rise in salary, were given new ranks specially created. When the Spanish Riding School was taken over and the status of *Bereiter* definitely established only the *Oberbereiter* held the rank of lieutenant, and the others were only second lieutenants. Under the new arrangement the *Bereiter* began his career as a lieutenant, and once he was an *Oberbereiter* became a major.

I succeeded also in fulfilling the riders' express wish by procuring for them the right to change into Wehrmacht service uniform when they were not on riding duty—partly on financial grounds—though I myself was not very attracted by the idea. All the same these uniforms did come in useful later for riding outside the hall in the Josefsplatz.

During my eight months' stay in Bad Nauheim, attended with great devotion by the best heart specialists, I became naturally more and more worried over the situation, and finally got permission to go back to Vienna early. If I could deal with the affairs of the school, as far as my strength allowed, my terrible depression might improve. When my spirits were at their lowest I received a letter from General von Pongràcz.

DEAR FRIEND PODHAJSKY,

Hearing you were ill, I went to the Rainer hospital, but you had already gone to Bad Nauheim. I had almost the same trouble when I was forty, and I am sure you were never as ill as I was. It was often so bad that even when I turned my head my heart began to thump, and I started to lose consciousness, and thought my end had come. Rest, and again rest, brought me back on my feet. But making a complete recovery was a slow business, and took me over a year. I was made adjutant to the Emperor, and with much care got completely better. But I could not cope with a horse, as in my youth, for a very long time. However, I even managed that in time. Last month I was seventy-six. Be grateful that you are half my age.

Don't lose heart; everything will be splendid!

With best wishes, dear friend,

Your very devoted
ARTHUR PONGRÀCZ

These lines from the Grand Old Man of riding gave me a tremendous lift and brought back some of my confidence.

By the end of 1940 I was at last back in Vienna, and could at least see to the administration of the school for one or two hours daily. I just looked at my horses and rejoiced to see them, gently patting their necks as I gave them titbits. I was like Prometheus bound to the rock: I had the horses within reach, and still could not ride them. I used to sit and watch the riders at work, and then discuss their mistakes with them. I became more than ever convinced that the character of the rider is reflected in his work. This period during which I was forced to reduce my physical exertion to a minimum gave me ample opportunity for observing people.

The affairs of the Spanish Riding School had naturally become even more complicated during my absence. Work had been interrupted for months at a time because the Lipizzaner had been ill, and then the school had been without a head *Oberbereiter* for a long time, for Zrust had fallen ill in the spring of 1940 and died in December of the same year. By the time I returned from Bad Nauheim he was already in his grave.

The appointment of a new head *Oberbereiter* was not easy. For this important post there was nobody to choose from but the ageing Oberbereiter Lindenbauer, who had replaced Zrust when he fell ill, and the slightly younger Oberbereiter Polak. The situation was even more delicate because the two riders could not get on either professionally or privately, and I was constantly trying to keep their mutual dislike within reasonable bounds. There was no doubt that both were outstandingly able, but Oberbereiter Polak was unquestionably the more productive and better all-round rider. I could not shut my eyes to the fact that to carry on without him would be almost unthinkable—particularly after the complications resulting from Zrust's illness. He was the only one in the school who could train the new horses in "Airs above the Ground", teaching them *levades*, *caprioles*, or *courbettes*. Lindenbauer confined himself to *haute école* airs on the ground, schooling a horse on long reins and on mezairs—all very classic, but a method rarely used nowadays. *Levades*, *caprioles*, or *courbettes*, the very backbone of "Airs above the Ground," he had never touched.

Now I had always felt that all promotions, even of riders, should be decided on merit only, and not on length of service or age. Checking back in the history of the Spanish Riding School, I found that this principle had always been followed, so I was upholding tradition. But how was I to tell my children?

I tried to be as tactful as possible and got each of them to write down his record since his entry into the Spanish Riding School. A study of these reports confirmed my choice of Polak, for responsible *Oberbereiter* of the Spanish Riding School can only be those with experience of all aspects of horsemanship, so that they can show the riders under their care whatever is required. I made the following official announcement to the assembled staff:

"The choice of head *Oberbereiter* was particularly difficult on this occasion, since it was between two riders of great ability and reputation, both nearly the same age. If in the end the choice has fallen on Oberbereiter Polak this is no reflection on the exceptional riding achievements of Oberbereiter Lindenbauer. But just as among a large number of outstanding generals there can be only one commanding general, so only one man can be appointed head *Oberbereiter*."

Polak strode over to Lindenbauer, hand outstretched, and said, "We can work together as good friends, can't we?" but Lindenbauer was never able to forget the supposed slight to the day of Polak's death.

But the final choice was right. Polak became the best head rider I have ever known, maintaining the correct relationship between us and bringing all important questions to me for thorough discussion, so that I could either fall in with his suggestions or at least explain the reasons for not doing so. His cheerfulness, humanity and, not least, his great ability both as rider and as teacher won the hearts of his subordinates, who worshipped him. He really was an ideal *Oberbereiter*.

Boundless optimism combined with an unshakable belief in the cultural mission of the Spanish Riding School was needed to combat the dreary, hopeless monotony of everyday life and summon the energy needed to carry on with the construction. The reception-rooms in the Hofburg were filled with baroque furniture, and here guests assembled before the performances and got used to the traditional atmosphere; on countless occasions these rooms have helped to create a feeling of gaiety. The office near by became at last worthy of the surroundings, which certainly could not be said of the little room near the stables previously used. The extra rooms previously occupied by the Master of the Horse's staff were turned into changing-rooms and bathrooms, thus rectifying a curious situation—a magnificent riding-hall, but absolutely no washing facilities for the riders.

By a rearrangement of space even the grooms now had reasonable accommodation in the Stallburg, and their appalling barrack-room existence in two small rooms, with ceilings so low that it was impossible to stand upright, disappeared for ever. The authorization for the proposed increased strength of sixty-nine horses meant that new boxes would be needed in the Stallburg. So six compartments, part of the old stables, which for years had been used as a store, were vacated by the old chemist's shop, and after various alterations these were restored to their original purposes. But there were endless negotiations and troubles before the stables in the Stallburg appeared in their former imperial glory.

An additional project was the creation of summer quarters. The illness of the Lipizzaner virtually every year, and the fact that they had not left the city since returning to the Stallburg over three months before, induced me to look for some kind of summer holiday quarters for the school—an undertaking that seemed almost hopeless in the middle of a war. But firm faith often moves mountains and helps to overcome the most improbable obstacles. And so I managed to discover a suitable place in the Lainz Zoo, and there, despite all opposition from the Gauleiter in Vienna, I set up summer quarters for the horses.

The Zoo, a magnificent stretch of parkland on the outskirts of Vienna, surrounded by a fourteen-mile wall and once an imperial hunting-ground, was declared a nature reserve after 1918. In this park is the Hermesvilla, at one time a favourite palace of the Empress Elizabeth, and here, in spite of her restlessness, she often spent long periods. There was stabling for twelve horses in the imperial residence, but to accommodate the Spanish Riding School a stable for sixty horses had to be built; its wooden construction on a concrete base blended well with the landscape. Two disused tennis-courts were turned into an open-air school, and several meadows were fenced in to provide grazing for the Lipizzaner. And all round was plenty of room for rides across the fields. As the Lainz Zoo was open only twice a week—as it still is—there could not have been a better health resort for the white horses.

At the end of July 1941 they made the journey from the Hofburg, some in great transport vehicles and the rest walking. A large crowd had gathered while the trucks were being loaded, and the rumour flew round that the Spanish Riding School was to be taken to Berlin, and this roused great indignation. Only when I assured the people that this was simply a transfer to the Lainz Zoo, and invited the greatest doubters to come and see the Lipizzaner there, did the muttering die down. But this little episode pleased me, for it showed how the Viennese had taken the school to their hearts, regarding it as their personal property, and the erstwhile imperial riding academy had a firm bond with the people—one of my main objects ever since my appointment.

During the months of the summer holiday the horses were alternately given training and taken out for rides, being left in the afternoons to enjoy the soft meadows undisturbed. They enjoyed this freedom immensely, and even in the oldest horses youthful memories stirred, for they frolicked about at first like children let out of school, dancing in the grass and leaping in the air with delight. Lainz had such an effect on these philosophical animals that in the following years they used to whinny with delight as they approached the Zoo at the prospect of the summer days in the open air.

The Lipizzaner were wonderful to ride round the countryside. Although not used to this kind of work they soon grew accustomed to it, trotting and galloping superbly up and down hill, clearing joyfully any obstacles like ditches, tree-trunks, or winding brooks and convincing their riders that the greatest earthly joy is without doubt to be found on a horse's back.

These rides in the wonderful, peaceful countryside, populated only by red deer and wild boars, which stopped feeding and stared in astonishment after the unexpected cavalcade, convinced even the most sceptical how well suited the Lipizzaner were for general work. To us also our stay at the Zoo was like Paradise. From then on the stallions kept very fit; gone were the recurring bouts of illness, and the rides were immensely valuable as training.

I noticed another crying need as soon as I took over the Spanish Riding School: a musical accompaniment worthy of the performance. For years there had been an excellent quartet to supply this, grouped on the second balcony above the entrance to the riding-hall, the musicians completely hidden by the high stone balustrade. But now these men were otherwise occupied and begrudged every minute, often with comic results. Oberbereiter Polak, a musician himself, often complained to me that during the public performances the quartet, due to the premature 'disappearance' of the musicians, became first a trio, and then a duet, until by the end of the show it was a violin solo by the lonely man remaining that was providing the music for the heavenly movements of the Lipizzaner. I tried to put an end to this state of affairs by engaging a first-class Army orchestra.

As the War went on the problem of musical accompaniment became more and more critical, for the constant changes of musicians meant a good deal of rehearsal for the orchestra, since the music had to fit in exactly with the movements of the horses. Realizing that this would get worse the longer the War continued, I decided to have records made of specially chosen pieces of music. I discussed the idea with the Equerry Dr Gustav Rau, but he turned down as absurd this "canned music," as he called it. But I refused to be deterred, and finally arranged a recording with an excellent orchestra. After much experiment we managed to adjust the gramophone and so place the loudspeakers that the recording sounded just like a live orchestra.

How well we succeeded was clearly proved in a conversation with Dr Rau after the first performance with the new music. He asked me whether I had really intended to replace the excellent orchestra he had just heard with canned music, so there was nothing for it but to tell him that the accompaniment had been a recording. He looked somewhat surprised and incredulous at first, but then said with a smile, "Well, you have managed to convert me to your way of thinking!"

But the reconstruction was not confined to material things. I was able to pursue my equestrian ambitions, thanks to the willing co-operation of Oberbereiter Polak (who later, under the new ruling, took the title of *Reitmeister*) and the other riders. Ever since taking over the Spanish Riding School I had dreamed of replacing a slightly dreary quadrille for four with a school quadrille of twelve riders, as a worthy living memorial to the accomplished school horse. At first sight this seemed a vain ambition, for it meant raising the establishment from six *Bereiter* to twelve, and this in the middle of an apparently unending war. What a hopeless undertaking! But the impossible happened: talented young riders were released from the Army, and trained for many months, making such good progress that in the spring of 1942 the new great school quadrille was shown for the first time. Its success was tremendous, enriching the programme and providing an added attraction. In reporting one of the first performances, French journalists who knew the Cadre Noir from Saumur said the new quadrille was unequalled in the perfect matching and precision of the horses.

The highest recognition, however, for the great school quadrille came from Dr Gustav Rau, who, at the very moment when we were fighting a battle over the Lipizzaner stud, said in a report to the Army Command:

> On November 29, 1942, a gala performance is to be held. The Spanish Riding School in Vienna is packed with spectators. Among the guests of honour are many leading personalities from the Army and the Party. Under the direction of Colonel Podhajsky the school, taken over after the union of Austria with Germany by the Army High Command, has made more progress than even the greatest optimist could have foreseen. Specially chosen non-commissioned officers and sergeants have been put on the strength of the school, and done so well that they are hardly distinguishable, either by their seat or by their riding skill, from the few old hands. The climax of the gala performance is a combined school quadrille by twelve riders. It can be said that this is of remarkable perfection. For hundreds of years the Viennese Spanish Riding School could never produce more than four riders and four horses.

But in 1942 the Spanish Riding School suffered a terrible blow through the totally unexpected death of Reitmeister Polak. On May 12 he rode as usual into the packed riding-hall in front of the young horses to begin the performance, and after the first step fell unconscious from his horse. The audience was paralysed with fear as the cheerful, nimble man—so young-looking—lay helpless in the sand and his riderless horse had to be led away. And even then nobody guessed that the first shadow of death had touched Polak and this was his last ride.

In the cemetery chapel at Hietzinger riders in traditional uniform kept watch over the bier. Then the funeral procession formed, with full military honours, and his favourite horse in its best trappings followed the coffin, which was borne by the grooms and escorted by the riders. Then came a long line of mourners, including two officers from Berlin representing the Army High Command, the City Governor from Vienna and representatives of the local command, many friends of the Spanish Riding School and admirers of the great master. During the burial service at the graveside the horse neighed loudly, as if saying a last farewell to his master. A rich and valuable life had come to a worthy end, and afterwards I paid public tribute to Reitmeister Polak's outstanding talents as a rider, his reputation, and the fine example he gave of the value of traditional training. All his friends, including the Lipizzaner, would miss him sorely.

The establishment of summer quarters at Lainz, the furnishing of the reception-rooms in the Hofburg, the construction and equipping of the stabling at the Stallburg, and the creation of a school quadrille with twelve riders had brought the Spanish Riding School by the beginning of 1943 to the height of its reputation. And the new supplies of uniforms as well as the golden trappings for the horses played an important part in making the Spanish Riding School opulent as well.

CHAPTER 6

Horse Stories

It may at first glance seem peculiar, even exaggerated to many people, to claim that horses, dumb creatures apparently destined only to serve man, should play an important part in his life. If we love and study Nature, however, we soon realize that some animals that are to be our companions through life cannot be carelessly ignored, but deserve a little attention. Their characters, if we learn to understand them, will open the doors of an unknown kingdom, and we might well follow their example of integrity, reliability, and devotion.

Of the quadrupeds horses and dogs are closest to us, for they often bring us pleasure and relief from the cares of everyday life. Which of them approaches us most nearly is a matter of opinion. I have often heard men say that dogs are superior to horses in intelligence and adaptability. I do not believe that any such comparison is fair, for in general we take more trouble to understand our dogs, have them with us much more, without always demanding that they work for us. We devote ourselves to our horses, on the other hand, for several hours a day at the most, and leave them in the stable for the rest of the time to themselves or their grooms. We barely give them the chance to get used to our habits, and in the few hours we spend with them, usually occupied in serious work, we ourselves have little opportunity to get to know them thoroughly. But this knowledge is essential for mutual understanding.

I have learnt to understand the horses I wanted to school for my own use by trying to put myself in their place in giving my commands. Thus I began to appreciate their latent intelligence and sensitivity, though they are unfathomable to so many people. My experience has been enriched, and I have found many of them excellent teachers. I am not afraid to acknowledge my debt to horses, for they have taught me self-control, patience,

72

and moderation in my duties. My dealings with them have been closely connected with my riding career, and are part of the general picture I am trying to give of my life, so I must deal rather more thoroughly with these devoted companions

I have spent my whole life with horses; my association with them and love for them resulted in my devoting myself to them. They have brought me under their spell and given me the strength to fight for them in the most varied situations. The golden words of the Koran come instantly into my mind: "Horse, thou art truly a creature without equal, for thou fliest without wings and conquerest without sword."

When we do succeed in penetrating the inner thoughts of our horses we appreciate the great wisdom of Mohammed. But what a bad impression these divine creatures, with their beauty and smooth movements intended to bring only delight, must often have of their owners! How lucky for many that the Creator denied them speech, or they would complain bitterly of the unreasonableness, brutality, injustice, and ingratitude of man. Because they are mute their disillusionment and sufferings are drowned in the great sewer of earthly injustice. This is true not only of the poor army horses, who often loyally endure severe privation through inadequate feeding, but of the many callously treated working horses who carry loads far beyond their strength, and countless saddle-horses who suffer so much through the impatience and vanity of their riders. It is a phenomenon of our age that every driver tries to learn all about the engine of his vehicle, but most people who want to make use of the motive power of horses rarely give them a thought, although, being living creatures, horses are entitled to be assessed according to their physical capabilities and to have their feelings considered. The longer I work with horses, the more I realize that an understanding of the intellectual capabilities of an animal is even more important in training than any judgment on his physical merits and shortcomings, though this latter is always easier to arrive at than an assessment of his inner qualities. But, conversely, no effort should be made to excuse an animal's bad manners or disobedience with psychological explanations, as many riders do, for this only leads to the same negative results as in badly brought up and spoilt children.

Many horses have been my companions, beginning in the First World War with my service horse Neger, into whose dimming eyes I looked as a young soldier, and ending with the gallant Pluto Theodorosta, who had the honour of bearing the Queen of England. They all guided me through the colourful world of horses, and I am indebted to all of them for many wonderful experiences.

Neger, a strong-willed black stallion, who earned me so many reprimands by his refusals on the parade-ground, and had been a real problem to me, later saved my life in the field with his powerful strides. Forced to retreat under enemy fire, I noticed only when he collapsed under me that he had been mortally wounded by a piece of shrapnel, but he carried out his duty to the last. Flecks of white foam covered his already cooling body, and his glazed eyes stared at me in such indescribably pathetic helplessness that tears came into my eyes—I am not ashamed to admit it. I had lost a true and loyal comrade.

Nero was my companion for more than twenty years, and the most amiable and reliable animal that I have ever owned. Thanks to these traits and his remarkable intelligence he took far less time to train than any of my other horses. All the same, as a four-year-old he had nearly killed a groom; the stable guard was found one morning unconscious in the gangway by Nero's stall. What happened in the night could never be established—the dragoon himself could not remember later—but undoubtedly Nero had been frightened by a sudden movement and in self-defence had bucked and kicked him on the head. How easily he might have gained a reputation for bad temper and been handled accordingly, although in fact it had been nothing but fear that had caused his behaviour. And Nero was a coward, as I had ample opportunity of proving.

Jumping for him was fraught with difficulty. As soon as he saw the obstacle he stopped a long way away, and could be persuaded neither by good advice nor by active help to go any nearer, much less to go through the motions of jumping. Endless patience was needed to get him to carry out even the obedience jumps in the dressage trials. In any case I had to practise these as little as possible because of his bad feet. But as he progressed in dressage training I began to detect a growing obedience overcoming his distaste, so that he would clear the obstacles. The performance that touched me most was after the 1936 Olympics when he had to jump a hurdle in the Advanced class event at Aachen. Although for more than a year I had not put him over a single jump, so as to nurse his feet, he followed my commands exactly, though I could feel his heart thumping, and soared over the hurdle to victory.

He was nervous, too, of the white lines in the Olympic stadium. To start with he stood trembling in front of them, or jumped over them in terror, thus risking being marked down by the judges, but I soon discovered that he would cross these lines quite willingly if he could look at them quietly. After that I always had similar lines drawn in the training square. He would look at them snorting, his front legs stiff and straight, but later he never even noticed them. These precautions were only successful, however, if the lines were made of exactly the same material as in the competition arena, otherwise his complex became noticeable once more.

I knew Nero very thoroughly, and he knew me just as well, as he showed one morning when, after a particularly long leave, I went into the badly lighted stable without being noticed by the soldiers working there. Only

Nero, who was being groomed in the gangway, noticed me at once and came straight up to me. On another occasion after returning to Fürstenwalde after a Christmas leave I thought I would visit him before I went to bed, but found his stall empty and learned that he had been moved to the regimental sick-bay in my absence because of a lowering attack of cellulitis. The guard did not know into which of the forty-odd loose boxes Nero had been put, and the light was so bad that I could not pick him out from the numerous other horses. Rather sadly I regained the entrance after walking through the stable without having found him, and made one last attempt, calling out "Burschi," which was my pet name for him. Then I heard a soft whinny from the far end, and there, sure enough, I found him at the door of his box waiting for me.

My close companion for so many years became as time went on a real character. He would look amiably out of his stall, then whirl crossly round when his saddle was shown him, and had to be persuaded to present his head instead of his croup! This dislike of being saddled must have come from having his girths too tight in his youth. He took such exception to this that several times when his saddle was uncomfortable he had rolled right over. Even work gave him no pleasure to begin with, and he was obviously one of those who are not at their best in the morning. Because of his gloomy mood and reluctance to be saddled he had to be given a very gentle start and plenty of time to settle down, but as soon as he warmed up he would perform all his exercises eagerly and with exemplary precision, obviously thoroughly enjoying himself. But he always tackled dressage trials like clockwork, rarely making even the smallest mistake, and, however stiff the opposition, was always placed high up. Still, I always made an effort to remember Nero's idiosyncracies when I gave commands, training him to obey joyfully by praising him often, and this is why he retained his youthful appearance even in his old age. He looked so very different from those old dressage horses whose obedience had been achieved through the whip, for they had joyless, often sorrowful, faces and looked much older than they really were.

In January 1939 at the Berlin International Horse Show the retired Commandant of the Cavalry School in Hanover, General von Dalwigk, then an old man, asked me how I managed to keep Nero looking younger every year without losing any of his friskiness—a tribute to my training, for General von Dalwigk in his position as Corps Commander had no reason to pay me an empty compliment.

Of course, I could handle Nero in this individual way because I knew him thoroughly, and could sense his moods and fancies. It is in some ways easier for an animal psychologist, for these creatures have not man's talent for pretence. One can always tell by the way his ears move whether a horse is of a friendly, mistrustful, or hostile disposition.

Nero loved the applause after he became a star, and played up to an enthusiastic audience, though without ever making mistakes in his excitement. He also liked to have his admirers, and particularly his lady admirers, press lumps of sugar on him after a successful ride. Then he behaved as if I were not there at all, merely trying to grab as quickly as possible the treats his fans offered him, for, of course, he knew that the rewards of his master would also be forthcoming. Nero was a real scamp, trying to increase his sugar ration by storing up the lumps of sugar between his cheeks and his jaw like a hamster.

But even he could refuse titbits if I had offended him in the course of our work. Oh, yes, this knowing animal rejected in his own way the method of 'bread and jam and a beating.' I noticed through the years that other horses, too, simply would not take sugar offered to them by their riders if they had been badly handled or overworked, often as a result of youthful overenthusiasm. For me this was always an alarm signal. I blamed myself, determined to be more moderate, and it frequently spoiled the whole of the rest of the day for me while I tried to find a reason, analysing carefully all I had said and done. Thus horses taught me self-control; my work became quieter and more mature, and my horses less often showed their displeasure by refusing their sugar. Our friendship and mutual understanding grew deeper, for, unlike many riders, I never ignored this refusal of sugar or treated it as the whim of a stupid animal.

If I felt guilty when I was impatient or inconsiderate, and aroused Nero's disapproval, he was equally sorry for the sins resulting from his high spirits. Once when, deep in thought, I was riding along with a slack rein Nero suddenly jumped to one side, throwing me anything but gently; later he sprang the same surprise on my wife. Both times he stood motionless at the scene of the crime, gazing with bowed head and horrified eyes at his prostrate rider, as if to say, "Forgive me: I didn't mean it." Moments like these gave me unforgettable glimpses of the inner feelings of my loyal companion.

With horses as with humans it is the problem children who become our favourites. And Nero, God knows, caused me problems enough through the years. There were his brittle, thin-soled feet, which repeatedly made him lame, and he was so afraid of the pain that long after the trouble had cleared up he did not dare to take a step. I noticed this after one particularly long period of lameness, for which ultimately the veterinary surgeon could find no reason; after a few moments of trotting Nero went quite lame. I let him go on, and noticed that he gradually took firmer steps, and suddenly went on quite happily. He had been so conscious of his pain that he was still nursing the foot after it was quite better. Or was he shamming? I was never quite sure, although I knew him so well.

One night Nero decided that Nora's tail was specially tasty, and chewed it for so long that in the morning there was hardly more than a bald stump left. This wickedness had two results: Nero fell ill with a severe attack of jaundice, which often recurred, and Nora, just before a stiff dressage competition, had lost her tail and become even less attractive. What a frightful situation! But the mockers jeered too soon at her unlovely appearance, for I had false hair plaited so skilfully into her tail that it looked real.

So for many years Nero and I shared our joys and sorrows and grew older together, merging in the riding world into a single unit. How widely Nero was known in Germany was obvious from the countless questions that came to me in letters during the War. I will only mention here the company fighting in Russia who had made a bet as to whether the gallant thoroughbred was still alive, as they wanted to drink our health, and the riding enthusiasts in the air raid shelter during the bombing of Hamburg who had a difference of opinion over Nero's pedigree and called me in to settle it. It shows how strong the love of the horse can be even at such a distressing moment.

Nero was with me to the very end. I had resisted all the many pressing requests to sell him, and was lucky enough to be able to give this faithful warrior a carefree evening to his life. He had been a regular stable companion to the noble Lipizzaner, so when he was twenty-six years old I put him out in the paddock, but the old gentleman indicated that he was not interested in being out to grass. His only concern was to instruct the white mothers and daughters of this noble race in the *passage*, gallop, and changes of leg; so, since I was bothered about his heart, I brought him back into the stables of the Spanish Riding School.

When the inevitable moment of parting came I felt as if I had lost something of myself. I stood sadly in front of the empty stall, and thought how often in silent gratitude after a successful ride I had offered him the sugar he loved so dearly. Involuntarily the poetic thought came into my mind that in the days to come I should not lack a devoted charger in the heavenly army, for Nero, the faithful companion of so many years, would bear me on his back through those Elysian fields.

There are horses who are completely materialistic, repulsing any show of affection from their riders to get their earthly sweets faster, others who ask nothing but to be treated kindly, taking even a loudly spoken word as correction and shrinking away nervously—in fact, they are all feeling. Nora, the other horse to accompany me on my ascent in the riding world, was such a sensitive creature that she took offence very easily and was not easy to pacify. She valued gentleness above all, and showed how much she needed it, particularly when she was ill and in pain. After that unlucky day's hunting when she strained her fetlock badly she had to endure long and painful treatment. It was very touching to see how patiently she bore the agony of the poultices if only some one would pat her neck and stroke her delicate nostrils, but became restless as soon as she was left alone; so the groom and I had to take it in turns to comfort her. It is not only humans who become children again when they are ill!

In my experience mares are more dependent on their riders than geldings. I schooled Judith, a general's charger, for some months. We understood each other incredibly quickly, and our work progressed rapidly. But this idyll was disturbed when her owner asked whether I could get Judith ready for the big dressage event at the 1936 Olympics, as otherwise he would not be keeping her. As I knew only too well the difficulties in the way of this high equestrian objective, although the general had the reputation of being a not very unbiased critic, I could not say yes, and the mare was sold in Switzerland. A year later I went to Thun for the Horse Show, and her new owner pointed her out to me standing listlessly in her box, taking no notice of her surroundings or the horses who had preceded her into the stable. I called to her, and shall never forget how she raised her drooping head a little and pricked her ears as if searching in her memory for the owner of the voice she had just heard. Then she turned slowly round and came up, greeting me with a quiet and very intimate neigh. Her owner looked on in astonishment, but simply murmured, "Amazing! She is an odd creature! She has never yet come up to me, though I have called her again and again." To be in sympathy with a horse it is certainly not enough merely to be its owner! A great deal of effort is needed to understand the peculiarities of any other being.

Of the many, many horses that through the long years I have schooled and brought up to a standard worth remembering, Otto was one of the few that I never really managed to get to know. He was a wild, long-legged devil, very temperamental and obstinate, and I unwittingly treated him more carefully than other horses and thus made slower progress with his schooling. Some people, including Oberbereiter Polak, whom I respected greatly as a horseman, did not agree with my training methods, and once asked to ride Otto, to show me how I could get along faster. The outcome was shattering, for Otto opposed his distinguished rider at every turn, until Polak lost patience and handled the horse roughly; the latter bolted up to a tree and tried to sweep him off under the overhanging branches, leading the riding-master such a dance that he was completely exhausted and had to dismount. Still out of breath, Polak gasped, "He is suicidal. He'd die rather than give in!" And he was absolutely right, for later, riding in the Prater, I had a difference of opinion with Otto, which he concluded rapidly by pressing me against the rather flimsy railing of a bridge, and when I tried to get him away, only pressed the harder. The railing was obviously giving way, and I had no option but to dismount and lead him from the dangerous spot. It was the first time in my life with horses that I had had to admit defeat.

To-day I realize that we demanded of Otto more than he was physically able to give, thus arousing his stubbornness, and, considering his intelligence and love of a fight, he was usually justified. There would certainly never have been such differences between us if I had not listened to other people's advice and had been satisfied with slower progress. My careful schooling was, though I did not realize it then, the right method, but I never succeeded in getting back on to the right track. However, in spite of everything, I did manage to train Otto for the Olympic dressage trials, but he was never as reliable as my other horses, and caused me endless trouble, always without warning. All the same I learnt a great deal from him, and remember this animal teacher with gratitude, sorry for the wrongs I once heaped upon him.

My experiences with Otto came in useful for his successor, Teja. He was a very showy, dashing Hungarian from Prince Ludwig of Bavaria's stud in Sárvár. He had a fiery temperament and was very difficult, hating the bridle, disliking being shod, and full of riding complexes. He would never willingly pass horses coming towards him, and actually spun round when he saw them. I ignored this piece of naughtiness and quietly urged him in the original direction, carrying on with my work as if nothing had happened. Since he often offended in this way Oberbereiter Polak asked why I did not administer the usual punishment. But this time I refused to be influenced, convinced I should get further by patience. It was indeed months before I cured Teja of this bad habit, but then he never did it again.

Later I understood the reason for his nervousness, for I learned that when an Austrian commission had been sent to Budapest to buy horses he had been tried out as a mount for a general. Teja was so frightened that he would not stand still while the unknown rider got on his back, and he was replaced at once. His next owner allowed all sorts of riders, quite indiscriminately, to mount Teja, and beat him if he made the slightest attempt to move. This rough handling so broke the horse's spirit that at the next muster he was quiet enough to be bought. But once in Vienna he still would not let his general get into the saddle! Unfortunately, teaching by force is not at all uncommon among riders; I knew one very famous rider who punished his horses by jerking the bit and similar brutalities if they even whinnied, until finally not one of them could make a sound. They all lost their stallion's fire and behaved like geldings, apparently indifferent to people, if not positively hostile. By forcing these creatures to submit absolutely to his will he had broken their spirit, and I myself saw one of them shrink into the farthest corner of his box at the sight of his master.

There are many roads to Rome: straight and crooked, easy and laborious, and various ways of making a horse obedient. Continual punishment will break an animal's spirit and teach it obedience through fear, but frequent rewards and careful understanding will win joyful obedience, which for the horse means also pleasure in work. An advocate of the latter method, I have always had completely friendly relations with my horses. I used to visit them in their stables whenever possible, and after hunting or other hard days' work always saw to it that they were well cared for, growing close to them, and being rewarded by their trust and lively interest in everything that happened. In short, I treated them as good companions, and they gave me many happy hours.

Once on a long hack a temperamental thoroughbred called Bengali bucked suddenly and landed me in the grass, and, enjoying his unaccustomed freedom, headed for his stable on his own—a very risky thing to do without an escort and several miles from home. Picturing the long walk and the jeering reception I should get in the barracks, I shouted his name but without much hope. To my astonishment he came galloping back in a great arc as soon as he heard my voice, and stood quite still beside me while I mounted: a truly chivalrous act not to take advantage of his momentary victory over me.

Another instance illustrated our good relationship still more clearly. Bengali, in spite of two years' racing, had little dash, and if he was ridden through the crowd in public without warming up he never hurried, not merely halting at obstacles, but going backwards at speed. Once in early October I was riding him along the Danube dam, stirred by the autumn day and a sudden longing to go hunting. I put Bengali at a small jump. He did not think much of this, and not only refused, but began to retreat rapidly. I sensed the river behind us, but was quite unable to halt his backward course, and in a matter of seconds disaster was upon us. His hind-foot slipped down the steep slope of the concreted dam, and he somersaulted with me into the water. I reached the bank with a few strokes, but was horrified to see Bengali being swept away into the middle of the Danube. At that moment I was sure I had lost my horse for good, feeling that to call his name would be a puny attempt to halt apparently inevitable fate. But my voice worked wonders; Bengali lifted his head, neighed feebly, and struggled mightily against the current in an effort to reach me on the bank. We both returned to barracks soaked and shivering, but inwardly I rejoiced at his great dependence on me.

When we succeed in understanding the animal world we discover the various characteristics and habits, the strength and weakness, of those entrusted to us. The hard-working horse will always do his best to please his master. My Neapolitano Africa was a typical example. If he made a mistake or learned a new exercise he became so excited by his efforts that his teeth would chatter, and I would ostentatiously ignore his confusion to calm him down again. Phlegmatic horses are far better in that they never take an unnecessary step and they conserve their strength.

The way horses behave together is interesting. There can be intimate

12. A Brilliant Rider and Teacher: Oberbereiter Polak
in the *Levade* on Neapolitano Adriano, 1928

13. Teja, 1945

14. American Army Spectators in St Martin, 1945

15. An Historic Moment: Colonel Podhajsky before
General Patton in St Martin, 1945

friendship or bitter hostility. I noticed this particularly with the Lipizzaner, for they are strong individualists, and their long association with human beings has stressed this characteristic even more. I was able to prove how much this contact contributes to the development of their personalities, for the Lipizzaner of the Spanish Riding School were far more alert and confident than the Lipizzaner from Italy and Yugoslavia.

They are incredibly proud as a race and obviously make friendships among themselves. I noticed repeatedly on our tour how little notice they took of the strange horses competing, but watched closely from the saddling enclosures the performances of their stable companion. Once at St Gallen I rode my horses Teja and Neapolitano Africa as an exhibition item; and as my groom wanted to watch Teja's entrance he left Neapolitano Africa tied up alone in an empty stall with open sides. But it began to rain, and other competitors put their horses under cover there, and I dismounted to find the Lipizzaner stallion surrounded by mares, and only separated from them by a few rails, but with no eyes for the fair sex in spite of several approaches, waiting impatiently for his companion Teja, and neighing in greeting as he approached.

But beware of a friendship that for some reason turns to hatred, for then the horses are virtually irreconcilable. Often horses came to the Spanish Riding School from stud bitter enemies already, unable to forget some upset in the meadows. Such stallions are never put near each other, for they would squabble unceasingly, but it can happen that the closest friends fall out after living peaceably together for a long time. Usually the drama begins when a stallion gets out and visits his neighbour. Before the stable lad can restore order the horse whose night's rest has been disturbed shows fight and there is pandemonium. But the foundation stone for permanent hostility is laid when the loser, who usually emerges from the tussle with a number of bites, waits patiently for a chance to avenge himself on his opponent, regardless of time and place, for a stallion never forgets a defeat.

In the Militär-Reit- und Fahrlehrerinstitut in Schlosshof two spirited stallions were at such loggerheads that they could never be taken out together, and had to be separated by at least the width of the street. Once their riders were so deep in conversation that they did not notice their horses gradually moving towards the middle of the road. As soon as the two got close enough one stallion reared up, fell on the other, and became completely uncontrollable. He threw his own rider, pushed his enemy's rider out of the saddle with his forelegs, tore the saddlery to shreds, and, seeing his chance at last, set about his foe with hoofs and teeth.

From the wealth of stories about Lipizzaner that I could tell I have chosen only a few showing what strong personalities these animals can have. Maestoso Borina was especially cunning; he had been for many years in the school, and reached the great age of thirty-three. He was one of the last stallions of the Spanish Riding School to have been born in the Royal Stud at Lipizza, and he had spent a carefree youth galloping over the Karst-plateau, playing and sparring with his companions. Countless scars and scratches on the old horse's coat were mementoes of his youthful battles.

His keen intelligence helped him greatly in training, and in a very short time he was an accepted favourite. As he grew older he was chosen to teach the civilian riders, and in this sphere too the clever horse managed to lead a comfortable and agreeable life. Whereas under his regular rider he would execute a brilliant *passage*, he tricked his civilian pupils by moving his back in a most peculiar way, but without actually lifting his hind-legs off the ground. Thus with the least possible trouble to himself he would send his rider away highly pleased with his 'splendid' *passage*.

Maestoso Borina was also one of the privileged few to appear behind the footlights of the Vienna State Opera House, dancing on to the stage to classical music with a famous prima donna on his back. He knew his part so well that as soon as he heard the music for the singer's entrance there was no keeping him in the wings, and he would hurry forward, once even jumping —to the not inconsiderable alarm of the singer—over a rolled-up carpet lying in his path on those boards that mean all that matter in life to so many people.

As the doyen by many years of the Lipizzaner herd in the Josefplatz he had his own special box, from which he would observe curiously and with great interest all that was going on in the stable, particularly in his last years, when he ate, so to speak, the bread of charity as a Spanish Riding School pensioner. He was completely at home in his box, which, although the door was open, he never left, and one day simply refused to accept that he must be put in another stall because a sick horse had to be isolated. He did not rest until he had succeeded in opening the barred door of his temporary box and got back into his old stable and his very own place. Who could be annoyed with the self-willed old creature?

His intelligence was obvious from the expression on his clever face, which never altered, even when his body was noticeably failing.

In his honourable old age Neapolitano Montenuova was another member of the noble company of those who take their duties very seriously and know exactly what they want. This thirty-year-old Lipizzaner, outstanding for twenty years in all the performances of the Spanish Riding School because of his great ability and poise, was given in his old age the task of testing candidates for the post of *Bereiter*. While he would willingly submit to the authority of capable riders and obediently perform every exercise in his usual way, he sensed with uncanny instinct the weaknesses of a rider and brought low many who thought themselves great artists. Frequently he would bring the tiresome game to an end with a mighty *capriole*, depositing the over-optimistic applicant in the sand.

There is no doubt at all that the Lipizzaner have been endowed with exceptional intelligence, but careful selection by riding tests in the Spanish Riding School and close contact with human beings have played a decisive part in the development of their outstanding characteristics. It is only their intelligence that makes the fiery horses, with their enormously powerful bodies throbbing with vitality, submit to men and try to understand their intentions. There was the four-year-old Lipizzaner Conversano Soja, who tore his tongue so badly playing with his neighbour that a piece of flesh two inches long was hanging loose and had to be removed. Although the veterinary surgeon nipped it off unceremoniously with a special pair of tweezers—a very painful business—Conversano Soja allowed this same man still in his white coat to stroke his head. Other horses would have been nervous for much longer, and certainly not have been so sensible.

There are countless stories from the land of the white horses about these riding teachers who have played their part in establishing and maintaining the fame of the Spanish Riding School. To some people the Lipizzaner may well be merely animals who have no right to a life of their own. But many, even in the middle of a war, have expressed a strong desire to get a glimpse of the inner world of these creatures, and it is for them that I have included these lines.

CHAPTER 7

——————◆◆◆◆◆——————

The War Years

From its earliest days there had always been a strong bond between the Spanish Riding School and the Lipizzaner stud, for training in the *haute école* was given only to horses that came from the Karst stud. The reason for the school's very name was that since its foundation only Spanish horses and their descendants, the Lipizzaner, had been used.

During the supremacy of the Moors in Spain Barbary and Arab stallions were crossed with Andalusian mares, and for centuries the resultant Spanish strain played much the same part in Europe as the English thoroughbred does to-day. Because of its exceptional aptitude for learning, and the delicacy of its movements in spite of its great physical power, the Lipizzaner was particularly suitable for training in the *haute école*, but after the expulsion of the Moors there was a general deterioration in this highly developed strain, so an effort was made in several European countries to preserve it by special breeding—just as the English thoroughbred is produced almost all over the world.

In 1562 Emperor Maximilian II stocked the Royal Stud at Kladrub with Spanish horses, but the breeding of Spanish horses in Austria did not become really significant until Archduke Charles founded the Royal Stud at Lipizza in 1580.

This stud, from which the Spanish Riding School was to obtain its horses thereafter, was able, except for a few interruptions necessitated by war, to carry out its task undisturbed for hundreds of years. The first decisive change came when the Royal Stud had to be evacuated in 1915 because of the war against Italy, but the worst blow it sustained was the collapse of the Danube empire. The Hapsburg court, which actually owned it, was condemned to dissolution, and the province containing Lipizza had to be ceded to Italy. After lengthy negotiations between the Austrian Republic and Italy all the available bloodstock in Laxenburg was finally shared between the two countries in 1919. Italy retained altogether 107 stud horses, which went back to Lipizza, while the 97 horses left to Austria for breeding purposes were taken to the Lipizzaner stud at Piber, in Styria.

The function of the Royal Stud at Lipizza since its inception had been to breed horses for the Marstall and Spanish Riding School in Vienna, which is why both the stud and the riding-school were the responsibility of the Emperor's Master of the Horse. It was for him to settle all breeding plans after consideration of the wishes and needs of the Spanish Riding School. Thus we read in the records of the Royal Stud that in the year 1591 Bereiter Zuan Caprina was posted to Lipizza to help the studmaster; in 1627 Count Mansfeld, the Imperial Equerry, set up a commission to visit and report on conditions in the Royal Stud; and in 1717 the *Oberbereiter* of the Spanish Riding School was sent from Regenthal with extraordinary powers to reorganize the stud. In 1812 Count zu Trauttmansdorff had laid down precise mating rules, "from which there was to be no deviation," with due regard to the requirements of the Vienna Riding School, and arranged for the renewal of the Lipizzaner strain by the purchase of the pure Arab stallion Siglavy, making the school's influence on the running of the stud quite plain.

The Spanish Riding School was naturally interested in obtaining first-class horses from the stud, and sent there to serve the mares only those horses with strength and endurance, the right character, temperament, and intelligence as well as the physical requirements for stud. The school is thus the proving-ground for the Austrian Lipizzaner, and is as important for this breed as the racecourse is for the thoroughbred. So in the interests of both there must be very close co-operation between school and stud, and this obviously depends largely on the Spanish Riding School, inasmuch as it schools the horses reared in the stud.

The horses who were permitted to remain in Laxenburg after the partition of the Royal Stud in 1919, because they had previously belonged to the imperial family and had no connexion with the country's horse-breeding in general, were after wearisome negotiations taken over by the Austrian Republic, and removed to Piber in November 1920. It was even more difficult to clarify the position of the Spanish Riding School after the Republic had decided to keep this cultural institution going, and it was not until the end of 1921 that it was given to the Ministry of Agriculture and Forestry, not because the latter had anything to do with equestrian training, but merely to ensure that there should be a central authority for both stud and school. After the Austrian Anschluss the Spanish Riding School came under the command of the German Army, while the Lipizzaner stud was given to the Ministry of Food and Agriculture.

In the First Austrian Republic the relationship between school and stud changed, as the former's position as senior partner in the business of rearing the horses, which she had acquired under the monarchy, was now seriously restricted. The influence of the stud became as important as if the Spanish Riding School had been created for the benefit of the stud, instead of the reverse. The best school horses were often dragged off to Piber to serve the brood mares without thought of the training requirements. On the other hand, the principle of selecting stallions for stud in the riding-school was no longer observed, for even horses who were rejected in Vienna as not up to standard later managed to get to Piber for stud. The result, of course, successfully proved their inadequacy, for not a single one of their sons was chosen to return to the Spanish Riding School. The rôle of stepmother, so to speak, to which the Spanish Riding School was relegated by the new Ministry, was made clear in the years between 1925 and 1930, when because of the country's economic stagnation there was talk of disbanding this ancient academy to save money, but this project was dropped under pressure of public opinion.

The domination of the stud over the Spanish Riding School at that time was so marked that after the Anschluss the stud's Director felt compelled to give the German Army some advice about the direction of the School in an article to the paper *Soldat in der Ostmark*: "It must be the constant care of the military authorities not to deprive the Spanish Riding School of its intimate character as stallion reservoir for the breeding of Lipizzaner in Piber, and not to give it too much scope for purely riding activities."

The elevation of the stud to self-sufficiency had a very bad effect on the supply for the Spanish Riding School, and from 1923 to 1939 it received an average of only four horses a year, and in 1935 there was only one; of these 60 per cent. had to be rejected because their ability or health was not good enough. The result was that the school horses were far too old, and lacked that homogeneity that the horses of the Spanish Riding School had had for centuries, since there was obviously no clear plan as regards breeding, and nobody paid enough attention to the experts in the school.

One of my first tasks was to re-establish the correct relationship between the two establishments, and a meeting of representatives of the Army and the Ministry of Food took place in Piber. Unfortunately, the stud did not put up such a good show as our tradition demanded, evoking from the German gentlemen some critical remarks, which were certainly justified, especially as German studs were models of efficiency, as I myself noticed on many occasions. Greatly upset by this experience, I tried to convince Colonel von Langermann that this exception to Austrian custom could not be taken as a yardstick, since it was in fact on attention to the schooling and care of its horses that Austrian horsemanship depended. The Colonel broke in:

"You need say no more. I have seen the orderliness of the Spanish Riding School, the glossy coats of the horses, and the gleaming saddlery, and felt that the great traditions and international fame of Austrian horsemanship were fully justified. That high reputation cannot be injured by the little irregularities we have seen here to-day."

Then I knew that the Spanish Riding School and I had won a firm friend. But nothing was changed, for the Director of the stud hid behind the Ministry, whose representatives were always at odds with the Army—all the more in this case because they could not get over the fact that the Spanish Riding School had slipped from their grasp. So relations between stud and riding-school grew even more strained, the young stock fell far short of our expectations, and, worse still, our increased requirements resulting from the improved standing of the Spanish Riding School were not considered at all. These facts and other disadvantages induced the military authority in 1942 to run the Lipizzaner stud like other Army studs. At this time Dr Gustav Rau, who at the beginning of the War had been promoted Colonel in the Quartermaster's department, had a considerable influence in the breeding of Army horses. Thus he had a big say in the establishment of the new Lipizzaner Military Stud, and our paths crossed again and our differing opinions clashed. Dr Gustav Rau's decisions were often prompted by what was going on behind the scenes, and he often sacrificed his expert knowledge to diplomatic intrigue, whilst none of my actions had any ulterior motive, which was perhaps easier for me in my less exposed position. In addition Rau was a man full of ideas, a passionate reformer who would not be stopped by tradition or experience, the main thing being to get something new. He said to me in all seriousness when I was appointed Director of the Spanish Riding School, "If you succeed in building up the art of classic horsemanship with Hanoverian horses at the Spanish Riding School your reputation will be made."

Although we often had different ideas and fought a good many battles, this made no difference to my great respect for him as a person, or his great service to riding in Germany.

He had been deeply shocked by the conditions at Piber, and in consequence had nothing good to say about this stud or its bloodstock. So it was quite understandable that he intended to make numerous reforms when the Army took over the Lipizzaner, buying new stock in occupied Yugoslavia and establishing a carefully worked-out breeding plan. But what was incomprehensible was his intention to send the Lipizzaner stud to Hostau, in Czechoslovakia, because of inadequate accommodation at Piber, for horses are, after all, raised on suitable pasture and not in well-cared-for stables. On this point in particular we held sharply differing views.

When in June 1942 I learned of these intentions I dispatched a report at once to the proper authority in Berlin setting out the whole story of the stud, and added that Piber until now had proved a satisfactory substitute for Lipizza. I concluded:

> If the Lipizzaner strain is to continue to be preserved in the interests of the Spanish Riding School, then at all costs any experiments which might impair its suitability for the classic style of riding must be prevented. In transferring the Lipizzaner from Piber to a lower-lying northerly district there is the risk of changing their true nature, and the Riding-School will not get what it needs. It depends absolutely on suitable Lipizzaner horses, and therefore I feel it my duty as its Commandant to give the strongest possible warning against transplanting the Lipizzaner to territory which in the light of centuries of accumulated experience has nothing to recommend it.

I tried to add weight to this report by the following personal letter on July 16, 1942, to the Divisional Commander in the High Command, Colonel Stein:

> I have already set out the reasons for my attitude on this matter, prompted only by my anxiety to preserve the old school. It is also worth noting that when I visited the late Reitmeister Polak for almost the last time and told him of the plan to transfer the mares, he begged me with tears in his eyes to do everything possible to prevent it, as he knew Hostau very well, and it was not at all suitable for raising Lipizzaner. Oberbereiter Lindenbauer, too, asks me on every possible occasion whether the danger of the transfer has passed. It is not merely coincidence that we three who know the habits of the Lipizzaner so thoroughly should feel such misgivings at the danger threatening the school that we love so much.
>
> Oberlandstallmeister Seyffert also made a significant remark about the proposed transfer to Hostau: that it was a good thing at least that the Spanish Riding School was now in charge of an Austrian, so it could be not said in years to come that the Prussians had destroyed the Lipizzaners. Seyffert seemed to be of the opinion that the transfer to Hostau had originated from me, or at least been approved by me.

For weeks nothing at all was said about the plan, and I concluded that my arguments had caused some second thoughts, so I had a terrible shock when on October 2 I learned from a private source that the mares had already been transferred from Piber to Hostau. I called Berlin at once and received official confirmation of this news and naturally expressed my annoyance that my report had remain unanswered and that I had not been given any information about the transfer. The official, rather taken by surprise at my attack, admitted that Dr Rau, who had the final say, had acknowledged my communication merely by writing in the margin that it was still far from being proved that the horse was a product of the soil, and had thrown it aside. Now there was nothing left for me to do but to end my call, full of bitterness, with a request to be sent officially to Hostau to supervise the newly arrived mares.

When I got there early in November 1942 my fears were more than justi-fied. This neighbourhood was climatically quite unsuited to the Lipizzaner, for the pasture was far too rich, and the soil so deficient in calcium that a supplementary calcium feed had to be given. But the most disturbing factor was that I felt on my journey as if I was in a hostile country, so clearly did the Czech people display their hatred of anything German. What would then be the fate of the Lipizzaner stud if one day . . .

To add to my worries I discovered that Dr Rau had been to Hostau a few days before my arrival and ordered a host of fundamental reforms: the rejection of a great number of the brood mares from Piber and their replacement by mares from Yugoslavia; the mating of closely related horses, very often brother and sister, allegedly to preserve the breed and good qualities of the single strain; the use of three-year-old mares for breeding; and many other innovations. In a word, the good doctor was once more in his element carrying out experiments. The great pity was that this time it was the Lipizzaner he was using, for the Spanish Riding School was the only place employing this breed, and I as its Director had to bear the brunt of this new scheme. To the Commandant of the stud I made no secret of my objections, and did not restrain my justifiable criticism.

Certainly the Lipizzaner stud during the centuries of its existence had had to endure many experiments, especially the many attempts at cross-breeding of various kinds, even with English thoroughbreds, to produce a larger horse. But in those days several hundred animals were available, so that the failure of such matings could be rejected without harming the stock. It was quite different in 1942, when there were so few mares that each failure must bring irreparable consequences and seriously endanger the continuance of the Lipizzaner breed as a whole. My arguments induced the Commandant to report our meeting to Berlin, and I was invited to a discussion of the whole affair by the Veterinary Inspector, General Schulze.

The Berlin meeting in November 1942 was very difficult, being my first open conflict with Dr Rau, before some fifteen officers under the presi-dency of the Veterinary Inspector. The odds, too, were far from even: Rau had great powers of rhetoric and a reputation as an expert on horses, was highly respected by most of those present and feared for his sharp, con-fident, and often somewhat taunting retorts; I, on the other hand, was certainly known as a successful rider, but was severely handicapped by not having hitherto been prominent in questions of horse-breeding, and being, moreover, an Austrian, too often treated in the mighty German Reich as something of a joke. However, I had with me to support my side of the case Oberbereiter Lindenbauer, the senior member of the old Spanish Riding School, but he proved a very inept business partner, although such a skilful rider. He could not be persuaded to utter a word, and would do no more than accompany my remarks with nods of approval. So I was on my own.

The Veterinary Inspector announced at the beginning of the meeting that the military authorities had taken over the Lipizzaner stud to ensure in every possible way supplies of horses for the Spanish Riding School, and ordered me to report on the muddle I had found in Hostau, so that a peaceful solution could be found. I thereupon stated that the co-operation of stud and riding-school could be certain of success only if the Spanish Riding School were given the same far-reaching powers of consultation as it had evidently had for centuries. Further, any breeding experiments were useless and should be resisted, since the extensive records of the stud were sufficient guide, and the achievements of the Spanish Riding School gave the best proof of the success of the present strain. In particular I stressed the necessity of taking special care of the Lipizzaner from Piber, so that this stud, which had been breeding horses for the Spanish Riding School without interruption for two hundred years, should not be destroyed through over-hasty decisions.

Here I was vigorously opposed by Dr Rau, who wanted the influence of the Director of the Spanish Riding School virtually eliminated. After a long debate the Veterinary Inspector decided that the Director must be consulted in all questions of breeding, and his wishes must most definitely be considered. I had achieved my first success, and perhaps kept the right to veto the proposed disposal of some of the Piber brood mares.

Obstinately Dr Rau clung to his ideas on interbreeding, one of his hobbyhorses. After a great deal of discussion, and my observation that it is years before experience can prove whether a *Landstallmeister* (provincial equerry) has been good or bad, which would possibly be too late for the Lipizzaner stud with its relatively small stock, the new breeding plans were rejected for the Piber Lipizzaner, and the stud was ordered to keep me fully informed of the matings arranged.

Dr Rau was particularly put out over my demand that the three year-old mares should not be used, as they were not fully developed. He pronounced my opinion old-fashioned, adding that the anticipated enlargement of the stud made this necessary. As I seemed to be making no headway I turned to the expert on thoroughbreds and asked him what he thought of having two-year-old mares served. He rejected the idea angrily, remarking that after all one could not use children for breeding, so I demanded the same treatment for the Lipizzaner, for years of experience had shown that they mature late, which is borne out by the length of their lives: the development of a three-year-old Lipizzaner is the equivalent of that of a two-year-old thoroughbred.

Dr Rau contradicted this passionately and said he thought that the late maturity of the Lipizzaner was one of those old ideas that were thoughtlessly repeated, parrot-fashion. There was no reason why the Lipizzaner, if it had more food, could not mature just as quickly as any other warm-blooded horse. Since he would not listen to any of my arguments, I could not resist reminding him that less than a year before he had bought a yearling Lipizzaner stallion in Yugoslavia to bring new blood to the breed, and it looked quite out of place at Hostau, being more like a mule than a Lipizzaner. There could be only one explanation for such a mistake by an expert like himself: a yearling Lipizzaner is far less developed than any other half-bred horse of the same age.

When Dr Schulze finally decided that the Lipizzaner from Piber should, as in the past, only be used for breeding after four years, Dr Gustav Rau sprang to his feet in a fury and announced that he might just as well have stayed away from the meeting, since all his suggestions had been turned down.

Thus I had succeeded in ensuring that no Lipizzaner from Piber would be rejected without my knowledge or used for experiments. Dr Schulze, however, told me at the end of the hearing, which had gone on for several hours, that I should have to agree to the transfer of the whole stud to Hostau in the end. And my success at that significant meeting was only a Pyrrhic victory, for Dr Rau was much too dictatorial to implement the resolutions, and tried to go his own way, so I had to continue to battle with him on behalf of the Lipizzaner breed.

Only a very few months after the Berlin decision I found out that he had not given up his plan for interbreeding, even going so far as to mate father and daughter. I managed to prevent this at least by dispatching a written complaint in January 1943, but not the pairing of brother and sister, which Rau thus defended to the High Command in February in 1943:

"The mating of full sister and brother fulfils the necessary breeding requirements. In animals it is not at all unusual, according to the most recent authorities on Heredity."

Many years later, when I had the Lipizzaner stud and the new stock from Hostau under my care, I asked for the rest of the mares and stallions dropped from mares served by brothers or half-brothers, but discovered that not a single example of these breeding experiments could hold its own either in the Spanish Riding School or in the stud.

The Austrian Lipizzaner stud from Piber was now combined with the Yugoslavian Lipizzaner stud from Demir Kapia, with the addition of numerous Lipizzaner bought by Count Elz in Vukovar and Herr Reisner. In the autumn of 1943 the original stud from Lipizza was added, and from it the Lipizzaner stud at Hostau was formed with something like 350 horses. Thus the descendants of the Royal Stud, scattered through the collapse of the Danube empire, were brought together.

I made full use of the authority given to me to keep in close touch with the Hostau stud by frequent visits, to prevent worse harm to the Piber Lipizzaner—in particular their transfer to studs in Poland or to private people.

So it was a personal tug of war with Dr Rau, whose dislike of the Piber Lipizzaner grew and grew. I was able to modify the mating experiments a little and almost completely prevent the Piber brood mares from being disposed of—at least until I lost contact with Hostau in the difficult final period of the War. In the few remaining months in which Dr Rau reigned unchallenged he practically decimated the Piber Lipizzaner stud by constant selling. It is interesting to note that after the retreat of the German troops the Czechs confiscated most of the Lipizzaner sold to private individuals and sent them to the Topolcianky stud in Slovakia, where there were also many brood mares from Piber.

My opinion of the shortcomings of Hostau for breeding Lipizzaner was very soon vindicated. The number of barren mares was on the increase, because, as the Commandant of the stud informed me, they had got too fat and refused to be served. So their food racks were put higher up, but in spite of this their excitement for the stallions never returned. Another disturbing factor was the noticeable deterioration of their good hard hoofs, which now became misshapen—hitherto unknown in this breed—and were often so bad that they were almost like goat's feet, and numbers of Lipizzaner had to be rejected because of this. Naturally this development was not concealed from the authorities, but they comforted themselves with the thought that Hostau was intended as only a temporary home, and dreamed of moving the combined stud at a later date back to the historic territory of Lipizza—one of the many dreams of the 'thousand-year Reich.'

But for any sensible thinking man there were obvious dangers for this ancient breed in the political developments that were rapidly emerging. If the War were lost and the Greater German Reich collapsed, what was to become of the Lipizzaner in a 'protectorate' whose people were filled with a bitter and enduring hatred? I was exceedingly worried, but could do no more than refuse the transfer of any more Lipizzaner stallions from the Spanish Riding School, regardless of the fact that I had far exceeded the number of horses allowed me, which was to prove rather difficult after July 20, 1944. Perhaps later there might be an exchange of stallions for mares, and in this way the Piber stud could once more be established. That was my idea through these gloomy days and months before the Second World War came to an end, and why I in the final year set my face firmly against handing over the stallions Dr Rau wanted for stud, sending him only inferior Lipizzaner instead. And I would not budge even when at a race-meeting lunch in Vienna he said to me, in the presence of several experts, that I ought to concern myself with preserving a good strain, which would only be possible with good sires. I even endured the criticism of these experts in order to prevent our good stallions from being lost to the Spanish Riding School at the very last minute.

However, this little success was unimportant compared with the serious threats that menaced the Lipizzaner stud. Although the original stud had through the centuries had to flee before an advancing enemy, it had always remained in territory over which the Austrian Empire had full power. But this time these valuable horses were outside their homeland, and there was no possible doubt that in the event of a collapse they would fare no better than after the end of the Danube monarchy. Thus the future of the Lipizzaner stud, and consequently of the Spanish Riding School, looked more serious than ever before in its history, and really only a miracle could avert the danger that threatened. But have not countless people through the years waited in vain for a miracle?

CHAPTER 8

The Spanish Riding School leaves Vienna

The triumphant frenzy of the first years of the War was succeeded, for Germany and her allies, by military reverses that began in Russia and gathered momentum until they ended in catastrophe. The changing situation overshadowed our daily lives more and more, and naturally could not but have an effect on the Spanish Riding School. I was forced to recognize that my work of reconstruction had reached its limit and that I must confine myself to holding on to what had been gained with so much effort, and build defence against the rising waters.

In the autumn of 1943 the Commander of Area XVII, General Schubert, informed me that the Governor of Vienna, Baldur von Schirach, had lodged a complaint in his capacity as Defence Commissar, that no steps had been taken for the protection of the valuable horses against air attack. Instead of remaining in the Lainz Zoo with the horses during the winter months I had foolishly returned to the city. When the General handed me the letter to read I commented that it was simply not credible that the Allies, who had so far spared Rome and Paris from the air, would not be equally considerate of the Danube capital with its great cultural tradition. Moreover, I considered the suggested transfer quite pointless, mainly because the horses could not be worked at Lainz in winter, let alone shown in public. General Schubert agreed with me in thinking that Vienna would not be bombed, but felt that we must take some note of the contents of the letter.

I had a difficult decision to make. An interruption in the training of the horses through their being kept all the year round in the Lainz Zoo would lower the high standard of horsemanship already achieved, while to stop the performances, whose success emphasized the whole cultural significance of the Spanish Riding School, might cause it to be forgotten, always dangerous for an institution of this kind. So I decided to keep the horses in the city, where in my view the *Pferdegang* in the school, with its thick walls on both sides, afforded better protection in an air raid than the wooden stables at the Zoo, and was in any case hardly an important target. In the end I had to take full responsibility for the valuable Lipizzaner on which the ancient riding academy entirely depended.

After much thought I reached a compromise that would satisfy everybody. The young horses were transferred permanently to Lainz, and the school stallions were brought back to the Stallburg for the winter. In this way the performances continued undisturbed until the spring of 1944.

These exhibitions of the classic style of riding attracted more visitors every year. People sought an escape from their everyday cares, letting themselves be transported into a dream world for a few hours by the performance of the noble Lipizzaner. Even General Schubert never missed, and once confessed to me that he was like a thirsty man eager to drink his fill at the spring of beauty before it dried up. So he came along to the last performance in the Festsaal at the Josefsplatz on May 24, 1944. On this occasion the enchanted spectators had no idea that they were saying good-bye for a long time to the magnificent horses and the beautiful riding-hall. The protracted applause at the end of this show sounded an unconscious farewell.

The unsuccessful attempt on Hitler's life on July 20, 1944, unleashed terrible reprisals, and even the Spanish Riding School felt some of the repercussions. Some of the men in Berlin responsible for the riding-school were replaced by particularly fanatical adherents of dictatorship, and these had little liking for the cultural mission of this Austrian institution. After long-drawn-out negotiations I was obliged to return to my previous numbers and send some of my horses to mounted Army units and a section of the young assistant riders between the ages of twenty-five and twenty-eight, previously exempt, were called up in the course of the winter.

The first heavy air raid on the centre of Vienna gave its citizens their first real taste of war, and destroyed the last illusion that the Allies would spare this European city so rich in culture and history. However pointless this destruction might seem, and however little influence it could have on the outcome of the War, there was no longer the slightest doubt that even the old imperial capital would have to endure the brutal methods of modern warfare.

The behaviour of the horses in an air raid was most interesting. They quickly recognized the alarm signal and came on their own to the entrance of their stalls to make the evacuation easier, allowing themselves to be led at the double into the Winter Riding School, where they had their air-raid shelter. There they stood quiet, even when the alarm or raid lasted for hours, as on September 10, 1944, when bombs fell all round the school— in the Michaelerplatz and Stallburggasse—and windows were shattered and doors torn off. At the worst explosions the horses cowered down, as men do when they fear some danger from above. It seemed to me that the clever school stallions had a peculiar expression on their faces, as if saying, "How incomprehensible humans are!"

I had not the slightest doubt about the result of the War, and was convinced that Vienna would be occupied by one of the Allied Powers. None the less I intended to stay in the city with the Spanish Riding School, which had never left Vienna since its foundation centuries before, but when I saw for myself the devastating effects of the air raids, which grew heavier and heavier, I realized that the War would not stop outside Vienna, since there was no thought at all either for the civilian population or for property. In these circumstances it was suicidal to keep the old riding-school in Vienna, and so I decided to leave with my Lipizzaner.

What seemed to me obvious met with strong opposition in high places, as I soon discovered at my first interview in the autumn of 1944. The district official told me that for the Spanish Riding School to leave would be like defeatism, which under the latest orders was to be severely punished. He attempted to weaken my conviction of the danger of leaving the valuable horses any longer in Vienna by giving me information on future military operations that were to bring about a complete change in the war situation.

I was not in the least influenced by this optimism, but realized that my only hope of success lay in circumspection and well-considered action at this time of great political tension, so a great deal had to be done secretly, on my own responsibility, and in some cases disguised as something quite different.

I had already taken the air-raid precaution of packing our valuables piece by piece in boxes by the beginning of 1944. In the autumn I packed all the remaining movable property of any worth, and then prepared myself for every emergency. I found a staunch ally in the District Commander, who put vehicles and harness at my disposal, so that I could at least leave Vienna under my own power if need be.

Then the Lipizzaner had to be harnessed and led without attracting attention and this could best be done in the Zoo at Lainz. It was most moving to see how these noble artists now adapted themselves to hard necessity, and pulled the carts patiently behind them, as if they realized what was happening, They forgot the delicate dancing steps of the *piaffe*, the lively leaps of the *capriole* and *courbette*, and the statuesque immobility of the *levade*, and willingly carried out their new tasks, obediently putting themselves between the shafts to pull the heavy loads that had suddenly been given them. What admirable creatures! It would now have been possible to set off almost immediately, but such a departure would have meant the loss of many valuables that would have to be left behind, so I decided not to wait until I was forced to flee from Vienna, but to make an orderly transfer of the Spanish Riding School. This was the beginning of a long and difficult road, filled with anxious and dramatic moments.

16. Snatched from Chaos: The Lipizzaner Stud in Wimsbach, 1946

17. Lipizzaner Mares between the Shafts, Wimsbach, 1947

19. Federal President Renner visits the Spanish Riding
School in Wels, 1946

The air raids on Vienna were increasing in number and severity. In one raid by American airmen bombs landed on the Lainz Zoo, only just missing the stables. I made use of this raid and our proximity to the battle-front in a new attack on the District Command, and this time succeeded in getting the official responsible for accommodation to contact the office of the Gauleiter for Upper Austria to secure alternative quarters for the Spanish Riding School.

Then I myself began to look around in Upper Austria, which, of course, at this time was already overrun with refugees. The few places with good stabling were already occupied by studs evacuated from Hungary, but I was more hopeful when I was told about the neighbouring castles Ebenzweier and Württemberg in the Salzkammergut. But I was pretty disappointed there; the stables of Ebenzweier Castle, an extraterritorial Spanish possession, were too small and too primitive, and quite insufficient to provide the space hitherto occupied by the personnel and equipment of the school. In Württemberg Castle, on the other hand, things were a little more promising, and there was even a small riding-school available, but I was not pleased to find that this was occupied by the Marine Hitler Youth, and their leader during our negotiations hinted that his pupils could take riding lessons on the Lipizzaner in return. I had so far managed to keep myself clear of all political organizations, and I did not want to be involved in a tricky situation at the eleventh hour by sharing quarters with a school sponsored by the Party.

So I dropped this idea, although I could have carried on the Spanish Riding School divided between the two stables. Fate undoubtedly took a hand in my lucky decision, for Württemberg Castle was completely plundered in 1945 by the occupants of the near by concentration camp, of whose existence I was absolutely unaware, and the Spanish Riding School would certainly not have been spared.

I sent two riders to find out about other castles and abbeys in western Austria that I knew, but both came back empty-handed. Soon after that I received instructions from the Gauleiter of the Upper Danube through official channels to transfer the Spanish Riding School to Castle Krumau, in Bohemia, as this would be particularly suitable accommodation for the precious horses. I was horrified, for what should I do with the horses in Czechoslovakia when the inevitable collapse occurred?

Clearly I could not simply refuse to carry out this order, so I sent a rider to inspect Castle Krumau in the hope that he would be able to find enough snags for me to turn it down. Unfortunately, this was not to be, for there was indeed adequate and excellent stabling, and even a large, well-equipped riding-ground.

It was difficult and not without danger to persuade the very obstinate Gauleiter, a fanatical apostle of the 'thousand-year Reich,' to give up his idea, for he arrogantly waved aside all my fears that the Spanish Riding School might be affected by disturbances in Czechoslovakia, saying that there were enough S.S. men to protect it. Now all I could do in the circumstances was to leave open the question of alternative accommodation, since I did not expect any change of heart from him.

At last the Landstallmeister of Upper Austria suggested Count Arco-Valley's castle in St Martin-im-Innkreis, and I set off at once, for it was now December and the war situation was even worse than before. With a permit from the motor pool I was given a lift in a dilapidated ammunition truck, and succeeded, after an adventurous journey enlivened by repeated dive-bombing attacks, in arriving late the same evening at Linz, whence I continued my journey next day by train.

The owner of St Martin, a victim of the Nazi reign of terror, was in a concentration camp. In his absence Countess Gabriele Arco-Valley took me over the property and showed me all the available accommodation. The main part of the huge castle buildings was occupied by several hundred refugees from the East, but as long ago as the time of Maria Theresa a relay station had been established here for changing the post-horses drawing the mail-coaches, so there was enough stabling, though it was full of Air Force stores at the moment. But the officer in charge, though personally in favour of mechanization, proved sympathetic to my requests, and was prepared to clear the stabling for us without higher authority, though the Gauleiter of the Upper Danube, who was responsible for the refugees in the castle, categorically refused to make room for the personnel and equipment of the Spanish Riding School. However, the Countess helped me to overcome these difficulties also by making available the necessary space in the part of the castle that remained to her and the administrative buildings. At last I had found possible new quarters, and all I had to do now was to get the necessary permit. But even this last formality proved very difficult indeed.

In the welter of worry over the existence of the Vienna Riding School I still had to fend off an attack on the riding-ground itself.

The staff of the Gauleiter of Vienna wanted to store potatoes there, and tried to override my objections by simply driving in the first lorries and ordering the *Bereiter* who was there to hand over the key in the name of the Commissar of Defence, but in vain—for, knowing the way things were done at that time, I had taken possession of the key to guard against any unpleasant surprises of this kind. Then it was pandemonium. There were unfriendly exchanges between the civilian and military authorities, from whom I had no support whatsoever in this matter, for they maintained more strongly than ever that the storing of potatoes was at that moment more important than the training of the Lipizzaner. It was only when I pointed out to them that the S.S. were still in possession of their riding-ground in

No. 3 district and could just as well have stored potatoes there that I had a short breathing space, but the next day a Government official phoned to say that the S.S. riding-ground was unsuitable for storage, as potatoes would perish in a very short time lying there on the ground impregnated with salt. I decided there and then to tell the white lie that in the Spanish Riding School too salt was mixed with the sand and sawdust. From the other end of the wire I was told sharply that a representative would call to inspect the riding-ground.

Now we had to move fast. I got our staff to scatter cattle salt all over, and when the awaited sniffer arrived he really did not know how to make his inspection. A member of the school who had just finished 'salting' the ground came to his aid by passing his hand several times over it, brushing away the dust, and inviting him to satisfy himself of the taste of salt. With the tip of his tongue the Government official reluctantly touched the outstretched hand that had just finished scattering the salt. He started back in horror. So that was the end of that, and, though the situation was far from amusing, I could not help smiling at the successful bluff.

Just before Christmas 1944 I was ordered by the High Command in Berlin to send in a requisition for the necessary transport for moving the Spanish Riding School. This order seemed to me a gift from Heaven, for I thought I had the green light for evacuation, so I was even more disappointed to learn that the intention was to transfer the Spanish Riding School to Ludwigslust, in Pomerania, because there was enough stabling there and also a large riding-ground. I opposed this, saying that towns—above all garrison towns—were the most subject to air raids, and the Spanish Riding School would be going out of the frying-pan into the fire, and urged our immediate evacuation to St Martin, which was very remote and also fulfilled the necessary requirements. But I could not get permission for this, only for the cancellation of the order to go to Pomerania, so the burning questions now were: How could I get away from Vienna? When and how could I set about it? And they pursued me for many sleepless nights like a dreadful nightmare.

The seriousness of the situation was further emphasized by an inquiry I had at this time from the Budapest Spanish Riding School, already in flight, as to whether their horses could be brought under my care. The Hungarian school had been founded in Örkénitábor, modelled on the Vienna school, and had removed in 1938 to Budapest. I willingly made room for them, and it was fairly simple, as I had the summer quarters in the Lainz Zoo, but my help was after all not needed, since the Commandant of the school, Colonel Haszlinsky, as he told me later, had in the meantime found satisfactory accommodation near Ödenburg and decided to stay there for the time being.

With the New Year the situation deteriorated still more. The air raids became more frequent and severe, the front line was coming nearer as it fell back, and there was not the slightest doubt that one day it must overrun Vienna. All my previous attempts to get the school away had been unsuccessful, and nobody in authority would hear of any transfer. Just as the Trakehner stud was a symbol for East Prussia, so the Spanish Riding School was a symbol for Vienna, and it was feared that its departure would bring home to the already uneasy population the hopelessness of the situation.

A lucky chance aided me in my attempts to get at least part of the school out of the threatened city. One day I saw great furniture vans standing in front of the museum, and learned that its treasures were being hidden outside Vienna because of the increasing air raids. But were not our old pictures, furniture, saddle-cloths, and traditional uniforms equally worth taking to a less dangerous spot? These arguments succeeded in persuading the High Command to let me transfer our equipment to St Martin, and my second assault, to occupy the stables that were free with some of the horses at least, was also successful. I was ordered to keep the numbers of the departing horses down to a minimum, to keep up appearances, for the Spanish Riding School had to stay in Vienna to keep up morale.

This was the first step towards my goal. Officially "removing valuable traditional equipment and partially occupying the alternative accommodation provided in order to prevent its being put to other uses," the first muster of seventeen horses and the most valuable equipment left for St Martin.

But there were still incredible difficulties to be overcome! From Berlin I had indeed been given permission for partial evacuation, but I had to get the necessary wagons myself, and try my luck with the Transport Command. The responsible officer, himself an Austrian and former friend from our old Army days, told me that the necessary transport could not be found, even if I had written authority from Berlin, because they were already short of thousands of trucks for the most urgent military transport. I knew that this was really the case, for the High Command had a month before unsuccessfully put in a requisition for a truck to take the Lipizzaner stallions chosen for Hostau, which I welcomed at the time, wishing to spare them an uncertain fate. But now it was a matter of saving whatever could be saved, so I told the Transport Officer the whole story and of the dangers that the school, as an ancient cultural institution of the old Austria, must suffer if it remained longer in Vienna. At last he agreed to do his utmost to save the Lipizzaner, even if military transport had to go short of yet another thirty trucks. And I must be satisfied with transport "a drop at a time," for my dream of one general departure would in no circumstances be practicable. I welcomed this only because at the moment I had not obtained an order for evacuation. A second muster followed the first in February with a further forty-five stallions, this time with the knowledge of my superiors. Sixty-two of the most valuable horses and all the equipment were thus safe, and a great stone fell from my heart. The Spanish Riding School was still actually in Vienna, but really only symbolically with fifteen horses and a few riders.

An evacuation order would have to be obtained before we could leave the city with the remainder, and I tried all of one day to get in touch by telephone with the High Command in Berlin, a great strain on my patience, for the lines were constantly down as a result of air raids. At last I managed to convince the Cavalry Inspector, General Weingart, of the impossibility of our position and that it was of the utmost urgency that we should leave at once. He promised to see the chief of the Reserve Army, a branch of the Waffen-SS, and let me have his decision immediately. The next day after hours of air attack on Vienna I received the telephone message that the evacuation of the Spanish Riding School to Upper Austria was authorized, provided that the Commander of the Thirteenth Division and the Commissar of the Ministry of Defence gave their assent.

I asked for the necessary trucks, which I was lucky enough to get immediately, set in motion the loading of the rest of the equipment still in Vienna, and went to the Commanding Officer to get the required permit, which I visualized to be merely a matter of form. General Schubert, having checked by phone with Berlin, agreed to the move at once and told me warmly that the sooner the Spanish Riding School left Vienna the happier he would be, as there were evil times coming for the city. He indicated that it would be much more difficult to get the agreement of the Commissar, and regretted that he could be of no help to me in this. A raid of several hours' duration the next day, which also interrupted the loading, made an immediate meeting with Baldur von Schirach impossible. As soon as the All Clear sounded I called up his adjutant, who named a date in three days' time and was very chilly when I asked for an immediate appointment. After a long discussion I managed to persuade him to deal with my request immediately, although I was understandably not willing to divulge my reasons. I spent some anxious minutes waiting by the telephone. How otherwise could I get at the well-guarded Party leader? What would become of the trucks loaded with my own hands? Was my plan really to come to nothing at the last moment? All these thoughts raced agitatedly through my head, until at last I learned, with immense relief, that the leader was ready to receive me at once in his villa at Pötzleinsdorf.

Baldur von Schirach, wearing a new uniform like that of the Wehrmacht, received me in a worried manner and asked if everything to do with the Lipizzaner was under control. So there was nothing for it but to state the reason for my visit and establish the necessity of an immediate evacuation of the school because of the heaviness of the air attacks and the nearness of the retreating front. The great man heard me in silence, and then replied that I must not lose my nerve and would consider what an adverse effect the removal of the Spanish Riding School must have on the people of Vienna. They would take it as an indication of the hopeless position of the city and be still more despondent. But there was no justification for this, for already in a day or two new military measures would be brought in that would bring definite relief, so I ought not to upset even more the very sorely tried citizens.

Luckily, in my despair at this intransigent attitude, I suddenly remembered the Party leader's letter to General Schubert. The contents of this missive gave me an opportunity to renew my attack, and I said that it was hard to understand why the Lipizzaner must remain in Vienna when he, the Party leader, had said even before the New Year that he thought it was madness to bring the horses back to the Hofburg, and had ordered that they should remain at Lainz. But even there it was not certain how the bombing would affect the stabling, so the only solution was to go to a more remote area, if the valuable horses were not to be sacrificed to the insane fury of destruction. Considering his interest in the survival of the Spanish Riding School, I could not understand why he now wanted to expose the Lipizzaner to the danger of bombing raids. After an agonizing silence the Party leader answered, obviously very deeply moved: "Looked at like that, you are right, but all the same it is not easy for me to agree to the evacuation, for I have always considered the Spanish Riding School to be Vienna, and with the departure of the Lipizzaner a piece of Vienna goes from us. But I love them too much to leave them in danger any longer. So go to Upper Austria!"

The next morning I was able to make the final arrangements for our departure, now at last legalized, without fear that any unlucky chance would bring all my efforts to nothing. While we were preparing to leave a courier from the Spanish Riding School in Budapest arrived to ask whether there were any free stalls for their horses. I replied that practically all the stabling was available since I was in the process of leaving Vienna. This news must have decided Colonel Haszlinsky to halt on his way to Vienna and meet the Soviet troops as they marched in, informing them of the cultural importance of his academy. In actual fact from that very moment the Spanish Riding School of Budapest ceased to exist; the personnel were made prisoners of war, and fourteen of the stallions were shot on the spot, because they resisted all attempts to harness them.

When finally, after all the months of agitation, the very last of the Lipizzaner was loaded in the afternoon of March 6, 1945, and I held in my hands the official permit to leave Vienna, I had a tremendous feeling of relief, but not of joy. The decision I had taken on my own responsibility to remove the Spanish Riding School from the city that it had never left in spite of many upheavals was a very far-reaching one, and there were plenty of friends and acquaintances who criticized my action and looked on it as incredible nervousness.

On the last day we were there Vienna was spared any raids, almost as if the good spirits guarding my Lipizzaner had snatched a breathing-space from the rapidly advancing troops. A fresh fall of snow mercifully hid many of the gaping wounds inflicted on the city by the fleets of bombers, but it was easy to sense that this was only the calm before the storm, and the piece of paper I had had in my pocket for only a few hours was valueless: my appointment as Commandant of the Hofburg Defence Sector. This military order was, of course, superseded by the evacuation instructions I had received.

After the heavy cares of the last months, which had allowed no time for personal thoughts and feelings, I now had a little time for reflection in those last moments in Vienna as I awaited the departure of the train. I walked once more into the wonderful creation of Fischer von Erlach, the buildings, that had always represented for me the true temple of horsemanship and for whose preservation I had trembled every time there was an air raid.

As I stepped into the Winter Riding School the sounds of the city died away, as they always did. A deep, almost uncanny calm surrounded me in the hall usually filled with light, but on this day sombre and dismal because all the panes had been broken in the September raid and paper had been pasted over the windows. And the wonderful crystal lustres that had been, as it were, the decorative crown of the riding-school could do nothing now to lighten the darkness, for I had secretly had them dismantled and packed away—not yet guessing that the precious crown chandeliers would thus be saved for the Spanish Riding School.

But even the half-stripped state of this superb specimen of baroque at its very best put me into a receptive mood, and all the magic that had been present here for hundreds of years took hold of me, and made me forget for the moment the pressing cares of the day. Now I had to take my leave of this wonderful place, whose simple beauty and noble elegance moved me so deeply. I prayed to the Almighty to protect the work of the great architect against the holocaust and preserve the home of the Spanish Riding School. Once again I absorbed its atmosphere, storing up every detail, so that I could take with me as real a picture as possible into an unknown future.

Standing in the Kobel, where not a breath stirred, I relived in spirit the fulfilment of my dream: the great doors opened, and in a blaze of light twelve snow-white Lipizzaner stepped into the hall to enchant all lovers of harmony and beauty with the graceful movements of the great school quadrille. Involuntarily the anxious question assailed me whether the blossoming of the ancient school in the past few years had been the last before it died for ever, and whether Fate had determined for me the rôle of last head of this school? A shiver ran through me, and I felt weak at the thought that the props of the Spanish Riding School were in flight with an inscrutable future before them, and the riding-hall was abandoned without protection against whatever the War might bring. Here in the course of over two hundred years there had been countless functions of unbelievable brilliance, magnificently staged and colourful tourneys and carrousels as well as gay balls and wild masquerades, and here Beethoven had conducted his great concert, and in 1848 the first sitting of the newly formed Parliament had taken place.

But my glance back into the past was interrupted by the announcement that the loaded trucks could not, as planned, leave that night, because the Transport authorities had postponed the journey indefinitely as the trains were overloaded. This new difficulty drove out all sentimentality and dreaming and awakened all my energy.

A call to Transport headquarters proved unsuccessful; the officer on duty suggested I try again the next day. Then I hurried to Franz-Josephs-Bahnhof, to find some solution through personal intervention. The West-bahnhof and part of the West Westbahnstrecke had already been so badly damaged through continuous bombardment that no traffic could leave from there, and the last part of the Spanish Riding School could only leave the city by a devious route.

When I protested the offiical on duty said he was quite ready to hitch up my trucks without special instructions on to the freight train leaving late that evening. Once more the situation was critical, for after the train had been made up the engine-driver insisted that additional trucks made the strain on his locomotive too great, but I managed with a few friendly words to persuade even this member of the State railway to look the other way, and at last, about midnight, the long train drew slowly out of Vienna.

In the early morning we reached Tulln—barely half an hour from Vienna by train. All the tracks were crowded with goods trains, but after a certain amount of sorting out order was restored and we waited patiently to continue our journey. When the halt seemed to me to have lasted really too long I discovered with great misgivings that my trucks had been uncoupled and were standing in a siding. I at once went to the Stationmaster, who informed me that our transport could not go farther for the time being because he had no instructions from Vienna. He really couldn't understand how these trucks could have got there, but he was quite prepared to call up headquarters. So there we were for the moment: Wait! But meantime we had to make a roster, for warnings and All Clears sounded practically the whole day long. Other trains kept rolling through the station, but we never moved. I demanded to see the Stationmaster, but a somewhat unco-operative official replied laconically that there were still no instructions for us to continue our journey. When he had waited until the following afternoon, still with no prospects of moving, I changed my tactics and firmly demanded that a call be put through to von Schirach, in the hope that this would shake the officials out of their indifference. But the call did not come through because the lines had been damaged in a severe raid on Vienna. However, I did manage to frighten the Stationmaster by telling him that appropriate quarters in Vienna would certainly not overlook this irresponsible endangering of valuable horses, and at last the next morning he sent the wagons on to Amstetten on the Western Line, even though they had no transport number.

We reached the Rangierbahnhof in Amstetten relatively quickly, but the sight that greeted us was hardly encouraging. On all the tracks stood long military transports, and the station staff were obviously nervous as the hour approached for the start of the daily air raid. The Lipizzaner provided an unexpected contrast in this picture of war-time tension and unwittingly attracted the attention of the people like a memory from the long departed days of peace. Making full use of this interest, I did all I could to get away with all possible speed from what seemed to me an undesirable spot, and succeeded in getting our train off among the first, so that we were already on our way before the usual time of the air raid.

As we drew into Linz the sirens were wailing; the train stopped suddenly, the locomotive was uncoupled and driven away, and all the people left the train and made for the air raid shelters at the double. I could not bring myself to leave my darlings, so my wife and I stayed in the truck and watched a rain of bombs pouring down on us. The impact of the exploding bombs was so great that we sometimes felt as if we were being thrown up into the air and derailed. The floor shook violently with the force of the explosions, and we and the horses trembled from head to foot. This inferno lasted for more than two hours, but a kindly fate held its protecting hand over the valuable cargo and our lives.

After the All Clear the locomotive drew us into the station and preparation was made for the next stage of the journey. But all of a sudden the sirens sounded again, a woman transport officer jumped on to the footplate and ordered the driver to uncouple his engine and take it outside the station to safety. This order filled me with such horror that I leapt out of the truck and called to the engine-driver not to expose the Lipizzaner to the danger of being killed here in the station when they had just escaped disaster, and, despite the orders of the determined official, he took the whole train out of the station.

Then slowly the train began to move westward, while over Linz a new shower of bombs rained down. Near a railwayman's cottage we were halted with the warning "Dive-bomber attack." According to regulations the locomotive should have left the train at once and made for open country, but the driver did not want to leave us in the lurch and asked for my advice. At this moment I remembered from my childhood the school journey I used to make every day; near by there was a railway cutting through which we had to pass, and I ordered the train to stop in this sheltered spot. We reached it unharmed and waited there until the hunters circling overhead had gone, either having not seen us or else having failed to find a favourable position for attack.

Throughout this journey I was aware of a noble spirit of comradeship among my countrymen, which awakened in each individual the greatest desire to help others. As Austrians they all felt bound to lend a hand to bring to safety one of our rare cultural treasures, of which they were very proud, and I look back on this experience with pleasure and with gratitude for the many great and small services I received from my compatriots.

Just outside Wels we had to stop again out in the open because there was a heavy American raid in progress. Waves of planes made a concentrated attack, bringing destruction, fear and unspeakable misery on the city in which I spent part of my youth and began my military career. As the All Clear sounded the twilight sky looked blood-red from the light of countless fires. The train had to halt outside the station, which had also been hit, but I revisited the town where the ancient houses still recalled their former splendour; I heard again the soft clinking echo of spurs as the elegant cavalry officers strode down the streets now filled with rubble, and walked sorrowfully through the little side-roads so dear to me.

Around midnight the last Spanish Riding School transport finally left the perilous main track of the Westbahn for its destination on the local line. The constant interruptions for alarms and air raids were ended at last, and the smiling landscape that we now travelled through was so peaceful that it almost seemed like waking from a bad dream.

After a four-day journey on the short stretch of barely 190 miles we arrived on March 10 safe and sound in St Martin-im-Innkreis, the first exile the Spanish Riding School had endured since its foundation.

CHAPTER 9

The Spanish Riding School between War and Peace

In St Martin, a little village near Ried, in Upper Austria, the homes of a peaceful peasant population of the fertile Inn district clustered round the powerful castle of Count Arco-Valley near to the church. The vast castle, built in the familiar square shape dating from the time of the Peasant Wars, with equally imposing outbuildings, stands in a large park.

When we arrived the place was like a beehive that had been disturbed, and I could not help wondering where all the swarms of people had come from. In the requisitioned part of the main castle alone more than three hundred refugees from the East had been billeted, but in addition all extra buildings belonging to the estate and forest administration, and every other kind of accommodation in the district, as well as the schools and many private houses, were filled with refugees and bomb victims. Thither came the many Polish and Russian prisoners of war who worked on the estate and for the farmers, so that the strangers vastly outnumbered the local population, which largely consisted of women and children, youths, and men who were old or sick.

Whatever our joy at getting the Lipizzaner out of the witches' cauldron that Vienna had become in the last few months, these conditions could not be overlooked in view of what must inevitably lie ahead. The weak resident population had had more than enough of the blessings of National Socialism, which in Austria had merely demanded sacrifice, and looked anxiously, some with paralysing resignation, into the immediate future. The refugees from the East, on the other hand, had made up their minds to victory at any price, since in this they saw their only chance of recovering their lost goods and property. They looked mistrustfully, even with hostility, on the Spanish Riding School, because want and personal sorrow had long ago robbed them of any feeling for culture and other spiritual values. Materialism

107

had gained such a hold that many said openly that the Lipizzaner might be used to improve the very small meat ration and the personnel sent off to fight the enemy.

The many prisoners of war, mostly men in the prime of life, stood detached from these events, and some of them hardly troubled to conceal that they were waiting for the hour of their deliverance. The bearing of the Poles in particular caused a good deal of ill-feeling, while the Russians, mainly officer prisoners of war, who had proved excellent workers, seemed much calmer.

Such moods and behaviour had to be taken into consideration by anyone preparing for the transitional period ahead.

I had to take precautions to be able to put up a fight if necessary to protect the Spanish Riding School, and with the few weapons at our disposal set up strong-points in the castle and outbuildings. These were connected by telephone and in sight of each other and could in the event of an attack from outside be defended simultaneously by cross-fire. A precisely worked-out plan would ensure co-operation between the two groups in case of danger.

The horses were put in the closed farmyard, and could, thanks to its position, be easily guarded and watched. To start with, because of shortage of space, twenty-four stallions were sent to Ried, seven miles away, and I was worried about their fate as defeat came nearer. But Countess Gabriele, then owner of St Martin, soon relieved me of this worry by vacating still more cowsheds so that I could collect all the horses into one place. She was exceptionally kind and helpful towards the Spanish Riding School and made very much easier the change from the civilized existence in the Hofburg to the somewhat primitive conditions we encountered in 'exile.'

The stabling, some of which had not been used as such for centuries, had to be repaired and restored to take the roomy boxes and high-screened stalls the Lipizzaner were used to. I had endless trouble in procuring the necessary permits for the wood. Hanging devices with wooden mangers were made out of thick posts, and temporary barriers of crossed poles were erected between the stallions. In the end their quarters looked really cosy, with clean straw beds, and the Lipizzaner, tired out after their journey, occupied them, neighing joyfully, waltzing delightedly round in the fresh straw and feeling at home immediately, so when I found them peacefully eating their evening meals from their mangers and heard the familiar sound of munching I went off to bed intensely relieved, still not dreaming what a surprise awaited me the next day.

In the morning there was absolute pandemonium in the stables. The newly erected barriers had virtually disappeared, the horses were walking without restriction down the central gangway or paying their 'specials' a visit, often resulting in a fight. What ever had happened? After their evening feed the horses sniffed the new wood, liked its freshness, and began to nibble it. The night was long, and the delighted chewing of the Lipizzaner was unrestrained, so that by early morning there remained only a few fragments of the solid wooden poles. The horses were no longer fastened up; it would be truer to say that the remnants of a single post were attached to the halter chains, which the Lipizzaner were dragging and rattling through the stable. The sight of this devastation sent me nearly demented, for now there would have to be more applications for fresh wood permits. By painting it with carbolic and ox's gall I tried to spoil the taste of my charges' newly discovered treat, but I was not entirely successful. However, the timber was never totally destroyed again.

Now I had to think about keeping the horses occupied. Obviously there could be no question of leaving muscular stallions at the peak of their vigour shut up in a stable; they must be given plenty of exercise, not an easy task, since the staff reductions during the last few months had left each rider with some ten horses in his charge. Moreover, since the covered school, a converted shed, was very small, only a few horses could be exercised at a time; so the majority of the stallions were taken out hacking in the surrounding country. There had for a long time been no question of training new school horses, but at least what had been achieved must to some extent be maintained.

Even these rides, however, were soon interrupted by the swarms of dive-bombers. Our route had always to be chosen so that the Lipizzaner could find shelter at once, either near a clump of trees or near a group of houses whenever the planes came swooping down.

The many refugees arriving from Vienna gave us such shattering news of events in the city that there seemed to be no ray of light to alleviate the general gloom. What was happening at the Front concerned us most deeply, for on the advances of the separate armies to occupy Germany hung our fate. Only by listening to the foreign radio could we clarify and fill in the confused picture of the situation given by the official Army news. The American advance had obviously slowed down, and that of the Russians greatly speeded up, so that the question of where these two allies would join hands became daily more urgent. It would be absolutely unbearable to find ourselves near the Front, so I decided to pick out some of the most valuable stuff and take half of it farther west to Bavaria, and I had more and more to do with the horses.

Then began a truly adventurous undertaking, which seemed to be ill-fated from the start. Naturally all preparations had to be carried out in the utmost secrecy to prevent a possible upsetting of my plan by the local authorities. This was no easy matter in those days when everybody was thirsting for news. However, we managed to load the equipment almost unnoticed into wagons put at our disposal by the Countess, and some of these were to be drawn by Lipizzaner and some by farmhorses, which were put between the shafts at midnight, and the wagons began to move quietly in the direction of Bavaria. But at the first really steep incline of the journey it was obvious that the wagons were far too heavily laden, so I had to send for trace horses. This was, naturally, not done without some noise, particularly as the wagon with the biggest load hit the kerb as it slipped backward in the darkness and tipped over. The heavy cases fell on a muddy patch of grass, and now I had to alert the rest of my people to raise the wagon and load it again. With all the delay dawn was beginning to break by the time we got under way again. Needless to say, the news spread like wildfire that the Spanish Riding School was moving westward. On this day, however, there were a number of successful air attacks on the village and its neighbourhood, so the nocturnal interlude was not specially noticed. The equipment arrived unharmed in Sassau-im-Chiemsee, where it was stored by relatives of the Countess, and even the horses returned in good shape to St Martin.

I went even farther in my precautionary measures, and bricked up in the castle the most valuable of our possessions in a fairly well-concealed space, dividing my reserves of oats and other stores between the peasants who seemed sympathetic. Thus it seemed probable that not all my treasure would be lost if looting were to follow.

I had also made careful plans about food. I must say that the Spanish Riding School supplies came through remarkably well in spite of the difficulties of the War and serious disturbances through air raids. We received punctually every fortnight the correct amount of oats, hay and straw. One of the wonders of organization of the Great German Reich!

Already by the second year of the War I had begun to reduce the ration slightly and add an iron ration, and I was able to increase my store with supplies from the Hostau stud, so I came to St Martin with two wagons of oats. I made up my mind to increase this reserve still further so that I should also have enough for an interim period. The fighter attacks on the road systems, which severely hindered the movement of traffic by day, and the difficulties of procuring the necessary lorries to transport the feed soon provided sufficient grounds for recommending the allotment of a two month's supply to meet any eventuality.

A further pressing need was to make arrangements to dispose rapidly of our Wehrmacht uniforms when the enemy troops arrived. For each of the staff I tried to put ready in the castle from our stores of civilian riders' clothes a suitable jacket, coat, and cap. I found out by asking or guessing the sizes of the various people, and then with the help of my wife laid out in one of the rooms set aside for the school the appropriate garments clearly labelled and ready to be taken. I took care not to involve anybody else in these preparations, for in these last days of the Third Reich there were orgies of denunciation, and I had to avoid anything that might limit my freedom of action. After all this I thought I had done everything humanly possible to safeguard the Spanish Riding School, so finally there was nothing to be done but to keep alert and await events.

In the last days of April the Cavalry Inspector, General Weingart, paid us one more visit. He had covered a long way from Berlin in his own producer-gas driven car to say goodbye, as he candidly admitted, to the Spanish Riding School and me. He watched the Lipizzaner at work in the impoverished covered school with close interest, and then walked quietly and thoughtfully through the stables, scrutinizing the individual horses once more. Over the whole scene lay the melancholy of leave-taking.

Before the dinner that the Countess Arco-Valley gave in his honour we discussed the military situation, walking up and down in the park, and General Weingart said to me, "You have found the best place imaginable to let the Front roll over you. I am not anxious about you, for the Americans will be coming, and with your Spanish Riding School you will succeed in putting these soldiers as deeply under the spell of your white horses as you have always managed to do with me."

When I expressed my fear that the riders, as members of the Wehrmacht, might be separated from their horses by the occupying troops and even taken off as prisoners of war, the General said, "I am going back once more to the High Command, which has now set up its headquarters in Bavaria, and will have a document drawn up for you, duly signed and sealed and to be put into immediate effect, removing the Spanish Riding School from the command of the Army and declaring it once more a civil riding-school, as it was before 1938. Perhaps this document may help you to cope with the transition period more easily. For me this final service to the Spanish Riding School will be the last good deed of my life."

Noticing my inquiring look, General Weingart continued: "My life comes to an end with the occupation of Germany, for I have no longer the strength to begin again as in 1918. We generals will be accused of allowing ourselves to become Hitler's tools, although from the beginning we were against him. But the struggle between trained obedience, respect for the oath we had taken, and anxiety about the welfare of the German people ended with our executing our orders to the letter, and that is where our responsibility began for the misfortunes that have struck Germany. After the resignation of the first set of generals there would not have been a second or third set available, and then Hitler would not have been in a position to pursue his plans for war. This will quite rightly be thrown up at us, and I am much too tired to endure again the experiences of the 1918 defeat."

The General thoroughly enjoyed his evening at the castle, and I was particularly delighted that the Countess Gabriele Arco-Valley had brought so much understanding to the arrangement of the dinner that I had suggested. As he took his leave the next day General Weingart said to me, "I was so happy yesterday to be able in the midst of this chaos to sit at an elegantly laid and cultured table not having to make small talk, and shall treasure this evening as one of the loveliest memories of my life. How wonderful it could be! I shall bring you the document in a few days, and so shall be seeing you again."

But it was to be the last time we shook hands, for the sound of thundering artillery steadily coming nearer announced that the end was upon us. From the Americans who marched in shortly afterwards I heard that a German general had shot himself on the Herreninsel in the Chiemsee and that an empty producer-gas vehicle had been found on the bank; the description fitted General Weingart's car. The distant rumbling of gunfire came even closer on May 2, and the last convulsions of the Great German Reich were plain to see. In these hours of disintegration I received my last military order, labelled "Most Secret": my appointment as Commandant of the Defence Sector St Martin. The laconic instruction took no account of the relation between what I had to do and the forces at my disposal. As things were now beginning to happen all at once and I had to make my final preparations for the change-over, I stuck the letter into my pocket for the time being. When the sounds of battle grew even louder in the afternoon St Martin got completely out of control. Order, which up to now had been kept with Draconian severity, seemed to be disappearing. Even the estate staff killed a fat pig without getting the necessary permission first, and the Countess invited me to a banquet at the castle, but asked me particularly to come in civilian clothes so that she could get used to what I should look like in the future. With the approach of darkness the sounds of battle ceased, and there seemed some hope that we should have a quiet evening, so I put on my civilian clothes and was walking with the other guests into dinner when I suddenly realized how deceptive was this apparent peace.

First of all the mayor, an active but harmless Nazi, asked for orders to throw in the Volkssturm, that wretched handful of badly armed youths and old men, too young or too old for general military service or even physically incapable of it.

From the news we had received it was obvious that the Americans, to spare their own soldiers as much as possible, would at the slightest sign of resistance plaster the area with their artillery. I had to try to forestall any unconsidered action, therefore, and so ordered the mayor to divide the Volkssturm into groups to prevent any attempts at looting. For if the people managed to empty a baker's shop they would not hesitate to plunder the butcher's and other shops, and then there would be no holding them. As the mayor himself owned the biggest butchery in the District, he received this order with obvious satisfaction.

20. The Lipizzaner show themselves again: Wels, 1947

21. Under the Pines on the Piazza di Siena in Rome, 1949

22. Giving Autographs

A little later a first lieutenant announced himself as head of a signals company and asked for orders. Since he had seventy-eight gunners, but no heavy weapons, at his disposal I gave him clear instructions to keep his soldiers at the ready in the local school, and by this means succeeded in preventing any accidental fighting, which might have been disastrous for the Spanish Riding School.

Hard on his heels appeared the Ortsgruppenleiter (local group leader) and Party Secretary, feared as a particularly fanatical Nazi throughout the village. Clearly embarrassed, he announced that he had received orders from his superiors in Ried to close all the street barriers to prevent the advance of the Americans, but was so uncertain that he wanted to leave the decision to me. As the Americans instantly shelled places where there were any kind of obstacles, I instructed him to post members of the Volkssturm at the barriers, but to await my orders before actually closing them. The group leader said he thought this order contradicted the instructions of the Kreisleiter (area leader), who had announced, with the severest warnings against insubordination, that he was visiting St Martin. I calmed the pale, distraught Party official by assuring him that I would justify my orders to the Kreisleiter in person.

Soon after the once-so-powerful man in the little district had left the castle he rang me in great agitation, begging me to come at once to the Party offices as the Kreisleiter was arriving at any minute. I tried to hide the civilian suit I was wearing under my military greatcoat, as there was not time to change, and set off, slipping a pistol into my pocket in case of emergencies. The faces of the Party officials gathered there were drawn and anxious, and the Ortsgruppenleiter looked a completely broken man. The uncanny silence that greeted my arrival was suddenly broken by the sound of heavy footsteps approaching; the door flew open and the Kreisleiter, preceded by two heavily armed S.S. men, entered the room. He raised his arm with a flourish and broke the silence with a "Heil Hitler," then turned to the Ortsgruppenleiter to ask whether the tank barriers had been closed as he had ordered. No answer—sheer fright had deprived the Ortsgruppenleiter of speech, so I answered for him. "No, or else your car would not have been able to get here." To this the Kreisleiter snapped furiously, "Why were my orders not carried out?" The situation was reaching its climax; the onlookers stood as if rooted to the spot and scarcely dared to breathe. The armed Party god with his two satellites fixed me with his burning eye, and I must admit that I feared the worst at that moment, but I was resolved not to die alone. The cool stock of the pistol hidden in my greatcoat pocket gave me a strange comfort in spite of the dramatic circumstances. After quick and calm deliberation I decided to stake everything on one card, in the hope that the military amateurishness characteristic of most Party men would come to my help. I said in an almost pontifical tone,

"When our troops brought the advance of the Americans to a halt, as indicated by the fact that the sounds of firing ceased, I did not consider that any useful purpose would be served by closing the streets, since this might hinder the freedom of movement of our own soldiers. But I have had the barriers manned by the Volkssturm and made the necessary arrangements for them to be closed in the shortest possible time when I give the order."

This was the greatest bluff of my life, for the closing of the very much improvised barriers would have taken quite a long time.

After a little thought the Kreisleiter said, "Then everything is in good order," and with a few threatening words to the bystanders he strode off into the murky darkness—and was never seen again.

Meantime it was midnight and I wanted to get back to the castle, but as I was passing the stables I caught sight of a cluster of men, and people darting away carrying packets and disappearing into the darkness. Horrified, I approached, and forced my way through the crowd, which reluctantly made way for me. It did not take me long to realize that it was not my Lipizzaner that were awakening all this interest, but some stairs that led up into the roof from the stable entrance. When I had forced my way through the room that ran above the stables I saw huge piles of cartons of cigarettes and pipe tobacco—an extremely rare commodity at that time—with a surging crowd fighting over them. So the looting had begun in earnest, and, moreover, right above the heads of my Lipizzaner! Needless to say, I was far from pleased by this discovery, and only managed to get the grumbling, cursing crowd out of the room at the point of my pistol. I realized that I could not control this mob for long, so I sent a message to the mayor to reach a decision as quickly as possible and by all possible means to prevent the crowd from becoming masters of the situation. Then I proposed a sharing out among the people to get this "inflammable material," which could all too easily prove the beginning of further looting, right away from my horses. The mayor agreed to my suggestion, thus—as I explained to him—maintaining the semblance of authority. So we began to distribute tobacco rations, and even included the troops marching through, so as to exhaust the stock as quickly as possible. I breathed a sigh of relief when during the morning of the next day the supply ran out and a dangerous attraction for evil elements was removed from the immediate neighbourhood of my stables.

That morning was relatively peaceful. The whole night through there had been a continuous stream of German troops and individual soldiers, but this had ceased, and even the rumours of the approach of the Americans had been almost silenced.

We were just about to sit down to lunch, which the Countess had prepared for me, remembering the delicacies of my spoiled evening meal, when a *Bereiter* rushed in in great agitation and announced that the first Americans had arrived and seized our Lipizzaner-drawn cart. Now was the time to set the prearranged plan in motion. I had everybody attached to the Spanish Riding School summoned to the castle at the double to change their tunics and caps for the civilian clothes ready for them, turning them from soldiers into civilians.

This metamorphosis was effected so rapidly that the first batch of American military police, who twenty minutes later were combing the stables, discovered nobody belonging to the Wehrmacht, and, seeing only 'civilians,' merely asked, "Hier nix S.S.?" which we were able to deny with easy consciences.

The Americans herded everybody they did find in uniform unceremoniously into an empty field, where they were kept all day under strict guard without attention or protection against the weather to await transportation to a prisoner-of-war camp. A typical example of the conqueror's always believing that he must repay past injustice! The sight of these poor men having to learn of their release in such an odd way through a radio announcement was just as shattering as the breaking up by the 'Amis' of the arms that were surrendered. A symbolic picture of total surrender!

In the first phase of the occupation I had already given my staff instructions to hand over our weapons and ammunition as inconspicuously as possible at the place announced over the loudspeakers, and then to disappear into their quarters or the stables, to prevent any of them being arrested by the Americans as a result of denunciations. For others too had, of course, had the idea of taking off their uniforms and changing into civilian clothes, but the Americans now began an organized hunt for these disguised soldiers and were backed up in this by the local people. So the order of the day was: Keep out of sight.

The Lipizzaner team seized in that first moment, together with its uniformed driver, was returned unharmed, for the fully motorized Americans really did not know what on earth to do with this unmodern vehicle, and their interest turned to other things. The vanguard rolled on to Ried, leaving a few sentries behind them, and we had to wait patiently for the arrival of the main forces.

In this little breathing-space many men hurried to a large building, broke open the doors with howls of delight, and fell avidly on the tobacco supplies stored there. There were disgusting scenes of unbridled greed, men were pushed over and trampled under foot, and the cigarette tobacco was scattered all over the floor. Nobody was in a position to check this pointless activity, and the few American sentries looked on amused or indifferent at this crazy looting and destruction. As soon as one store was stripped another was located with triumphant howls, and the same wild game was repeated. The rioters did not even confine themselves to the local shops, and under the pretext that the owner was a Nazi the looting became general. I was relieved that this tumult was not too near the horses, for the unleashed mob could only too easily have fallen on the quite considerable treasure of the Spanish Riding School. The Lipizzaner, oblivious of world events, chewed contentedly at their hay, and only occasionally did the distant yells of the excited crowd disturb the stillness of their stalls.

In the late afternoon of this day, May 3, several Army cars left the unending columns pouring through St Martin and approached the castle. The Chief of the General Staff of the Twentieth Corps, General Collier, came with several officers to set up his headquarters there. I presented myself to the General as head of the Spanish Riding School, but saw immediately that he had not the slightest idea what kind of an institution that was. He walked past me with a "How do you do?" and examined in detail all the castle accommodation.

With the arrival of the staff of the Twentieth Corps events began to move really fast, and while I was still puzzling how to make the Americans understand the significance of the Spanish Riding School, since our future fate depended upon it, one of my riders rushed in great agitation into the castle and announced that an American major who had made inquiries about me and Nero was in the stables.

Naturally I hurried down at once—to meet an officer who had seen me riding at the Berlin Olympics and was delighted to have found Nero here. While he was still asking what had been happening to me since 1936 General Collier appeared with the Corps Commander, General Walker. The major introduced me once more, and informed the General that the Spanish Riding School was very famous and that I was a well-known competition rider. After a short talk General Walker asked me whether it would be possible for me to arrange a performance for the next day, as he intended to invite General Patton. I assented and was ordered to make the necessary arrangements.

First I had to hurry back to the castle, for meanwhile General Collier had given orders for its immediate evacuation. He did, however, allow the Countess, my wife, and myself to remain, a quite remarkable concession at that moment, but we had to change our rooms for smaller ones. Soldiers began at once, working with local labour under the command of officers, to get the headquarters in order. A large hall, which was filled with furniture from the remaining part of the castle allotted to the refugees was to be the officers' Mess, and had to be cleared immediately. What a fright I had, for only hours before the abandoned uniforms of my staff had been hidden behind this very furniture. My wife began to lend a hand with the clearing so that she could get hold of the wretched uniforms and have them removed in laundry-baskets under curtains and covers, and while she was doing this General Collier arrived to see for himself how the work was getting on. So Countess Arco-Valley had to engage him in conversation to prevent this sharp-eyed officer from showing an interest in the contents of the laundry-baskets. Thus, literally under the eyes of the Americans, we managed to take the German Wehrmacht uniforms, which could easily have been considered possessions of the dreaded ghost "Werewolf," to another hiding-place.

I passed a very uncomfortable first night in 'liberated' Austria. I had to make do with a large child's cot, and twisted and curled myself up to get in my long legs. To my physical discomfort was added the planning for the forthcoming performance and the anxious question as to what impression it would make on the American general, for I was fully aware how much the future of the old school depended upon it.

But I was not the only one to be worried about the arrangements, for General Walker, who knew Patton's eccentricity, was having second thoughts about the invitation. In fact, he was committing the busy Army Commander to a journey of over four hundred miles, and realized that he would have to justify the long trip to his guest. So he wanted to see a re-hearsal as early as possible, but was quite horrified by the condition of the room where it was to be held, and at once ordered an officer to help me with preparations for the performance. More than a hundred civilians had been collected in St Martin, a very mixed and workshy crew, and I set the majority to cleaning the riding school, the courtyard, and the entrances, and then to gathering branches from the nearby wood, to hide to some extent at least the bare, dilapidated walls. The rest helped me to bring the prec-ious saddlery and uniforms out of their walled-in hiding-place so that the riders and horses could be traditionally dressed. The many beautiful pic-tures and costly saddle-cloths would play their part in transforming the modest covered school into a fairly attractive setting, recreating with a little illusion the atmosphere left behind in Vienna.

These preparations were no more than the indispensable details; it was the riders and horses that were my main concern. Since our departure from Vienna we had confined ourselves to keeping up roughly the required standard of horsemanship and were far from contemplating any sort of public performance, so I had to draw up a hurried programme, taking this into account as well as the lack of space and the limited number of riders, and begin intensive training right away. I therefore welcomed the news that General Patton's visit would be somewhat delayed. General Walker appeared frequently during the next day or two to see for himself how the decoration of the riding-school was progressing, and always stayed to watch the rehearsals. I was pleased to observe his growing interest, and saw in it a good omen for the fateful visit to come.

After two days' hard work at last everything was ready to receive the important guest. The riding-school was transformed into a sparkling fresh green grove, the old engravings and saddle-cloths giving the normally dreary building, now brilliant under powerful electric lights, a gay and festive appearance. Even the music was unpacked and set up, so that, once riders and horses had been busily got back into form, everything humanly possible for the success of this important performance seemed to have been done.

The god of the weather too bestowed his special mercy, and assumed his party clothes for May 7, 1945, covering St Martin in brilliant sunshine. The great courtyard, in which the released prisoners of war with the local people and refugees had set up a regular market to barter the results of their looting, was to-day completely empty, since all the entrances had been barred by American soldiers. After repeated cleaning by the civilians who had been pressed into service order and cleanliness reigned as for an inspection in peace-time. The white horses with their gold-brimmed bridles and the riders in their traditional uniforms presented an unusual picture, pushing the prosaic world of everyday into the background and evoking the picture of a dream stretching hundreds of years into the past.

But at that moment there was little inclination to dream, for everybody belonging to the Spanish Riding School was too busy wondering whether the magic of the white Stallions would do the trick in this hour of destiny for the oldest riding-school in the world.

Into this expectant atmosphere in the courtyard—the riders having taken their position at the entrance to the school—the important guests stepped at about eleven o'clock, having flown from Frankfurt. Even they made a ceremonial arrival. In front came the standards of the Fourth Army and Twentieth Corps flanked by military police, and followed by Mr Patterson, Secretary of State for War, accompanied by General Patton and his suite of four generals and four colonels. The General, tall and thin, and of imposing appearance, indicating clearly the personality of the famous soldier, strode past the lined-up riders with his hand in the air, curtly acknowledging their greeting, into the covered school, and took his place with the other gentlemen on the little platform with the standards on either side. The performance could now begin.

I must admit that a certain nervousness filled us all. We had to present a type of art bound up with tradition, and, like the ballet, built not on sensation but triumphing in the harmony of movement and music, to these foreigners from distant lands who up to yesterday were our enemies; and we had to do it in such a way that they too would appreciate it as art and respect our work, which der.1anded a degree of expert knowledge to be fully understood. On this demanded ultimately the future existence of the Spanish Riding School.

The first item was a *Pas de Deux*, ridden by Oberbereiter Lindenbauer, at that time the oldest rider of the Spanish Riding School, and another *Bereiter*. General Patton at first watched the movements in the little ring with some indifference, almost boredom, but I could see his interest awakening as the horses went by in the *passage* and becoming still greater as *piaffes*, *levades*, and *caprioles* followed one after another. But the quadrille completely enchanted the spectators. I could not help noticing the pleasure on the faces of the General and his followers as they attentively watched each figure, but my beloved Lipizzaner were really marvellous. As if they understood how important it was, they willingly gave of their best and confirmed the great reputation they had already won in Germany as bewitching dancing horses. After the quadrille, with which the ice seemed effectively broken, my wife and Countess Arco-Valley, who had been watching from the other side of the ring opposite the guests of honour, came over while the horses were being changed to tell me that General Patton had watched each separate item of the performance with great interest, and in particular had never taken his eyes off me. Encouraged by this, after the exercises on long reins and "Airs above the Ground" I rode Neapolitano Africa on a curb, the bridle in my left hand and a switch held upright in my right in the classic manner, taking him through the most difficult exercises: walking sideways, pirouetting, changes in the air, *piaffe*, and *passage*. General Patton, who rode himself, was fascinated by each separate movement, and his excitement was undoubted even without the loud applause. This made my next move much easier.

I finished my performance, riding in the *passage* up to the platform, then halted, taking off my hat after a short *piaffe*, and presented my petition to the General. It was one of the most important moments of my life: in a little Austrian village in a decisive hour two men faced each other, both having fought for the Olympic crown for their countries, the one in Stockholm in 1912, the other in Berlin in 1936. Although they now met on such unequal terms, the one as triumphant conqueror in a war waged with such bitterness, the other as a member of a defeated nation, the aura of the Olympic spirit hovered over this meeting, and I was so conscious of it that I managed to make my speech with greater ease than I could otherwise have done.

"Honourable Mr Secretary and General!

"I thank you for the great honour you have done the Spanish Riding School and myself by your presence. The Spanish Riding School, this ancient Austrian cultural institution, is today the oldest riding-school in the world, and has managed to survive wars and revolutions throughout the centuries and by good fortune has lived also through the recent years of upheaval. The great American nation, which has been singled out to save European culture from destruction, will certainly interest itself also in this ancient academy, which with its riders and horses presents, as it were, a piece of living baroque, so I am sure I shall not plead in vain in asking you, General, for your special protection and help; for protection for the Spanish

Riding School, which will pass the difficult period of transition under American military command, and for help to locate and bring back the Lipizzaner stud, which is at present in great danger on Czechoslovakian territory."

General Patton, who had risen to his feet as I began my address—a gesture of respect very rare among Americans, as I was later told by officers —seemed rather disconcerted by my appeal. He had a short, whispered discussion with Secretary of State Patterson, and then replied that he was placing the Spanish Riding School under the special protection of the American Army in order to restore it to the newly risen Austria. This official declaration was far more than I had dreamed, so I was bold enough to ask the gentlemen before they left the school whether I might show them the Lipizzaner in their stalls, an invitation General Patton was happy to accept. As we walked past the riders drawn up as a guard of honour in front of the ring I asked the General whether I might present them, but he refused curtly.

The General showed an exceptional interest in the horses in the stables, inspecting tack closely and asking for information about details of equipment and schooling. I naturally made up my mind to mention again at the psychologically right moment my anxiety about the Lipizzaner stud. The opening came when he asked whether we used stallions also for training in *haute école*. This gave me a chance to explain that in the Spanish Riding School only stallions had ever been used, the mares being exclusively kept for breeding. This situation was at the moment particularly disturbing because the stud was in Czechoslovakia, and Austria would probably lose it for good. Then the salvation of the Spanish Riding School with American military help would be of short duration indeed, for without new stock from the stud the centuries-old academy must cease to exist after the death of the stallions now belonging to it. This had been my reason for making what might have seemed an inopportune appeal for help in getting back the Lipizzaner stud.

General Patton listened attentively to my explanations, and then asked why the stud was in Czechoslovakia. I told him that the Austrian branch of the Lipizzaner strain in Piber had been transferred by the German authorities in 1942, in spite of my protests, from Styria to Hostau, in Czechoslavakia. Patton asked his Staff Officer for a map, and asked me to show him the little village near Pilsen. I was very impressed by the speed with which his order was carried out and the excellent plastic map on which I was able to find the right spot in spite of my understandable agitation. After a short consultation with his officers the General promised to see what he could do for me, and left the stable and the Spanish Riding School. While I was still telling my friends and the riders what had happened General Walker came back from seeing off the guests of honour and said that

General Patton had talked of nothing but the Spanish Riding School during lunch at the castle, as he had enjoyed the show so much. I asked him whether there was any hope of getting the stud back, but he only replied that General Patton had already given his orders, and I should hear more about it shortly. I heard later that General Patton issued strict orders before he left St Martin to ensure at all costs the safety of the Lipizzaner stud regardless of the demarcation line.

General Walker took this opportunity to give me back also the guest book of the Spanish Riding School, in which all those present had signed their names. I had asked the day before whether I might bring out the book for signatures, pointing out, however, that although Hitler's name was not in it many other personalities of the Nazi German Reich were represented there. General Walker took it away to look at, so that he could decide whether it could be presented for General Patton's signature. In the meantime I had to listen to a good deal of cynical opinion that this interesting book would be lost for ever, since the Americans were great collectors of signatures and souvenirs. Immediately before the arrival of the guests General Walker dispelled this fear by announcing that of course General Patton would write in the visitors' book, for his signature in it would record a piece of the history of the Spanish Riding School.

Years later I remembered all this when a distinguished man still living in the past refused his signature when he visited the Spanish Riding School, saying that he did not want to put it in a guest book that contained names from the Nazi period. I was so annoyed that I merely commented that the victorious General Patton had not hesitated for a moment to add *his* name, although at that time, standing so close to events as he did, it would have been quite understandable for him to refuse. Having said this, I was going to slam the book shut, but the hesitant guest now put out his hand and signed his name.

This little episode reminds me vividly of the hysteria which seized many people in those unsettled days of the collapse and often caused me a great deal of work. For instance, the Oberbereiter was much offended after the visit because Patton had not spoken to him, and he announced in a tone of resignation to the younger riders, "The King of England shook hands with me during our festival tour in London, but I am not good enough for the American general." He quite overlooked the fact that because of the veto on fraternization not a single American officer had shaken hands with me either, although I had a great many negotiations with them, nor did he stop to consider that this unjustified remark was bound to sow unintentional mistrust and stir up bad feeling, which was beginning to undermine the excellent spirit that had prevailed in the Spanish Riding School during the War.

It was a further symptom of hysteria that some of our riders insisted on having demobilization papers from the German Wehrmacht, because they were afraid they and the entire school might be taken to America. All my protests that there could be no question of this and that in a few months' time nobody would be asking for such papers were received with scepticism, until at last one member of the Spanish Riding School did go to the Americans, and then had to wait weeks for his release in a prison camp in an open field, hungry and unprotected from the weather. It was a most salutary lesson.

Though these unfortunate incidents were more or less unimportant, the impression of a few individual members of the school that the wealth of this institution was booty, a remnant of the German Wehrmacht, forced me to take into my personal charge all material assets, for in a time of total defeat the simplest objects were suitable for bartering for goods in short supply, and to replace even such things as curry-combs or other cleaning equipment was well-nigh impossible. So I preferred to look after all my 'treasures' personally, a severe burden on my already over-occupied time.

However much General Patton's decision had delighted me it did not relieve me of the many pressing problems resulting from it. First the new financial arrangements had to be made, for the financial position of the Spanish Riding School had to be put on a new footing, since the pay offices of the German Wehrmacht, to which we had been previously referred, no longer existed. An interview on this matter with the Twentieth Corps only elicited a promise to consult a higher authority. Nor could the Bezirkshauptmann (district officer) or the Mayor, the first representative of the Austrian civil authority, help me in this matter, but because something had to be done immediately, I set up a communal kitchen with my wife's help to ensure that my people would be fed. The mayor of St Martin helped with the distribution of food.

Then there was the horses' feed to be considered. I asked the Americans for permission to supplement my reserves from the stocks captured from the German Wehrmacht, and in due course received authority to collect these supplies, but often discovered that the local inhabitants, unauthorized, had been there already, and cleared the place, and when I appeared took up such a menacing attitude that I had to remove the remaining and very much depleted stores under American military police protection.

In addition there were vitally important problems of personnel. It is true that I had saved the riders from military service on the grounds that they were irreplaceable experts, but the grooms able to fight had been called up for military duty and turned into what at least looked like soldiers, inasmuch as they could display some knowledge of horses. These naturally came mostly from the country, and by the end of the War the majority of the grooms were farmers' sons or farmers, most of whom after the collapse thought only of their deserted holdings and wanted to get home as quickly as possible. A number of these characters did a midnight flit from the Spanish Riding School in the general confusion of the liberation, so that each morning I found myself with a smaller number of grooms, but there were also men with a sense of duty who allowed themselves to be persuaded to carry on a little longer. Indeed, two owners of large properties—one is to-day mayor of his local town—remained voluntarily until July, declaring that during the War they had found a good job with the Spanish Riding School and would not leave it in the lurch now when it was in difficulties. They were obviously moved when they later said goodbye, saying with tears in their eyes, "Be strong, Colonel, so that you can lead the school out of danger and into a better future!"

At first I tried to replace the deserters with demobilized soldiers who did not want to return to their homes in the Eastern Zone of Austria. But these men often changed their minds after a few days and moved on, their longing for their families driving out all thoughts of personal safety. Next I tried to find replacements among the many disarmed Hungarians, who had enjoyed particularly favourable treatment from the Americans, but was not at all lucky. These people were rough with the horses, though they themselves expected kid-glove treatment. One evening I heard the sharp crack of a whip coming from one of the stalls and the rattle of a halter chain, and noticed a stable-lad standing there hiding a whip behind his back. I asked him for an explanation, and he told me that the stallion had kicked him. I knew my Lipizzaner very well, and was certain that there was not a kicker among them. On the other hand this did explain the increasing nervousness of the horses in the last few weeks. I ordered the man to leave the Spanish Riding School at once, and stood my ground when he threatened that his comrades would stick by him and leave the school at the same time, and in fact the entire Hungarian stable staff downed tools. Still, I simply could not tolerate such rough treatment of my Lipizzaner!

Then I tried my luck with the German soldiers who could not get back home coming through from the Eastern Zone. With these too I had some unpleasant experiences. One morning I discovered that most of the stallions had very whispy tails, as their long hair had been very skilfully cut away—horsehair being a rare commodity fetching a very good price. I did manage to secure the capture of the culprits, who had run away, but the bushy hair styles of many of my charges were lost for a long time. On the whole, however, I was well satisfied with the German grooms, until one day the Americans collected them out of hand and forcibly repatriated them to Germany. Then an American colonel in near-by Schärding was willing to help me by sending an Army truck filled with some thirty ethnic Germans from Roumania and Yugoslavia. But my joy was fleeting, for I saw facing me sullen and unwilling men who declared angrily that the Americans had simply lined them up and brought them here without asking, but though I tried to talk them into staying and dispatched them to the district office to get ration cards, only three came back of whom two left St Martin in the course of the evening. The remaining one, who had stayed the night, was so lonely when he woke up that he too made off. The colonel, whom I informed of these events by phone, calmed me down with the familiar "Take it easy," and sent me yet another truck full of ethnic Germans, but this time the whole lot ran off as soon as they were unloaded, and I gave up expecting help from this quarter.

At the Labour Exchange I was met merely with regretful shrugs, and when I took my complaint to the Military Governor of Ried he led me to the window and pointed to the many idle youths lounging in the streets, so I got no help at all there.

Then I heard that prisoners of the Waffen-S.S. would be pleased to get more freedom by working at the Spanish Riding School. The appropriate American officer, to whom after a long interview I managed to convey our difficulty, at last declared himself willing to help, if I would bring him a declaration from the Labour Exchange in Linz that there were no grooms available. But there I met officialdom at its most obstructive, for the head of this department told me very politely that, though at the moment he had not in fact any workers to offer, he hoped in a few weeks to be in a position to do so; therefore he could not issue the declaration demanded by the Americans. He stood his ground, even when I retorted sharply, "Sir, remember the Lipizzaner are living creatures that have to be fed and tended every day, and not porcelain horses, which I can stand in the shop-window when there is a shortage of stable staff, and take them out a few weeks later, dust them, and set them to work again." The sum total of my success was an apologetic gesture indicating that there was nothing to be done!

I had, therefore, to seize every opportunity of seeking our grooms singly, a tedious and often humiliating undertaking. For more than six months the staff question was my worst worry—there were brief periods when there were only three or four grooms to deal with my seventy horses—until the growing shortage of money after the first currency reforms stimulated the desire for work, and men came to me delighted to find a job with the noble beasts. This solved one of the many problems that robbed me of many a night's rest in that troubled period of transition.

One day I was horrified to discover that when the surrender of weapons and ammunition was ordered some hundred cartridges in the castle had been overlooked in the general confusion, for the amnesty period was long past. This stock of ammunition right in the midst of the Twentieth Corps must be spirited away as quickly and as unobtrusively as possible to prevent it from being discovered accidentally and perhaps considered by the still obviously suspicious Americans as a secret arsenal of the "Werewolf" so excessively feared. My courageous wife at once announced that she would smuggle this dangerous material out of the castle on her own, so that in the interests of the Spanish Riding School I should not be involved in any way with this risky business. But it was exceptionally difficult, as all entrances to the castle were guarded by American sentries and civilians were not allowed in the building. The few remaining occupants, the Countess, ourselves, and the very small staff, had to show passes (which were frequently changed) as we entered or left the castle. Parcels or brief-cases we carried were often searched, so my wife began to take the ammunition out over a long period in small quantities in her handbag or shopping-bags, smiling and scurrying past the sentry as fast as she could with her often very heavy burden. But once her heart nearly stood still when a particularly conscientious soldier whom she had already passed called her back and ordered her to show the contents of her shopping-bag. She pictured herself, her mission almost completed, being arrested, as a "Werewolf," and began anxiously, but with as impassive a face as she could manage, to open the bag. Suddenly the sentry thought better of it and waved her away, allowing her to leave unmolested, with her suspicious ballast. After many alarms and excursions the risky material was at last removed from the building and thrown unobserved into a canal.

We were not entirely spared unpleasant experiences with the occupying forces either. For instance, in the early days of the occupation a captain came into the stables and ordered one of the most valuable stallions to be saddled for him on the morrow, and I was to provide riding-breeches for him. When I pointed to the "Off Limits" notice at each entrance he roared at me to carry out his orders without argument or he would enforce respect another way, and showed me his pistol. Naturally this had to be reported to the Staff Commandant to prevent a disagreeable clash the following day, but he could not answer for the person of this particular captain, so he directed the head of the military police to take up the matter. The captain never appeared again, for his behaviour had been censured in the Corps' routine orders. The attempt of the Military Governor of Lambach to ride a Lipizzaner fizzled out even more harmlessly. When I told him that he could get permission to do this only from General Walker he replied that I was in charge of the school, so he had come to me and not to the General, who, in his opinion, had no possible right to exercise authority over the Spanish Riding School. When in spite of this flattery I remained insistent that he get a permit from the General he, like so many others, finally gave up his idea to ride a Lipizzaner, for nobody wanted to go to the Corps Commander. Thus, with the exception of the school horse Favory Africa, which Patton had ridden for a few minutes, not a single Lipizzaner was ever used by the occupation forces.

The Spanish Riding School even in those months of 1945 also enjoyed special consideration, and was visited by many Americans who came from even the farthest corners of the German occupied zone to see the wonder horses. The high regard in which the school was held was demonstrated by an order from the Military Governor of Ried, under whose authority I was placed after the departure of the Twentieth Corps, to refer to him all applicants from American units or headquarters for public performances, so that he could refuse them, for the Spanish Riding School was not a circus available at any time for the convenience of sightseers. So, indeed, the prophecy of General Weingart was fulfilled; even the Americans surrendered to the magic of the Lipizzaner stallions and showed their appreciation of them.

CHAPTER 10

The Lipizzaner Stud returns Home

One of the particularly significant events in the long history of the Lipizzaner breed, and thus of the Spanish Riding School, was also one of the greatest successes of my life: the Lipizzaner stud, threatened in the chaos at the end of the Second World War with destruction or removal, returned safely to Austria.

This event, a near miracle, has excited the imagination of many and provided material for many fantastic and dramatic legends, even featuring clashes with Czech partisans and battles with Soviet tanks. The prosaic truth, however, was exciting enough, even without any shooting, and as it did concern the actual return of the stud I will describe it.

May 7, 1945, undoubtedly counts as one of the memorable days of the Lipizzaner stud, which at this particular time could look back on a history of 365 years. When after that memorable performance General Patton decided to comply with my request concerning it this was the first glimmer of hope after nearly three years of worry and anxiety about this noble breed, but there was no means of telling how much fate would interfere with the General's intentions, for every day many important factors played their part in the chaotic conditions. The following week I was called out of my wearisome speculations—for, after all, the continued existence of the Spanish Riding School was involved—to see General Collier. He put his plane at my disposal so that I could get to Czechoslovakia as rapidly as possible to inspect several hundred horses captured by the American troops. I mentioned that there were also Lipizzaner from Yugoslavia and Italy in the Hostau stud, but he replied that for General Patton Lipizzaner meant Austria, so in somewhat unusual circumstances I made the first flight of my life. It was a lovely, sunny day, the peaceful landscape lay below us, and it was hard to believe that after years of waiting this peace had become reality only a few days earlier. After nearly an hour the pilot pointed to a large building below us, circled round it, and landed with incredible skill on a small meadow in the park. We had arrived at the estate of the Skoda family in Zinkowy.

A major received me in well-kept quarters and informed me that Colonel Reed, Commander of the Secondary Cavalry Group, would be back to dinner and would give me further information, and led me at once into the room allotted to me for the night. Here, now that I found myself alone and quiet, I was able to do a little thinking. I did not look forward at all to dinner at the castle, for the Americans everywhere observed the rule against fraternizing so strictly that they did not even permit Count Arco-Valley, freed from a concentration camp at the very beginning of the occupation as a well-known figure, to sit at the officers' table, but let him eat with the staff. So I thought Colonel Reed would receive me some time later and probably behave to me over the Lipizzaner in the same way as Count Arco-Valley and I myself had so often been treated in St Martin.

At six o'clock, however, the major came back and brought me to Colonel Reed, who held out his hand—I could hardly believe my eyes and ears—and introduced me to the officers who had come into the Mess with him, calling me 'Colonel.' With this noble gesture the cavalry officer from the United States created an atmosphere that reminded me of the Officers' Mess of the Austro-Hungarian Empire, the Austrian Republic, and the German Reich. He placed me on his right at table, while young Skoda, our host, sat on his left.

Our conversation soon showed how full life is of interesting coincidences. Colonel Reed mentioned that my name was very familiar to him, and at first I smiled in embarrassment and some astonishment. I pricked up my ears, however, when he went on to explain that his brother had ridden a horse bearing my name, and added that the captain of the U.S. riding team had been so impressed with my riding at the 1936 Olympic Games that he had called one of the horses in the Cavalry School at Fort Riley after me, and Reed's brother had achieved many successes on it in the spring of 1942. This personal contact naturally gave us common sporting ground, which I knew so well from the great international competitions. It not only gave the evening in Zinkowy a special charm but proved very propitious for the negotiations that followed.

Colonel Reed confided to me that he had ensured the safety of the Lipizzaner stud in Hostau on the orders of General Patton, and in doing so had been forced to advance into territory that later would probably be evacuated by the Americans. Therefore he had already had the horses temporarily moved to Schwarzenberg, on Bavarian soil, to insure against any unpleasant surprises, and he wanted to take me there next day to be able to make the necessary arrangements after we had inspected them.

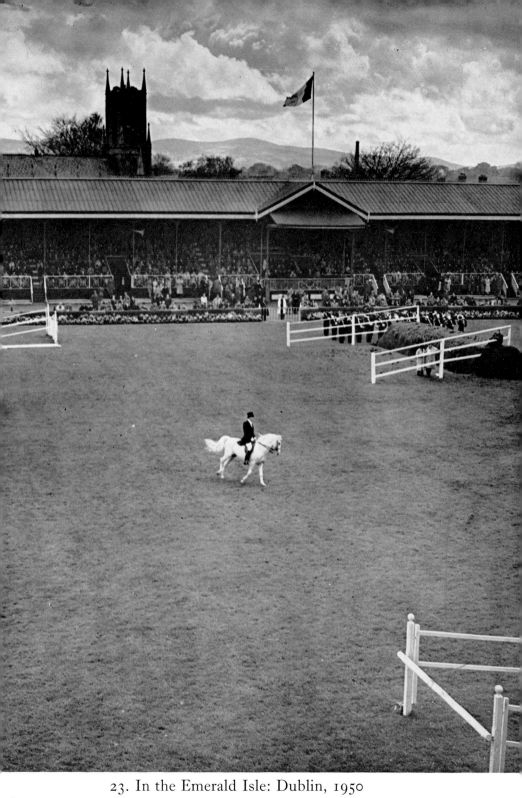

23. In the Emerald Isle: Dublin, 1950

24. Solo on Neapolitano Africa in Frankfurt, 1950

25. Pluto Theodorosta in a Round of Honour between
Otto Lörke and Willy Schultheis: Frankfurt, 1950

How wise these speedy measures had been was already evident during the transfer of the stud from Hostau to Schwarzenberg. The horses were moved out escorted by five tanks under the command of an infantry captain. To provide the additional grooms needed the Americans, determined to do everything properly, pressed into service a large number of captured German officers, a measure that was to lead to one of the first mishaps, for the officers fancied themselves as horsemen, and could not be restrained from riding the young stallions instead of leading them. All warnings from the stud staff were ignored; the two- and three-year-olds were saddled, and after sundry interludes in the stud yard, only to be expected with young unbroken stallions, the column finally moved off. Within minutes the inevitable happened: the horses shied at the slightest thing, the riders flew off, and there was an appalling confusion of uncontrolled, riderless stallions and mares defending themselves. In this whirling mass of biting, kicking horses, the attendants, some of whom were totally inexperienced, had the greatest difficulty in halting the excited animals and avoiding being trampled under the hoofs of the now frenzied herd. Finally thirteen young stallions, tiring of the rough game, left the rest and bolted home in the direction of their stables, but the Americans were glad to have the situation in hand once more and never thought of recapturing the rebels high-tailing it back to Hostau, but moved off again after this unfortunate interruption. So of the 247 horses that left Hostau 13 two- and three-year-old stallions were lost.

Some miles short of the Czech-German border some members of an Allied Commission overtook the column in a car and ordered the leader to halt immediately until the ownership of the stud was established. The captain replied that this question did not interest him in the least; he had his orders to carry out and would crush any resistance to them. Then he indicated the five tanks scattered round and got the column on the move again without listening to any further protests, so the Lipizzaner stud arrived safely in the much more peaceful surroundings of Schwarzenberg, in Bavaria.

Next morning Colonel Reed drove me there in a jeep. In all the places we passed there were great banners bearing the words "We greet the Red Army." When the American colonel noticed me looking up at these he commented with a bitter laugh, "The inhabitants of this country do not love us much, and can hardly wait for the Russians to arrive. Now you will understand why I had the horses brought to Bavaria as quickly as possible."

In Schwarzenberg I found our Lipizzaner grazing peacefully in a temporary enclosure. The Arab herd from Hostau, as well as other breeds that had got mixed up there, incidentally, were now located here as well. The Commandant of the stud had remained in Hostau, and the Staff Veterinary attached to the stud had taken over command. He was not at all pleased to see me, and at once informed me that he intended to leave a disintegrating Europe and make his way to America. How far he wished to involve his private ambition with the fate of the stud I was soon to learn from the interview that followed, when he expressed to Colonel Reed the opinion that the next step must be the transfer of the horses to what was at that time the Army Remount sections of Bergstetten and Mansbach, since the pasture in Schwarzenberg would last no more than a fortnight. I opposed this, saying that yet another stop was quite unnecessary, since the horses were to be taken to St Martin and Lambach until they could return to Piber for good. Then the Staff Veterinary said that Austria was much too small to retain the Lipizzaner stud, and proposed that he should take the entire stud to America, as there this noble race of horses, which had survived the Second World War with such difficulty, would most safely be preserved for posterity. I objected strongly and stressed that the Austrian Republic would appreciate the cultural importance of the Spanish Riding School, as well as the generous help of General Patton, sufficiently to look after the Lipizzaner stud herself. In any case any further argument was superfluous since General Patton had already decided in St Martin to give back to the new Austria the stud that belonged to her. Colonel Reed then brought the distasteful negotiations to an end and decided that the Lipizzaner should be taken in trucks to Upper Austria, and the Staff Veterinary was given the job of making the necessary preparations.

When we got back to Zinkowy and before I flew off I tried to thank Colonel Reed for his help and great understanding. But he stopped me, saying, "I have only acted as a fellow-rider should, and I am convinced that you would have done the same if the positions had been reversed."

Once again it was the genuine spirit of riding comradeship that had come to my aid over all my difficulties at this time in my struggle on behalf of the Lipizzaner.

Back in St Martin I had to arrange rapidly for the transfer of the stud, which was far from easy, as all the larger accommodation was still occupied by refugees, and all the usable stabling was filled with the Hungarian stud, as was also the Stallion Depot in Stadl-Paura, near Lambach, where I had managed only with great difficulty to get six boxes freed for the stallions. But some two and a half miles from St Martin, near Reichersberg, there was a disused German military airfield, with stabling where the Luftwaffe in the last phase of the War had kept draught horses, bringing in supplies with them to save petrol. I got permission from the Twentieth Corps to take this over for the stud, but when I went round with an old caretaker a horde of released Polish prisoners of war, who had settled themselves here and terrorized the entire neighbourhood, forced me with curses and threats to leave the airfield. When I returned the next day with an American colonel accompanied by military police it transpired that my obliging guide of the day before had been murdered by the Poles after I left. Police reinforcements were instantly called and swiftly surrounded the buildings. Then they rounded up all the men and took them away, so I was able to carry out undisturbed all my preparations for the arrival of the Lipizzaner stud. The huge hangars were comparatively easily converted into stabling, water could be obtained from the flowing stream near by, and the barracks provided sufficient room for the stud personnel. Rather reluctantly I recognized that I should have to break into my carefully accumulated supplies of straw, but the Lipizzaner must have a decent bed after their long journey.

Colonel Reed had intended the transfer to take place in two or three days, but gave clear instructions that I was to be informed in plenty of time of the stud's arrival. Still without any news by the late afternoon of May 18, and having had an exhausting day in Reichersberg, I was planning to have dinner and go straight to bed when I received a telephone call from the Twentieth Corps telling me that the convoy with the horses would arrive around ten that evening. I went along to the airfield and waited. It was a beautiful, starry, and very cold night with no moon. In my understandable excitement—now the Lippizzaner I had believed lost were really returning to Austria—the minutes dragged slowly by.

At last, shortly before midnight, the distant sound of engines broke the stillness, and on the horizon an ever-lengthening line of headlights came into view. Driven by German prisoners of war, forty trucks arrived on the airfield, which lay in complete darkness, because the floodlights had been destroyed before the occupation. There was a good deal of confusion, for the drivers, weary from their long journey, had simply left their vehicles without a thought wherever they could halt.

I had provided a temporary ramp in a hollow to facilitate the unloading of the horses, but the drivers refused to take their trucks there in the darkness, as they were afraid of mishaps on the uneven ground, so I ordered the loading bridge to be used. In the German Wehrmacht this had always been brought along when animals were being moved, and one of the men said, "We haven't got it with us! We could have done with it on the journey when one of the trucks fell over, and the mares and foals were tipped out into the street. One mare was so badly injured that she had to be shot. The other horses stayed behind because we could not get them back into the truck."

Meantime the Lipizzaner were beginning to grow restless and kick the thin boarding uneasily with their hind-legs so we could not wait for dawn to unload. Searching round with my pocket torch, I found a bridge that had been used for loading petrol-cans, and we now tried with this to free the horses, growing more and more impatient from their confinement. It was a precarious business, for the bridge left a long drop to the ground, and the horses had more or less to be pushed out. The whole operation was carried out by the light of the headlamps of two trucks—the only illumination we had. It was a most tedious business, and it was quite three o'clock before the horses, now thoroughly nervous, were deposited safe and sound in their stalls. The brood mare Trompeta III was the only one who could not wait her turn. She wrenched herself free from the attendant and jumped out of the lorry in the darkness, landing so badly that she broke a leg and, like the mare on the journey, had to be shot. In spite of this regrettable loss I was pleased to have brought the remaining 159 horses—47 brood mares, 38 foals, 32 young mares, and 42 stallions—into their temporary quarters at last, where they rolled delightedly in the fresh straw after their long journey. Dog-tired I went back to St Martin, with conflicting feelings of joy that the return of the Lipizzaner had been accomplished, and anxiety as to whether I should be able to overcome the difficulties that lay ahead.

A week later the second transport, which this time encountered no difficulties, arrived in Reichersberg with the rest of the stud, so that 216 horses had been lucky enough to reach Upper Austria.

The transfer arrangements had been made by the Staff Veterinary responsible with a really unparalleled lack of forethought. Although food for men and animals had been brought with us from Hostau to Schwarzenberg, the Lipizzaner arrived in Reichersberg not only without halters, blankets, saddlery, and other such equipment, but even without any veterinary instruments or medicines. And that at a time of great shortage, when even procuring a simple nail for a horseshoe became an affair of state!

Moreover, the 216 horses were accompanied by 70 men, most of whom were idle and mutinous and foreigners into the bargain, and from the very beginning they were a great nuisance to me.

This unfortunate state of affairs reached its climax when I discovered that some of the young stallions had glanders. If the horses had been handed over to me properly I should have been informed of their condition. As it was this illness, not unnaturally, spread to the sound horses because immediate precautions were not taken.

As soon as I inspected the horses I noticed that two more stallions and twelve mares were still missing, these having remained behind in Schwarzenberg, allegedly with the permission of General Patton, to be used for breeding in the Arab herd. To what extent this measure actually represented the American general's intentions I could not determine in those turbulent days, and I also had to resign myself to the fact that the Staff Veterinary had given work horses to sundry people and dispatched two Lipizzaner mares of the Piber strain as riding and carriage horses for Colonel Reed in Nuremberg.

The Arab stud from Hostau and the dispersed Lipizzaner were taken a year later to Fort Riley, in the United States, as Army property, actually accompanied by an American Veterinary Officer. But as the Army no longer employed horses, this stud, except for what was required for restocking while the Poles were being repatriated, was given over to the Ministry of Agriculture, which showed no interest whatever in these displaced animals and sold them in the open market to private people. The Lipizzaner that are to-day to be found in the United States are in the main descended from these horses missing in May 1945.

With the return of the Lipizzaner stud there began for me a trying period filled with apparently insoluble problems. The first difficulty was the question of feeding the stable-staff. In Schwarzenberg they had received Army rations on the intervention of Colonel Reed, a solution that the strictly correct head of the General Staff of the Twentieth Corps found unacceptable. He referred me to the Reichersberg district office for an issue of civilian rations, which meant considerably less for the stable personnel. Kitchen staff had remained in Schwarzenberg, and a cook who had been attached to the stud in Hostau could not be employed in the new kitchen because she had been accused by the grooms of dishonesty over food and discharged for open embezzlement. The strong-minded woman from Berlin, however, determined to get the job, managed to turn one of the notoriously susceptible American lieutenants against me, so that once more a time-wasting interview with the Twentieth Corps was necessary to keep the tiresome kitchen-fairy and her energetic protector under control.

But this little episode lay on the fringe of the countless problems that the stud raised and caused me many sleepless nights, for the second transport had barely arrived and been joyfully installed before General Collier summoned me and announced that the airfield would be taken back into service by American troops and I must look for other accommodation for the Lipizzaner. He put a captain with extraordinary powers at my disposal, and with him I was to search the whole neighbourhood for suitable quarters. This was shattering news for I knew from my search for accommodation for the Spanish Riding School how hard it was to find room for so many horses in the overcrowded land. Obviously one could not billet stud horses out singly in farmyards.

My first thought was the Federal Depot in Stadl-Paura, near Lambach, which had more than enough stabling, but this was still occupied by the Hungarians, and when vacated would accommodate farm stallions. My one-time regimental comrade and old friend Landstallmeister Ulrich, who was in charge of it, at once suggested the foal ranch near by and the Wimsbach estate. In both places, however, there were still saddle and draught horses belonging to the Hungarian Army, which enjoyed preferential status in the American-occupied part of Upper Austria. Although the American captain came with me our entrance was barred by hostile-looking characters much feared in the neighbourhood, so we drove on to the appropriate Military Governor. However, he received us very ungraciously and announced categorically that the Hungarian horses would remain there, and even

General Patton could do nothing whatever about it, so we had to return to St Martin, having accomplished nothing. But the somewhat autocratic Governor of Wimsbach had not reckoned with the energy of the Twentieth Corps Chief of Staff, for the very next day the captain urged me to repeat our fruitless journey of inspection to Wimsbach, and this time, in spite of sullen faces, every door was open to us. Even the Governor had turned completely round and agreed, once I had decided the accommodation was suitable, to have it vacated in two days.

I could, however, transfer only part of the stud there, and had to go on looking until I managed to find at Heidegut, on the Löfferhof, and in Otterbach, near Schärding—thus fifty miles in opposite directions—accommodation for the rest of my horses; and on May 29 the transfer of the 40 brood mares with 19 foals chosen for Wimsbach began. The Americans put at our disposal a convoy of captured German Army lorries with German prisoner-of-war drivers under the supervision of a strong detachment of military police commanded by an officer. The loading was uneventful, and the long convoy moved off slowly in accordance with its instructions.

But first one unpleasant matter had to be settled. I had been told that the 35 Polish stable-lads were particularly discontented with their lot, trying by every kind of complaint and refusal to work to obstruct Army supplies. When these attempts were fruitless they made secret preparations for flight, requisitioning wagons and harness in the neighbourhood and starting to load up their possessions. As they had nothing to draw their carts I was afraid for the Lipizzaner, which had already been hitched up in Hostau, as these grooms naturally knew, so I got permission to keep the threatened horses in the Reichersberg abbey for a few days before we left as this was under special military protection. But when I was having these horses collected the Poles overpowered my own picked men, harnessed some of the horses, and charged off with three wagons at a wild gallop. I immediately alerted the lieutenant in command of the Military Police, but had reluctantly to remind him forcibly of General Patton's orders to protect the horses and prevent the loss of individual animals before I could stir him to action. But then a sergeant with two Military Policemen stormed off in a jeep and half an hour later brought back the three wagons, whose passengers now looked very pathetic. Taking advantage of this, I had the Poles lined up at once and made it clear to them that I would crush unauthorized action, but would consider reasonable requests. Then they all told me at once that they had nothing against me, but wanted to return to Schwarzenberg, in Bavaria, because their compatriots were there. I promised to put forward their request, and late that evening after my return from Lambach I went to General Collier, who ordered the 35 Poles to be sent back the next day to Bavaria—not, indeed, to Schwarzenberg, but into a camp where that kind of behaviour would not be tolerated, so I was relieved of one intolerable burden.

A day later 47 mares with 38 foals and 18 young mares from Lipizza were loaded up and brought to the country estate in much the same way as before; so another and exhausting day passed.

Next morning the mares from Piber and Demir Kapia without foals were to be transferred to Lambach. The loading took a very long time, for both the stable staff and the escort were showing noticeable signs of fatigue after the strain of the two previous days. At last the trucks moved off about mid-day. I as usual driving my own car at the end of the column. The heat was intense, and the journey had to be frequently interrupted for long rests. I felt a fearful, almost sick weariness, my thoughts grew more and more dizzy, until the present seemed to be far away. I came out of this misty haze to find myself lying on a stretcher. What could have happened? Overcome by sleep, I had lost control of my car, which had swerved to the middle of the road and had been hit by an American Army truck coming in the other direction and was a total wreck. I was dragged out unconscious by the Americans, and brought back in a military ambulance to the castle at St Martin, now converted into a hospital, where I regained consciousness. The regimental doctor, who was forbidden to deal with civilians, gave me first aid and sent me by ambulance to a civilian doctor in the next village. The latter, after a thorough examination, discovered numerous scratches on my face and cuts on both kness and several broken ribs, tended me as well as he could with his meagre supplies, and sent me back to St Martin. But I had hardly got into bed in my own room, hoping to restore my bursting head to normal with a little rest, when General Collier appeared and had me taken back to the Army doctor who had given me first aid. He then took all the dressings off again—if the procedure had not been so painful I should have smiled at the comic situation—washed the wounds again, stitched them, and laid a fresh strapping round my ribs. Then he said, almost reproachfully, "Why didn't you tell me that you were the gentleman with the white horses, then I should have looked after you myself without any orders from the general."

This mishap put me out of action for several days, and the rest of the transfer from Reichersberg could not be completed until I was up again; then the young mares and stallions were brought to Lambach and Otterbach, so I had done my best for my lambs for the time being, even though they were scattered over an area of fifty or sixty miles.

At last I found time to give the horses a thorough inspection, and made a horrifying discovery. It was quite easy to see from the combined Lipizzaner stud how much Dr Rau had disliked the Lipizzaner from Piber, for in the short period of two and a half years things had come to such a pass that of the stud horses sent to Hostau hardly more than 50 per cent. were able to return to Austria. Through sales, particularly in the last half-year of the War, the Piber stud was severely depleted, and of the remaining mares more than 60 per cent. had not been in foal for a year. The Italian and Yugoslavian section of the Hostau stud were not in such a bad way, because the studmasters Stopar and Matoff, who had accompanied this group, could look after their horses and prevent any large selling, while the Lipizzaner from Piber had remained without a protector from the moment I lost contact with Hostau during the fighting. They were so unexpectedly reduced that the Piber stud as a unit was barely functioning at all, a situation that certainly demanded much thought in view of the coming division of the combined Lipizzaner stud.

With the completion of the transfer to their various destinations the Lipizzaner could now at last lead a somewhat more peaceful existence after the great upsets of the month before. Moreover, this rest was now absolutely necessary, for the health of the horses, particularly of the younger ones, which had been badly affected by the glanders they had brought with them, left much to be desired.

The peace that had come to the Lipizzaner certainly did not embrace the director of the stud, whose job now had to be combined with that of the Spanish Riding School, for the care and provisioning of the many horses involved endless worry in the weeks and months to come.

The store of fodder that I had begun to accumulate for a rainy day even during the War was an appreciable help for the stallions of the Spanish Riding School, but quite inadequate for the many stud horses. Austrian officialdom had a sort of Platonic love for the Spanish Riding School, but was very hesitant in all practical questions, and most of the time took refuge in the usual answer that this was some one else's responsibility. The provisional Provincial Government gave me to understand that the stud was a Federal responsibility, but I was not able to get in touch with the central authority in Vienna for some time. When later a very poor connexion was made I was referred back to the Provincial Government, but without being able to give the latter any instructions. Few people in authority had a clear idea of the importance of the lucky return of the Lipizzaner stud and I often had to listen to such questions as: "How can Austria possibly cope with all these Lipizzaner when fodder is so short?" "Why were these horses brought back to Austria in such a hurry?" The fact that only the return of the Lipizzaner stud, an undertaking in which a few hours played an essential part, could ensure the Spanish Riding School's future was completely overlooked.

But it would never do to give up because of lack of understanding. In those days everybody was fully occupied with his own concerns, and countless problems of vital importance were clamouring for attention. On the other hand I could not shuttle aimlessly between the central and the local authority, for the creatures committed to my care needed feed and attention. It was these two necessities that caused me most worry; there were often moments when after fruitless negotiations I thought I could no longer stave off the destruction of this valuable bloodstock. After restless and sleepless nights, however, I always began looking for a fresh solution, and in the end my obstinacy was rewarded, but in the meantime it was a severe strain on my nerves, for I certainly could not stand aside indifferently and watch the rescue of the Lipizzaner being abandoned half-way.

From the moment the Lipizzaner stud returned I had always visualized Piber as their ultimate home, and, as some of their new quarters—those like the ones at Fohlenhof, Weidegut, and Löfflerhof—were unsuitable for the winter and there was such a severe shortage of supplies, I suggested transferring the stud to Piber, but could never extract a definite decision from the Americans. It was only later that I learned from a document belonging to the Provincial Government that the military authority regarded a transfer to the stud into the British Zone with the strongest disfavour. A few days later I dispatched a written inquiry to the American Second Corps, under whose authority we were later placed, as to whether I could count on the return of the Lipizzaner stud to Piber before the arrival of winter, as otherwise I should have to look round for winter quarters right away. The reply stated that there was no question of the stud's returning to Styria for the time being, as in this zone there was no fodder ration available. However, the Military Government of Upper Austria and Salzburg promised to give me every aid in finding suitable winter quarters. I suggested the cavalry barracks in Ried and the dragoon barracks in Wels as suitable accommodation, but there were immediate difficulties, for the buildings in Reid had been converted into living-quarters and the dragoon barracks in Wels were full of Hungarians, so there was no alternative but to make more or less draught-proof three large exhibition halls in the Volksfestplatz in Ried, which were vacated for me. Double walls and a false roof were fitted, and during October we managed to take 82 mares with 8 foals and 55 fillies over there. Thus the most pressing problem seemed to be solved for the winter.

And now back to what seemed to me the everlasting gargantuan problem of fodder! The supplies belonging to the former German Wehrmacht left me by the Americans lasted the stud for only a brief period. An allocation from the civil authority, in charge of the various requisitioned stocks and the new harvest, was unfortunately not forthcoming until the American military authority intervened.

Their orders were complied with by the issue of fodder for one month, so that every four weeks I had to endure the same time-wasting pilgrimage, until finally in the autumn of 1945 the Military Government ordered the local authority to supply the Spanish Riding School and the Lipizzaner stud with a half-yearly fodder ration. When I called the appropriate official he told me that the local regulations allowed them to issue permits only every fourteen days for the time being, so I was in fact worse off than before!

Things got so bad that at times there was neither hay nor oats available for a couple of days. Repeated representations to the local authority in Linz were unsuccessful, so the great support of the Americans did not help me much at first, for I could not grumble to them about my own countrymen. These moral scruples cost me many hundreds of miles in the car, and whole days of waiting without meals, simply to evoke a little official sympathy for my four-legged charges with all the rhetoric at my command, and extort the fodder for the next fortnight.

At the beginning of December one of the periodical unannounced inspections by the military took place. I was not present at the time, as I was in the process of begging for supplies in some office or other, so the captain learned from the stable staff about our difficulties, was shown the feed house, which was once more completely empty, and left the stud without awaiting my return. But he reappeared in St Martin two days later, and, though on other occasions he was always friendly, this time his manner was distinctly chilly, and he bluntly demanded an explanation as to why I had not claimed the six-monthly ration of fodder as arranged. When I replied that I had he interrupted me with a retort that he had been informed by the food office in Linz that because they had not received my requirements they could make no allocation. I invited the captain into my office and showed him copies of all my applications. He made a note of the dates, and then remarked, once more friendly and smiling, "I thought there must be something wrong, for it would not be at all in keeping with the impression I have of you if you had forgotten feed for your horses."

The very next day I received a written order for the necessary six-monthly supplies, though I had to collect the ration in separate consignments from various widely scattered distribution centres, but the distributors simply said they had no more because the farmers had not fully honoured their delivery quota. In this fashion I finally managed in January and February 1946, after I had chased about and procured additional permits, to store up the fodder ration for the period to the end of May.

I had the same trouble over the stable-lads for the stud as I had experienced with the school. Of the staff who had come from Hostau, the Ukrainians left after the Poles, and could be replaced only by a dwindling number of ethnic German refugees. But there remained the studmaster Stopar from Lipizza with twelve trained stud-grooms, so, though the tending and care of so many horses was very difficult, at least it was assured for the time being. It was a real catastrophe, however, when the entire Lipizza personnel announced that they were homesick and could stay no longer, and all my powers of persuasion and promises were useless; in December 1945 these thirteen men departed after saying good-bye, leaving me in a hopeless situation. Despite various applications to every possible office, and newspaper advertisements, only a few replacements could be found, and many, having received their ration cards, deserted at the first opportunity. When I thought of my dependent horses on the one hand and my powerlessness on the other I was often near to despair, for there were times when I had no more than three men in the stud, with whose help the horses could barely be fed and watered, let alone groomed.

Luckily the health of the horses in Ried was magnificent, so the mares in foal endured the winter well without special attention. The many births took place in the main without complications, and in these not very favourable surroundings a fair number of good foals saw the light of day. Some of them are now stars of the Spanish Riding School, and bear not the slightest trace of their turbulent and difficult childhood. Full-scale mating was also carried out, in such circumstances with a total of 82 mares undoubtedly an achievement, and the brave Lipizzaner ladies did their best to repay our human efforts, and brought 55 lusty foals into the world.

In arranging mating I not only considered the general appearance of the partner, but also took the opportunity to refresh the various sections of the stud with suitable crosses, which was particularly urgent in the interests of the weakened stud from Piber. That these measures were completely successful can be seen to-day in the National Stud at Piber, which mainly consists of the descendants of those born at this particular time.

The Lipizzaner stud in Reid, in spite of its decidely wretched outward appearance, attracted many admirers, and the noble, intelligent horses radiated, even in their exile, an unmistakable glamour. Bruno Brehm wrote in his book *Am Rande des Abgrunds (On the Edge of the Abyss)*:

> One of my first trips was out to the Trotting Race course of the little Upper Austrian town. Down each side of it stretched barracks in which Estonians, Letts, Lithuanians, and followers of Wlassow were living. But on the track stood young, almost black, Lipizzaner. I lured one of the friendly mares to the hedge, stroked her, and let her sniff my hand. It was the same feeling as one used to get touching with a trembling hand the marble head of one of the horses in the Parthenon.
>
> I stood thoughtfully looking at these horses. The days of horsemanship were over. The days that are to come have none of the mild goodness of a horse's face, as Leonardo and Baldung Grien drew it, realizing what this animal meant to man, and what man will lose, if he forsakes it for machines.

It was obvious to me that the situation in which the Lipizzaner stud found itself in the winter of 1945-46 was no more than temporary, a little breathing space. Therefore as early as November I tried to set in motion with the Ministry of Agriculture and Forestry the return of at least some of the Lipizzaner to Piber. My suggestion met with such sympathy that April 1946 was set as a target, but first I must get into direct negotiation with the Director of the stud, Dr Besel, and then take the necessary steps with the military authorities for Upper Austria.

Dr Besel, an admirer of the Lipizzaner for many years, was enthusiastic about the proposed return of his former darlings. He made available far too many stalls, which in the main stood empty, and agreed the intended date, provided—yes, provided—I delivered some oats with the horses, otherwise he would not be in a position to take over the Lipizzaner before the autumn. So once more I stood before a closed door, since the Military Government did not permit fodder to be sent forward into another zone. In any case I was amazed at being expected to provide fodder for Piber as well, but this load fell on my already burdened shoulders. People in Upper Austria, where there were so many 'foreign' horses to be fed, were quite justifiably of the opinion that Styria also could make some contribution for 'their' Lipizzaner. The Ministry of Agriculture finally decided that pasture must be found for the Lipizzaner in Upper Austria—easily said, but extraordinarily difficult to accomplish.

Once more I had to go in search of quarters with possibilities of grazing, as the horses in Ried, where there was no available pasture, could only stay until the spring. It meant starting all over again: searching, waiting in outer offices, negotiating, and begging, until after almost incredible and repeated efforts, irritations, and disappointments I finally managed to find refuge on the Wimsbach estate.

The castle and estate of Wimsbach belonged to the Hermann Göring works in Linz in its time and was considered to be German property, administered in trust under the supervision of the Americans. After many months' efforts I managed to procure a lease of this property through the Ministry of Agriculture and Forestry, but, fortunately, thanks to the exceptional helpfulness of the trustees, I had secretly arranged that the horses could be taken there in May and June—in fact, long before the negotiations were completed—for my rations came to an end in May, and I could not have procured any more fodder before that year's harvest.

Anticipating this state of affairs, I had already begun to make drastic cuts to make the ration go a little farther. I transferred 34 fillies to Hinterstoder, 48 miles away, and the yearling stallions to the mountain grazing at Rauris, near Salzburg, seizing every opportunity to rid myself, even if only for a short time, of some of my 'eaters.' So the combined stud in Ried broke up at the end of May.

The negotiations over leasing the estate dragged on, as I have said, for a very long time, and there were delays in vacating the stabling still needed. It was most inconvenient when at the beginning of August the agent of the Prince Eulenburg estate in Hinterstoder withdrew overnight the pasture that had been offered me. The stables in Wimsbach that could be used at this time were filled to bursting, and to pack any more in, particularly considering the many mares with foals, was quite impossible. Very reluctantly—but even my love for the Lipizzaner, not only in the Platonic sense, was exhausted—I was forced to gain time by holding up the negotiations until in October I was able to transfer the 34 mares provisionally into other villages.

But the delay in leasing the Wimsbach estate had also reduced the fodder supplies for the Lipizzaner, for the herds of cows could not be taken away until the deal was closed—in October instead of May—and in the meantime had to be given the feed intended for my horses. Still, all these difficulties were small compared with the previous mishaps and the everlasting uncertainty in the past, for now at last the Lipizzaner had a real place of their own where they could remain until they finally returned home.

I have set out in detail the problems involved in directing the stud in the first two post-War years, not to emphasize my devotion, nor to criticize others and complain of the conditions, but only to put on record all the significant details about the Lipizzaner stud. Unusual events create unusual situations. The new Austria rising from the chaos had so many problems to solve that on calm reflection it seems fairly understandable that the Lipizzaner in those days should not have excited the same interest that they do now, when everybody announces proudly, "We did this for the Lipizzaner." But at that time I was alone in the wilderness with my anxiety over this noble breed. People who live in the settled conditions that were restored to us will never understand, or have forgotten, what happened in the period after the War years, and therefore can no longer appreciate how often in those days the existence of this institution that had grown so dear to us hung by the slenderest of threads.

In April 1946 the first requests to return became effective, and with them the impending dissolution of the combined Lipizzaner stud began to take shape. Anyone who knew precisely the numbers of horses in this combined stud realized that on the way in which the division was made depended the continuance and future of the Austrian Lipizzaner stud, since this had returned from Czechoslovakia severely weakened; so the forthcoming negotiations with the Reparations Commission became of supreme importance. I was well aware that the individual countries were pressing their requests most inconsiderately. In those post-War days a great deal of fresh injustice was being created under the title of reparation, and it was by no means rare for horses sold to Austria during the War in the ordinary way to be demanded back by their previous owners without compensation. In this period of unrestrained legal quibbling I had to uphold unaided the Austrian point of view, but perhaps this very circumstance was fortunate for the Lipizzaner, for I was able, unhampered by bureaucratic restrictions of any kind, to fight with all my devotion for the retention in Austria of this ancient breed of horses.

At my first interview with the Americans I was made to realize that according to the strict letter of the law we could expect no replacement from the other two sections of the stud for the losses sustained, and that our demands for restitution could be made only to Germany. So from Germany, who lay in the dust, her life-blood ebbing away, were to be demanded the Lipizzaner that had been sold by the so-called protectorate, and had already been for a long time back in a national stud in Czechoslovakia. Obviously a completely pointless undertaking!

The Yugoslavs raised claims to the former occupants of the two studs at Lipizza and Demir Kapia and their descendants. While the demands over Lipizza were held up because of the still disputed territory of Trieste, the negotiations with the American Reparations Commission began at the beginning of May concerning the return of the horses from Demir Kapia. But, in addition, the Yugoslavs demanded replacements for the horses that had been brought at one time from Demir Kapia, but later pushed into Hostau, and the Yugoslav officer accused me in a very aggressive manner of forcing the grooms from Lipizza to go home so that I could have a free hand in the stud. Since the departure of these men and the consequent difficulties were still very green in my memory, this intentional distortion of the facts made me furiously angry, and I rebutted the unfair charges with great vigour. The American officer in charge of the negotiations cut short any further reply from the Yugoslav by saying sharply, "I would recommend you, instead of levelling charges at Colonel Podhajsky, to propose him to Marshal Tito for a medal, for if he had not got General Patton's help Yugoslavia would not be seeing a single Lipizzaner again to-day."

During the autumn of 1946 Italy also succeeded in its claims on the horses from Lipizza, and put in a long list of returns, including many stud horses actually sold long before Hostau. Since I had repeatedly tried to get the Americans to throw out the foreign horses to ease the fodder and supply difficulties, the question of the return to Lipizza now became acute. It was decided that Italy should retain the former inhabitants of Lipizza, with the proviso that she should settle the eventual claims of Yugoslavia by direct negotiation. December 1946 was proposed as a final date, but I waited in vain long after that time for the horses to be removed.

The shortage of roughage was particularly noticeable in the winter 1946–47 because of the abnormally dry summer, so the prolonged stay of the Lipizza stud was specially grave. I reiterated my urgent plea to the Americans for the immediate return of the horses to Italy, but was told that the situation had completely altered and that the Lipizza territory had been awarded to Yugoslavia under the peace terms; the latter had once more raised their claim to the stud and announced the arrival of the former studmaster Stopar with suitable proof; the return to Yugoslavia would then follow in May.

Again weeks and months passed, without anything at all happening. The summer of 1947 also was exceptionally dry, the fields were eaten bare, and the blades of grass scorched by the sun. Any hope of producing the necessary hay steadily receded, particularly after the control of roughage was abolished in June.

Deeply concerned over the worrying shortage of fodder, I pressed the military authorities and the American Reparations Commission once more for the immediate removal of the Lipizza stud, and was finally given an assurance that the horses would be collected on October 28, 1947—but by the Italians! At the very last minute before the agreed date the removal was cancelled once more because of protests from the Yugoslavs. At this point I wrote a letter to the High Commissioner of the United States in Vienna, General Keyes, refusing to take any further responsibility for the Lipizza stud if it remained because of the disastrous fodder position, using the loss of a mare which had broken a leg in the meadow to drive home the intolerable situation still more emphatically.

This letter proved effective, for on November 18, 1947, the Lipizzaner were handed over to Italy and taken to Fara Sabina, near Rome.

With the departure of these horses the Odyssey of the Lipizzaner ended. For me ended also the weary years of care and anxiety over these noble creatures, with the comforting knowledge that I had done everything humanly possible to save the Piber stud. Only my love for the white horses had given me the determination to achieve complete success, setting aside all personal feeling to surmount every obstacle. There is really no need for me to say this, for the Lipizzaner stud in Piber provides a living proof.

In the spring of 1947 to ease the feed position one section of the mares together with three stallions to serve them returned to Piber. The Director of the Stud, Dr Besel, was delighted with the beautiful foals, the results of careful mating. The rest of the Lipizzaner stayed right up to September 1952 under my supervision in Wimsbach, and, indeed, the responsibility for this section after all the terrible difficulties of the years that had passed was an easy matter. In particular the fodder position changed fundamentally for I succeeded in procuring from the Italians 125 tons of oats, 145 tons of hay, and 85 tons of straw in repayment for feeding the horses from Lipizza.

When, therefore, the last stud horses left Wimsbach in 1952 I looked after them with proud joy, for I knew that successors for the Spanish Riding School and therefore its existence were now assured; all the same, I watched the departing horses with a somewhat melancholy eye, for the hard times with their attendant worries had united us in friendship.

The dissolution of the stud in Wimsbach had been decided by the Ministry of the day without a single word of acknowledgement, so little value did it put on what had been achieved there in the seven years. This curious phenomenon in my own country upset me greatly, for foreigners like the Italians were not unaware of the saga of the Lipizzaner stud, and the general responsible for the breeding of horses in the War Ministry in Rome awarded me the bronze plaque of that celebrated reviver of Italian riding, Captain Caprilli, with the following inscription:

> Ministero Difesa Esercito Italiano—Ispett. Ippico e Veter.
> Al Colonello di Cavalleria Alois Podhajsky
> in ricordo dei Cavalli Lipizzani amorevolmente custoditi
> Roma—Dicembre 1946

(in recognition of the Lipizzaner horses looked after with such devotion). This honour was accompanied by the following letter:

REPUBLICA ITALIANA
MINISTERO DELLA DIFESA—ESERCITO
ISPETTORATO DEL SERVIZIO IPPICO E VETERINARIO.
IL GENERALE ISPETTORE

Rome, 12 December 1947

DEAR COLONEL,

I have the honour to inform you that the Lipizzaner horses that were entrusted to your care have arrived in Italy in fine fettle.

I should like to put on record my appreciation to you personally and your colleagues for your exceptional ability and great devotion and express my recognition of your outstanding knowledge of horse-breeding. It is thanks to your knowledge and ability that we are once more in possession of this valuable breed.

As a rider and passionate lover of horses permit me, honoured sir, to express my gratitude to you and your staff. I would like to bring to your notice that your efforts have been much appreciated in Italy and will continue to be so.

It will give me great pleasure to make your acquaintance when you come to Italy and show you the Lipizzaner horses that were entrusted to your care.

Once again, with appreciation and thanks, please accept this simple medallion as a memento of Italian riders.

With equestrian greetings
IMPERIALE, GENERAL

26. On the Way to the New World: Bremen, 1950

27. Welcome in New York: General Tuckermann with
Neapolitano Africa

28. Favory Calais in *Caprioles* in Madison Square Garden: New York, 1950

29. "A Rose without Thorns" from Mrs Patton in Madison Square Garden

CHAPTER 11

The Spanish Riding School in Exile

W hen we left Vienna in March 1945, deserting it with such heavy hearts, we quite expected to be able to return very shortly, and at the longest several months after its occupation by the Allied forces. This belief remained unshaken by battles and upsets, for Vienna and Austria must be freed and led towards a happier future—this was at least the tenor of the foreign radio transmissions for many years. But the fulfilment of this promise was disappointing, and the general situation cast its shadow over the Spanish Riding School too. At the moment there could be no thought of returning, so a temporary control of the school by the Military Government of Upper Austria, to ensure essential supplies for the next months, seemed the only solution. Certainly a Federal Government had been set up in Vienna immediately after the occupation, but nobody in the new headquarters bothered about the Spanish Riding School, so it floated like a piece of driftwood on the flood of destiny, and at first there was no alternative but to take great care that it was not smashed on one of the many reefs.

As I have already indicated, the interest of the Americans in the Spanish Riding School was very great indeed. The news of the performance for General Patton had spread to the farthest corner of the occupation zone, and the numbers who wanted to see the horses that had had such an effect on the normally stolid Army Chief grew daily greater. The Austrians, affected by the general deprivations and the division of the country, with the difficulties over the demarcation lines, were the least informed about the Spanish Riding School, except for the occupants of the little village in Upper Austria, who with pride and delight noted the interest of the conquerors in the Austrian cultural academy. And, of course, it must not be forgotten that the newspapers and journals had first to be revived. The

145

Oberösterreichischen Nachrichten on July 16 brought the first news of the performance given before General Patton and of the rescue of the Spanish Riding School. This article gave the first public intimation that the school had luckily ·survived the devastating storms of the preceding months. Letters began to arrive from various parts of our country, from which I was able to assess how far this institution had become a symbol for Austria and had secured a place in the hearts of the widest cross-section of the people. This naturally encouraged me greatly, and gave me strength to carry out my tasks, often so heavy.

The first weeks of the occupation were so completely devoted to ensuring the existence of the old school that the question of horsemanship was of necessity pushed into the background. I had to employ the personnel of the Spanish Riding School to carry out also the various movements of the stud and to collect fodder I had secured. Only gradually could we turn again to an intensive riding training to bring the horses to a suitable standard for public performances. When I was repeatedly pressed by the Americans, who had been most helpful to me on various occasions, for performances for "ordinary mortals" as well, I decided to arrange some similar exhibitions for the American troops. The school in which we had performed for General Patton would hold only a few spectators, so I fitted up a meadow near to the castle as a showground, where I had the advantage of being able to warm up the horses unseen behind a hedge surrounding the park, so that the performances went without a hitch. There were sometimes one or two thousand soldiers present at the shows in June and July. The Americans took responsibility for cordoning off the area and saw to it that the sections of troops from the various garrisons were kept in order. But Austrians too interspersed with the Americans, or, as 'hedge guests,' managed to follow the performances. The success of the Lipizzaner with the American Army General was repeated also with the ordinary soldiers: they were all captivated, and even the informal and easygoing Americans always respected the decidedly ceremonial atmosphere.

This was particularly noticeable when Colonel Dwight Colley, Commander of the 238th Infantry Regiment, ordered a performance in August for a number of American generals, including General Patton. A daïs was erected beside the show-ring for the guests of honour, and decorated with boughs and bunting in the Austrian colours. A deputation of officers from the Second Corps in Salzburg discussed the programme with me, and the 328th Infantry Regiment collected a guard of honour from the companies in Reid, Schärding, and Braunau. A few days before there was a rehearsal, at which the drill and presenting of arms aroused my admiration, for during the whole three months' period of the occupation I had never seen the American soldiers drilling at all, so, as an officer, I was expecting something slightly ridiculous. I was therefore much astonished when at the word of command several hundred soldiers presented arms with a precision that would have done justice to a Prussian battalion.

About midday General Patton arrived in St Martin, followed by eight more generals. The band played an old military tune, and General Patton walked along the line with his entourage, here and there straightening the steel helmet of a soldier. After the military ceremony the Bezirkshauptmann from Ried greeted the General in the name of the Austrian Government and thanked him for the great help he had given to the Spanish Riding School. Boys and girls stepped from a group in national dress and presented General Patton with a gift from me: an album bound in red and white leather with photographs of the Spanish Riding School and a huge bouquet of red roses. After lunch at the castle the performance began. The guard of honour marched in, forming a square round the edge of the arena, presented arms when the General appeared, and then sat down to watch. A more festive background could not have been provided in those days for the gallant Lipizzaner, whose art now had to justify all that had been done for them.

The guests and soldiers applauded loudly, and the Austrians, some of whom had come a long distance, were no less enthusiastic. The accompaniment was provided by our musical staff of records, and in the intervals the American military band played. The records sounded so good that the newspaper reporters thought that a secret orchestra, part of the military band, had been playing. At the end of the performance I rode up to the daïs and thanked General Patton for his tremendous support, and with this the improvised show on the castle meadow reached its climax and fitting conclusion. Before the General left St Martin he expressed a wish to see the horse that Hitler had intended to give to the Emperor of Japan, and asked me whether he might also ride it, and was obviously delighted to be able to execute various movements with it.

Gradually the news of the rescue of the Spanish Riding School spread throughout the country, and now a great many Austrians too, experts and admirers, began to visit St Martin, to satisfy themselves that the Lipizzaner had really survived the holocaust. The other occupying troops also began to take in interest in us and sent their representatives, the French in uniform and the Russians, unknown to me, in civilian clothes. It was only later that the Military Governor of Ried drew my attention to these incognito visitors. The British, however, sent two officers to fix up festival visits of the Spanish Riding School to Carinthia and Styria.

I informed these gentlemen that the school was under military control; thus visits to other places, particularly in a different occupation zone, could never be undertaken without the permission of the American authorities. The British officers went immediately to the Second Corps Command in Salzburg to fix things up on the spot. What followed was really most extraordinary.

A week later I was summoned to the Second Corps headquarters and invited to lunch with several high-ranking officers, and in the course of conversation the Chief of the General Staff, General Willems, asked me whether it would harm the health of the Lipizzaner to transport them by train. Quite truthfully I said no, of course, but immediately noticed that this was not the answer he wanted, so he put the question to me in a slightly different form. I suspected this had something to do with the proposed tour in the British occupation zone, but stood my ground, for I wanted to avoid having the Spanish Riding School blamed in the event of a refusal. As an Austrian it was my task to remain on an equally good footing with all the occupation Powers. We then talked of other things, and I left Salzburg without having really discovered why I had been summoned.

After the second performance for General Patton the Chief of the General Staff of the Second Corps gave orders as he left that any transfer of the Lipizzaner to another place must have the written authority of the Corps. Oral permission was not valid, no matter who gave it.

One August day about noon two British officers came to me beaming with delight and instructed me to make riders and horses ready for loading, as three trucks were already waiting for them at the station. When I asked whether they had got a permit for the tour from the Americans the older officer replied that they had come straight from Salzburg and were prepared, though somewhat reluctantly, to get written authority if I insisted while I got on with the preparations for departure. At ten in the evening the two returned weary and downcast from St Martin, having failed to procure written approval from the Americans. I was sorry for them, for they had wasted the whole day—I knew from personal experience how bitter this was—so I asked them to share our humble supper, and about midnight they set off back to Carinthia very depressed over the failure of their mission.

In these troubled times I found my private life, now reduced to an absolute minimum, enriched in a strange way. A little creature had literally forced his way into my life and adopted me as his master. Count Anton Arco-Valley had a delightful short-haired, liver dachshund called Lumpi, who adored his master, and I having been a dachs-owner in the days of my youth, always made a fuss of him whenever we met. But these fleeting interludes naturally made not the slightest difference to Lumpi's devotion to his master, but when the Count was killed in a motor accident involving an American truck there was a complete change in the dog's attitude. He came up to our room in the castle, accompanied me wherever he could, and in the evening it was almost impossible to get him to go to his accustomed sleeping-place in the kitchen. After he had settled down in his basket and been covered up he would often return to our door and beg to be let in, scratching and whimpering. To avoid any ill-feeling I informed the Countess of Lumpi's nightly excursions; the kitchen door was then shut to restrict his wanderings.

A few days later we again heard the familiar noise at our door, but did not open it, so as to make it easier for the little creature to return to his own bed, and after some time we heard no more, so assumed that Lumpi had gone back to the kitchen. Judge of our astonishment and distress, therefore, when next morning we found him lying outside our door, wrapped in the slip-mat because he was cold. Countess Arco-Valley, who heard all about it, then gave him to us, as he had taken us so completely into his little heart after her husband's death.

For three years Lumpi was our inseparable companion, bringing us nothing but happiness. The only trouble the little dog gave us was when in 1948 he suddenly died in the car as I was on my way to my office. The loss of this loyal companion upset my wife and myself so much that Count Ferdinand Arco-Valley brought us a dachshund like him from Bavaria, and he managed to take over our hearts and fill the gap left by his predecessor. Out of loyalty we called him Lumpi also, and Lumpi II, who shared our lives for ten years and, one might say, brightened it, gradually developed into a real character, until all our many friends almost considered Lumpi and Podhajsky as one.

The first official information from Vienna was in October 1945, to say that the Spanische Hofreitschule had been placed once more under the protection of a Government department, and was to bear the name Spanische Reitschule. Not a word more! I read this not without bitterness, for while the school had been fighting for life, the people in the new Ministry considered its change of name of more importance than the care of its personnel and horses. However, for the majority of Austrians, what- ever their political party, this was of no importance, for the title Spanische Hofreitschule has remained in common use ever since.

But I was particularly shocked to discover that with three demobilized grooms and a war-time *Bereiter* a kind of branch office of the Spanish Riding School without horses had been set up in Vienna—just when I in Upper Austria was having the greatest difficulty in finding grooms for the Lipizzaner. The climax of this remarkable sequence of events came with the demand to bring the school back to Vienna. An official had been negotiating with representatives of the Russian occupation forces and in- duced them to clear the riding-hall of the wrecked cars that were in it, and then, presumably with Soviet authority, had prepared the school and stables for the return of the horses. The cost involved had later, incidentally, to be borne by the Ministry of Agriculture, but this bill had nothing to do with me.

I went in the middle of November 1945 to Vienna, to clear up on the spot the question of the Spanish Riding School's return. When I heard that an official had promised that the school could function undisturbed in Vienna once it had sent a few horses to Moscow, and only now and again would any of the generals come to ride, I stated categorically that I would do everything possible to prevent its return at that time. I rejected even a compromise plan, to send at least four to six stallions to Vienna, despite many pleas and threats, but I did go at once to the American headquarters in Vienna to discover their attitude, which was quite clear: all the horses of the Spanish Riding School were to remain in the American Zone in Upper Austria. The officer I saw then added, "Now you will understand why we did not allow a tour of the Spanish Riding School in the British Zone not long ago. We were anxious not to establish a precedent." And that unpleasant interlude was over, but my journey to Vienna made me realize that the dream of a speedy return home, a dream that had never left us since our departure, would not be realized in the immediate future.

St Martin provided a splendid substitute in the last months of the War, but as things returned to normal it was able less and less to meet the demands of the school. The opportunities of riding, particularly during the bad weather, were insufficient and not enough to keep the school horses in trim, let alone to train the young horses. Moreover, the place was off all the main transport routes, so that in the first post-War months any contact with the outside world had been established by the occupation troops and now grew rapidly weaker, and we stood in danger of being gradually forgotten. I thought first of a move to Salzburg. There the Felsenreitschule and the horse-ponds were a reminder that the powerful Archbishops of this city had once cultivated the classic art of riding in their princely households, and the annual festivals would have provided the necessary audiences. But when I heard that the fodder position was even more precarious in Upper Austria I dropped this plan, though years later it was resurrected by the *Landeshauptmann*[1] of Salzburg.

Towards the end of the winter I discovered that the Dragoon barracks in Wels, where I had wanted to transfer the Lipizzaner stud in autumn 1945, had at last been vacated by the Hungarians. I hurried over at once, and my idea to move with the Spanish Riding School was warmly welcomed both by the mayor and by the *Obmann* (Chairman) of the local farmers. The latter was so excited over the project that he promised me the best possible fodder for the horses, a promise that was, unfortunately, not always honoured later.

The dragoon barracks in Wels are some of the oldest cavalry barracks in Austria, where for many centuries the former 4th Dragoon Regiment, in which I had begun my military career, was stationed. They are divided into three squares, with the stables at ground-level and the living-quarters

---

[1] In addition to the actual government and parliament each province has its own assembly (*Landtag*) and elected governor (*Landeshauptmann*).

on the first floor, and were occupied by the Austrian Army in 1918 and then by the German Wehrmacht, but after the collapse were set aside as a receiving centre for refugees and were badly damaged and virtually stripped. All the windows, doors, light-fittings, and circuits were the objects of pointless vandalism. Everything looked so depressing that I agreed to consider the transfer of the school only after I had been given suitable promises. In fact, the necessary stables and some accommodation, but above all the great covered school, were then put in order, and my oft-repeated wishes were in the main taken into consideration; a satisfactory and positive work of reconstruction.

My application to the military authority to make the move was not immediately answered, but as the first signs of spring were already appearing I decided out of hand on a transition stage, sending the first of the horses to Wels at the end of April 1946.

The school was specially prepared for the public performance, which I wanted to begin in early May; seating for some seven hundred people was erected. Our reception was enthusiastic and interest in the Spanish Riding School immense, so everything appeared to be going well—until on the day of the first show permission to give public performances was refused by the Military Government in Linz. As so often during the occupation, I could not fathom why, but our premature move to Wels must have been the reason. When I was later in Linz on business I tried to get the project going again, for this decision had halted it completely, by proposing a show for the High Commissioner of the United States, General Clark. Because of political duties at the time he had not been able to come to St Martin for the second performance given for General Patton, and my suggestion was received with delight.

As soon as the High Commissioner's visit was arranged the last outward signs of damage were removed at top speed, and the school and the barrack square gleamed in the splendour of a hasty coat of fresh paint. There was much discussion as to the importance of the proposed arrangements, but I did not form a very favourable impression of the organizing ability of my colleagues, for they turned down most of my suggestions, particularly the representative of the Commander-in-Chief, whose counter-proposals, however, were still less valuable. The results of the hours of discussion were meagre indeed and in the end achieved nothing.

On May 7, 1946, General Clark arrived in Wels by car from Vienna with his wife and daughter escorted only by Military Police. The town had put out the flags, the school was decorated with fir boughs and the flags of the United States and Austria; everything suggested a special occasion. The heads of the occupying Power and Austria, the Landeshauptmann, Bezirks-hauptmann, and Mayor, lined up as planned to await the illustrious guests. My suggestion of an official greeting before going into the school was turned down, as was my intention to accompany the General as he left the car and escort him to his place. This duty was to be taken care of by a colonel, but at the proper moment he was not in his place, so the General had to look round and find the right entrance to the school for himself, with the somewhat unusual result that he had to be welcomed by the local dignitaries from the other side of an eighteen-inch partition. The first flaw in the arrangements!

The performance went according to schedule and was obviously well received. When the horses were drawn up I dismounted and presented General Clark with an album of pictures of the school.

Then the second hitch occurred. I was to wait for him at the exit to the school to show him the stables. A colonel was to bring him to me, but once again was not in his place! The General got up, could not immediately find the way out; there was a very painful and embarrassing pause; then I quickly sent a man to the door to free the General from his incarceration. This poor organization resulted, incidentally, in the Americans' giving me a completely free hand in all future arrangements, because I could "organize everything much better anyhow." General Clark, tall, elegant, almost youthful in appearance, asked me whether it would not harm the horses to bring them to Vienna. The British High Commissioner had, in fact, asked his permission for the Spanish Riding School to take part in the tattoo in the park at Schönbrunn. I already knew about this because while we were still in St Martin a British major, on the instructions of General McGreery, had come to me with the same question, but I had sent him on to the American headquarters in accordance with my orders. Because I did not want to appear unwilling in any way, I answered that transport to Vienna could not hurt the horses. Clark stood still and looked at me with a smile, saying, "I will put it differently. Do you think it a good idea for the Spanish Riding School to endure the consequences of the invitation?"

Then I replied, "No, it would be folly to give the performances in the British Sector in Schönbrunn but to refuse to return to the Hofburg because this is occupied by the Russians!"

He said he felt the same, and therefore had not agreed to our visiting Vienna.

In the stables the General met the individual horses and listened to a detailed description, and then left the town, obviously content. Before he left I managed to obtain permission for other public performances, telling him that these had so far been denied to the general Austrian public.

This performance in Wels was valuable to the Spanish Riding School since its success affected the establishment's immediate future, but it was also important for me personally, since it recalled my past. In this school I had taken my first riding lessons as a child, certainly never dreaming that the foundation of my later career was being laid, but I saw myself here in spirit some years later also in the ornate uniform of the 4th Dragoons, hung about with weapons and other accoutrements, at the head of the cavalry troop destined to be disbanded for a field regiment, to be given in a so-called passing-out inspection the blessing of my elders for the realities of life that lay before us. Though as a child I had allowed myself to be introduced to the basic principles of horsemanship, my teeth gritted with pain; at this inspection I sat proudly on a horse I had schooled myself, dreaming of deeds of heroism and—believed myself a great rider. And now, at the zenith, as it were, of my life, I once more set foot in this school at a third important moment. Behind me lay a vast number of experiences, disappointments, and ruined castles in the air, but before me lay a mighty task that so far I had managed to handle. Occupied with thoughts like these, I faced this performance with deadly seriousness.

Now the school horses of the Spanish Riding School were appearing for the first time for many years before the Austrian public, the country folk and people from provincial towns, who, of course, knew of the existence of the Vienna Riding School, and were proud of it as peculiarly symbolic of Austria, but had seen only isolated shows in Vienna. We had to bear in mind that this was a completely different type of audience, but on it too the play of controlled power, the grace of movement, the result of the physical and mental fusion of two living beings, had its effect. These performances, watched with an expert eye, gave pleasure to many as a nostalgic reminder of the proud tradition of this old cavalry garrison which once had two mounted regiments, but the majority merely accepted with obvious delight the development of the movements into a dance of intoxicating beauty without analysing it. The new Austrian Press told even the most isolated of our countrymen in long articles about the performances that the Spanish Riding School, saved from the chaos, was flourishing by its own efforts, true to its traditions.

Countless letters too from people quite unknown to me revealed how greatly our skill had stirred their emotions, and I was particularly surprised and moved when after a show in Wels a beautiful statue of Our Lady was presented to me with the following letter:

> As it has pleased the Lord God to create art and artists, so that men may delight in them, I should like to express my great admiration and joy at the genuine beauty that I have seen, and my sincere thanks by making you a present of a likeness, given to me by a priest, of the Mother of the Son of God made man. It is my earnest wish that the embracing love of God and the protection of Our dear Lady may always watch over your performances, and your efforts be crowned with perfect results.

But, unlike these uplifting moments, the problem of daily life remained in the foreground, and I was therefore glad to be introduced in the middle of May to the Minister of Agriculture and Forestry, Josef Kraus, the economist, showing him the school and laying my troubles before him. I was fortunate enough to find in him a true friend for the Spanish Riding School, for as a former horseman he was able to set a proper value on our work. When, on a later visit, he lingered in the school watching silently one could tell from his face that his was the enjoyment of a real rider. When he had seen for himself the significance of the Spanish Riding School I was certain of his support over any important matter. When I had put him in the picture he even finally closed down the superfluous inactive 'branch' of the Spanish Riding School in Vienna, which had lasted for nearly a year.

One performance at the beginning of June was particularly important because of the presence of the President, Dr Karl Renner. It was the first time for decades that the school had had the opportunity of performing for the Head of State. The President was cheered as he arrived with his wife, and followed the programme with great interest and obvious delight, often clapping spontaneously anything particularly well executed. Afterwards he made an entry in the Spanish Riding School visitors' book, the first important person of the second Austrian Republic to do so:

Whit Monday, June 10, 1946

With pride and pleasure at the cultural property restored to us, and sincere thanks to its deliverer.

Dr Karl Renner, *Federal President*

Some days later my wife and I received an invitation to dinner at Feyregg castle, where we spent a most interesting evening. The President, the type of man who in spite of his modesty commands respect by his learning, praised the performance again, saying how fortunate it was that the old academy had been saved. The remarkably lively old man made a fascinating and vivid succession of observations, recalling experiences from the past and present, and did not see us off till long after midnight, sending us home in his own car.

Naturally the school was also visited by numbers of Americans during its stay in Wels. Among them was a divisional commander, notorious for his harshness to German prisoners of war. He asked among other things under whose command the Spanish Riding School had been during the War, and, when I told him, remarked rather sarcastically, "Was it not a dreadful thing for the riding-school to be under the administration of the German Army?"

I thought it unfair to take up this stone and cast it at the defeated Wehrmacht, and answered, "I should be ungrateful if I were to agree with you, for I was given substantial funds to build up the school, and the greatest possible support. Moreover, the riders, even the youngest, were exempted from military service until the very end of the war."

At this he replied rather thoughtfully that the Americans would certainly not have released the young riders.

As the quarters in Wels were still not ready for the transfer of the entire school, I went back to St Martin in mid-July with the show horses; it was no longer practicable to have them divided. With the preparations under way for the moves, I learned one day that the dragoon barracks had recently been requisitioned by the Americans to be reconverted into a refugee camp —a danger to which all large property standing empty was subject. An official protest against this measure had already been in vain, so it looked very much as if my plans, so painstakingly prepared, might come to nothing at the last moment. I went at once to the highest military authority in Salzburg and, thanks to the reputation that the Spanish Riding School had already won for itself, managed to get the refugee camp transferred to another place, but was advised to move at the earliest possible moment, so at the beginning of October 1946 I started to transfer from St Martin to Wels, but could not finish until the end of the month as the work on the stables and quarters was held up again.

By the summer of 1946, sponsored by the occupation troops, the first signs of riding as a sport were beginning to appear. It was not easy to revive civilian riding in a country well-nigh stripped of all her territory, for she had already sustained a severe shock in 1938, the year of the Anschluss, and had gradually lost all that remained of her horses through the War. But there were enough enthusiasts to overcome all difficulties, particularly resulting from the lack of a national bloodstock strain, and with the sympathetic help of the occupation authorities to get the sport on its feet again even in Austria.

The British organized the first great International Riding and Jumping Competition in Vienna towards the end of July 1946, in the grounds of Schönbrunn Castle, with the Gloriette in the background, and I was invited by the British general to judge. Apart from some Italian and Swiss riders, most of the competitors were French, British, and American officers from the armies of occupation, but a few Austrians took part as well, and some Russians came as spectators. I soon realized the widespread interest in the Spanish Riding School, for I was constantly surrounded by compatriots and foreigners asking about the Lipizzaner.

At the end of August 1946 the second great Horse Show in Austria took place with American help on the Trotting Course in Salzburg. I was asked to give an exhibition ride on my competition horse, Teja. There was a record gate, and the racecourse was so crammed that many visitors could not get in at all. The spectators were very stimulating and appreciative, enthusiastically applauding my exhibition of *haute école* riding on Teja. The occupation troops acknowledged my riding skill, but the Austrians felt proud as well that it was one of their compatriots finding such exceptional favour.

This appreciation of my work gave me great satisfaction, and a pleasurable thrill, reminding me of my many triumphs in competitions before the War. Of course, I was used to generous applause for the Spanish Riding School's performances, but then I was always surrounded by the splendour and atmosphere of the historic rooms, which were certainly partly responsible. But here in my modest civilian clothes I managed on a not very attractive bay horse to captivate the audience with my riding skill alone, and my success awakened in me a competitive desire that I had believed long dead.

In addition to the American Military Governor the French Commander-in-Chief, General Bethouart, himself a passionate rider, was present, and invited me at a party afterwards to come to Innsbruck with my horse for the Allied Horse Show.

Towards the end of September we—that is, Teja and groom, my wife and I—set out, and I was taken to a hotel in Igels reserved for the Allies only and fed in the officers' mess. Here I met all the riders and guests of the four occupying Powers together, but was the only Austrian present. It was moving to see how attentively and carefully the waiters served me, demonstrating their delight at having once more a countryman among their guests.

The French pampered us and showed themselves to be most charming hosts. They assigned an officer to look after me, and carry out all my wishes about exercising ground and stabling. They even went so far as to take out one of their horses from the box to make it free for Teja.

My exhibition rides became the main attraction of the Horse Show, and were advertised by leaflets scattered over the city from a plane. Behind all this outward show there was in fact, the hidden purpose of awakening the interests of the civilian population, who had so far been decidedly unenthusiastic over the riding activities of the occupying Power.

The ground in Reichenau, once an airfield used by the Luftwaffe, provided ideal turf and, surrounded by the soaring mountains of the Tyrol, a wonderful view, and here the French also held their races and played polo. On the day of the show the ground had an unusually festive look: the flags of the Allies and, for the first time, the red-white-red colours of Austria fluttered in the gentle breeze and brought back long absent memories of international meetings. Crowds of people streamed past in the glorious sunshine, the local people quietly dressed and on foot, while the then masters of Austria drove by in shining cars and were received according to their rank by the guard of Moroccans, who presented arms to the accompaniment of a roll of drums. The various uniforms of the officers and the elegant gowns of the ladies were a gay sight.

My ride followed the jumping, before a polo match that had been specially arranged. A French military band took up its position—naturally we had rehearsed this together the day before—and I rode across the vast arena at a collected canter to a musical accompaniment, as in Salzburg, up to General Bethouart and his guests, including the heads of the Austrian Government, stopped, and saluted. In dressage the mood of the rider plays an important part, as it involunatrily communicates itself to the horse. At the sight of the colourful ground and the many thousands of spectators falling silent in expectation as I appeared, a mounting tide of excitement filled me with a determination to prove my ability and the riding skill of my country so rich in tradition. The knowledge that I was now riding for Austria gave me an unconscious fillip, and made me firmly determined to give of my best. General Bethouart congratulated me afterwards, and made me a presentation; a little girl broke through the barriers to offer me a bouquet on behalf of the Austrians. When I galloped past the rows of spectators, saluting again, there was protracted clapping, and I saw tears in the eyes of many of my countrymen. It was an especially memorable moment, knowing I could give so much pleasure and stir the emotions so deeply.

I dismounted and was taken to the guests of honour, including some Russian Officers who had come as spectators, and welcomed enthusiastically. The Russian general offered me his personal congratulations through an interpreter, then refreshments and delicious cakes were handed round. At this moment my glance fell on the Austrians standing behind the barriers; their sad eyes in their haggard faces expressed more than words. In particular the huge eyes of the children, looking longingly at the sweets, gave me a lump in my throat; without a word to each other my wife and I edged slowly to the end of the reserved seats and surreptitiously put the sweets we had taken from the tray into the children's outstretched hands.

On the last evening of the final day of the show the French Commander-in-Chief gave a large party in the Burg. Moroccan soldiers greeted the guests' arrival with a roll of drums, and then stood on each step of the staircase to the first floor in their picturesque uniforms, lances in their right hands, springing to attention at a curt command each time a guest appeared. As I walked up the stairs through this line I involuntarily compared the following scenes:

Vienna 1937: A reception at the Rathaus during the International Horse Show. On every step to the entrance to the great hall men in the black uniform of the Ostmark (Austrian) S.S., who as the guests passed clicked their heels together and saluted. What a pompous parade of mighty power intended to deceive!

Berlin 1939: A reception in a Ministry to mark an important riding event. Flanked by S.S. in black uniforms with silver braid, the guests made their way to the hall. A curt command rang out, followed by brisk movements, a dead stop as right hands shot upwards as a mark of esteem.

And now *Innsbruck* 1946: Nearly the same ceremonial; only the uniforms had changed.

I found this pomp rather excessive as I watched General Bethouart receive his guests in the hall. Standing under the bright lights of a chandelier, wearing an ornate uniform covered with decorations, he looked like a modern God of War, at a time when German militarism could not be condemned strongly enough. Was this scene outwardly any different from a reception in the Hofburg by a *Reichsstatthalter* of Vienna? Probably once a Caesar had received his guests of state in a like manner.

The party in the Innsbruck Burg was very splendid, with an abundance of rich courses and champagne. It reached its climax at midnight when the lighting was provided by innumerable candles, taking those present back hundreds of years. This theatrical setting was uncommonly effective and impressive, and one could have delighted in its sheer beauty if—yes, if—the candles had not been proof of the decided shortages among the civilian population living in such penury.

I returned with mixed feelings to St Martin: proud of my equestrian success, happy over the many pleasant things that had happened to me, bitterly upset, however, by the great contrast between the feasting and the poor living conditions of the citizens of Innsbruck.

These three trips re-established my contact with the sport of riding, which, at least in Austria and Germany, was at first carried on mainly by riders from the armies of occupation, and awakened in me the long buried hope of being able to take part once again in the Olympic Games, and so the training of my horses received special attention.

The transfer of the Spanish Riding School to Wels began after my return from Innsbruck. Settling into our new place of exile took such a long time that the official inaugural performance could not take place until the middle of December, but at the end of November we were visited by a Senator from Oregon, and put on a show in his honour. When I expressed surprise at the extraordinary preparations a colonel explained that in the United States there were hundreds of generals, but only ninety-four Senators, so this visit was of special significance. Senator Wayne L. Mors, a passionate horse-lover, was so impressed by the Lipizzaner that he said after the performance and a visit to the stables, "Austria and the Spanish Riding School have given me my pleasantest impression of Europe."

The occupation army chiefs turned up in full force to the inaugural performance in the new quarters, along with many important Government officials. To make this a special occasion I welcomed the guests of honour with a short speech before the show, expressing my exceptional pleasure as one of Wels's sons that the Spanish Riding School, one of Austria's cultural treasures, should have found asylum in this town so rich in equestrian tradition.

Only two days later we had a very interesting and, from a riding point of view, valuable visit from the officers of the French Cavalry School at

Saumur, known to the riding world as the Cadre Noir, making an auspicious start for our stay in Wels.

The French officers watched the performance with a critical eye, their applause getting louder and louder and reaching its climax at the end of the quadrille. The chief instructor, Commandant Margot, then expressed his admiration at the unbelievable precision of the quadrille, so paying me the greatest possible compliment, for precision was the forte of the French school quadrille, as I had noticed on many occasions before the War.

These performances, and one for the workers of Wels and its surroundings, showed that the school in winter was intolerably cold for the spectators, so we had to stop them, in spite of many protests, until the warmer weather. Even so, more and more Americans dropped in on their way through, for it was, so to speak, the done thing not to drive through Wels without having taken a peep into the school and seen the work being done, even if there were no performances.

The public shows arranged for May and June 1947 were splendidly received and always sold out. In addition to the civilian population for Upper Austria there were many Americans from as far away as Germany. At the first performance the barrack square and the street outside were so crammed with the most beautiful cars of all colours and sizes that a visitor might have thought he had come to a motor show rather than a display of riding.

One of the June shows was visited by an Allied Commission, in which all the four occupying Powers were represented, and this was the first time that representatives of the Soviet officially inspected the school. The Russian officer leading his country's delegation was much impressed and asked the departmental head of the Ministry of Agriculture who was with him, "Why are such wonderful horses hidden away in the provinces instead of being allowed to come to the capital where they belong?" He turned to me on the way to the stables and asked the military importance of the Spanish Riding School, and when I replied, "None at all," he added, "Then why does Austria maintain this riding-school if it has no military value?"

"Why does the Soviet Union maintain a ballet, although it has no practical significance?"

He interrupted me with great fervour: "Our ballet is the embodiment of a great culture, and culture must always be sponsored."

I was then able to answer, "Look, the Spanish Riding School also preserves an ancient culture, so does it not follow that it is Austria's duty to keep up this institution?"

This seemed to enlighten him, for he nodded his agreement.

During the stable inspection he never stopped asking questions and monopolized me completely, which did not please the other members of the commission. First the American and then the British officers whispered to me that I should not allow myself to be cross-questioned in this fashion —the first sign of the tension that was later to develop between the Allies.

At the beginning of July French officers brought me an invitation from General Bethouart, for the Spanish Riding School to take part in the International Horse Show in Vienna. As the Cadre Noir from Saumur was also coming to Vienna, but the two schools ought not to compete against each other, they decided that the Spanish Riding School should demonstrate the "Airs above the Ground" and the French Cavalry School the school quadrille. They also expected me to give an exhibition on my horse Teja.

As the Americans would not in principle allow the Lipizzaner to be taken into another zone, I also declined to go to Vienna with Teja, but travelled there on my own, having accepted an invitation to be one of the judges.

This great international competition took place in the wonderful park of what had been an archducal palace in Hütteldorf. The natural setting was beautiful, the decoration of the ground first-class, and I again came to the conclusion that the French are past-masters in arranging festivities. This impression was confirmed by the social arrangements, for a cocktail party in the grounds of the palace occupied by General Bethouart, at which the horn quartet of the Parforce hunt club from Rambouillet in their elegant riding dress added to the spirit of the occasion with musical interludes, and for an enchanting farewell party in the Palais Palavicini.

The competition itself took a very interesting turn, when the Austrian riders, who this time had appeared in much greater numbers, were still overshadowed by the outstanding Allied jumpers. The public—particularly the Viennese riding enthusiasts—had flocked in to see the Cadre Noir and an exhibition ride by me which, in spite of my early refusal, was announced and not cancelled until the last moment, but we were all rather disappointed in the French Cavalry School, for little remained of the old glamour except the becoming black uniforms.

The autumn shows in Wels, although far removed from world events, were just as successful as the spring ones, and prominent visitors who came there solely for the Spanish Riding School continued to arrive. The former heir to the throne of Egypt, Prince Abd el Moneim, and his wife came from Salzburg to Wels "to see another wonder of the world on Austrian soil," and the U.S. Chief of the General Staff, General Balmers, came with high-ranking officers of his staff to take a look at the Lipizzaner because "it would be a shame to go back to the U.S.A. without having seen this bit of Austrian culture." And the new United States High Commissioner, General Keyes, visited the Spanish Riding School with the newly appointed divisional commanders and generals and later conveyed his good wishes for the school in a very friendly letter of thanks.

30. Governor-General Lord Alexander with Pluto
Theodorosta in Toronto, 1950

31. Carrots for Dessert

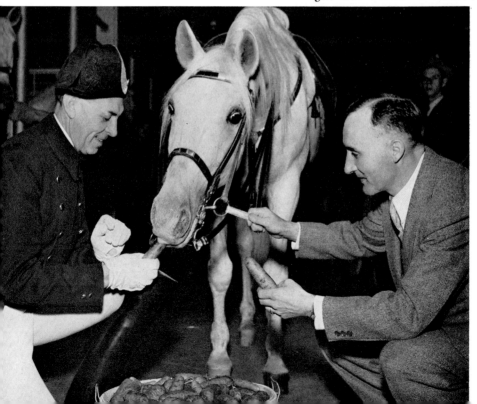

32. Rehearsing in Private: the Picturesque Ground at Klein Flottbek

In November 1947 we had a chance of performing before the head of the Austrian Government, Chancellor Dr Leopold Figl, who had come to Wels with members of his Cabinet and the heads of the local administration. After the performance, which was much applauded by this exalted company, I expressed my satisfaction that this time it was to the men responsible for Austria's destiny that the Lipizzaner had been able to show their skill. The Chancellor said he was pleased to see the Spanish Riding School again after ten years, its high standard unimpaired, but he would not be completely satisfied until he could once more admire these wonderful horses in Vienna. As he said this I noticed a slight cloud in the faces of the representatives of the Upper Austrian Government, but he went on: "Still, Colonel, we must never forget, must we, in looking forward, the hospitable province that has given the school shelter and support in the time of need, and we promise here and now that even after its return to Vienna the Spanish Riding School will be at the disposal of Upper Austria once a year."

This announcement was received with cheers by all present.

The Chancellor then took a good look at the horses in their stalls, even going into them and showing a lively interest, as I could tell from the many questions he asked. He wrote in the visitors' book, "Very delighted to see again after ten years that the Spanish Riding School has retained its great skill."

The strong impression that the Lipizzaner had made on him was echoed in a very kindly phrased personal letter of thanks, reiterating the wish to bring back the Spanish Riding School "to the place of its former glorious activity."

In spite of the great interest of many important people both at home and abroad, I realized that with the growing tension between East and West the possibility of returning to Vienna was more remote than ever, and thus the position of the Spanish Riding School must become more critical. The reduction of the occupation forces in Austria soon began to have an effect on the visits to the school; the sightseeing urge of the civilian population round Wels was satisfied by the many shows in less than two years, and general tourist traffic in Austria was at that time in its infancy.

This must in the long run have sore effect on us, and in particular there would be less incentive to work if there were no devoted experts visiting us, and this would be detrimental, for as a cultivated plant needs the correct nourishment in the soil to thrive, so the art of riding must have the proper surroundings and atmosphere. In Wels these could only suffice as a start after the restricted amenities in St Martin, and for a very short stay.

There was also the question of the primitive accommodation, which was definitely an improvement after the end of the War compared with St Martin, but its inadequacy was more and more stressed by the rebuilding of our district, and our quarters contrasted sharply with the scrupulously traditional appearance of our performances. They brought home to the staff living in overcrowded conditions the gnawing, almost demoralizing, conditions of drab everyday life, but the organization of a weekly horse and cattle market in the yard of the dragoon barracks was the greatest of the many inconveniences. For the profit-greedy visitors to these markets the Spanish Riding School was merely an unnecessary burden, and the brave Lipizzaner, who perhaps often wondered about their neglected fellows, were increasingly exposed to the danger of infectious diseases.

These distressing facts and the hopelessness of an early return to Vienna made me consider the idea of taking the Spanish Riding School on a Festival tour out into the world, to get riders and horses, at least temporarily, away from surroundings fast becoming intolerable. At the same time any successes abroad should help not only to maintain the school's reputation at home in spite of the increasing difficulties of the times, but to enhance it. This was the extent of my thoughts, but practical realization of them proved much more difficult. Because of the long isolation of Austria our country's national organizations had been quite forgotten abroad, and the results of the War waged over the whole of Europe still restricted thinking in the majority of cases to the events inside the various frontiers. Certainly the Spanish Riding School could not present itself simply as a source of entertainment, so a great deal of diplomacy and delicate handling was necessary to accomplish my purpose.

Two things, however, helped me greatly: the great interest that the performances had awakened in the occupation forces and the many riding contacts I had managed to make everywhere at pre-War competitions. The news of the existence of the Spanish Riding School was echoed in countless letters from all over the world, spread by the occupation forces, and the well-known Swiss team captain Colonel Haccius wrote to me, having himself once been sent over to the school. With this officer, who had got to know me through riding competitions, I now began to work out a plan for the Spanish Riding School to visit Lucerne, and the unusually sympathetic Minister of Agriculture and Forestry, Dr Kraus, helped me to overcome Government opposition, and so in the spring of 1948 we set off on our first post-War foreign tour, which was to be such a striking success that it laid the foundation for the drawing power of the white stallions throughout the world. Thus the exile crisis, which seemed to threaten the whole future of the Spanish Riding School, was happily surmounted, and with the many successful performances abroad its popularity increased also among the Austrian nation. What I once set out in a talk to the youth of Austria took a long time to accomplish:

"Foreign countries envy us our ownership of the Spanish Riding School, so I should be very happy if you were as full of pride as I am that this cultural treasure belongs to Austria."

Before the start of the Swiss tour I had a further pleasant surprise in the shape of an official invitation in April from the Italian War Ministry to go to Rome for the Seventh Concours Hippique.

After consulting Dr Kraus, who considered this a great honour, I accepted and set off for Italy with my wife on May 2, 1948.

It was an exhilarating feeling to set foot on foreign soil once more after nearly ten years of isolation from the outside world, and to be able to look at it from a different angle. There was the added pleasure of having a chance to pay a personal visit to Rome, that historic city on the Tiber of which I had already heard so much and dreamed so often.

I had my first surprise after my arrival in my beloved Venice on the lagoon where we had a few hours to spend. Totally untouched by the events of the last decade, this eternally youthful and ever-enchanting pearl of the Adriatic offered itself to the beholder dreamily in the brilliant sunshine of a wonderful May day, inspiring him to dream also.

This radiant picture, however, changed completely on the long trip to Rome. Most of the stations were damaged, and many districts had become devastated areas, but already new life was springing up everywhere—comparing very favourably with the reconstruction in my homeland where the struggle for daily bread and the shortage of raw materials of all kinds, and often also the occupying Powers, stifled any initiative.

In Rome we were given a reception that surpassed all our expectations. Colonel Riccardo Turina greeted us in the name of General Imperiale and presented my wife with a huge bouquet of red and white roses. A War Ministry car that we were given for our personal use had once belonged to the King of Italy, and it took us to a luxury hotel where the colonel detailed to look after me during my stay then discussed our programme with us. In addition to the official presentations and receptions of the visiting sporting representatives a detailed sightseeing tour of the city had been planned; Colonel Turina, having been born in Trieste, spoke perfect German, and his wife had studied the history of art, so Rome was shown to us as very few foreigners see it.

It was just like a peace-time city: not a trace of the War, no foreign uniforms, most people well, and some luxuriously, dressed. Here throbbed an untroubled life of gaiety and pleasure; walking through the streets with one's eyes open, one was forced to the conclusion that Italy had once again been victorious, in spite of having lost the War.

The friendly Turinas showed us ancient Rome as well as the recent works of art of this city. We wandered about as in a dream, tirelessly drinking in all the beauty, and our enjoyment understandably pleased our charming guides, encouraging them to show us even more. As we stood in front of the famous Trevi fountain Signora Turina urged us with a friendly smile to throw in some coins, "for we want you to come again."

Colonel Turina also showed me the villa where Field-Marshal Kessel-ring had set up his headquarters, saying, "He was certainly strict, but did not deserve to be tried after the War. Foreign occupation troops are never popular, but the Germans at least kept order and severely punished any excesses by individual soldiers, unlike the Allies, who managed to make themselves still less popular in a very short time."

The International Horse Show at the Piazza di Siena, one of the loveliest showgrounds in the world, is unique. Even the visitors in the shade of the pine-trees indicate by their elegant clothes that it is a special occasion. It was a sight for sore eyes to watch so many lovely women in beautiful clothes. At least for us the Italian women at that time were by far the best; there was nothing at home that could compare in any way with the setting of the competition, and there was some impressive riding, showing not a trace of the effect of six years of war.

Of particular interest to me also was the inspection of the stud in Fara Sabina, thirty miles from Rome, which General Imperiale showed me personally. I immediately noticed with astonishment the different enclosures, with mares classified according to their breeds, including some Trakehners and Hanoverians. I asked the General about these, and he explained: "The War had left us with empty studs, and our horse-breeding was non-existent, but there were thin, broken-down horses to be found scattered all over the country, the remains of the defeated German Army. We made an exact muster of these immediately and brought all the available bloodstock that could be used for breeding to build up the stud." I must admit that it was an ingenious solution to the problem, for I saw some beautiful mares in the enclosures.

Then I caught sight of the Lipizzaner once in my care. They were frolicking happily in the tall meadow grass, and it gave me great satisfaction to hear the experts praise their outstanding quality and the splendid foals, the first to be born on Italian soil, and the results of the matings I had arranged in Austria.

I was praised and congratulated by everybody and introduced as the man who had preserved the Lipizzaner for Italy. A huge reception at the Palazzo Barbarini brought our visit to a brilliant conclusion, and the Army Chief of the General Staff thanked me in an official speech for my efforts on be-half of the Lipizzaner breed:

"We are very well aware that to-day we should not have a single Lipiz-zaner in Italy if you had not succeeded in bringing the stud back from Czechoslovakia."

I returned to Wels full of my experiences, and had to adapt myself rapidly to the drab surroundings where the troubles of daily life were suddenly once more of prime importance. As a result of the exceptionally dry summer in 1947 there was virtually no hay to be had, and all my appeals for help to the appropriate Ministry remained unanswered, so I had to cut the ration to a minimum to eke out my meagre supplies. It was noticeable that the horses, in spite of plenty of oats, constantly longed for their normal portion of hay.

The renewed fodder difficulties were, however, not my only anxiety in these days. The upset in the barracks resulting from the aforementioned markets was growing worse now that each week a pig market was set up in front of my stabling and a garage was opened very near the noble Lipizzaner. Often there was such a racket in the square from lorries and every kind of animal that it was difficult to lead the horses from their stalls to work in the school. All protests, comments, and pleas were in vain—in fact, I was given to understand that I was only making myself unpopular; we were living in a time when good relations were more important than actual necessities. Although the heads of Upper Austria and the town of Wels welcoming prominent foreign visitors to the Spanish Riding School —shocked by the scene that greeted them—always took great pains to get the guests as quickly as possible into the school or the stables, where order reigned supreme, nobody helped me afterwards in my losing battle for cleanliness and tidiness.

This unpleasant situation made me look forward to the first foreign trip of the Spanish Riding School with exceptional pleasure: a chance to get away at last from our miserable surroundings and ride before an audience of experts who could really appreciate our efforts. The performances before spectators with a knowledge of riding must both create a standard of training and be of vital importance for the existence of the old academy.

The success of the first foreign tour after an interval of eleven years surpassed our wildest expectations, and its effect on the school's reputation in its own country was clearly recognizable. After the stirring reports in the foreign Press no journey was too long for the Austrians to visit the fabulous white wonder horses in Wels. The Spanish Riding School had now truly become one of the country's national shrines.

Thus what had once been the Vienna Hofreitschule could still fulfil its high purpose in exile; its efforts made it a good advertisement for Austrian culture abroad and attracted an ever-growing circle of admirers. Not only many public figures, including accredited diplomats in Austria, came to Wels to see the Lipizzaner, but a great many ordinary horse-lovers as well. Especially valuable was the interest of youth, which was given an introduction to our national heritage and learned to look at the animals in a new way and to love them. I often showed these young people round myself and was amazed at their perception.

The Spanish Riding School's success was based on three things: the achievements and beauty of the Lipizzaner and ancient tradition. All three are essential to keep a proper balance. The cherishing of tradition had almost taken care of itself in the sacred atmosphere in Vienna, but it was much more difficult when we were forced to work in what could have been dull and degrading surroundings. What in Fischer von Erlach's hall was taken for granted had to be kept up here by sheer determination. The riders, creators of the performances, had thus to be constantly protected from the effects of the disillusioning surroundings. Having to live at such close quarters in the barracks encouraged dissension, which grew daily more serious, transforming close friendships in a trice into bitter hatreds, endangering the integrity of the *Bereiter*, so firmly established in Vienna.

Added to this, the results of my efforts through the years to improve the riders' financial standing were nullified at one fell swoop because the Ministry in Vienna in taking over the riders as personnel of the Austrian Republic had gone back to the pre-1938 rates of pay. It was clear that the consequent financial losses and the absence of any chance of a rise shook those pillars of the school, nor could I understand why all my representations and hints about the risks incurred were merely shrugged off.

The loss of everything that I had managed to win by hard battling under the Germans had hit me hard. The architect who has to stand by helpless while his house burns down cannot suffer more than I did. Now we were back to the older grooms earning a higher wage than the younger riders, at a time when material values threatened to outweigh ideals, and in a place where every Saturday the horse-trading brought the money simply rolling in.

Paradoxically these difficulties were magnified by the school's success on its various tours. The triumph of the white horses abroad, and the glitter and excitement that surrounded us there, brought me the greatest personal problems, for the riders felt that the contrast between all this profusion abroad and the poor living at home was too absurd. They were also persuaded by many tempting offers to leave merely for money the place where their skill had been systematically matured and where they had worked for many years, even during the war raging in Europe.

That they often overrated their ability was quite understandable in view of the enthusiastic applause for all our performances, but those who believed they could buy a similar success for their own horses with riders from the school, through their selfishness merely tore out from the machinery of the Spanish Riding School several cogs that could be replaced in time, but did not gain the big wheel that would bear them up to the heights they dreamed of. The riders found out that they could achieve greatness only as part of the Spanish Riding School, and the speculators, cheated of their hopes, were forced to realize, thank God, that in this world there are still things that cannot be bought. Naturally I took none of the deserters back, however contritely they begged, for loyalty to the old home of tradition is one of the cardinal virtues that an apostle of the horsemanship cultivated here must possess.

I made use of these regrettable losses to force a breach in the incredibly stubborn and stupid wall of bureaucracy, and finally succeeded in obtaining a slight financial improvement in the shape of bonuses for riding and performing. But naturally these adjustments did not add up to the allowances won during the War.

From the very first moment that I became responsible for the Spanish Riding School I focussed my whole attention on safeguarding its future, and managed even during the War to acquire a large number of young military riders as trainees so that losses due to age could be made good and a still larger staff built up. After the War ended, however, recruiting riders became quite another matter. From the very beginning most of them had come from the Army, and until the First World War the best riders from fifty-six cavalry and numerous infantry regiments were available. Even in the First Republic replacements could be found in the small but well-commanded reserve of six squadrons and artillery divisions. This arrangement had the great advantage of making it possible to throw out the utterly useless after a trial ride. A long probationary period then decided who was to be considered for a definite appointment, but this way of keeping the *Bereiter* up to strength was no longer possible, for the Second World War had administered a death-blow to the cavalry, a branch of the Army with a splendid history going back hundreds of years.

Out of the ruins of the German Army I tried in the first post-War years to get replacements for the Spanish Riding School, and was gratified that in fact many officers and aristocrats applied for positions. But I realized fully that social position and a good name could not give by themselves any guarantee of ability to maintain a highly qualified body of riders, so I insisted on some kind of test. As there was at the same time a chronic shortage of grooms, I made a virtue of necessity and stipulated that the applicants during their riding training should also do grooming and stable duties. But my incurable optimism suffered a severe blow, for the supposed riding enthusiasts, including officers up to the rank of captain, and aristocrats up to that of prince, soon showed a disinclination for work and carelessness in their stable duties, and I made some really unpleasant discoveries. They were all only attracted by the glitter of the performances, but had no heart for the work involved, so I finally gave up the idea of taking trained riders as replacements.

This decision was certainly not resignation on my part, although during an interview about personnel the spokesman of one of the highest authorities told me, "We have no longer a cavalry, so you must get used to the idea that you will get no more replacements, and the Spanish Riding School will sooner or later cease to exist."

I forced myself to a decision to tread quite new paths and start by training lads who loved horses but had never ridden : a tremendous undertaking, but the only course open to me. The rejections were now very numerous indeed, either because of physical awkwardness or defects of character that came to light in the course of training, but at the same time I noticed that riding pupils make faster progress the younger they are, so I began to recruit boys of fifteen to sixteen as soon as they finished school. They applied in great numbers, and I was astounded over the rapid progress of these youths who were not spoilt by faulty training. Another advantage of this method of keeping up the strength was a noticeable drop in the age of the *Bereiter* corps, for while formerly the junior officer posted to the Spanish Riding School would not become a *Bereiter* until he was twenty-eight to thirty, the pupil who starts early can take this post at twenty-three or twenty-four.

Another problem was that of pupils. The school had from the beginning taken pupils to utilize its great equestrian value for the benefit of horsemanship in general. To take lessons here was considered a great honour, and exceptional ability or a high-sounding name were usually conditions of acceptance, and to start with only officers were given advanced riding training. Later important civilians received permission to ride at the Spanish Riding School, but after it was taken over by the German Wehrmacht the training was once more limited to officers, then the War prevented any consistent ruling. After the War, with the slow resurrection of riding as a sport, the Spanish Riding School had to re-establish its connexion with horsemanship in general by taking pupils. In the meantime, however, every army had lost its mounted troops, and in many countries even the horse itself had disappeared, so we could no longer count on details of foreign officers, who in any case had already decreased greatly in number since 1934.

An overwhelming proportion of the civilian pupils came until 1938 from our own country, but as a result of foreign tours, my personal participation in riding competitions abroad, and not least my publications, in which I repeatedly mentioned the instruction available, after 1948 there was no country in Western Europe, and no part of the globe from which pupils did not flock to the Spanish Riding School.

While the school in exile, in spite of all its troubles, received the greatest possible publicity far beyond the Austrian border, and was very highly spoken of, its home in Vienna lay empty and derelict. The summer quarters in the Lainz Zoo on the outskirts of the city in particular had suffered from the chaos after the War. The rooms of the former imperial Hermesvilla had been plundered and devastated, and the great stalls erected during the War with such difficulty had quite literally gone on the fire, and, for fear they might collapse, the ruins had to be cleared away. My representations to the mayor of Vienna, General Körner, had no effect, for even the highest authority cannot work miracles, and the gates of the Lipizzaner paradise closed for ever. I shall certainly never succeed again in making the Lainz Zoo accessible to the Lipizzaner; for us all it remains paradise lost.

The stabling, the school and its ante-rooms in Vienna remained empty for the first few years, but understandably attracted a great deal of interest in a city suffering from a serious shortage of accommodation. The old Hofapotheke took back the section taken during the War to extend the stables, and ruthlessly tore out the precious fixtures, which I had taken so much trouble to collect in difficult days. It was indeed to be a long and hard struggle to prevent further inroads by the Hofapotheke into the stabling of the Spanish Riding School. Not less attractive was the lovely riding-hall of which various sports clubs tried to get permission to use through their political connexions. It was a lucky coincidence that the National Theatre, on the lookout for a scenery store, had the same idea, and had the hall allotted to them temporarily, for scenery would definitely be easier to transfer elsewhere at a later date than a sports club installed there. The sama thing happened to the other rooms, so that there was at least a prospect of getting these back if the Spanish Riding School was allowed to come back to Vienna.

But when would this become a reality? The years were passing with no plans for return, and my hope of living to see the day of the Spanish Riding School's entry into Vienna grew steadily fainter, so we carried out with inflexible determination our duty of maintaining the Spanish Riding School even in exile. But in our pensive moments our thoughts sped nostalgically and we dreamed of all our work there, which now had every semblance of belonging for ever to the past.

CHAPTER 12

The White Dancers conquer the World

B y the beginning of June 1948 all the preparations were at last sufficiently advanced for the Spanish Riding School to begin its first foreign
tour after the Second World War. It had been fully eleven years since
its members had last set foot on foreign soil—and think of all that had
happened in that time. A whole world had collapsed, and out of the unending fields of ruin a new life was only timidly springing. We were going, true
enough, to Switzerland, an island of peace in the heart of chaotic Europe,
and did not expect further disturbances, but we must accustom ourselves
to contrasts resulting from a fundamentally different way of life for many
years. But above all there was the great question as to how the Spanish
Riding School, coming for the first time under such unusual conditions to
Switzerland, would be received. Little was known about it there from the
Vienna days, but the six years of war had put an end even to those visits, so
most people had no knowledge at all of its existence. So much had been
obliterated in Europe!

As we crossed the Austrian border we could not stop marvelling at the
peaceful atmosphere conjured up by the clean, well-tended, and lovely
villages and pleasantly dressed people.

The reception given to us personally was most moving. The white
Lipizzaner caused a sensation when they were led through the streets of
Lucerne to the stadium, and the people whispered to one another that
these were the horses from Austria that by a miracle had managed to survive the inferno, and many stroked them as if they wanted to satisfy themselves that they were real.

But the most important thing still lay ahead: the equestrian proof of the
great reputation that had preceded us here through the occupation troops,
and this could not be achieved by emotional demonstrations alone. The

Concours Hippique International Officiel in Lucerne had been considered in the past one of the biggest riding fixtures, and after the Second World War had become even more important. Here there gathered a pampered cosmopolitan public with a wealth of expert knowledge, accustomed to demanding a high standard of performance; there were also representatives of many nations, some of whom were already on their way to London for the Olympic Games, a rendezvous for the riding élite of 1948, American, Mexican, English, French, Italian, Irish, and Swiss.

The stadium is considered one of the most beautiful if its kind in Europe. The well-tended grass, covered with the gaily coloured, attractive jumps— with the lake as a backcloth—looked in the blazing sunshine like a casket of jewels. Our hearts were light as we exercised our horses here and prepared them for their great début. Our delight evaporated decidedly on the day of our first performance, for it began to rain in the morning and never stopped at all. The jumpers went round the course in the streaming rain, the spectators watched the events dismally from under their umbrellas. Shortly before it was our turn there was another cloudburst. We stood waiting under the awning in our traditional uniform, the Lipizzaner with their gold-trimmed trappings polished till they shone, and with anxious faces watched the clock hands moving on, and the rain coming down faster and faster. Apart from the far from ideal conditions—for in the rain everything can so easily look grey, and why should our performance be any different?—there was the practical problem of what we were to do with our soaked gala trappings? Should we call off our appearance? Any decision of that kind would certainly disappoint the many who had come long distances specially to see the Spanish Riding School—that was how the official had explained to me the unusually large crowds! But the heavens had pity on the old Riding School, for just before we were due to start the rain stopped, the sun's rays broke through the stormy clouds and shone on the Lipizzaner as they made their first world appearance. We gave a complete programme of leading work and "Airs above the Ground" and ended traditionally with the school quadrille by eight riders—the remains of the twelve quadrille instituted during the War. The excited applause, often accompanied by stamping feet—for the Swiss, usually so reserved, were really roused by the Lipizzaner—showed us clearly that the Spanish Riding School actually did possess what the illustrious spectators had expected, and they had jumped successfully off the springboard into the big world.

It was noted with approval that the Ministry of Agriculture and Forestry accepted my suggestion that no fee should be asked for the performances, but that these should rather be considered as thanks-offerings for the tremendous help given by Switzerland to Austrian children, especially as the organizers were bearing all the extra expenses of the tour.

The weather remained very bad for the next few days, though when the Lipizzaner entered the ring it did at least stop raining, as if Heaven wished to show these horses its especial favour. But the ground was soaked, soft, and muddy, and the horses sank in beyond their fetlocks, often slipping during difficult exercises. Their precision in executing their tasks in spite of these terrible conditions greatly astonished all the experts and gave me the deepest satisfaction, for this was clear proof of correct schooling: only a perfectly balanced horse could show such controlled equilibrium on such ground in all steps, including the *passage*.

The success of the white horses affected their riders too. If we had been spoilt hitherto—perhaps partly out of pity for the fate that had befallen our country—we were now promoted heroes of the hour. The glamour that suddenly surrounded us was almost too much for many individuals who identified the teamwork of the Spanish Riding School with their own performances.

I was a centre of interest in the splendid social engagements connected with the show, and was mobbed by horse enthusiasts, newly made friends of the Spanish Riding School. The American officers who had come previously to performances in Wels all greeted me with an excited "Hello" and took as personal an interest in our success as if I were one of them. I had a chance to shake hands with many riders whom I had known from pre-War competitions, greeting them as old comrades, and to meet many competition riders of the new generation and accept their congratulations. It was the first time after years of solitude and discrimination that we could operate once more as full partners in an international riders' guild without being divided into victors and vanquished or 'liberated.' I spent many happy hours of real contentment during these days in Lucerne, which after all that lay behind us did me a tremendous amount of good, particularly when I realized the pleasure we could give to others. Even in Lucerne I kept hearing people say that the Spanish Riding School absolutely must go to Thun for the Horse Show, one of the most important national events in Switzerland; and, indeed, straight after our last appearance the organizer of this show, the Commandant of the Eidgenössische Pferderegienstalt, invited us to take part. I could not help feeling that public opinion alone had influenced Colonel Thommen to reach this decision and that he issued his invitation with mixed feelings. Not, indeed, that he had anything against the Spanish Riding School; on the contrary, he had been one of its admirers for many years, and was always sending Swiss riders to Vienna, but the so-called main event at Thun was always provided by riders from the Pferderegienstalt, so our appearance there would mean an encroachment on his preserves, with all the consequent comparisons and criticisms. This made me refuse at first, but Colonel Thommen tried his very best to persuade me, and finally said, "You do not seriously imagine that I can show the quadrille I have rehearsed to my public, most of whom have been to Lucerne, after they have seen the Spanish Riding School!" So I agreed, and we went to Thun. For me personally this decision brought special pleasure, reviving my happiest memories of the place in which I had made my first appearance abroad.

After fourteen years I returned to this city with its delightful situation on Lake Thun, where its happy life seemed quite unchanged. The stadium too, looked after by the Regienstalt, was just the same, like a meadow of flowers which back in 1934 had made such an great impression on me: a military ground that did not stop at mere tidiness, but made a gay picture with the luxuriance and abundance of its flowers of every variety. Even then I had been struck by how different it was from grounds in Austria, and it stressed clearly the prosperity that a country preserved from war can enjoy.

The Eidgenossische Pferderegienstalt had long been responsible for providing a steady stream of mounted officers and riding horses for the artillery and infantry, but when we came to Thun the impending closure if this institution was already casting its dark shadows, and seriously affecting the mood of the people connected with the horses there. Nor did we find the early days very exhilarating, for it had been raining in torrents for days, and we could only work our horses in the covered school. Even the beautiful scenery and perfectly tended ring seemed grey and sad in such weather, and as any picture can be improved or spoilt by its frame, so the performances of the Spanish Riding School gain or lose their sparkle according to their surroundings and lighting.

But on the day itself all these gloomy ideas and thoughts were driven out by brilliant sunshine. The flower-edged, sap-green grass showed up in glowing colours, and a large crowd streamed in, happy and excited. Anybody who was anybody, all the important people in Switzerland, seemed to be gathered here. Against the imposing background of mountains the effect was unusually festive and gay, and the "shining silver Lipizzaner, these vigorous stallions, conjured up a wonderful atmosphere of equestrian tradition," as the Zurich paper *Sport* wrote.

Even the riders of the Spanish Riding School felt inspired with a special vitality—a rare and happy experience which life occasionally gives the truly serious and hard-working dressage rider—as they stepped into the arena in ceremonial step and the many thousands of spectators grew silent in admiration. The whole performance went like a dream; the Lipizzaner, as if they were conscious of their bewitching effect, gave of their best, and were spurred on to even greater efforts by the frenzied applause that continually broke the silence. We reached here the climax of our tour in Switzerland, and the Press wrote in superlatives of the "unforgettable presentations of the Spanish Riding School." They spoke of "equestrian chamber music," of the "beneficial effect of classic riding on the dressage riders of the country," of "ravishing living baroque," saying that "the experience of a wonderful work of art was reflected in the faces of the admiring spectators".

So the first foreign tour of the Spanish Riding School after the Second World War ended with a unique triumph. The Press throughout the country was full of praise, assuring the inhabitants that art so flawless as the performances of the Spanish Riding School can only very rarely be enjoyed.

This ancient academy thus succeeded in fulfilling its cultural mission beyond the frontiers of its homeland and making good propaganda for the classic art of riding. My secret wish was fulfilled: the Austrian public would be stirred by this success abroad, and reminded that our land still possessed treasures envied by other countries, and that we Austrians, who in the last ten years had truly had little reason to be proud and happy, should be grateful to destiny that the Spanish Riding School, a living memorial of a brilliant past, had remained as a legacy to a better future.

Practical good, too, resulted from this festival tour. The Swiss did not limit their enthusiasm to words, but provided in addition a vast quantity of provisions, rice, sugar, and chocolate, which I gave to the Wels district, and it was then distributed among several hundred needy children. This naturally also had a good effect on the Spanish Riding School, greatly increasing its popularity. Our riding achievements in Switzerland had also made many riders from that country eager to be taken as pupils, and in this way the reputation of the Spanish Riding School was enhanced abroad.

After their agreeable first trip abroad the riders were to have their leave and the horses enjoy a well-deserved rest, but for me intensive preparations for the Olympic Games in London were now beginning, giving the final polish to my horses.

The Olympic crown for me, as for every sportsman, was the highest goal, and so my old passion for competitions flared up again when I received the invitation to take part in the Games, the more strongly because after many years of careful training I had in Teja a magnificent dressage horse for this stiff challenge. He had become famous, partly through the occupation troops, and, as I discovered particularly during my stay in Switzerland, was considered a hot favourite for the big dressage event in London. For me it was the realization of a long-cherished wish—indeed, a dream—in whose fulfilment I had no longer dared to believe because of the political events of the years that had passed, but, as so often in life, how differently it all turned out!

Teja was given the best possible training for the big dressage trials. I took Neapolitano Africa as well—as my reserve horse, to be prepared for any eventualities. There was one drawback: that the test as compared with previous Olympics had been made decidedly easier through the omission of the *piaffe* and *passage*, for mature experience teaches that the easier the test the harder it is to judge fairly, as it is actually only the difficult exercises that make a better discrimination of ability possible. But Teja had a remarkably vigorous action and a rare suppleness, so in spite of everything I went to the 1948 Olympic Games full of expectations.

As a good beginning I accepted the invitation of a horse-crazy Swiss friend, Alexander Clavel, to break my long journey to London with a few days in Basle, as there would be opportunities to ride my horses on another ground in different surroundings, so the first stop on this memorable journey was Wenkenhof Castle in Riehen, near Basle. Wenkenhof, set in the middle of a large cultivated park quite secluded from the outer world, and built in the style of the old French castles, seemed a refuge in the modern, bustling times, and was as if created for the gathering of strength. The surroundings provided an atmosphere that seemed just right as a preparation for the great occasion. The stable and covered ride were royally furnished, and fitted harmoniously into the cultivated park landscape. It was truly the loveliest place that anyone could wish.

On the day before my departure I rode my horses for a select audience invited by my host. Only important people were invited, including the leading horse experts in Switzerland and many members of the Diplomatic Corps, headed by the Austrian Ambassador.

I rode Neapolitano Africa first, and then Teja, and was extraordinarily well received. Everything went—the experts thought—so smoothly that I was able to leave for the Olympics with a feeling of absolute confidence. Indeed, this demonstration of the well-ridden dressage horse had been so successful and convincing that I was invited to repeat it on the return journey from London at the riding competition in St Gallen.

A fairylike celebration was given in the castle and park—like a dream of a long departed age. All the arrangements, from the tasteful decoration to the choice of the guests, showed my host's exceptional taste; one could have imagined oneself at one of the feasts of the Sun King. Dull reality was forgotten, and unrestrained beauty and joy held sway. Small wonder that the next day, as I hastened towards the Channel in the train, I felt like Adam after he had been driven out of Paradise.

The contrast was really too great. Yesterday unclouded joy in the midst of refined luxury, in surroundings symbolic of lasting peace, and to-day, wherever I looked, a cheerless landscape full of memories of the hideous war with all the signs of destruction. The fields, in poor shape and neglected, looked as if the whole place was deserted—and that in the summer month of July. The longer the journey lasted, the more clearly the signs of war stood out concentrating in Dunkirk harbour in a heap of ruins, where only a few remarkably ugly essential buildings indicated the beginning of a new life. The change was certainly too sudden, but proved merely the prelude to a series of disappointments.

I crossed the Channel on the same boat as my horses, and on arriving at Dover was horrified when the British Customs officials had the good hay I had prudently brought with me thrown into the sea, in compliance with quarantine regulations. I saved the oats from a like fate by giving them to a railway official for his hens—certainly a worthy cause. But my horses had to be satisfied with much worse fodder, which, moreover, I had to buy, so once again I realized that red tape is truly international.

We then travelled separately to London, the horses on a goods train, and my wife and I on the last passenger train. At two in the morning we reached London Bridge, and had a fairly long journey to Grosvenor House, Park Lane. My very limited supply of English money had been appallingly reduced by the unexpected expense in Dover, so I watched uneasily in the taxi as the clock ticked up and finally showed an amount greater than my supply of ready cash. I felt like a cheat, especially as this was happening to me in a foreign city that had for years hated everything German, and was very relieved when the porter paid the driver as a matter of course, as was quite usual here in the early post-War years because of the currency regulations.

The next day I went to look for my horses in Aldershot. Here I saw several most disturbing things, reminiscent of the Olympic Games in Berlin. I found no announcements about the great sporting event, and the people I asked in my search for my horses looked at me in astonishment when I mentioned the word 'Olympiad,' as if they had never heard it before. As the civilians could give me no information I turned to a military policeman, for I assumed that the many horses would have been taken to one of the barracks. The term 'Olympiad' was unfamiliar to him also, but he showed the way to what had once been cavalry barracks, thinking that foreign horses might be there; and there, indeed, I came across my two, which had been put into roomy boxes. The space, however, was the one good thing about this rather derelict building. Whereas in Berlin the stabling had been rebuilt, here quantities of nails had to be knocked out of the partitions before the horses could be put in, and all the buildings were very shabby, as they had not been used for years.

My return to London after the Second World War was interesting in many respects. My first impression was that it had outwardly changed very little compared with 1938. One had to go a long way through London to find even odd souvenirs of the fury of war. But the food was quite another matter, being much worse than in Austria, and involuntarily I remembered a remark made by a British officer in St Martin in 1945: "It is possible to win twice, and still lose the war both times."

I was immensely impressed by the people, who endured all the shortages with exemplary discipline, and displayed a politeness that had long disappeared on the Continent through the brutality that followed the two wars.

33. Wenkenhof Castle at Riehen, near Basle

34. A Festive Setting for Classic Riding: the Riding Hall
at Christiansborg Castle: Copenhagen, 1951

35. The "Porcelain Horses"

36. President Heuss confers the Grand Service Order of the Federal German Republic: Dortmund, 1954

The English waited patiently at the stops of the overcrowded buses, and if a foreigner tried to push forward he would be told with an almost apologetic smile (my God, a foreigner!) that he must take his place in the queue.

After the years of strife between the nations the Olympic Games in London were to demonstrate their peaceful intentions to sorely tried mankind. Again—as once in Berlin—the Olympic flame of peace went out on the way to London and again in London itself. One could almost see this as a symbol of the unsettled times, with man's general longing for peace, like this Olympic flame, flickering and in constant danger of being blown out by the storm of political events. The attitude of the people to this great festival of sport, held only every four years, was quite different from that of 1936. Then every one in Berlin followed the events closely, and the whole city took part for a fortnight in the classic contests, but in London this sporting occasion was nothing like as popular as in 1936, and only a very limited number, mostly foreigners attracted by the Olympic Games, followed the sporting results with interest.

Even the opening ceremony was a disappointment for anyone who had been present in Berlin in 1936, both as regards organization and in the actual ceremony. The long speeches bored the sportsmen, and they began to sit down and fidget about. I still had nine days in hand before my appearance, and all the riders used this period for last-minute training. It was the first opportunity the competitors had had to get together and weigh up their opponents. It was immediately obvious to me that the standard of horsemanship was considerably lower than in Berlin, and I looked forward to the coming conflict with some hope of success. My work had also quickly attracted a crowd of hangers-on, much to my regret, for I would have been only too glad to train my horses in peace without an audience, but even in the farthest corner of the great polo ground which was put at our disposal for exercising I could not be alone.

For the first few days there was lovely weather with tropical heat, but on the day of the big dressage event it began to rain slightly. I was number four, and Teja went through his programme with great precision except that his right ear irritated him in the walk—perhaps a drop of water had got in—which caused him to shake his head once or twice. A surprisingly good round of applause greeted the end of my performance. Although it is generally a disadvantage to be one of the first in a dressage competition, I was now able to watch my opponents very closely. Once again I noted the lower standard of horsemanship in comparison with 1936 and really faced the result confidently—although I am not given to overestimating my own efforts or to exaggerated optimism.

After the last rider had completed his programme it was more than an hour and a half before the results of the event, which had lasted two days, were finally announced to the anxiously waiting riders and spectators. Then I experienced the greatest disappointment of my life, for I was put in eighth place, and, worse still, I could get no explanation from anyone as to the reason for this poor result. I did not share the anger of the many experts and and spectators who came excitedly up to me, but was overcome with an uncanny feeling of stillness; in me yawned an indescribable emptiness as the hopes and expectations of more than twelve years lay shattered at my feet. Still more the question as to whether the method and the purpose of years of work had perhaps been wrong after all, since I had had such a crushing decision, shook me to the depths of my being.

Before returning to London I visited my horses as usual in their stalls and gave sugar to Neapolitano Africa and Teja, and my groom, who had been with me for many years, looked at me and remarked that Teja certainly had earned the sugar, having given of his best. Then, turning to the horse, he said with a sob, "It's lucky you can't understand how unfairly you have been treated to-day." So, decidedly in no mood for laughter myself, I had to comfort my tearful groom.

The newspapers had plenty to say: they wondered why, contrary to all expectations, I finished only eighth in the main dressage event. It was generally felt that the standards applied were inferior to those of former years; and it was some small consolation to see from their generous references to my skill that the English Press, at any rate, seemed to acknowledge my abilities.

The Zurich paper *Sport*, although this event was won by a Swiss rider, reported:

> Colonel Podhajsky was Number Four, riding his Hungarian gelding Teja, which we had a chance of admiring in Lucerne and Thun during the performances of the Spanish Riding School, which is commanded by Colonel Podhajsky. Apart from a few uneven steps in the walk his programme was very elegant, and nothing astonished us more than to learn at the close that he had been placed only eighth, with 437 points. There must have been some mistake.

But these representations in the Press and the arguments of experts on the same theme in subsequent months did little to alter the fact that my riding had suffered a severe setback. I was completely thrown off my balance as by a heavy blow.

The next day I was invited in the name of the British Horse Society to give an exhibition ride on Neapolitano Africa after the end of the military dressage event. Influenced by the rainy weather and the after-effects of the dressage results—everything seemed so grey and joyless—I refused the invitation at first. But I changed my mind when the Society's spokesman asked me to consider that this request represented a recognition of my ability in British riding circles, and that there had been quite a struggle behind the scenes to get the General Secretary of the F.E.I. to withdraw his opposition to this extraordinary idea. So as not to cast this sporting and noble gesture back at the British Horse Society, I agreed, not dreaming what a great triumph awaited me.

When the last competitor had completed his programme I rode Neapolitano Africa into the stadium where I had suffered defeat two days previously. The tiers of seats were packed, and many riders and officials crowded on to the grass near the corner to be able to watch me closely. The rain, which had been coming down all day, had ceased and a few timid shafts of sunlight conferred their blessing on the performance on the Aldershot polo ground.

I completed a programme of particularly difficult exercises and delicate movements, containing everything that could be asked of a well-ridden dressage horse, beginning with the spirited natural walk to the *pirouettes*, jump changes, and *passage*. The public followed in respectful silence the difficult movements of the noble horse and clapped and cheered in a manner quite unprecedented in this stadium during the Olympic struggles when I raised my hat at the end of my performance. I dismounted and received congratulations and gave autographs for over an hour. My success was so tremendous that I was asked to repeat the performance after the hunters' jumping event.

The *Daily Telegraph* of August 12 in a brief account of the competition mentioned that

> After the judging at Aldershot was over Colonel Podhajsky from Austria showed some advanced dressage on his Lipizzaner horse, Neapolitano Africa. This was a beautiful and faultless performance, emphasizing very clearly the elementary standard of the competitions we had witnessed earlier.

The judging in the main dressage event was examined under a microscope and subjected to exhaustive analysis, with the result that my unjustifiably low placing was unanimously rejected. Since this concerned opinion in a foreign country which had no need to be sentimental on my account, I found in it some small consolation for my heavy defeat.

Many years have passed since then, and at this distance of time I can judge the whole situation more clearly. The year 1936 saw the start of the great period of competitive dressage, fostered by exaggerated nationalism, which outweighed objective judgment. In 1948 this weakness for one's own compatriots had, in spite of the shaking that the Second World War administered to the whole of mankind, grown even more in London. By this time several nations were already turning away in annoyance from this branch of the contest, and there began to be suggestions that the dressage events should be dropped from the Olympic programme. These were then considered eight years later by the International Olympic Committee, because this disciplined training "always caused ill-feeling." When in 1952 in a speech in Warendorf I predicted this development I had no idea that my prophecy, thanks to lack of serious purpose or else of judging skill, would be so quickly fulfilled. It is, in fact, an important moral task to judge objectively the years of work done by a dedicated sportsman. Only a judge who has himself been a rider can assess which struggles reveal a rider's faulty judgment, and will therefore be more aware of his reponsibility than so many of the judges who have never shown how far they can themselves master what they are criticizing. But what a sad end for the noblest and finest of all sports!

After the Olympic dressage results I felt it would be out of place for me to ride my horses in St Gallen, in the native land of the winner, so I posted my refusal from London, and received the following telegram:

, What do you think we are? Of course we expect you. Please give time of arrival. Rennklub St Gallen.

On the strength of this I did after all break my journey in St Gallen before returning home, and not only received a warm welcome but gave highly successful exhibitions on my horses. I first showed Teja, and then Neapolitano Africa in two different programmes which made still greater demands than the Olympic Dressage event, and I managed to enthral the masses of spectators, as was proved by the stillness that reigned throughout my performance. What a marvellous feeling for any performer! The *Schweizer Kavallerist* reported that "Colonel Podhajsky delighted the excited and attentive audience with two brilliant performances on Teja and Neapolitano Africa."

After six eventful weeks abroad I took my horses home at the end of August 1948 with very mixed feelings. My conflicting experiences, my riding defeat on the one hand and the jubilant successes that far outweighed it, had rather thrown me off my balance, but there was plenty of room for deep depression. There was no reason for an official welcome, and so we returned to Wels quietly and unobtrusively, to the accompaniment of lively articles in the Austrian Press. All the papers, whatever their politics, made no secret of the disappointment that my downfall had caused, but all were correct in saying that the decision in London was very controversial.

Life and the duties of the Spanish Riding School continued as usual regardless of my emotional or physical condition. Only a few days after my return the High Commissioner of the United States of America with a large number of high officers attended a show; they were completely captivated. At the performances given as part of the Wels Volksfest, at the Trabrennplatz, the many thousands of spectators vied with the visiting Americans and French in expressing their approval, and at one of the September performances the Chancellor, Dr Leopold Figl, was present with several of his Ministers, and later wrote in the visitors' book: "One can only marvel and admire! That it may continue to be so is my earnest wish!"

In May 1949 the Spanish Riding School began their second foreign trip. This time the tour was to Italy, the traditional home of show jumping. During the London Olympics, after Neapolitano Africa's exhibition ride, the President of the Italian Fédération Équestre, Count Campello, had already said that he hoped to welcome the Spanish Riding School to the great International Horse Show the following year—doubtless a very flattering but decidedly risky invitation—for the *haute école* of dressage to appear in the greatest European show-jumping ground, where dressage riders had never before entered. And, indeed, the precepts of the famous Captain Caprilli, the architect of the modern style of jumping and founder of the Italian success in this sport, were opposed to the ancient school of dressage, once cradled in Italy. We must be quite clear that we should meet a very critical public in Rome, but a rider should always form a precise picture of his own ability and the receptiveness of his public, so this festival tour would be an experiment—in fact, a crucial test of the persuasive power of the Spanish Riding School.

When I was staying with the Italian War Minister in 1948 I had already dreamed of presenting the Lipizzaner in the beautiful Piazza di Siena to the pampered and elegant public and bringing them under the spell of the white dancers, but now, as with a nervously beating heart I entered the fairylike arena beside the Villa Borghese at the head of my riders, 35,000 pairs of eyes full of curiosity, excitement, and perhaps also scepticism turned towards the unfamiliar picture. The cream of Society, headed by President Einaudi, and the leading generals were all present, stressing the importance of the occasion. The temperamental Lipizzaner, who were perfectly attuned to the wishes of their riders, gave an indication of their controlled strength only in the proudly held heads and dancing steps, and contrived to capture the audience's attention from the very moment of their entry. But when for the first time since the War the Austrian national anthem was heard in this square, and the powerful stallions stood completely motionless like statues, apparently as proud as their riders that the red, white, and red banner fluttered beside the flags of the other nations, there was a stir of surprise in the crowd which was accustomed, when the competitors were drawn up in a line, to seeing the horses, quickly wearying of standing still, causing embarrassment to their riders by all kinds of escapades. The first impression that the Lipizzaner made on the exacting visitors to the Piazza di Siena was therefore exceptionally favourable, and the execution of all the steps and turns of the *haute école*, the handling and the "Airs above the Ground," succeeded in riveting the attention of the thousands so closely that all the chatter faded into a respectful silence, broken only by great bursts of applause after each individual item. The public, more and more carried away, became ecstatic over the final school quadrille, and acknowledged with frenzied clapping the harmony of movement displayed. That it was the quadrille, not even the *caprioles* or *courbettes*, that managed to rouse such wild enthusiasm, was in keeping with the Italian love of music: for them the eight horsemen rhythmically flowing and weaving in and out created a musical picture. The Lipizzaner here in Rome gave a new meaning to the words of the Koran, "And ye triumph without sword." The public fêted us enthusiastically, and the Press gave details of the triumphal progress of the Spanish Riding School in the land of show jumping. One daily paper waxed lyrical:

> Quite suddenly there breathes over the picturesque arena an atmosphere of the sixteenth century. Horses in magnificent trappings and saddlery. Riders in traditional uniforms make us think involuntarily of fragile porcelain figures carefully placed upon a green carpet, beneath the brilliant sky of a Roman spring. Suddenly these figures come to life; to the irresistible strains of the music they begin to execute their movements with dignity, grace and incredible precision, as well as a rare delicacy. They trot and gallop—no, they dance—these white porcelain bodies brought to life, and it seems like a fairy-tale from the *Arabian Nights*. These temperamental and powerful horses, which move like ballet dancers and excite us with their leaps into the air, then freeze into immobility like some of our many exquisite Italian statues. When the riders doff their cocked hats in salute they recall a far-off age of an old and civilized Europe, and all are conscious of the strength of tradition displayed here under the pines.

And from the riding publication *Il Cavallo Italiano*:

> Every rider ought to remember that the skill of the Spanish Riding School displays the experience of the work of many centuries, and has no connexion with any passing fashion. At the recent Olympics in London the Lipizzaner stallion Neapolitano Africa gave an exhibition, and the English Press wrote more about this ride than about the winner of the main Olympic dressage event. The Spanish Riding School will always be considered throughout the world as the example of the art of *manège* riding.

During the many receptions where those connected with the show got together to talk informally a Swiss diplomat made a significant remark to the Austrian Ambassador: "In the Spanish Riding School your country has the best ambassador in the world."

A highlight for us was our special audience with Pope Pius XII. After the last day of the show I went with my riders in traditional uniform and several grooms to Vatican City, where the Commandant of the Swiss Guard was waiting for us. The decorative uniforms of the Spanish Riding School fitted harmoniously into the brilliant scene provided by the colourful uniforms of the papal dignitaries and guards. As we stepped into this historic territory so obviously endowed with a great past we were captured by the compelling atmosphere and filled with a strong sense of occasion. While we were waiting in the ante-room for our audience I looked out of the window at the Eternal City, lying so to speak at our feet, and became aware of the greatness and power of the Catholic Church. The might of an uncompromising tradition was displayed also by every gesture and movement of those in attendance on the Pope. The Commandant of the Swiss Guard talked to me a great deal and told me many interesting anecdotes about his service in the Vatican.

Countess Habig-Thun, for many years a friend of the Spanish Riding School, and our family, my wife, and the members of the School were standing waiting to be received when the door opened silently and the Holy Father in white robes appeared in the lofty doorway, like a supernatural figure. As a beam of light pierces the darkness and in an instant transforms the whole scene, so much stillness preceded his appearance that one could hear one's own heart beating. It was one of the very few sublime moments afforded us in this life, and I shall never forget the Holy Father's approach, walking silently as if his feet were not touching the ground. He held out his slender hand for me to kiss, but without waiting for this raised me from my kneeling position and said in fluent German, "I have heard what a great success the Spanish Riding School has had here in Rome. How are things in the land of beautiful mountains? I love Austria so much."

I answered that conditions had gradually improved, and the Holy Father replied, "I have already heard this and rejoiced."

Then I presented my companions individually, and as we walked from one to the other answered various questions about the Spanish Riding School and the nature of our work. When we reached the grooms, who in their quiet civilian suits were something of an anticlimax after the riders, I said, "I have taken the liberty of bringing along to the audience the grooms, who never share the splendour of our performances, but whose work is so necessary for their success." And the Pope answered with a benign look, "You were quite right to bring these men to me as well." Some of the men actually had tears on their cheeks, so much were they affected by the moment when they could shake hands with the Holy Father.

After a short conversation the Pope charged me to give his warmest greeting to Austria, and gave his blessing to us and our homeland. As we knelt there deeply moved there was not one of us who did not realize that it was one of the highlights of his life. When we raised our eyes again the place where the Pope had stood with outstretched arms was empty. One could almost have believed that what we had just experienced was only a vision.

We left the Vatican filled with emotion, reverence, and happiness. There could not have been a more wonderful conclusion to our triumphal visit to Rome, and our success was widely recorded in the Austrian Press and given publicity that greatly affected the attendance at the shows arranged in Wels.

As soon as these were over I had to go to Cologne in early June 1949 at the invitation of the Kölner Reitverein to act as dressage judge at the contest there. It was my first return to Germany since the holocaust that had lightly touched her two neighbours, and the impressions that I formed on this occasion were exceptionally interesting.

We had been horrified enough over the destruction that the larger Austrian cities had suffered from bombing, but I now realized how small this damage was compared with what the Allied bombers had caused in Germany. When I arrived in Munich I was profoundly depressed by the great misery that I saw all around me. Whole streets were razed to the ground, and out of a vast heap of rubble emerged only a few primitive barrack buildings where the first beginnings of a new commercial life could be discovered. The people, shabbily dressed and badly fed, some living in the cellars of ruined houses, provided a striking contrast to the occupation personnel, who drove about with their families in luxury cars, covering these wretched people with dust. Colonialism in its worst form seemed to be celebrating its revival, and it was all so dreadful that I heaved a sigh of relief when I left this Bavarian capital, once so gay.

But other cities on my journey presented a similar picture of senseless destruction and endless distress and were barely recognizable. This was specially true of Cologne, the city that I knew so well and remembered with such pleasure. I stood before the old cathedral soaring like a memorial above the ruins, and could no longer find my way. What severe trials had been imposed upon the German people! How lucky we were in Austria by comparison, in spite of all the shortage that still existed in the early post-War days!

But I felt not only sympathy for these hardly tried people, but a great admiration for their patience, moderation, industry, and determination to begin again—a thought that obsessed every stratum of society from the humblest worker to the greatest scholar.

In these far from exhilarating surroundings one of the first big post-War horse shows in Germany was held, and there was a remarkably high standdard of riding, a living proof of the Germans' great affection for the horse. If the opening ceremony was very modest, the performances were of the highest quality, a quality rare amid the low living standards in the country. In Austria at this time riding as a sport was barely out of its infancy.

I have no words to describe the warmth of my reception in Cologne. The hospitality was beyond expectations, and everybody was ready to make my stay as pleasant as possible, and to obliterate in some measure the impression of prevailing poverty. Friends gave us a carefully chosen dinner in one of the newly erected restaurants, with a series of courses that would have compared favourably with those of peace-time.

The relations of the people with the occupying Powers were most remarkable. Whereas in Austria there was a brisk traffic between civilian population and foreign soldiers, this was still absolutely forbidden in Germany. Moreover, except for those of the police, there were no uniforms to be seen on the showground.

At this competition I met Dr Gustav Rau, with whom I was acting as judge in various dressage trials. It was amazing to see this man who had lost everything in the course of the recent hostilities devoting all his strength and energy to rebuilding the sport of riding in Germany. He managed to inspire active riders with his spirit and enthusiasm, and to resurrect the sport in the defeated and prostrate country just as he had once wrested the country riding clubs from the very ground itself. He has done so much for German riding that his name deserves to be inscribed in letters of gold in the annals of this sport.

He asked me so cordially to visit him after the show that I followed up his invitation and went to Dillenburg with my wife on the return journey. He had found sanctuary there and lived in the humblest circumstances, thinking of nothing but the restoration of riding in Germany. We spent a delightful evening. Frau Rau served one of the geese she had raised herself, and he sacrificed his last bottle of champagne, kept for a special occasion, a truly hospitable gesture. We talked far into the night about horses, riders, and old times, both of us carefully avoiding the old bone of contention, so that no discord should spoil the harmonious hours. In Dillenburg I sat opposite a man whom the fearful happenings of the preceding years had certainly not robbed of his energy, but had bestowed a gentle mellowness that was reflected in his great tolerance of all human weakness as well as in his obvious goodness. In those hours I was truly aware of his greatness as a person and as an expert.

At the beginning of July I was next to embark on one of my most interesting tours with my horses Teja, Neapolitano Africa, and Pluto Theodorosta. The British Horse Society, under the patronage of the King of England, had sent an invitation on February 8 via the Austrian Embassy in London to the Chancellery in Vienna to send the head of the Spanish Riding School as a guest of the Society to the International Horse Show in London in July, to demonstrate the training of horses up to the stringent demands of the *haute école*. This invitation gave me the greatest possible satisfaction after my experiences at the Olympic Games the previous year, for the British experts had not invited the Olympic winner or any of the medallists to give an exhibition of *haute école* riding to the horsemen of their country—as is often done—but me, the national of a state that had never been represented on this island before. This gesture of British fairness was a remarkable honour not for me alone, but also for my country, a view shared by the Austrian Press and given wide publicity.

Thus I was given a very rare opportunity to show my skill to a public that had been for generations passionate devotees of the sport in all its forms. The knowledge that in spite of the judges' decision I had succeeded at the 1948 Olympic Games in attracting so much attention that the British public wanted to see me perform again, thus paying a tribute to Austrian horsemanship as well, filled me with particular pride.

I once more broke my journey to London in Basle, where I was to give an exhibition on the occasion of a big celebration at Wenkenhof Castle. This time also all the important people were there, and seldom can there have been so many representatives of the Diplomatic Corps at a private party as on this afternoon. The leading Swiss riding experts were also among the guests, so I could not have wished for a finer dress rehearsal for my important appearance in London. I led the two Lipizzaner horses into the decorated hall, which seemed made for equestrian chamber music, and Teja to a large Olympic dressage arena. I made up the programme to show to the best advantage the physical virtues of the different breeds, Lipizzaner and highly developed half-breed, and also to prove that classic riding is not basically limited to any particular breed of horse. It was a complete success, as the loud applause and the remarks at the wonderful garden party afterwards indicated, and I received nothing but congratulations.

In England I was first taken with my horses to the private residence of the President of the International Horse Show, Colonel Williams, at East Burnham Park, near Windsor. In this charming country house surrounded by superb grounds with old trees, playing water and the inimitable well-kept English grass, I was received with kindly hospitality like one of the family, and felt as if I were in another world: no hurry, no nervous strain, no politics, only a patriarchal community life in a cultured home with passionate sportsmen.

My horses lived in roomy boxes and were obviously delighted with surroundings so much pleasanter than Wels; through a large window they could see everything that was going on in the open square in front of their stable. But my host was particularly considerate in putting a part of his beautiful turf at my disposal for training my horses. I had rarely had the chance of working in such lovely, well-kept surroundings and felt an exhilaration such as I had not known for years.

On the working days before the show a large number of visitors, knowledgeable about horses, came to watch the schooling of my mounts, often travelling long distances to get there. Colonel Williams had very cleverly invited the most sceptical, to prove to them by the evidence of their own eyes and by talking about it that their ideas of classic riding were in many instances mistaken. I have already observed how conservatively the English kept themselves apart from any Continental influence in all riding matters, but now came to the conclusion that England with her outstanding horses would be unbeatable in the international competitions if only her riders would abandon their primitive methods and pay greater attention to the training of their horses. How right I was then was proved only a few years later when British riders, adopting Continental methods, reached a standard in jumping and general competitions adequate for the most severe international riding contests.

I was in no doubt that there were not a few sceptics among the daily spectators, only waiting for an opportunity to have their rejection of this dressage training proved right, so I tried as I talked to them to discover their doubts so that I could show them the very things that were troubling them. My real task, I considered, was to dispel the idea of the 'cruelty' of dressage riding, perhaps an exaggerated survival of the outcry once caused by the rough methods of the Duke of Newcastle. My work, which was conducted in public and without any concealment, succeeded in transforming the severest critics into interested spectators, so I had achieved my first success on English soil, but the great test before the general public in the White City still lay before me.

The White City, one of the big London stadia, with a capacity of 80,000, had some years before displaced Olympia as the scene of the big annual International Horse Show. During the rest of the year greyhound racing is held there, and certainly attracts an entirely different public from that of the Horse Show. To the latter, the equestrian event of the 'season,' come all the best people, for it is considered the done thing to be seen there, and the grandstands provided a picture of the greatest elegance and gave the somewhat out-of-date stadium a gay and festive appearance.

The organization of the show was also noteworthy, having been thought out to the last detail to ensure that everything should run smoothly. The officials and organizers, in morning coats with top-hats, carried out their duties in an exemplary manner; there were no raised voices nor any nervous rushing about; the whole affair was an example of discipline without obvious compulsion, worthy of this noblest of sports.

Each afternoon and evening I was to ride first a Lipizzaner and then Teja. By this means the spectators would be taught the true nature of the classic art of riding and at the same time be shown that horses of an English type like Teja were just as suitable for *haute école* riding as the Lipizzaner.

The size of the gate on the opening day surprised the organizers, and the success of my first appearance was overwhelming. I would never have believed that I could succeed on my own in conquering the hearts of the English at my first assault, and thrill so many thousands.

Interest grew daily, the applause in the crowded stadium became louder and louder, and the Press surpassed itself in the extravagance of its praise.

I was the most popular rider of the show, fêted on all sides, and repeatedly asked for autographs, and when I crossed the street on my horse on the way to the ring children ran after me, shouting, "There's the dancing horse."

Among the many compliments paid me one from a landowner and sportsman, who himself kept twelve horses, impressed me particularly. He introduced himself and said, "I have always disliked dressage riding, not because I know nothing about it, for I have seen Lörke and many other famous riders in Germany. But you are the first to make me change my mind. I have admired you every day, and become more and more enthusiastic about you, for you are the very first rider I have ever known to ride with his heart and soul!"

At one of the first evening performances I was asked by the organizers whether I would not like to ride a Lipizzaner by spotlight. I had never tried it, but agreed, trusting to the obedience of my gallant Neapolitano Africa. The well-known British show jumper Colonel Llewellyn warned me in a friendly way that he himself had had a most unfortunate experience doing this. He wanted to complete his round of honour after his first victory at the White City in the small circle of light from the spot, but found that his horse was reluctant to step into the gaping darkness ahead and tried to jump his own shadow.

"So how in such conditions will you show your horse in controlled movements that require perfect balance?" he concluded.

As there was no chance to try it out, I agreed to ride into the stadium in the spotlight, but made it conditional on my horse's behaviour as to whether I should then give my performance with the same or full lighting. I galloped into the inky blackness on Neapolitano Africa, surrounded and followed by a circle made by four powerful spotlights lighting up only horse and rider. I had to pick out little landmarks as I went so that I should, in fact, arrive at the correct place of my performance. I found the centre line of my arena, thanks to the flame from a lighter being used in the Royal Box, and this gave me my direction. Riding in, I could sense the complete obedience of my horse entrusting himself implicitly to my directions, so I decided to begin the performance in the spotlight.

I could only see two yards ahead. When one of the tubs of flowers that marked the corner loomed up in the cone of light, that was the sign to turn, so my horse had to keep an absolutely straight line not to become disorientated in the extensive space by missing the markers. This exhibition also provided a searching test of the basic schooling of the horse, made still more difficult by the lateral work and *pirouettes*. But everything went marvellously; Neapolitano Africa followed every command perfectly, and only the white foam that covered his body betrayed his nervousness and tension. The crowd went wild.

This evening performance was so well received that there were many requests for a repeat, but the President of the Horse Show turned them down, giving as his reason that the skill displayed was far too great to need emphasizing by lighting effects.

So on all the following evenings I rode into a stadium as bright as day, as with this lighting people could "follow all the details of the movements much better."

It was a special honour for me to be told on the third day that Queen Elizabeth was to pay a short visit to the White City and had expressed a wish to see me ride. It was one of the main days of the show when the Queen appeared in a horse-drawn landau, drove round the stadium where there was not an empty seat, and then took her place in the Royal Box. I was very impressed to see how affectionately and proudly the packed crowds of people stood to greet their Queen, as she drove smiling past the tiers of seats.

The show jumping was interrupted for me to give my exhibition rides. On this day the applause reached gale force, and when after bowing to the Queen I raised my hat again to the crowds of spectators, the cheers went on and on. As I dismounted I was surrounded by excited people asking if I had seen how closely the Queen had followed every movement of my horses, and had spontaneously clapped exercises particularly well done, and when I saluted her at the end had waved to me. As if I had noticed all this—in a stadium crowded with spectators who looked to me simply like a black wall!

Here in the White City in London the greatest success of my life had been achieved, and I should have been very happy—if only I had not felt so wretchedly ill for days. Life can sometimes be so cruel! On the one hand it afforded me the greatest possible triumph, and on the other took all the pleasure out of it.

In the final days of rehearsing in East Burnham Park a distressing weariness had begun to trouble me, so when I came to the White City I already felt very ill, but was immediately shocked at the thought of how disappointing it would be if I put off my performances, and how many hopes would be buried after such a promising beginning. For England, which had invited me, and had spared no expense in connexion with my appearance on behalf of my homeland, which for the first time had been given the opportunity of sending an apostle to preach the traditional gospel of horsemanship, an Austrian heritage; and for me, since it gave me the chance to prove that my efforts at the Olympic Games in the previous year had after all not been so poor as the judges had ruled. I resolved to grit my teeth, therefore, and let nobody see that anything was wrong! But to carry this through required more energy than I had foreseen; not only to have to ride when one longed to rest, but to smile and show interest in trivialities when one was dead tired!

Summoning all my strength, I began by warming up my horses, and when I grew warm myself, and was stirred by the atmosphere of the excited audience, I could forget all my troubles for a few moments and give of my best, at one with my horses. But as soon as I dismounted tiredness and such a feeling of wretchedness flowed over me that it could not be counteracted by the enthusiastic people around me, and I had to sacrifice what strength remained to hide how I really felt. So even after my performance before Queen Elizabeth I was not at all pleased to be hauled out of my dressing-room for a presentation in the Royal Box. Then champagne—French champagne!—was handed round, and the waiter, who had already told me how thrilled he was with my "show," wanted to give the poor Austrian plenty of this delicious drink, and could not understand why I sipped it so half-heartedly.

Under this burden I longed for my rides to end, although they brought me everything that a sportsman could desire. On one occasion Teja galloped out and tripped over the coconut-matting covering the concrete, and we stumbled. The fall was an easy one, indeed elegant, for my top-hat did not even leave my head, although I lay for some moments under the horse; the sympathy I received from everybody was not welcome, for I had only one thought: to creep away somewhere and be left in peace!

As my last appearance drew near I was particularly nervous, for my weariness had reached shocking proportions in the preceding days. I could eat nothing, and only ice-cold drinks gave me any relief from my discomfort. Moreover, I had to avoid any slackening of effort in my final performance, since, although every rider's form varies constantly, I had so far not had to record even the smallest black mark. Should I manage to conclude this series of successes with a flourish?

Since the success of an exhibition of horsemanship depends ultimately on the correct preparation of the horses, I began on the last day even earlier with this task, hoping to be able to rest a little before my actual appearance. Proper warming up is, in my opinion, an art in itself, for it involves loosening up rider and horse without making either tired, and increasing efficiency so systematically that it reaches its peak during the performance itself. On the final day, after wonderful weather with tropical heat, there was a noticeable drop in temperature, to which my horses reacted with unusual friskiness, so that it took twice as long to get them into the right condition, and there was no question of taking a rest before my appearance. I summoned up all the energy that I was still capable of commanding to make a worthy finish. That I had succeeded was obvious from the applause as I left the White City for the last time at a full gallop with loose reins. Many people told me I had surpassed myself that evening.

During the formal closing ceremony in which the heads of the teams and I had taken up our positions in the arena near the flagstaff for the farewell by the Duke of Beaufort, I felt so ill that the hauling down of the British flag seemed almost the termination of my own riding career. I finished my highly successful stay in London a very sick man, and flew back to Zürich exhausted, worn out, and almost unhappy, filled only with a longing to get home, but I still had before me the task of directing the performances of the Spanish Riding School in Dornbirn, in Vorarlberg, and showing my horses there as well. When my wife met me at Kloten Airport in Zürich she was horrified at my appearance.

"Good heavens, you've got jaundice!" were her first words.

Until then I myself had not noticed how yellow I looked, as I was far too tired to look closely at myself, and the other people cannot have noticed either.

With no more than a weary smile I acknowledged a pleasant gesture at the Customs. I wanted to declare a box containing a presentation souvenir of my London appearances: a glass decanter with the hand-painted head of Teja, and glasses with the portraits of Neapolitano Africa and Pluto Theodorosta on them. However, the Customs offical stopped me, raised his hand in greeting, and said, "It's all right, Colonel, we've read all about your great success in London."

When I reached Dornbirn I was absolutely at my last gasp. If I decided to ride in spite of everything, it was only because I did not want to spoil the items which had been rehearsed with me taking part, and perhaps also I feared the reproach of my own countrymen that I had ridden abroad again but the Austrians had had little chance to see me. It was not an easy decision, but I could not leave the Spanish Riding School in the lurch making its first performance in Austria away from its home in exile, however hard for me.

The first two performances took place as part of an international riding and jumping competition on the occasion of an Export and Sample Fair at the beginning of August. The weather was wonderful, but man and beast alike sweltered under the intense heat, and this temperature was almost unbearable for the fit, but for me real martyrdom. Later I wondered myself how I had managed to greet the guests of honour, to face the journalists and the radio and still ride my horses, and during the first performance I even had to endure a long interview for the Bavarian broadcasting system. My life in those days was restricted to little more than my sickbed, the trip to the arena, and riding my horses. Our visit passed as in a dream; the vast crowd from Germany, Switzerland, and many parts of Austria left me as unmoved in my apathy as the applause that thundered around us. It sounded to me as if it came from a long way off, while an inner voice kept on wailing, "Go home and rest!"

Only later from the Press notices did I learn how well we had done. While the riders and important visitors celebrated the successful conclusion of the competitions with a large party I dragged myself back to my sickbed in the hotel and collapsed completely. The duty that had spurred me on to use up the last of my strength was now fulfilled, and my energy, strained to the uttermost for many weeks, gave out. I wanted to do nothing but go home and see nobody.

My wife called in a doctor, who diagnosed a severe liver complaint and said the journey home to Wels would be dangerous, but consoled us by saying that luckily there was an outstanding specialist here in Vorarlberg, and he would be a great help. As he examined me the doctor told me that he had noticed my yellow face during the performance, which he had enjoyed greatly, but he had had to smile when the two foreign women sitting beside him ended their enthusiastic comments on my riding with, "What a pity he is an Asiatic!"

So I went into the sanatorium at Röthis under the care of the teaching professor, Dr Albrich, at one time assistant to the famous Professor Eppinger. My arrival was not without its comic side, for we had our dachshund Lumpi with us in Switzerland and in Vorarlberg, and now did not know what we were to do with the dear creature, as my wife was staying in the sanatorium to be with me. She asked hesitantly if she might bring Lumpi with her, but the doctor on duty at first indignantly said no, but then, moved by her sudden desperation, said with true Austrian kindliness, "Oh well, we certainly can't turn the animal into sausages, so you take him with you, but please take care he isn't seen."

Lumpi really proved himself in those weeks, for he would only leave my sickbed for the most pressing reasons, and captured everybody's heart; even the stern sister in charge and the specialist could not resist him.

My illness took a very serious turn, and I hovered for a long time on the brink of death. For three weeks I had to be artificially fed, and spent nearly three and a half months in the sanatorium. Luckily I was in the best hands with Dr Albrich, and I found him an attractive man who became a true friend. Faith in my doctors and the possibility, in this meeting-point of three countries, of getting the necessary medicines—still a problem in Austria—some from Switzerland and some also from Germany, proved most helpful to my treatment, so thanks to outstanding medical care, I managed to get over the illness quite well. My wife, too, played an important part in my recovery, for she gave me spiritual strength by her devoted love and unfailing sense of humour. I was particularly grateful for the care given me by the consultant's assistant, Dr Gmeiner, who carried out the instructions of his chief conscientiously, and I also came to respect him greatly as a man.

Once back in Wels I had to take up all my work at once, for the Spanish Riding School was to go to Zürich and Geneva in November, and there was a great deal to straighten out and improve. My horses had only been led during my absence, as was usual, so I had to get rid of the accumulated effects of their idleness and overcome their muscular stiffness before I

37. Farewell Round in Aachen, 1953

38. Successful Dressage Debut of Maestoso Alea in Dortmund, 1953

39. Neapolitano Santuzza in a Perfect *Ballotade* in London, 1953

could take up the training where I had left off three and a half months earlier. It was a great deal more troublesome to get the riders back into form after having been left to themselves for so long.

Our second festival visit to Switzerland was specially important, inasmuch as we had to confirm our success of the spring and must in no circumstances be disappointing. And the measure of that success had in the opinion of the Swiss far surpassed anything that had preceded it, but I knew from experience that hard-won achievement is usually harder still to maintain.

The entire riding world dreamed and raved over the brilliance of this widely known and traditional tourney, the Mecca of all horse-lovers. I too had for many years followed it with interest, and often secretly wished to be able to ride there just once, particularly after reading of the great success of the winner in the main dressage event in the 1932 Olympics, the French Commandant Lesage, when he exhibited his dressage horse Taine here in the stronghold of show jumping. Still, I was fully aware that the Spanish Riding School would be watched with a much more critical eye, probably even with a good deal of scepticism in this French part of Switzerland, which had become the domain of the Cavalry School of Saumur because of the frequent appearances of the Cadre Noir.

The setting was incomparably lovelier than in Zurich. The horses were brought right near to the Palais des Expositions, and there was ample opportunity to exercise them in the great exhibition hall and in the covered ride round it. The only difficulty we had was with the orchestra, which could not play our accompaniments, and tried to compensate for their shortcomings by playing extra loud, which shocked the sensitive Lipizzaner and several times threw them off their mental and physical balance. After this unfortunate experience at the dress rehearsal we fell back once more on the specially recorded gramophone music.

Our performances were usually considered as the climax and conclusion of the evening. The audience in the crowded hall was elegantly dressed and spoke mainly French, so that one could imagine oneself in Paris. Unfortunately the programme did not run to time, because the jumping with its jump-offs to decide the winner was often so long-drawn out that the Spanish Riding School, instead of beginning about 11 P.M., never did so until after midnight, often as late as two in the morning, so there was a great deal of grumbling from all those who had long journeys by public transport, and had no reasonable means of getting home after the show. Thus many had to forego the pleasure they had been anticipating for months. The Finnish Field-Marshal Mannerheim, who was in a sanatorium, sent his regrets to me that because of the lateness of our appearance he would have to abandon his long-held intention of seeing the Spanish Riding School again after many years.

As the hands of the clock passed midnight during one of the first performances I was afraid that we should have to ride to empty stands, but then I realized that nobody was leaving, and had further proof of the extent of our reputation. We were greeted with a mixture of concentrated attention and wild ovations, and the Lipizzaner truly did their best, as if they guessed that their prestige was involved. My horses, too, showed as much poise as if they had been training for this for weeks.

Their precision caused some of the Swiss experts—as I accidentally gathered from the whispers of the competitors—to ask who had really been exercising my horses during my illness, for it was quite incredible that they had only been led while I had been away. This was easy to refute, since we had Swiss pupils in the Spanish Riding School at that time, who had daily evidence to the contrary.

I was especially gratified and delighted when the elderly captain of the French team, the famous show jumper Colonel Laissardière, came up to me at a reception and said: "I have watched your performance every evening and enjoyed them very much. Before I came to congratulate you on the quite tremendous success that you have enjoyed in Geneva I inspected your horses in the stables. Here I found the stallions fresh and lively, interested in everything, standing on all fours, not bandaged nor tied up, and with no signs of thickening or galling. This proved to me how correct your training is, so here I am to express my sincere admiration."

It was a noble gesture, too, when on the closing day, after we had finished, and the cheering rang in our ears as we saluted, Captain Chevalier, Olympic winner for France in the 1948 military event, one of the most active competition riders, came to me and thanked me most sincerely; then he and his riders shook me firmly by the hand.

In barely eighteen months the Spanish Riding School, since they had crossed the Austrian border, had managed to break the ring, a remnant of the past, that still surrounded our country, and bring to other nations a fragment of Austrian culture. Could the old school have any better justification for its very existence? Did not these successes clearly prove the rightness of the decision to bring the Lipizzaner out of their restricted surroundings into the wide world?

That autumn the Ministry of Agriculture received an official invitation to send me to the Royal Dublin Society's Spring Show in May 1950. This request, involving no expense at all to the Austrian state, was not just an acknowledgment of my riding skill, but a special honour to Austrian horsemanship, for Ireland had hitherto maintained close ties only with the French Cavalry School of Saumur.

In the second half of April 1950 my horses Pluto Theodorosta and Teja —Neapolitano Africa had to stay behind because he was not well—made the long journey via Switzerland and England to Ireland. I went first with my wife to friends in Lausanne, to deliver Lumpi, whom I could not take with me because of quarantine regulations, and then flew from Geneva to Dublin. Though the flight to London by Swissair passed without a hitch, the second stage to Dublin was almost adventurous. We were the only passengers in the small aircraft, which did not seem too safe, the lighting was meagre and the weather stormy, so we were glad to be back on firm ground around midnight.

We stayed in an old castle as guests of the well-known rider Colonel Dugeon, and there got to know something of the romantic and elegant life of this island steeped in legend. When the storm rattled the windows during the night, and the old room creaked at every joint, one was inclined to believe in ghosts. This fantasy was heightened still further next morning when in the grey dawn light a white-haired woman glided through the room, like the ancestress of the castle, and brought early-morning tea. Without a word she left the room, as she had come, with hardly a sound, and only the steaming tea showed that it could not have been a castle ghost after all. The view from the window was unforgettable. In the park grazed some thirty horses in the misty morning light; some had spent the night in the open air and were later caught and saddled for the pupils who came there to ride.

Organization of the famous show was perfect to the last detail under the direction of its elderly President, Judge Wylie, who ruled his workers with a rod of iron. But he said with a smile, "In competitions I am a dictator!" and so I found out when my horses did not arrive for the dress rehearsal. He ordered the band to play, and instructed me to walk the course from the stadium gate to the ring, where I was to give my exhibition ride, so that the music and the rider should combine perfectly. When I said that I should be quicker galloping than on foot he silenced me abruptly.

"Who says you will come galloping into the ring? You will walk in!" And he took no notice at all of my remark that this might be rather tedious, merely saying, "You must give the spectators a chance to watch you in peace, and that is only possible if you walk. I know my public."

The national competition was part of the annual Agricultural Show. The ground, in summer used for the great international jumping contests, lies in the centre of the exhibition district of Ballsbridge, on the outskirts of Dublin. Surrounded by halls and paddocks, in which the classification of the animals takes place, the riding ring, completely closed in by tiers of seats and high fences, gives the impression of being a complete world of its own. Carefully kept turf, which is allowed to be trodden on by horses only twice a year, at the Spring Show and the International Horse Show, stretches like a soft green velvet carpet over the spacious arena, and seems to muffle any shouting. The barrier in front of the spectators consists of a hedge of flowers of all kinds, blending together like a symphony of colour. When I rode for the first time on to the then virgin turf it was the best natural ground that I had ever trodden, truly worthy of this horses' paradise.

The exhibition of cattle, agricultural products and machines was, as always, a national holiday in Ireland, and drew a noticeably larger crowd than the International Horse Show. Mingling with the business representatives were landowners, horse-breeders, and country people who daily filled the stands. The gate this year was a record one of 169,000.

The flower exhibits and animals made the greatest impression on me of the entire show. The rarest blooms had been massed together with remarkable taste into a unique garden in one of the huge halls, providing a wonderful scent and sight. But among the animals we saw quite unknown breeds of cattle with stocky bodies and short legs, intended solely for meat production, and the most striking thing was their condition when they entered the ring. We Austrians, and the Spanish Riding School in particular, pride ourselves on the care we give to our horses, and have always believed it unsurpassed, but what I saw here in the way of animal care really put our tremendous efforts in the shade. Early in the morning the animals were washed—often completely covered with suds—then brushed and combed, the hair was clipped, then finally their coats were rubbed with oil to get a good shine. The prize animal was then always shown in the ring before the individual events.

The national competition included, as well as the various classes for hacks, the main competitions over the famous jumps, classified in a most extraordinary and controversial manner. Jumping skill varied widely and could not be compared with the style on the Continent. The national characteristic style of riding was retained here, though England, greatly to her advantage, was beginning to abandon it; there were several unattractive scenes with riders struggling with their horses, themselves executing almost acrobatic movements as they cleared the jumps. It was remarkable that these riders, who, God knows, did not treat their horses gently on the course, tugging unmercifully at the reins, and with bits not unlike instruments of torture, should tell me they did not approve of dressage because it was too cruel and a session meant suffering for the horses. From this I realized at once what points I must emphasize when I rode my horses to demonstrate the absurdity of these fallacies.

The entire ground was always very crowded. When I prepared my horses I used an enclosure kept free for me and this was always quickly surrounded by a mass of spectators. My riding attracted the people like a magnet, and as soon as I was summoned by loudspeaker to make my entry quite a stream of people made for the stands, which were completely filled. The organizers later confirmed that the places filled up as soon as I appeared on the ground.

I had to take up an unseen position before the high gate until a fanfare heralded my entrance. Then the announcer gave a concise explanation of the horsemanship that I should be displaying, and at the words "Colonel Podhajsky" the gate opened, and I had to come on to the grass and stand still until I was introduced to the public with some brief details about myself and my riding career.

Then the fanfare sounded again and I rode at a walking pace to the arena prepared for my performance. The quietness and precision of my horse's pace, undisturbed by any nervousness, made a strong impression on the very knowledgeable spectators. After the preliminary applause there was complete silence, and I executed my programme to Irish marches and waltzes played by the Guards Band, which provided the best orchestral accompaniment I have ever had. The conductor adapted his tempo exactly to the rhythm of my horses, because he was a rider himself. On Pluto Theodorosta I concentrated on the airs of the *haute école*, but without neglecting the basic steps, and left the ring in the *passage*. On Teja, on the other hand, I emphasized more the freer airs, but also showed the *piaffe* and *passage*, then leaving the ring at a gallop with a slack rein, thereby convincing the last doubter of the value of dressage.

My success was manifested in many ways. Even the President, normally cool and matter of-fact, openly showed his enthusiasm and proudly introduced me to all the important people in political and business life. I became a popular figure; people who knew me offered me their places in crowded restaurants, and the waiters looked after me marvellously, particularly an elderly cavalryman, who watched each of my performances closely, and showed me pictures of himself on horseback. I had one pleasant experience when I went on a free day in ordinary clothes into a Dublin shop to buy something. When the bill was made out I saw that I had not enough money on me and asked the assistant to keep the parcel for me, but the proprietor begged me to take it with me there and then and pay him the rest later. When I asked him in astonishment why he was so trusting he answered, "Everybody knows you; the whole of Dublin is talking of nothing but you as the rider in black and white." (I rode in a black riding-jacket and top-hat on a white horse.)

In addition to the many glowing notices in the Irish Press I received via the Foreign Office and Ministry of Agriculture a letter from Judge Wylie that ended, "The greater part of our record gate is due to you. You have done a great deal to encourage the love of riding in Ireland."

I had also made many new friends over there, who raved about my performances for years and brought Austria nearer to the somewhat remote people of the Emerald Isle.

On the return journey we visited our friends Colonel and Mrs Williams in England. As I was going through passport formalities at the airport the apparently unapproachable official looked at me, studied my passport with an inscrutable face, and said, "It's wonderful that you saved the Lipiz-zaner!"

Very surprised, I asked him what he knew about them.

"More than you think. Don't imagine that checking passports is my whole pleasure in life. In my free time I also do some riding, and as a rider I have been following with great interest your efforts to preserve the Lipiz-zaner!"

An account of this trip would not be complete without my mentioning an interlude on the way home. My horses, which for days had been the centre of interest and been tremendously spoilt, obviously found the journey in the somewhat dreary boxes of the French State Railways irritating, and were downright restless at the unaccustomed rattling and banging. For a time they allowed themselves to be soothed by the groom, until Pluto Theodorosta found it all too much, broke free, and began to thrash about so wildly that the man could only save himself by flight. He squeezed through a narrow crack, shut the door again, and, standing on the footboard, tried to attract the attention of the guard, which he managed to do at last. The train had to be stopped while the horses were calmed down again, and at the next station the box was changed. Luckily, except for a few slight scratches, the horses were not hurt at all.

I, on the other hand, had a wonderful and unforgettable return journey. Inwardly content with my success, the satisfaction of a task well done, and the echo of the praise I had received, I enjoyed spring for the third time that year. When I had left Wels it was still cold and unfriendly. In southern Switzerland, however, spring had already made her entrance and delighted the human eye with the splendour of her flowers. In Dublin the trees were already in bloom, and now in my homeland a wealth of blossom greeted me. Could there be a lovelier homecoming?

At the beginning of June the Spanish Riding School embarked on its first tour of Germany after the Second World War. This was in many respects of great importance. With the dispatch of the Spanish Riding School the first cultural links were once more forged between these two states with so much in common, and thus began the breaking down of the barrier that had been unnaturally erected in 1945 between two countries with the same language. The tour had, moreover, another purpose: to give the necessary impetus to the sport in Germany, for it had been introduced by teachers from both countries. It must now be lifted as quickly and steadily as possible from the depths into which it had sunk with the country's collapse.

In the years immediately preceding and during the War the school had excited interest among a very large number of German riders and had succeeded in winning many friends, who in their hearts had never for-gotten the old academy, in spite of the turbulent events of the last decade and the bitterness of present want. Now it had to prove itself to the Germans, and on its return demonstrate that the white horses had not lost their extraordinary, almost magical, power. Expectations were undoubtedly very high!

We shall never forget our return to German soil. We were received with indescribable cordiality and at the same time welcomed as a symbol of the culture that had been preserved for Europe. Words are much too poor to describe all the emotions that assailed us or to tell how many old friends of the Spanish Riding School had tears in their eyes when they saw their darlings again and stroked them, as if to convince themselves that the living animals truly stood before them.

These warm human relationships contrasted sharply with the other conditions. Up to now we had in every country had all necessities found for us, but here we discovered that we were much better off in Austria than in Germany in spite of all our prevailing shortages. Our accommodation was very much simpler than at previous festivals, and what was considered comfortable was, by Austrian standards, very poor. From the ruins of Germany the normal conditions of a civilized land could only very gradually emerge.

Overshadowing all else, however, was the eagerness to give us the very best; the Lipizzaner were taken to the Mummschen Villa in Frankfurt-am-Main, where the mounted police had to vacate some of their stabling. What an example of hospitality!

Our performances on the fairground formed part of the Horse Show at the touring exhibition of the German Agriculture Society. The arena seemed poor and bare, and a layer of sand had to be spread over the much too hard ground before the Spanish Riding School could use it. But, as there were no sprinklers available, the rising wind whirled the sand about in clouds of dust. On huge flagstaffs fluttered the flags of the various states of the West German Federation, and leading the foreigners the red, white and red flag. This attempt at festive decoration of the very unsuitable ground was somewhat spoilt by countless advertisements.

In contrast to the setting was the incredible support given to the competitions by riders and horses from all corners of the Republic. There were even a large number of carts drawn by two or more horses, and the turn-out of the drivers, animals, and vehicles hid the still numerous deficiencies; but compared with the spring, even the riders had changed for the better. The converted uniforms were now used for exercising and warming up horses, but the riders once more appeared in public in black or scarlet coats. The exceptionally large numbers of visitors who filled all the seats and standing room—the papers spoke of a daily attendance of five thousand— emphasized the German people's old love of riding, for there were many of the spectators who had gone short of food to save their entrance money.

A further proof of the great love of horses was the preparation of two horse-boxes for the Lipizzaner, since "we could not expect the white stallions to walk for an hour to get to the ground." In Zurich they had had to make just as long a journey on foot on a paved surface! But in Frankfurt, where Heaven knows there were plenty of essential things to be done, care for the horses was not pushed to the bottom of the list.

The reception given to the Spanish Riding School outstripped our wildest expectations. Certainly we were acclaimed in every country, but here an atmosphere of admiration and enthusiasm surrounded us, putting all our previous successes into the shade, although we had thought often that we could not better them. People pressed round me when I dismounted just to shake my hand fervently in gratitude, and the policeman whose duty it was to keep the space clear for the Spanish Riding School could not stop them.

One day when I was making a rapid change—I took part with Pluto Theodorosta in several dressage trials in civilian clothes—my physician from Bad Nauheim, Dr Wachter, came to see me. He held my hand for a long time, and stammered, his voice filled with emotion, "That I should have lived to see you ride again and ride like that!" In a letter he sent later to Wels he begged me to take half as much care of my heart as I did of my horses.

We had performances in Frankfurt on five consecutive days. On the third day the sky grew dark and threatening during the programme, and I tried in vain to get on the telephone to the organizers, to suggest that the performance should be cancelled because of the approaching storm. With an anxious heart I stood in the ring at the head of the school quadrille and sent up an urgent prayer to Heaven to keep off the thunder for twenty minutes more, but we had barely broken into a trot after the salute before a gust of wind swept through the arena and amid screams from the spectators tore off one of the awnings over the stands. The rain came down in torrents, and the tightly packed spectators began to flee from the ground. Now I had to decide in a matter of seconds what we were to do. We had walked in ceremonial step towards our admiring public, doffed our cocked hats with a flourish by way of salute, and were now faced with a choice of rushing away with the spectators like wet poodles or carrying on in spite of the weather. I decided on the latter course, and gave my riders a sign to begin the quadrille.

I shall never forget the effect of this decision on the public. The fugitives halted when they saw the white horses quite undisturbed by the merciless cloudburst, turned back to their places, and overwhelmed us with cheers and deafening applause.

The weather had not finished, however; after the streaming rain followed a sharp hailstorm. The gallant Lipizzaner willingly followed their riders' commands, though perhaps the way they all shook their heads to protect their ears was not so much for this purpose as in mild wonderment at the unusual conditions under which they were expected to show their grace and beauty. It was obviously their endurance and efforts that made even the terrifying god of the weather change his mind, for as we moved in the *passage* into the closing phase of the quadrille a few shy sunbeams pierced the dark sky and harmonized, as it were, with the clamorous cheers around us.

The effect of this wet ride was tremendous, and it was a proud day for the Spanish Riding School, for one paper wrote that the Lipizzaner executing the figures of the quadrille in the hail recalled the days of Prince Eugène when, in spite of a raging storm the victory had been won. As I left the ring a young man ran up to me and called out, "Thank you, Colonel, for showing that we Austrians will not be beaten either. I am an Austrian living here in Germany and am so proud of this impressive performance by the Spanish Riding School."

A lady pressed my hand and said, "What we have just seen was like a promise for the cultural life of Europe. True art must overcome all storms and bad weather, and the sunbeams which at the end stroked the wet coats of the Lipizzaner meant that, after the deepest humiliation and darkness, light returns to us once again."

The practical results of this quadrille, described as a "keen ride," were, however, less happy. We could hardly strip off our soaked chamois leather trousers, and drying uniforms and saddle-cloths was the problem next day, in spite of the sunshine; since we had become the most fêted figures of the Show we manfully disguised even these discomforts. One of the flood of newspaper articles will serve to round off the picture of our first festival visit to Germany after eleven years.

The *Frankfurter Rundschau* of June 15 said:

> The quadrille gave one the impression that the porcelain in a giant shop window had come to artistic life. Yet these are no fragile figures, but superb, robust stallions, shining white and with intelligent heads and legs. . . Ballet is an understatement. It is a magical feast for the eyes, grace and effortless strength, a complete fusion of man and horse. Not merely horsemanship comparable with a work of art, but the highest equestrian culture.

After the final performance in Frankfurt the horses were entrained and taken on to Hamburg. I myself, although I was not recognized on my journey thither, heard many complimentary remarks about the Spanish Riding School's appearances, and was really astounded and delighted over our success.

In the Hanseatic city a fitting welcome had been prepared for the old Vienna Riding School. The joy over our arrival was not restricted to Platonic endearments. Members of the Flottbeker Riding Society put their horse-boxes at our disposal so that the Lipizzaner could be transported comfortably all together, heroically undertaking to transfer their own treasures for the period of our stay to less good stabling.

The buildings in Klein-Flottbek showed signs of the unshakable resolution of the residents of the Waterkant to build, although they had suffered so severely from bombing raids: only a few years after the end of the holocaust a badly damaged riding-hall was restored, and beautiful airy stables were erected close by. In the city, too, one was aware of the pulsating life everywhere, and in the Alster in the heart of the city there was barely a trace of the destruction of the last war. But the road out of the centre to Klein-Flottbek passed through incalculable devastation where buildings had been razed to the ground. The rubble from the houses had been cleared away, it is true, but even so it gave one an idea of the boundless suffering endured by many hundreds of thousands of people.

Some of our performances were given in the Flottbek Riding Hall, which had only limited room for spectators, and some on the traditional Springderby ground, the event having been staged here for the first time thirty years earlier. Whereas in the modern bare-looking hall the wealth of bloom created the right atmosphere for a horse-loving and rapturous audience, outside it was the trees that provided an impressive background. We riders of the Spanish Riding School were so pampered that each managed by cheerful individual effort to demonstrate his maximum skill.

The first performance was given in the riding hall before invited guests, and was repeated the next evening for the general public, attracting so many spectators that there was room for only a very small proportion of them. But the organization, particularly the control of the entrance, worked magnificently in spite of the crowd. The students posted there took their duties so seriously that they even prevented me from getting in, because I happened not to have my pass on me. Even when I opened my coat to prove by my riding-boots and white leather breeches that I belonged to the Spanish Riding School, one young man told me that he could only let in people with valid tickets or passes. I had to wait until an official, seeing my predicament, allowed me to get to my horses.

And these performances and the parts of our programme shown at the Springderby ground between the individual riding events were just as enthusiastically received, although the clerk of the weather was not as kind as he might have been.

I also took part in the big dressage events on Pluto Theodorosta, and tied for first place with Willy Schultheis on Pernod. As it is usual for the winner of this event to give his programme before the general public two arenas were prepared for us side by side so that we could carry out our tasks simultaneously.

This afforded a magnificent opportunity to compare the two horses, and

I too found this most interesting. In the trotting I noticed that Pluto Theodorosta far surpassed the thoroughbred Pernod in impulsion and adaptation of his step, and Schultheis would have to exert himself to pick up lost ground, particularly in the repetition of the extended trot, although I had as usual taken my corners very precisely, which could certainly not be said of my companion. But I had made my mind up that in the canter Pernod with his thoroughbred dash would leave my Lipizzaner far behind, and was astonished when this did not happen even in the extended canter on the diagonal, and the action of the Lipizzaner was able to hold its own against that of the thoroughbred. From the point of view of schooling this discovery gave me particular joy and satisfaction.

The climax of our tour was undoubtedly the floodlit evening performance on the Springderby ground. The whole day had been cool and showery, but towards evening the sky lightened, and by ten o'clock there were such crowds streaming towards Klein-Flottbek that the ground could not accommodate them all. Twenty thousand people had already got into the ground, the tickets were all sold, and there were still masses of people milling around the gates. But enthusiasm can reach such a stage that it seizes at means that would normally be prohibited; in several places the crush barriers were broken, and the people who had vainly tried to get in at the gates forced their way into the ground.

The show turned out to be one of our greatest triumphs so far. The respectful silence during the actual performance was broken by frenzied applause at the end of the separate items, and put us all into a cheerful and happy mood, which spurred us on to still greater efforts.

It is a wonderful feeling to be able to bring thousands of people under your spell and fill them with such excitement! When we drew up in front of the V.I.P. box after the quadrille and were given flowers to the accompaniment of prolonged applause, there was scarcely a single rider of the old school whose eyes were not glistening or brimming with tears. As we rode round the arena for the last time the spectators broke through on to the grass and came up close enough at least to touch the horses. At the same time they kept on calling out to us, "You must come again," and followed us to the stables. A lovely day ending fittingly on a great triumph.

The papers devoted whole pages to "fairy-tale horses from Vienna," "the joyous dancing horses," "the ballet of the white stallions," and "the festive hours with the Lipizzaner."

The farewell evening in the Hotel Atlantic was a big social occasion, where, for the first time since the Second World War, I saw full evening dress in Germany. Dr Rau, the much-respected Equerry paid special tribute to the Spanish Riding School by presenting me with the Golden Spurs of the Central Commisson for horsemanship. I was only the third to receive this high honour.

Our first tour in Germany had stirred the feelings of the sorely tried population to the depths, as I learned from countless letters long after we returned home.

Spiritually uplifted and richly rewarded, we returned from our festival tour to our much less attractive surroundings in exile. The echo of our successes and the memory of the reverberating cheers of the excited people compensated somewhat for the primitive conditions of our temporary home, and gave us an unexpected fillip and the urge to work at the noble art of riding with still greater fervour. Thus were laid the foundations of the preparations for our big American tour.

Before what was undoubtedly the most significant post-War experience of the Spanish Riding School the 1950 performances in Salzburg saw the fulfilment of a plan that had been mooted a long time before.

The conditions prevailing in Austria after the Second World War ended resulted in a noticeable transfer of the cultural events of international importance to the western part of our country. The Salzburg Festival, which already in the twenties had aroused world-wide interest and had not been disrupted by the deep political waters since 1938 nor the war years, carried on straight away in 1945 under its old flag. It became of exceptional importance, the more so because of further cultural extensions.

This had been in my mind from the beginning in my efforts to locate fertile soil for the Spanish Riding School, and as far back as spring 1946 the first discussions about an appearance in the festival city took place. Colonel Paul von Matić-Dravodol, at one time in my regiment and a very good friend, who as Squadron Commander had since given a strong impetus to riding in Salzburg, took exceptional trouble to arrange for performances by the Spanish Riding School in the Felsenreitschule, now restored to its former glory. Our idea found unanimous support from the authorities, including the Landeshauptmann and the President of the festival, but carrying it out involved almost insuperable difficulties. The Provincial Government wanted the financial risk of our undertaking to be borne by the Ministry of Agriculture in Vienna, but this department announced that it was not interested in sending the Spanish Riding School on those terms. To a certain extent this attitude was quite understandable, for in 1931 and 1932 the school had finished its festival seasons in the Felsenreitschule with a quite considerable deficit.

It took years of effort before our united wish was at last fulfilled, for Colonel Matić, as President of the Salzburg branch of the Österreichische Compagnereitergesellschaft, was responsible for the invitation and the whole organization of the visit. Unfortunately we could no longer use the Felsenreitschule as a certain amount of reconstruction had been done and it was now unsuitable for riding displays, so the performance had to be given on a football ground, not exactly a perfect setting, in spite of the

Feste Hohensalzburg in the background. But the Lipizzaner so recently acclaimed in Germany managed to project their charm even in this prosaic
place, and so to enchant the spectators and make them forget their surroundings, and everything on that grassy carpet but the dance of the white
horses.

The tumultuous applause from the pampered public—there was a large
and select audience of Austrians and foreigners—showed the extent of the
triumph, and the Austrian Press demanded in long articles that the appearance of the Spanish Riding School should become a regular feature of the
Salzburg Festival.

In fact, we did appear for five years running in the festival city until our
return to Vienna, and each time our performances showed a considerable
profit, which was of real value in promoting the sport of riding in Salzburg.

The Spanish Riding School made a farewell appearance before thousands
of spectators, predominantly country folk from Upper Austria at the Wels
Volksfest before embarking on their long journey to the New World. The
enthusiasm of our own countrymen and the many good wishes that the
excited crowds shouted after us as we left the ground gave us courage for our
new undertaking.

The *Wiener Zeitung* wrote a long article, which said among other things:

> If Colonel Podhajsky with his riders and Lipizzaner do undertake the
> voyage across the sea at this time as representatives in the New World of a
> part of Austria it is absolutely certain that he with his refined skill in horse-
> manship will show this gigantic country with all its technical progress some-
> thing that is unique.

Thus the echo of our last appearances in the Old World served as a good
omen for the great task that lay before us.

CHAPTER 13

The Lipizzaner captivate America

G eneral Patton had been so delighted with the white horses that he intended to show his countrymen the Spanish Riding School by means of a long tour through the United States, and was even ready to be responsible for the necessary expenditure. His sudden death at first put an end to this project, but it was not forgotten. Various interested parties kept returning to it, until in 1949 an official invitation for 1950 gave it tangible form.

The Horse Association of America and the Royal Agricultural Winter Fair in Toronto, Canada, invited the Spanish Riding School to give an exhibition of the classic art of horsemanship at the three big international riding events of 1950 in Harrisburg, New York, and Toronto. For the first time the oldest riding academy in the world, with eight riders, fourteen horses, and four grooms, set foot outside Europe. This fact in itself was a milestone in the eventful history of the school, and the tour gave the Spanish Riding School the opportunity of thanking the American people for the help of one of her greatest sons, who had done it an inestimable service through his quick thinking in the memorable days of 1945. The farther we moved away from the days of surrender, the more obvious became the part the American Army Chief had played in the preservation of this essential item of European culture. It was undoubtedly due to him that the Lipizzaner stud returned from Czechoslovakia to Austria, saving the bloodstock for the school and thus ensuring its continued existence. The fact that we were already using some of the horses returned from Czechoslovakia in 1945 on the foreign festival tours shows how important his decisions at that time were to be for the Spanish Riding School.

On the first overseas trip, however, it still had another mission to fulfil: to make propaganda for our little country, once a centre of culture in

Europe, and of the art of horsemanship cultivated there for hundreds of years. The Spanish Riding School must prove by its performances that the European method of riding developed over many years could still claim to be the best; a tremendous task, for the New World had also worked out its own style of riding.

I need hardly say that this trip involved a vast amount of preparation. It was intended that riders and horses should travel to the United States on the same ship, but unfortunately, this was not possible, as the *American Importer* could take only four attendants. This was a nuisance for during the long crossing the fourteen horses would have to be fed, groomed, and exercised every day if they were to arrive in America in good condition. The ship had to be fitted with separate boxes for its valuable cargo, and some means of exercising the horses on board had to be arranged. Early in September 1950 fourteen Lipizzaner stallions left Wels by rail and were taken on board the *American Importer* at Bremen. The shipment of the horses aroused great public interest, radio and Press reporters following the proceedings and trying to give their hearers and readers the fullest possible details of the first transatlantic journey of the Lipizzaner. These went rather suspiciously one by one into the special box prepared for them, and with curiosity or uneasiness allowed two safety belts to be buckled on, bowing their heads as the crane hoisted up the crate with a jerk; as they hung suspended they saw their companions already on board and began to neigh loudly. This whole procedure was really a sight for the gods and attracted a great many curious spectators.

The Lipizzaner had settled down fairly well by the time the freighter sailed. Unfortunately, the ship had engine trouble even before it reached England, and had to be taken into London Dock, where the horses had to remain on board because of quarantine regulations. The repairs took twelve days, with the horses taking their short daily walk in the restricted space between the boxes. Some thoroughbred mares were also taken on board at the last moment, and this badly upset the now rested stallions. The walks between the boxes were no longer possible, and careful arrangements had to be made to prevent the fiery Lipizzaner seeing the "beautiful creatures."

The voyage to America was an unfamiliar experience for the riders, for at that time few Austrians were accustomed to making a luxurious crossing in the *Washington* and leading for a few days the life of international travellers. I myself flew to New York by Scandinavian Airlines from Munich via Frankfurt, Hamburg, Glasgow, and Gander. The shortness of travelling time was impressive when one thought that the riders had taken six days and the horses eighteen days, while the aircraft, after its last landing in England, crossed the ocean in one flight of ten hours. Having travelled many thousands of miles on horseback, I had the disturbing and distressing thought, as I considered this gigantic technical achievement, that as a rider I was perhaps a representative of a passing generation. This idea was, however, dispelled in America, where I saw the happy combination of the most modern achievements with riding.

The journeys of the three parties were so arranged that they would arrive at much the same time, but the events on the *American Importer* rather upset this plan.

When I landed on September 19 at Idlewild Airport I was received by representatives of the Horse Association, the acting Austrian Consul, Dr Helmut Leitner, and reporters. These last monopolized me, so that I had hardly time for greetings, and met for the first time one of the most familiar American sayings: "Keep smiling!" The photographers did not want a serious face, but a friendly smile. Soon I learned also the second watchword, "Take it easy!" though this is not always apt, for the constant bustle to which the people of this part of the world are subjected makes this maxim anything but easy to follow.

The day after my arrival the big dailies showed pictures of my reception at the airport, with detailed articles of welcome. Since the Press in America has a vast circulation this warm reception was widely publicized.

Because of the delayed arrival of the horses in New York I had several days to spare, which, apart from the interviews that had been arranged, I was able to spend in taking a look at the New World for myself. The Sonnenbergs, with whom we had become friendly, helped to open up this strange world to us.

The first impression of New York is overpowering. The skyscrapers, which one imagines would be cold monsters hemming one in, somehow fit into the general picture and do not seem so gigantic flanking the wide streets, and it is astonishing how quickly after leaving the city by one of the highways one reaches such wonderful surroundings. Above all we noticed the absence of pedestrians. If anybody is walking about enjoying the lovely ordered scenery of the Westchester countryside the inhabitants say jokingly that he must be European.

There are, however, plenty of men and women to be seen taking their exercise in long rides, enjoying the beauties of Nature. Since in America the sport is not restricted to the 'upper ten' I had to get used to the unfamiliar sight of riders concerning themselves as much over their appearance as their riding. In spite of widespread mechanization and the disappearance of horses from the Army, people have retained a desire for and enjoyment of riding, two factors that provide the best conditions for building up the sport. So there, just as in England, where in spite of the breaking up of many private establishments the number of riders had markedly increased, there is a very strong horse-loving public, and it is noticeable in the U.S.A. as in England that in the main it is women and

40. *Caprioles* by Neapolitano Santuzza: Stockholm, 1952

41. The Majesty of an Ancient Breed: Pluto Theodorosta, 1955

children who enjoy riding, because, as I was jokingly told, the man has to earn money to pay for his family's hobbies.

Riding in America had many more styles than in Europe, having developed from different tradition. The vast prairies of the West, with their herds of many thousands of horses and cattle, have created the cowboy, the daring natural rider, who controls his horse by force, 'breaks it in,' to use the technical term. This type of riding, which is demonstrated in rodeos, is not for those with weak nerves and sensitive souls, and is also not particularly economical, for the animal that tries to regain its former freedom has two choices: bend or break.

The horse, once it can be ridden, has to help in rounding up the cattle, and from this rodeos developed in the West, but gradually spreading throughout America and Canada. Originating from the practical demands of life, they demonstrate also how tremendously riding is influenced by a country's tradition, just as dressage riding in Europe owes its development to the customs of chivalry, where riders in individual combat demanded special manœuvrability and dexterity from their horses.

Later, when the rider wanted to be carried across country, hunting emerged and, as a further development, jumping. In the early days of American history individual combat on horseback as it was practised in Europe was never necessary. Here it was much more important to put the many wild horses to use, and, if they could no longer tackle their work, to change them for others. This idea lies behind the whole structure of the rodeo.

Each year several hundred such events take place, ending with the big rodeo in Madison Square Garden, in New York, which is for the championship of the United States. I had a chance to see the twenty-fifth rodeo in New York, which, both in lay-out and cruelty, reminded me in spite of myself of a bullfight. This equestrian festival opened with a colourful parade of all the participants, which numbered some hundreds. Horses of every possible colour, including the modern Palomino, a pale buff, had, in the Western manner, richly ornamented bridles and saddles. The riders in picturesque cowboy and cowgirl clothes wore long bright trousers or jackets, with bright silk scarves, huge golden spurs and, of course, large cowboy hats.

This parade, during which the most successful cowboys and cowgirls of the separate states were introduced through the loudspeaker, was followed by three hours of very varied events, the breaking-in of saddled and unsaddled horses, the riding of steers, the catching and roping of calves and young steers, with a quadrille ridden by cowboys and cowgirls, and the High School of the famous Number One Cowboy, Gene Autry, who displayed his white stallion in a fair imitation of *haute école* and circus tricks, and sang sentimental songs. Gene Autry is reputed to have become a millionaire through performing at rodeos and riding for films and television.

To get the horses to buck their girths were put round their flanks and fastened very tight. The poor animals leaped with fright and tried to unseat their riders. These wild struggles between animal and man are quite unfamiliar to us, and I cannot say that I got any pleasure from the spectacle, but there are very many people in America also who avoid this kind of riding display. When one sees how the horses leap clear off the ground with pain, or how terrified calves often cannot stand up again when they are untied, or how the young steers stagger out of the arena, their heads hanging sideways after being mastered by humans, there is very little to choose between rodeos and the highly controversial bullfights. This spectacle causes the public to stamp its feet and scream with delight.

The thought that in about a fortnight, in the same Madison Square Garden, I was to show my Lipizzaner with their controlled and measured movements to this excitable public was not a particularly agreeable one, and it raised in me very serious doubts as to whether the Spanish Riding School would really succeed in the New World.

But the horses were still on the high seas, and so I had a short breathing-space for sightseeing, for I realized that I should have no free hours once the Lipizzaner arrived and the performances started. The reality surpassed all my expectations, for my obligations in connexion with the Horse Show utterly exhausted me, and there was no possible question of "taking it easy."

In the meantime the riders arrived in New York on September 30 after their luxurious crossing in the *Washington*, and were welcomed by representatives of the Horse Association, the Consul General, and the Press. The group was photographed, names and ages of each individual taken, and they were repeatedly told not to look so serious, but "happy," for they must not forget the famous watchword "Keep smiling."

A few days later the *American Importer*, with its valuable cargo, the long-awaited horses, tied up at the New York pier. Once more all the officials had made arrangements to give a specially festive air, so the riders put on their traditional uniforms. I was glad to see that the horses had stood the voyage well, and greeted the people from the other side of the globe with joyful faces.

The first impression made by our gallant Lipizzaner in the New World was an excellent one, everybody present being just as astonished at their freshness after their long and in part very stormy voyage as at their wonderfully polite manner and boundless faith in human beings. Newspaper reporters, television, and newsreels saw to it that the whole of America quickly learned of the arrival of the world-famous Spanish Riding School.

The horses were taken direct from the dock in the most modern motorized horse-boxes to Rye, a lovely part of New York in the Westchester district, where there was good stabling with American experts who came daily to our morning work and watched the training of the horses with close interest. Among the daily visitors were also many refugees from all parts of Europe, who often came from far away to cheer themselves up with a sight of European riding culture. For them the dear white Lipizzaner were more than animal artists; they represented, so to speak, a greeting from the old country. Many of them greeted us as compatriots, although they had only recently arrived from Czechoslovakia, Hungary, or Galicia; in America they felt like Austrians again.

The resumption of the training interrupted through the four weeks' voyage was a major problem, for to give the horses plenty of chance to become acclimatized I wanted to begin with short periods of work and gradually increase them. I got the surprise of my life, however, for the stallions were high-spirited, forgetting all their schooling, and made it difficult for their riders to avoid kissing American soil quite against their will—which would certainly have raised a hullabaloo among the spectators. They were just the same the second day, so I realized that the strength of my Lipizzaner was unimpaired and seized on a universal remedy: high spirits are best quelled by plenty of work, so by the third day we were already doing full and normal training. Since the Lipizzaner had not actually forgotten anything they had learnt I was able by the fourth day to agree to a film being made for the newsreels and Press photographs taken. To simplify matters all those interested were invited to a sort of Press photographers' reception.

I was aware that the free Press in a democratic land is of great importance, but I had never dreamt that its omnipotence could reach such proportions. In America, of course, everything is gigantic and larger than life. More than fifty selected people of very varied temperaments appeared with photographic gear and film cameras, well-nigh tearing me, my riders, and horses to pieces, for each wanted to see a different step from a different angle. The fastidious wanted *levades*, *caprioles*, and other difficult exercises on a conveyer-belt; some shouted to us to come here, while others wanted us on the opposite side of the ground. I tried to bring this mass of gesticulating and screaming people to some kind of order and reconcile their various requests. And, believe me, I succeeded; even the most insistent did what I told them, the reporters were satisfied, and the horses spared as much as possible, but it took several hours before the greatest reportage of the Spanish Riding School up to that time was complete. And once again opinions were expressed in superlatives. The strips for the newsreels were shown with texts in twenty-six different languages, and the combined Press of the United States and Canada provided with a generous supply of pictures. This was publicity such as they rarely afford a presentation of this kind.

This mass taking of photographs was not without its comic side. One snapshot showed a *Bereiter* in a *capriole* having rather lost both his balance and his cocked hat; this venerable headgear floated, like a juggler's master-piece, on end above the rider's head. This so bewitched the journalists that they preferred this picture to any number of others showing *caprioles* correctly executed. A magazine even chose it for its cover picture, to the not inconsiderable annoyance of the subject, who tore up the publication as often as he could lay his hands on it—only to find on his bedside table that evening another copy bought by his companions.

A week later the first performance was given with a reception for the Press, attended by the Presidents of the three organizations in Harrisburg, New York, and Toronto, along with the reporters of the most important dailies and many prominent members of American riding circles and of society—our first appearance in America before the critical eyes of those responsible for the tour. We showed a complete programme, and were able to gather from the applause during the performance itself and then from the enthusiastic Press notices that the Spanish Riding School had brilliantly won its first battle in the New World. But how would the broad masses of the public, the deciding factor in the attendance and therefore in the success of the Horse Show, receive a display of the embodiment of a high equestrian culture comparable only to ballet? This open question exercised the organizers and myself equally, for when I considered the nature of the rodeos, where in the dangerous breakneck riding of wild horses and steers the primary consideration was sensation for the spectators, I was compelled to ask myself whether the presentation of a highly developed art of riding with no breathtaking highlights would be understood at all.

But, indeed, I had little time for reflection, for with the arrival of the horses and the start of work in Rye the pulsating life of America had laid a thorough hold on me. Interviews with the organizers, receptions in connexion with the Horse Show, Press interviews, talks on radio and television, followed one another without a pause. In the vastness of New York these duties meant repeated dashes by car from one end of the city to another, a constant changing of clothes, and so forth, so that by the end of the day I was really tired already, but it was not until the evening that the many social functions really started, and these are of great importance over there.

My first experience of television, at that time not so widely known in Europe, was almost a tragicomedy for me. For the first interview of my life the time of the broadcast, which was intended to last six minutes, was precisely fixed beforehand. But I had almost to cross New York from end to end to get to the studio, and was very nervous because of the traffic that was holding us up. My companion calmed me down—"take it easy"—saying that all the details would be discussed carefully before the broadcast. The receptionist at the studio received us in great agitation and whispered to me that I was on next, and because I was late the broadcast would only last three minutes. Preparatory discussions or rehearsals were naturally quite out of the question; with his finger to his lips he signed to me to keep silent, held three fingers before my eyes to emphasize the shortened period of time, and gave me a sign to walk within range of the camera.

What a dreadful situation! The studio, in a huge room, seemed at first glance to be utter chaos, cameras everywhere, several revolving stages and several rows of spectators against the walls. I now stood in the merciless floodlights opposite a gorgeous television star, and suddenly became conscious not only of the eyes of those present, but also of the millions of New Yorkers looking at me, and subjecting my behaviour and words to severe criticism. And, to make it worse, the conversation was in a foreign language without any preparation! Not knowing how noticeable my discomfiture was, I struggled to master even this situation, and when my partner asked if she might try on my cocked hat I remembered that some one had told me of an American custom where the woman who tried on a man's hat had to give him a kiss. I drew her attention to this condition as I handed over my hat, and she answered with a smile, "What a lot you know already about America!" But as she handed back my hat she came right up to me and said, "I am an American and keep up my country's traditions!" and kissed me firmly. The interview had lasted ten minutes, because the producer, who put his arm round me afterwards and congratulated me, enjoyed it so much. A few weeks later a fashion paper brought out a design for a woman's hat based on the shape of the traditional cocked hat with the caption "Model hat *à la Podhajsky*."

Among the many interviews a discussion with the editor of *New Yorker* was of special importance. This magazine has, of course, a reputation for handling every subject with brilliant satire, and is often feared by society for its comments, which often border on biting ridicule. I saw facing me a somewhat surly man, accustomed to achieving his object by the shortest possible route. He told me at once that so much information had already been given about the Spanish Riding School that he did not intend to cover the same ground, but the school had a soul to which it owed everything, and about this soul—he meant me—too little had been written, so that he wanted to remedy this deficiency. I had to give him full details of my career, and when his article appeared under the heading "Dressage Expert" those familiar with this magazine were astounded to find it an article without mordant irony, if anything slightly flattering.

After the first performance of the complete programme in Rye, as had hitherto always been done abroad, the three presidents fixed the order for the coming public performances. "All the gaits and turns of the *haute école*" were to be demonstrated by me, "Airs above the Ground," and, in conclusion, the big school quadrille. These three items must be carried out in quick succession without pause in twenty-five minutes, time being usually of great importance in America, and at competitions with exceptional attendances, where the punctuality is unbelievable, this is quite an important factor. In compiling the programme the organizers allowed themselves to be led by public taste, for their plan was not only to attract them to the Horse Show, but to excite them so much that they would come back in later years.

It was no easy task for us to shorten the three sections almost by half without spoiling the general effect and the quality of the performance. Every rider knows too well how easily the polish of a performance can be lost by hurrying, and how extraordinarily difficult it is to demonstrate the most difficult exercises one after another. Now we should see whether the horses had reached the highest standard of obedience—I might almost say split-second obedience.

On October 20 the Lipizzaner were brought in wonderfully equipped horse-boxes to Harrisburg, in Pennsylvania, where we were to begin our series of presentations in the United States at the International Horse Show there. In a large hall accommodating over ten thousand people the event lasted six days, and 460 horses took part. There were afternoon and evening performances every day, and the Spanish Riding School items were fitted in between the most interesting events. I could not help noticing uneasily that in the preceding competitions the spectators applauded, as at the rodeos, by whistling and stamping their feet, and even during the tensest struggles there was a good deal of noise. What an anomaly it would be for the riders of the Spanish Riding School when they came into the arena and formally doffed their hats to be greeted with whistling, even if it was the usual way of expressing enthusiasm in this country. Would not this contrast ruin the first impression?

So we had a tremendous surprise when the public, contrary to their custom, acknowledged their appreciation by clapping when the Spanish Riding School appeared, and there was an almost ceremonial atmosphere, which was not unpleasantly interrupted by the slightest movement or noise. Could there be better proof of the refining influence of culture?

The interest grew from day to day, and the public's close attention was increasingly obvious from its respectful silence, broken only between the items and at the end of the performance by tumultuous applause.

Pluto Theodorosta opened every show with a solo, as my faithful Neapolitano fell ill with a raging fever just before the show. The hall was completely dark, and in the merciless circle of light the gallant Lipizzaner executed the most difficult exercises with complete obedience, untroubled by the strange surroundings and unusual lighting. Tunes played by a string orchestra provided a background for the performance, and the announcer discreetly gave short commentaries on the individual exercises. To my great surprise, the audience always stopped applauding at the right moment when a movement was particularly difficult or was not absolutely harmonious, as they later did with the "Airs above the Ground" and the school quadrille.

All the American papers carried banner headlines and accounts of the first appearance of the Spanish Riding School, full of praise and appreciation. The *New York Mirror* printed a long article under the headlines: "The White Horses put the Rockettes to shame." The Rockettes were a well-known New York ballet company renowned for their exceptional precision.

Many visitors came long distances to see the famous school from Austria. Among these were many officers who had formerly belonged to the occupying Power in Austria, and I found it unusually moving when the mother of an American Army captain fighting in Korea presented me after one performance with a large bouquet of roses as a thank-offering for the pleasant reception her son had had from us in Wels. She had not let the distance of nearly a thousand miles deter her, and had come in by plane.

Among the visitors to the Horse Show who had come a long way were a couple with horse-mad children. The parents hoped that their elder, exceptionally talented daughter would get the chance to ride a good school horse. Naturally I had to deny this request, but invited them when I saw their disappointed faces to find a half-ridden horse, then I would give the daughter a few hints. The girl arrived the next day with a pony, and I had to give up an hour of my extremely overburdened time—the day usually began with the first telephone calls at nine o'clock and ended with the last party between three and five in the morning—to this horse-besotted creature, but was disappointed in the talent of the twelve-year-old rider and her exceptional willingness to learn. There was a somewhat comic moment when, after the riding lesson was over, the parents asked about my fee and I replied that I did not give riding instruction for money. These honest people were horrified and begged me to forgive them for taking up so much of my time. They simply could not grasp that for once time was not money.

The visitors to the performances overwhelmed me with a flood of questions, and I must say that we very rarely had so many attentive spectators as in America. They noticed every button, every piece of braid on the uniforms and saddle-cloths and asked about them. The seat of the riders and the behaviour of the horses were admired, and everybody wanted to know how this unity with the horse could be acquired. One remarkable question came from a trainer of "five-gated horses," as to how long our horses had to be tied up in their stalls to hold their heads so beautifully during the performance.

But, to my great delight, the young people and their teachers showed the greatest interest in the performances of the Spanish Riding School. One afternoon a teacher with about a hundred boys from eight to thirteen appeared in the saddling enclosure and asked if he might introduce his children, and whether I could answer some of their questions. I stood with the lads round me for a while, with the Lipizzaner ready saddled for the show in the background. It was one of the strangest interviews I have ever had to give, and when I found an account of it in the *Evening News* I thought of the illustration of Gulliver with the Lilliputians. Indeed, a tape recording of three-quarters of an hour for the school radio was much more exhausting, for I had to explain off the cuff and in English the nature of the Spanish Riding School, its duties and the objects of the training, having had no time to prepare my speech. I was really faced with some most extraordinary questions, but the enthusiasm that greeted us on all sides gave me an unexpected thrill and helped to solve the toughest problems.

At the Harrisburg Show we were introduced with pride to more and more people at various receptions and parties; but even enthusiasm, when it reaches such proportions, can be burdensome and very wearisome, especially after the physical demands of two performances a day. After the final afternoon performance I wanted to eat in peace, at last, in the restaurant in the hall, and not even talk to my wife, for we were both completely exhausted. Three elderly men also sat down at our table in the overcrowded room and discussed the show. Suddenly one of them turned to me and asked, "Wasn't it wonderful? Did you see the horses from Vienna too?" As I was not sure whether this question was serious or whether perhaps he had recognized me, I hesitated a moment. This he took as a "No" and added excitedly, "What, you haven't seen the white horses! Then I can only beg you to see them this evening at their last appearance, otherwise you will regret having missed such a unique and perfect performance as we Americans have never seen before."

My answer, "Yes, I know the Lipizzaner," seemed to him so illogical that he went on; "How can you know the Lipizzaner if you have not yet seen them?"

So there was nothing for it but to add, "Because I am the Director of the Spanish Riding School."

The effect of my words was quite indescribable. The three sprang up, said they had been breeding horses for many years, and were quite beside themselves over the great honour of being permitted to sit at a table with me. So that, of course, was the end of the quiet meal, but the little episode was one of the pleasantest experiences I had in the United States.

We appeared for the last time in Harrisburg in Saturday evening, and by early on the Sunday all the competition horses were being taken to New York in huge horse-boxes. As the Show did not finish until 1 A.M., and as there was a farewell party afterwards and I already had been invited to a large lunch in New York that same day, I was moving at what was by European standards almost unbelievable speed.

The journey to New York will remain an unforgettable memory. I sat at the wheel for over two hundred miles fighting against sleep, as had happened to me before after great days of strain. When I drove up to the Waldorf-Astoria Hotel in New York there was a long line of cars waiting with the competitors just climbing into them. A colonel noticed me and waved, "Hello, there he is now!" So I was just in time to change cars before the procession moved off.

The lunch was given at the headquarters of the First Army on Governors Island, one of the outlying islands of New York. The military commander gave a particularly splendid reception in honour of the teams of the nations taking part in the Show, and many of his officers appeared in full-dress uniform. The guests were brought from the Waldorf-Astoria in Army cars, the convoy headed by a police car that tore through the streets with its siren howling and stopped all the traffic to let us through. It was my fastest journey through the streets of the capital.

The American officers showed themselves to be perfect hosts in the very elegantly furnished casino-rooms. I was surrounded at once by high-ranking officers and had to answer questions about the Spanish Riding School, of whose successes in the U.S.A. they had already read in the papers, and about the rescue of the Lipizzaner. The general in command of the Air detachments of the district of New York talked to me for a long time, as he had himself started in the cavalry. He ended our conversation with the comment that he would have been much happier if he had only had to deal with horses instead of horse-power.

The eve of our première in New York was both exhausting and exciting. First there was a big reception at the Waldorf-Astoria, at which I had to stand in the receiving line and greet some hundreds of guests as they appeared. The ladies moving about in their evening dresses and the men in tails made a splendid picture in the brightly lit banqueting-rooms of this mammoth hotel. As soon as dinner was served I had to leave this fine party and hurry to Madison Square Garden to put on traditional uniform and do my celebrating at the dress rehearsal with music and lights. My wife helped the musical director, a famous conductor from New York, to fit the orchestra to the movements of the horses, for we were all doing our utmost to prepare for the opening day, and then it was nearly midnight.

Madison Square Garden is a hall in the centre of the city used for all kinds of exhibitions; the great rodeo was followed by conventions and these by ice-skating. This finished on Sunday evening, and the ice had disappeared during the night, and right up to Monday evening the surface was being prepared for the horses. This was why we could not hold our dress rehearsal until late at night.

The transfer of the show horses into the basement stables of the great building was not very agreeable, for they were very depressing. Still more difficult was the problem of warming up the horses; for this only the great hall was available whenever it was not being used for performances or rehearsals, thus in practice only early in the morning.

The Lipizzaner were then transferred to a marquee with specially constructed boxes in a car park quite near to Madison Square Garden, a solution to which I had agreed because I preferred fresh air to the atmosphere of the basement and also could have separate stalls for my beloved horses. The beautiful mild weather was very kind to us, and even when a positive cloudburst flooded our temporary stables as it passed over I still had no cause to regret my decision, for this misfortune resulted in our getting an immediate supply of fresh straw.

Undoubtedly the most exciting moment in America was our first performance in Madison Square Garden. It is true that we came crowned with success from Harrisburg, but here we had to appear before the highly critical public of a capital city. The very appearance of the crowded hall was gay: full evening dress and tails predominated in the boxes and in the circles, and the whole luxurious display indicated that it was a highlight of the season. An intent, expectant stillness filled this vast hall with its fifteen thousand as the white horses with their riders in traditional uniform entered the arena. Thunderous applause greeted the individual climaxes of the performance, and went on and on when we left the hall after the school quadrille. There was no doubt at all that the Spanish Riding School had won all hearts at its first appearance in New York. It was a wonderful feeling, for its riders had come to the U.S.A. with the firm intention of bringing the Americans a part of our lovely Austria, something that the inhabitants of the New World do not possess. The applause showed that we had succeeded.

The performances in Madison Square Garden made a colossal hit, but a life of undiluted joy is not anybody's lot on this earth. A few horses had already had coughs and high temperatures in Harrisburg, and with our limited number of horses any more trouble would be a catastrophe. Every day I went anxiously into the stables to discover whether the number of patients had increased. Three first-class veterinaries were found by the organizers of the Horse Show, and they looked after the horses with touching devotion and speeded up their recovery so successfully that the performances did not have to be modified. The veterinaries were full of praise for the behaviour of these horses, who willingly submitted to daily injections without the slightest sign of flinching as if they knew that people were trying to help them. Not only as patients, however, but also as artists the white horses from Austria caused astonishment and admiration. An expert with horses who had been connected with the mounting and dismantling of the Horse Show for nearly twenty years said to me, "Do you know, your Lipizzaner aren't animals at all. They act like human beings. They go into the arena, look left, look right, and when they are sure they have the attention of the interested spectators they begin to dance. What beautiful creatures!"

An elderly visitor to the Horse Show in Madison Square Garden remarked, "I have noticed for a good many years that there are always people who want to talk even during the most exciting jumping competitions, but when the Spanish Riding School appears even the worst chatterers stop. The influence of your lovely horses is too strong for them."

The visitors were anxious to understand the reason for everything they had seen; they wanted to know how such an erect and supple seat could be achieved and how it was possible for the tails of the riders' coats stretched out smoothly on the horses backs to remain undisturbed from the moment of mounting until the end of the performances; or even how the riders made their horses understand, since they did not appear to give directions. They noticed too the minutest details on the trappings and uniforms and asked for explanations. The countless questions and the way in which my answers were received revealed a wide understanding of the niceties of the equestrian art. This impression was confirmed when I myself once asked an American why the applause broke out in the quadrille at the change from the walk to the gallop, something we had not met before. His prompt answer impressed me particularly as a rider: "Well, it is hard enough to strike off at a canter from a walk with one horse, but to have eight horses doing this at the same time without the slightest raggedness is to my mind a work of art."

The one thing that did not work out, through lack of space, was the preparation of the horses before their entrance. There were, as I have already said, no facilities for a preliminary ride. We tried to warm up the horses to some extent as they came out of the stable along a gangway of some twenty yards, covered with cocoa matting, if even this small space was not crammed with curious spectators. When once one of my riders, to help me, asked some particularly insistent enthusiasts to make a little room, all he got was, "We are not in Europe but in free America, and won't be given orders as to when and where we can speak to the Colonel!" They then stood in my way regardless of the inconvenience, and asked their questions, so the less sensitive pushed into the background many pleasant and polite people to whom I should have liked to speak. One of these was the captain who in 1945 had brought the stud from Czechoslovakia to Austria, and had come a long way to see the Lipizzaner and me again.

But there was much to admire in the organization. Everything ran punctually and smoothly, and without wasting a second. For our performance the whole arena was cleared of jumps; this was done incredibly quickly with four jeeps and small trailers, which rushed into the arena as the last showjumper had left the ring, loaded up the obstacles like lightning, and disappeared again. Another jeep towing a harrow levelled the surface, and the tubs of flowers marking out the square were quickly in position and we could begin. This transformation was effected in under ten minutes; the public, delighted over the quick, neat work, applauded the attendants as well. How tedious and complicated in comparison the ring-clearing for our appearance often was at European festivals, where the spectators' view was frequently spoilt by obstacles not removed, whereas at the New York Horse Show everything was planned down to the smallest detail, as if following Napoleon's famous precept: "Soignez les détails!"

As soon as every performance finished crowds of people surged round me for autographs or wanting to shake hands. The many refugees from Austria in particular seized my hand, seeing in the Spanish Riding School treasured messengers from their lost homeland, and most of them were so upset that they had to struggle with their tears. In spite of my previous exertions I always tried to fulfil their requests with a friendly smile and great patience, though these often took more than an hour, until my officer guide extricated me from the clutches of the excited spectators with his "Colonel, it's time to go," and took me along to one of the many parties.

New York was unbelievably exhausting. The telephone calls started at nine and often reached the record number of fifty by one o'clock. One of the last calls was usually from the officer acting as my aide to tell me that famous people who had come to New York specially wanted to lunch with me—another hour and a half filled more with conversation than eating. Then I had to change for the afternoon performance in Madison Square Garden. After this there were autographs to give, short interviews in the stables, another quick change, a cocktail party, which was frequently followed by some dinner that I usually had to leave before the end to rush back to Madison Square Garden and change for the evening performance. After that I had to meet public figures who wanted to talk to me. As our evening shows usually came on after ten o'clock, and often not until nearly midnight, it was very often three or four in the morning before we finally got back to our hotel room. This went on day after day, and I always had to watch my behaviour, show no weariness, smile all the time and be "happy," for every move was carefully observed.

A remark made by the President of the Horse Show, General Tuckermann, at the farewell party showed me how true this was: "I have admired you not only as a rider, but have come to like you as a person! I have watched you giving autographs and shaking hands after your performance, although there were still drops of sweat on your forehead from riding, and it impressed me particularly and brought us closer as human beings that you were just as friendly to the poor refugees as to the ladies in full evening dress."

Our performances in Madison Square Garden reached their zenith on November 4, when there was a gala evening and the hall was crammed to capacity and unusually brilliant: the evening dresses of the ladies and the black and red coats and top-hats of the men. On this occasion General Patton's widow was present.

Just before our appearance General Tuckermann asked me whether I would welcome Mrs Patton briefly in the arena, but did not explain what kind of meeting he thought it should be, so I quickly made a plan of my own, rode at the head of my riders into the brilliantly lighted hall and turned towards the box from which Mrs Patton, accompanied by General Tuckermann, was walking into the arena. The riders followed me in single file, and ten paces from her I sprang from my horse and went towards her. My riderless horse, left on his own—it was Pluto Theodorosta—followed me for a few steps, then turned back to his companions. Then came a surprise, filling me with admiration for the adaptablity of the lighting crew. Although the whole scene was improvised—I had only thought of it as I was warming up my horse and could not tell anybody else about it—the Garden was plunged into darkness as I stood near Mrs Patton and the spotlight directed on us. There I stood in the circle of light facing the widow of the man who in the May days of 1945 had shown such extraordinary sympathy for my requests. Around us was total darkness and such stillness that one could have imagined oneself in the open country. It was a moving and impressive moment, and I spoke from the depths of my heart: "I am very happy to be able to show you the horses that General Patton, a great American soldier, saved for Austria."

Mrs Patton answered, "I would give anything if only my husband could be standing here instead of me, for he loved the Lipizzaner so much. In nearly every letter he wrote enthusiastically about the white horses from Austria. I should so like to give you a rose. May I?"

With these words she took a red rose from the bouquet she held and fastened it in a buttonhole of my brown tail-coat. This was a signal for the thousands of spectators, who had watched the scene in complete silence, to break into a wild burst of applause. This simple and completely unrehearsed ceremony so caught the public interest that for days afterwards it was talked about even in the hurry and bustle of New York. A picture of the scene was circulated to the world Press with the caption "A rose without thorns."

But this rose almost led me on to a thorny path, for during the closing quadrille I noticed with horror that it was gradually slipping farther and farther out of my buttonhole, and threatening to fall. Its loss would certainly have destroyed all the glamour of the preceding scene in the eyes of the observant public, so I tried to slide the independent flower back with a gentle tug and rode a very tense quadrille. I could not take my eyes for a moment off the rose, which with the rhythm of the horse's movement began to rise in my buttonhole, and had to keep pulling the stem down carefully, but I did not lose it!

The performances of the Spanish Riding School in New York were an unparalleled triumph. Because of them the Horse Show had had the biggest attendances since its foundation, and even on the so-called poor days, like November 6, when the Metropolitan Opera opened its season at the same time, Madison Square Garden was virtually sold out. Everybody was talking about the Lipizzaner. The Press published more articles about the wonder horses from Vienna, and in the windows along the great New York shopping streets there were pictures of them. In addition their performances were televised every day.

Newspaper reports in America and Canada reflect public opinion even more than with us in Europe, and this publicity is not only of great importance for every entertainment, but it alone indicates accurately not only every success but, quite mercilessly, every failure. It was considered quite sensational that *Life Magazine* had in three numbers devoted six pages inside six weeks to the Spanish Riding School, and the professional paper *The Rider and Driver* brought out a special fully illustrated supplement about the school, giving information about its history and functions and the careers of each individual member of it. In all the illustrated papers so many pictures appeared that this appreciation of our efforts put all previous ones in the shade.

From the many interviews with interesting people only the remarks of the last commandant of the former Tsarist Cavalry School in St Petersburg, are reproduced here. This distinguished old gentleman, who had tried for days to be introduced to me said: "For days I could not get near you, but I did not want to leave New York without telling you how deeply moved I have been by your polished riding. I would not have believed that the art of the cavalier could have survived in such perfection to the present day. Your presentations are still better than when I last saw your academy when Vienna was still the capital of a great empire. I am delighted to have lived to see real horsemanship again and thank you with all my heart as an old cavalryman."

Every day countless letters arrived, and flowers and other gifts in such quantities that our apartment in the Waldorf-Astoria was very nearly too small to accommodate all these marks of appreciation.

The white stallions were wildly applauded for the last time on November 7. This brilliant sporting event, with Austria, through the Spanish Riding School, the centre of interest, ended with a tremendous banquet that lasted till early morning. On the morning of the next day the Lipizzaner were ready for loading, and earlier I had revisited the scene of our singular triumph.

Dreary and bereft of its pulsating life, Madison Square Garden lay before me in the dawn light. Trucks were removing the last traces of the Horse Show, the few remaining pieces of floor-covering. Overnight the most remarkable hall in the world had been transformed from being the scene of equestrian combats into a forum for the coming World Championship fight. Ended and dying away into stillness was the lightfooted galloping of noble horses, over and forgotten in the shortest possible time all the glamour that has surrounded them and the joy that they had managed to excite. A slight feeling of sadness assailed me as in days gone by when, after big sporting triumphs, I used to visit the empty competition ring before I left. Over and forgotten? Certainly not this time for years later I kept meeting people who raved about the performances of the Spanish Riding School in Madison Square Garden.

The Lipizzaner were taken to Toronto in big Pullman coaches, luxuriously fitted with padded boxes for twenty horses, compartments for the grooms, and space for luggage and feed. And, of course, heated. I myself still had two full days ahead of me winding things up in New York and fulfilling social duties, and hoped during the flight to Toronto and on the first day in this city to be able to be alone at last to collect myself a little after the bustle of the past weeks. But as soon as I stepped into the plane the stewardess said, "Hello, Colonel! I have admired you so often on television and am glad to meet you personally," and an American show-jumper immediately begged me to sit beside him throughout the flight of some hours, and discussed thoroughly and in detail with me whether horses are intelligent or only use their instinct. Since I argued in favour of the intelligence of horses, a view on which we differed, I had to prove my point with examples. There was no further question of a restful flight, and I breathed a sigh of relief when we touched down in Toronto. And I had so hoped to remain anonymous.

While we waited for the somewhat lengthy passport and Customs formalities I suddenly heard over the loudspeaker, "Colonel and Mrs Podhajsky, please come at once to the office."

There I was told after a brief look at our passports that everything was in order and we were at liberty to set foot on Canadian soil, but the President of the Olympic Committee for Horsemanship was already waiting for me. I was highly delighted that everything was settled so quickly, but somewhat surprised at the reception, since I had deliberately kept secret the time of my departure from New York.

The President said as he met me, "It has been a great nuisance finding out when you would arrive. You must come with me at once to the Colosseum, for there are several hundred riding enthusiasts waiting for you. You are to give them a lecture on the basic principles of the Spanish Riding School and the connexion of this teaching with riding in general, with practical illustrations."

My heart sank, and I tried to put him off by pointing out all the technical impossibilities of this unexpected request. But I made no headway, for all he said was, "Everything is already arranged. Your *Oberbereiter* is waiting for a telephone call to tell him which horse to get ready for this demonstration. This is the only chance for a lecture, as once the Horse Show has begun there will be no time to spare for it, so come to the telephone and give your instruction!"

When I had thought out the necessary arrangements at top speed, and had made my call, we got into the waiting car. I was put in the back, for my companion remarked, "You have an hour and a half's journey ahead of you, and you can easily take a nap if you are tired." As if I could have thought about sleep at such a moment—one certainly cannot give a lecture to a knowledgeable audience in a foreign language just like that!

In the Colosseum many of the seats were, indeed, filled. A microphone was ready, and the Lipizzaner and their riders were waiting. The show could begin. Anybody who has ever had to address a large audience without adequate preparation will know how I felt.

I then tried in an impromptu lecture lasting over an hour to explain our training methods, and with the help of the Lipizzaner to give practical demonstrations, from lunging work right up to pillar training. Here a good idea came to me in my need: to use riders in place of the missing pillars. This inspiration was most effective, as it dispelled the erroneous notion that in the Spanish Riding School the horse was simply fastened between the pillars and then driven with a whip to teach it the *piaffe*; the living pillars clearly proved that this work certainly could not be done by using force. I was generously applauded, and so had won my first round on Canadian soil.

Sporting conditions were distinctly better in Toronto than in New York. The riding competition formed part of the annual Agricultural Show. There was an arena accommodating 14,000 available for the performances, this very Colosseum. The horses were taken to a big, well-heated hall and put in magnificent permanent boxes, and could be exercised in a ride provided just near. This amenity was particularly welcome, as we had had no chance to work our horses except during the performances since we left Rye.

In the few days before our first appearance there was a great deal to be done, which, with the social functions, the welcoming of the competitors in the Town Hall, and receptions, filled the time completely. Two military bands were to take turns in playing the musical accompaniment: the better one at the evening shows, the less good one in the afternoons. As there was no conductor of the standing of the directors in Harrisburg and New York, a grand rehearsal for the band was arranged in some barracks. Both were assembled with their bandmasters and tried to sight-read the musical accompaniment for our performances. It took nearly two hours before it seemed that the Canadians had mastered the old Austrian rhythm of our horses' movements, and I had to give them the beat. The dress rehearsal in the Colosseum with both bands accompanying us went splendidly.

42. In the Land of their Forefathers: the Bullring in Seville

224

43. · · · and in Barcelona, 1954

At the first afternoon performance, with the help of the weaker band, everything went well, and I assumed that the second band, generally considered far superior, would make a good job of accompanying us that evening at the ceremonial opening. But it was not so, for during the quadrille the accompaniment got thinner and thinner, although the conductor waved his baton vigorously and tried to stir up the flagging musicians. What happened behind the scenes after this intermezzo, which luckily the white horses managed to conceal with their captivating movements, I never discovered, but the next evening this band too played as one man and was no longer shamed by the weak ones.

Of the many social engagements the reception at Lady Eton's home was particularly interesting. Throughout the journey to the hostess's castle riders in hunting pink waited at the various crossroads to direct the traffic.

Some three hundred people had assembled in the beautiful reception-rooms, with the Governor, Lord Alexander, as the guest of honour. As soon as we had been received his adjutant took me to him. His Excellency, an imposing figure with a particularly friendly manner, told me that in 1919 he had been with the British occupation troops in Vienna, and still remembered with pleasure the time he had spent in this charming city. But he had not been able to see the Spanish Riding School then, so he was specially pleased about the performances of which he had heard so much. He asked me also whether he might inspect the horses in private, and arranged to come to the stables at ten o'clock on the day after the opening performance. His adjutant was less delighted, because of the various functions and inspections at the Colosseum that had been planned for that morning.

The opening ceremony was a special occasion of the first order. If the spectators did not quite have the luxurious appearance that we had seen on gala evenings in Madison Square Garden, tails and dinner jackets predominated, and everybody of note appeared. A guard of honour was drawn up in the centre of the arena, and saluted as the Governor-General appeared, and the band struck up the national anthem. I was specially moved to see that Lord Alexander, himself a soldier, took the parade in civilian clothes. But he looked wonderful in top-hat and tails, and was warmly greeted by the crowd.

He sat down in his box, the guard of honour marched off, and the ceremonial parade of riders taking part in the competition began. The separate nations were presented to the large audience by the playing of national anthems. When it was the turn of the Spanish Riding School *Oh, du mein Österreich* was played, as then nobody knew the anthem of the Second Republic.

Our performance was made the highlight of the evening. We could tell at once, as in the preceding afternoon, that the Lipizzaner pleased the people here too. We gave the same programme as in the United States, but for the first time on our tour I was able to show Neapolitano Africa, for he had recovered quickly from his serious illness, thanks to penicillin, and in spite of the long break—he had not been able to be worked at all since he left Wels—he moved with perfect precision and such brilliance that he fully justified his high reputation. His efforts were warmly applauded, and his name was given special prominence in all the Canadian papers. At that time I did not guess that this success was to be the last of his many triumphs, for an infection resulting from the pencillin injections in one of his forelegs prevented him from appearing again in Canada, and a progressive emphysema of the lungs after his return to Austria terminated the unusually brilliant career of this noble Lipizzaner. My brave Neapolitano Africa's rise was meteoric, and his art reached its zenith and ended in Toronto in the fullness of beauty.

The Lipizzaner had made their début in Canada with flying colours, as was obvious from the cheers and clapping during and at the end of our performance in the Colosseum, and the Governor-General confirmed this when he inspected the horses the next day. He appeared punctually in the stables with a small *entourage*, announced by an officer who whispered to me that my distinguished guest's programme was very full, so he could spare only ten minutes for the Spanish Riding School. Lord Alexander came straight up to me clearly still under the influence of the previous evening's performance. His first question was about Neapolitano Africa, whom he had seen on his way in, but he asked about Pluto Theodorosta too, and liked him even better; this horse had also improved remarkably during the tour, for he had to take over the solo work from Neapolitano Africa during the latter's illness, he had appeared four times every day, and seemed to be aware of the importance of his mission, for he got better and better and devoted himself completely to his duty.

I was asked to show the Field-Marshal the rest of the horses, explain the *levade* and *capriole*, and the method of training, and answer a host of questions—not from the Governor-General but from Lord Alexander the rider, who, in spite of gentle hints from his adjutant, stayed with the Lipizzaner for over an hour. Before he left he met all the personnel of the Spanish Riding School and asked them several questions in German— the first German words after the Second World War from his Excellency's lips—to the astonishment of his staff.

Thus the school's success in Toronto was a worthy follow-up to its New York triumphs. There was the same attention and appreciation during the performances, which were attended by everybody prominent in public life. The Press gave almost daily reports on "The Wonder Horses from Austria." The Lipizzaner and their performances were extolled in poems as animal personalities. "Visitors of all ages admired and loved these gentle, well-mannered white horses, which seemed to love the public's attention," wrote the professional paper *Hoof and Prints*.

The big daily the *Globe and Mail* gave a complete page to an interview with me, emphasizing the patient labour that lay behind the splendour of the presentation: "Force could not have persuaded these noble stallions to develop their talent, but only patience and reward with sugar or carrots."

The day after this article appeared two men representing Dutch settlers came to me and in gratitude for the wonderful performances wanted to provide carrots for the horses, an offer that I was glad to accept. I could not specify the quantity on the spot, so the two men asked if it should be twenty-five or thirty bushels. As I thought this figure meant the vegetable bushels customary in our markets, I naturally asked for thirty, slightly surprised at so much fuss over a few carrots. Shortly afterwards a whole truckload of thirty baskets, each holding more than forty pounds, arrived, this amount being called a bushel in Canada. Although at first we were appalled at the enormous quantity of carrots these delicacies came in very useful later during our stormy crossing back to Europe.

For many weeks the Spanish Riding School was news in North America. A rare gem of ancient European culture, welcomed by the *New York Times* as "the last living example of baroque," had won a sweeping victory in the New World. Riders and horses were fêted and pampered wherever they went, and the Lipizzaner received many titbits and other delicacies, as the many traces of lipstick on their milk-white noses proved. For weeks we led the lives of people free of everyday cares, for on all sides we were offered nothing but beauty, kindness, and love, and felt in consequence the satisfaction that we in our turn had been able to give something to these affectionate and sympathetic people: pleasure in the beauty and harmony of the Lipizzaner stallions schooled and trained by us.

The triumphal progress of the Spanish Riding School to the United States and Canada ended in Toronto. It was gratifying to discover that the interest in the school did not lessen with the number of the performances, but on the contrary grew greater still. The hall was repeatedly sold out, as on the final evening. A feeling of pride and joy filled us all as after the quadrille we moved for the last time in the *passage* and doffed our hats in a ceremonial salute to the shouts and cheers of the excited crowd. As the riders then left the Colosseum in measured tread the now familiar voice of the announcer rang out, above the applause, quietening it a little:

"With the quadrille a monument is erected to the incomparably skilled horses trained by the fine riders of the Spanish Riding School of Vienna under their active and outstanding chief, Colonel Podhajsky."

After these words the white stallions disappeared from public view, and the sound of protracted applause accompanied us right to the saddling enclosure.

So the last page was turned of a remarkable chapter of the long history of the Vienna Riding School. For more than three months the gallant Lipizzaner had held the New World in thrall and sent it into raptures, stealing the hearts of the normally bustling North Americans. The countryside had finally shed its summer robes after a colourful interlude of lovely autumn months, and the first storms of winter were lashing the last leaves from the trees, and Christmas was sending out its first harbingers.

The Lipizzaner left New York harbour on December 6, to return to Wels after an unusually stormy crossing not merely in good shape, but lively and cheerful, while the pæans of praise over their achievements continued in the Press for a long time.

So the Spanish Riding School on its first American tour, which brought many more invitations, had completely fulfilled its mission. It had been excellent publicity for the ancient riding culture of Europe, and had succeeded in persuading the New World of the rectitude of the principles of classic riding. Indeed, such was the power of its persuasion that the doyen of the sport in Canada commented that it was the first time he had ever seen happy horses at a horse show: the white stallions of the Vienna Spanish Riding School.

CHAPTER 14

The White Horses dance again in Europe

waiting me on my return from America I found not only vast numbers of enthusiastic letters and congratulations, not to mention addresses of welcome in the Press and on the radio, but also many invitations for more festival tours, which were later to take us right through Western Europe, although not all the requests could be considered. Of the various projects a repeat tour of the United States and a similar one to Spain had to be refused, for in all assessments of the importance of foreign festivals the duties of the Spanish Riding School as the nursery of the art of classic riding must decidedly not be overlooked or neglected.

Thus there was no resting on the hard-won laurels of our grand tour; indeed, it seemed as if the faster tempo of America had stuck to our feet. The impact of our visit to the New World was more enduring and far-reaching than I had thought, and was not without its effect in other countries and Austria itself, which now saw in the Spanish Riding School one of its most valuable possessions. One report instigated another, and I was asked to give a radio talk on our great triumphs for Austrian listeners, and to describe our tour in a series of lectures in various provincial towns. Foreign journalists came specially to Austria to visit remote Wels and to see the famous white horses for themselves. They asked me about the American tour and a host of other questions concerning the Spanish Riding School, while the feature-film people decided that in a proper Austrian film there ought to be something about the school and set about getting the co-operation of the Lipizzaner. The principal cities wanted to do the same as Salzburg and deprive their citizens no longer of the widely acclaimed horses from Lipizza. So the motto for 1951 was *Tempo, tempo*!

Early in March the newly appointed High Commissioner and U.S. Ambassador Donnelli had his special train halted at Wels so that he could see the Lipizzaner, and he, his wife and staff thoroughly enjoyed themselves. When he received me in his salon on the train to say good bye I was fêted like a hero, so great was the excitement over our success in America and the performance witnessed.

The shooting for the film *Verklungenes Wien* (Vanished Vienna) took place at the beginning of May. The Lipizzaner were treated as stars, as the script-writer and director, my old friend and comrade in arms Ernst Marischka, was handling the negotiations with the Spanish Riding School. Filming with horses is always more difficult than with people, as the animals cannot understand the frequent repetition of scenes. The cameraman often missed the best *caprioles* and similar difficult exercises, thinking the Lipizzaner could perform movements requiring so much strength and determination one after another. But Marischka overcame all difficulties with unshakable calm, and the dreaded four days of filming went splendidly and proved a wonderful experience. The Lipizzaner had taken their tasks very seriously and shown themselves so well in this film that they stole the hearts of the cinema audience, and the official première of the film was spontaneously applauded.

Indeed, the shots taken in Wimsbach were perfect both from a technical riding point of view and as pictures, and especially was this true of the skilful introduction of slow motion for the most effective movements. This technique was again employed a year later in the Austrian film *1 April 2000*, in which the Lipizzaner also took part, riders and figures this time looking just like white porcelain figures.

The next milestone of this exciting year was the Salzburg Festival, which took place again in brilliant sunshine, a great rarity in this rain-soaked city. The idea got about that the arrival of the Lipizzaner was the best guarantee of good weather, since it had been just the same the previous year, and we performed once more on the football ground in Nonntal at the foot of the Feste Hohensalzburg.

The next stage of our long festival tour took us farther north to Copenhagen, and the Spanish Riding School touched Danish soil for the first time since its foundation. Equestrian contacts between Austria and Denmark had so far been only slight, and in the long list of foreign pupils of the Spanische Hofreitschule, which goes back more than a century, there is hardly a Danish officer to be found. So we were treading completely new territory.

If our first impression of the clean little country with its well-swept streets and pretty houses decorated with flowers was a pleasant surprise, our reception surpassed all expectations. The horses were quartered in the royal mews at Christiansborg Castle, and we were to perform in the baroque riding-hall in the same castle, more than two hundred years old. On hardly any of our previous tours had we found a setting so authentic in style. But this arrangement had one great drawback for our hosts, the

Danish Riding Club: the accommodation for the spectators was limited to a thousand in spite of the erection of stands and the provision of seats. This meant a tremendous financial risk for the organizers, for the expenses of the Spanish Riding School tour were quite high, and would have been much easier to recover in one of the big sports arenas than in this little riding-hall. Very high prices had to be charged for tickets, particularly as our performances were not, as had usually been the case, part of a horse show, but quite on their own. All the same the influential members of the club chose the Royal Riding Hall as the worthiest setting for the Spanish Riding School. How lovely to find so much idealism in these hard-headed times!

Our personal reception was in keeping with this attitude: every single member of the Vienna Riding School received many attentions, and there were magnificent social engagements. The brilliant parties, some of them in old Patrician houses, like our general impressions of the country, all suggested a well-ordered prosperity.

With Danish thoroughness the Spanish Riding School, of which many had never heard before, was introduced to the Scandinavians by the Press for weeks beforehand, and we were given the sort of advance publicity that reminded us of America. When we arrived in Copenhagen all four presentations in the Royal Riding Hall were sold out.

The first one was an important social occasion. Many members of the royal household and the Diplomatic Corps mingled with the important people in festive mood. We performed in an exceptionally cultured and expectant atmosphere before a very knowledgeable public. Before the start of the performance the President of the Club, Mr Lemwigh-Müller, welcomed the visitors and gave a short explanation of what they would be seeing. Then the riders of the Spanish Riding School entered the floodlit arena to begin the dance of the white horses on historic Danish soil.

In the restricted space the public sat very near to the ring, so we had to be careful not to hit those sitting in the first rows with our switches, while the spectators watched us very closely and were able to see the slightest move or direction.

The opening on Scandinavian soil was a great success, and our tour a special attraction in this northern corner of Europe, enjoyed not only by the Danes, but by the Swedes, the Norwegians and even the Finns as well. For many days the Press published pages of reports, with pictures taken during the performances, about our appearances, had interviews with me and individual riders, and told very varied stories about the Lipizzaner, and proudly announced that my stallion Pluto Theodorosta was descended from Pluto, who had in his time served the mares in the royal stud in Frederiksborg. No less numerous were the letters, some of them attached to bouquets of flowers, full of enthusiasm, appreciation, and good wishes for the future of the school. In the pile I found the following:

MY DEAR PLUTO THEODOROSTA,

Unfortunately I cannot see you and your wonderful brothers personally, but I love you all. I have always dreamed about you Lipizzaner, and I send you all my love, admiration, and these sugar-ration cards.

When I went along to get the sugar with them I was asked with astonishment who had given them for they represented a whole month's ration. What an example of self-sacrificing love for the Lipizzaner! Thus these horses had won the hearts of the reserved people of Copenhagen, and their affection so grew during the following performances that I was besieged on all sides to arrange an extra show one afternoon on the big square at Christiansborg Castle—once a riding square—to give a chance for the crowds who had not managed to get tickets to see the Spanish Riding School after all. This impromptu show, for which the old royal castle provided a very effective background, attracted more than six thousand spectators, although there were no seats available, but they were not at all tired or cross with standing so long—many had come more than two hours before the start of the show to be sure of good places—and did not move from the spot during the ninety-minute performance, and were really thrilled.

The last presentation in the riding-hall was outstanding because of the visit of the royal family, who had specially interrupted their stay in their summer residence. The appearance of the King, since he was a passionate devotee of water sports but was rarely seen at riding events, was considered a phenomenon. I awaited him with the other dignitaries at the entrance to the royal box in the front row. The royal couple, cheered on their arrival by curious crowds outside the hall, seemed strikingly unassuming and simple. Queen Ingrid, a brilliant figure with a very friendly personality, replied in French to my words of greeting, while King Frederik expressed in my mother tongue his pleasure at seeing the Spanish Riding School at Christiansborg. As at that time in Denmark German, as a result of the Second World War, was deliberately avoided, this speech by the King was a particularly graceful gesture.

The Queen and her daughters, who adore riding, were generous with their applause, and the King was so enthusiastic that he repeatedly leaned out of his box and clapped.

When some days later I want to Christiansborg Castle, where the Cross of Commander of the Order of Danebrog was conferred upon me, the Master of the Horse, whose name was Schaumburg, said to me, "Do you know, His Majesty was so excited by the Lipizzaner that first thing this morning he started to talk about yesterday's performance, which says a good deal for some one not greatly interested in horses."

This honour was also significant for the upholding of European culture, as it was the first order to be conferred on an Austrian citizen after the Second World War—so to speak, the first step in bridging the yawning abyss between the two peoples through the last war. Our success in Denmark, hailed by the Press as triumphant and unique, was of such tremendous importance because, of the ten thousand spectators, the vast majority were experts, and had it not been for the limited space the greater part of the population would have been present. Many who could not get in came every morning to have a look at us at least while we warmed up the horses on the open riding square; but they came, in spite of the No Entry notices, into the stables as well, and were delighted if they were allowed to stroke the coats of their "White Majesties" and ask us questions; although the mass of visits were often inconvenient we had to accept them because of the enthusiasm, and this was attributed to our "Viennese charm."

Leaving Copenhagen in triumph, we went to Cologne, where we appeared with the Riding and Jumping events at the Agricultural Show.

Before our performance in Cologne I had a most pleasant experience. I used a rest day during training to meet friends from America in Holland. At the border the German Customs officer asked if I had a currency clearance, which I had left behind with my Austrian change at the hotel in Cologne, but was supposed to give up when I left German territory. So as not to have to go back to Cologne unnecessarily I tried to persuade the Customs authorities to change their mind, explaining the situation and my reason for crossing the border. In the course of our conversation the official asked me who I was, whereupon I modestly mentioned my name and handed over my passport. I was most astonished when his stern official expression brightened and he asked me, without looking at my passport, "Are you by any chance the colonel who was given a red rose by that American lady that I read about in a picture paper?" When I said I was he explained, "That's quite different! And if you are coming back into German territory in a few hours or so, then I will let you go without giving up the declaration, only you must shake hands with my colleagues as well, for we all admire you so much after what we have heard about you." So I was able to continue my journey in spite of my lack of papers.

After our last appearance in Cologne we went to Rotterdam to finish our festival tour of almost eight weeks. During the International Horse Show performances were given both on the perfectly laid out and tended showground and also in a covered school. The Horse Show was a social event, and Queen Juliana and Prince Bernhard of the Netherlands were present. There were also a great number of experts in this illustrious crowd, and these rewarded our appearance with a certain scepticism, as was obvious from various remarks which reached me, sometimes at second hand.

Out visit began with a gala performance in the covered riding-hall before invited guests, with all the very best people and the Diplomatic Corps much in evidence. That bare covered school looked this evening like an enchanted grove of flowers out of a fairy-tale; under strong but by no means trying lighting the eye feasted on a riot of colour that in its luxuriance and tasteful arrangement did justice to Holland's high standard of flower culture. Mijnheer A. Klebe, responsible for our visit and the moving spirit of the organization of the Horse Show with his rich experience and warm feeling for the noble art of horsemanship, had certainly provided a worthy setting for the performance of the Spanish Riding School.

Our première on Dutch soil before invited guests was a splendid success, as the congratulations at the reception afterwards proved but the second performance in the same place before spectators who had had to pay a high price for their tickets was really a triumph. Excitement knew no bounds, and when the riders rode out after the quadrille the applause went on and on, so Mijnheer Klebe begged me to show myself once more. When I tried to refuse, saying this was not customary, he said almost pleadingly, "You don't know the Dutch. When my countrymen are so carried away as this there will be no peace until they have got what they want: to see you again. You can hear how they are stamping their feet." So I took off my greatcoat and decided to do something we had never done before: we walked into the ring, bowed, and acknowledged our thanks for the demonstration, and the applause grew still more tumultuous.

The remaining two performances were given in the open to show the Spanish Riding School to the general public. As the highlight of a programme carefully built up to a climax our performance was to begin at the end of the competition day at five in the afternoon, but the jumping dragged on so long that our turn came pretty late and the light soon became very bad. As our programme went on it got darker and darker, and during the quadrille we could not see the spectators at all. Only the sudden burst of applause reminded us that we were being watched in admiring silence.

This was one of the strangest quadrilles that I have ever ridden. In the advancing darkness we could see nothing at all by the end so that we could only form the familiar figures by feeling and instinct, the shining whiteness of the horses of our opposite numbers giving us our only direction. But it was a unique spectacle for the audience too, as we were often told later. With the approach of darkness a light mist began to swirl round the ground, gradually blurring the outlines. The riders in brown coats were swallowed up more and more by the dusk, so that finally all that could be seen were riderless white horses dancing and swaying in a milky haze. It must have been enchanting, an unreal picture that appealed to the spectators' emotions; the outside world seemed far away, and they were lost in a dream abruptly broken by the first sounds of thunderous applause.

Prince Bernhard apologized the next day for the delay, and explained that he had already seen to it that we should never again have to ride in such a bad light. Our performance was then put between jumping events, so instead of at five we now came on at three, delighting much fewer people than on the previous day. When we had finished a still larger mass was still crowding the entrances. Prince Bernhard came to me and said resignedly that whatever one did was wrong, for now a great many visitors who had come specially to see the Spanish Riding School had been disappointed, because they had missed the performance owing to the change of time. He begged me on the last day, when the Prix des Nations was to be decided, and we were not intended to appear because of lack of time, to give a short programme, so that the many dissatisfied visitors would have a chance to see the riders from Vienna after all.

As a matter of fact, these performances, at such different times of the day and under the most unfortunate lighting conditions, caused some of the experts to revise their preconceived ideas. One official who had seen the Spanish Riding School in 1928 at the Olympic Games in The Hague, and had then noticed that the Lipizzaner were affected by their surroundings and shied at puddles on the ground, had had to change the opinion he had then formed that the Lipizzaner are only show horses, as opposed to dressage horses, for there are only very few dressage mounts so obedient that they will submit to their rider in spite of a variety of surprises and unfamiliar surroundings. One of the pleasantest remarks a dressage rider could hear.

On the penultimate day of the tournament Prince Bernhard, at a large banquet, conferred in the Queen's name the Cross of Commander of the Order of Oranje-Nassau, not only in recognition of my efforts to preserve the Spanish Riding School, but also to heal the unhappy memories left in Holland by the activities of the Austrian Seyss-Inquart. Once more it was our beloved horses that made it easier to forget angry memories and offer the hand of friendship.

I asked when I might thank her Majesty the Queen for this high honour, and Prince Bernhard said quite simply, "My wife is coming tomorrow to the Horse Show, and you can talk to her then."

So the next day the Lipizzaner showed their skill to the Queen of the Netherlands, and I wore the new decoration as the only ornament on my brown tail-coat. After the quadrille my riders walked in a line behind me, I dismounted and went to the Royal Box. Queen Juliana rose from her seat and thanked me in French for the performance, but I decided to answer in my mother tongue:

"May I offer my grateful thanks for the high Order that your Majesty has been gracious enough to confer on me. This distinction fills me not only with pride and pleasure, but compels me to promise to devote my strength and skill still more to the preservation of a cultural treasure of the Europe that we all love, and for which we are always ready to fight." The Queen gave me her hand and said—to the astonishment of her entourage—in German. "Thank you for those beautiful words."

Our festival appearance in Rotterdam was once more a triumphant success, showing yet again that in the United States and Canada the Spanish Riding School had not in fact yet reached the climax of its foreign tours. Our experience was a sensation for Holland, variously reported in the Press; the papers even published 'interviews' with the Lipizzaner and told of admirers' dreams in which as centaurs these horses had enjoyed the cheers of the masses of spectators. So greatly stirred were the emotions of the normally stolid Dutch.

In August came the event of the year: our visit to Stockholm. I went ahead to Helsinki for the Olympic Games, but this time only as a spectator. It was remarkable how much this little people, so cruelly handled by fate, had contributed in the way of financial outlay and magnificent organization to the success of this great sporting event.

I had a pleasant experience in Helsinki, which had really begun a year earlier in Copenhagen, when the famous Danish dressage rider Lis Hartel asked me to ride her horse Jubilee. I was amazed at the great ability of this brave mare, and when she asked me if her horse was ready for the next years' Olympic Games I had no hesitation in agreeing. The only thing then lacking was a consistent *piaffe*, but this could be improved with time. I followed by correspondence the progress and setbacks that Lis Hartel met in her work, and tried to advise her on paper. At the 1952 Whitsun Show in Wiesbaden I was appointed judge for the big dressage competition, in which riders from Germany and such distant places as Chile and the United States took part. Back from there I found a message from Mrs Hartel that her efforts to teach Jubilee the *piaffe* had been fruitless, so she had decided not to go to the Olympiad. As I had just seen the majority of the probable Olympic competitors in Wiesbaden and even judged them, I knew that the other riders' *piaffe* was really poor as well. This I told Mrs Hartel and managed to persuade her to come.

As I entered the riding stadium in Helsinki a very worried Lis Hartel rushed up to me.

"It is due to you that I am here, and now Jubilee cannot do the *piaffe* at all. I have only myself to blame."

Understandably the rider's words and her condition gave me a terrible shock, especially as I had already heard how many experts had confused her on the preceding days with their contradictory advice. As she was not to appear until the second day of the trials, we planned that she should ride for me in a quiet corner. I tried in the short time left to calm the rider and to build up her self-confidence again, but realized that I myself was very nervous when she rode next day into the dressage square, so I left my place among the great critics and carpers to watch alone in a corner. Lis Hartel noticed me there just before she began and found great comfort—so she told me later—in my presence and the memory of my advice the day before. She performed her tasks brilliantly, and I and many of the experts considered her, in spite of the poor *piaffe*, quite the best rider, but, as so often happens in dressage, she only came second.

When she stood on the right of the winner to receive her Olympic medal tears of joy ran down her cheeks, for it was undoubtedly the most important moment of her life to be able to win an Olympic crown after being ill with polio some years before. As I watched this scene with the other spectators the captain of the Danish team, moved to tears also, came to me and thanked me for my help, for without my advice Jubilee would never have come to the Games. Then I slowly left the stadium, but I suddenly heard a horse's hoofs behind me and saw Lis Hartel galloping towards me. She reined in, bent down from the saddle and gave me a kiss—thereby offering me the Olympic crown.

It was rather interesting that the Hamburg *Welt* should write about Lis Hartel: "Those *piaffes* and *passages*, with the help on the previous day of the Austrian Podhajsky, were superbly executed." And I thought nobody had seen us training!

Our visit to Sweden represented one of the severest tests for the Spanish Riding School, since for decades Swedish officers had been seconded to the Spanish Riding School, until after 1930 there began to be a marked preference for Saumur. Moreover, I had to take into account that among the spectators there were many riding experts who would visit the Spanish Riding School on the way back from the Olympic Games, so the Austrian riders would be watched with particularly critical eyes.

Our reception in Stockholm was quite remarkable in every respect. The horses were stabled in the King's castle, and in the passage leading to the stables a "Welcome" was written in sawdust to greet the white horses from Austria. An officer of the Swedish Army acted as permanent aide to look after our comfort, attending to our every wish in the most friendly fashion.

We stood before the same great door that in 1912 had opened for the first time when the participants in the Olympic Games, including also for the first time riding teams from ten countries, marched in for the ceremonial inauguration. It was a thrilling feeling as this door opened into the completely darkened stadium before us; then four spots found us and followed us to the space where our performance was to be given. Only by the thunderous applause could we guess at the size of the audience that filled the huge circle to capacity. After a short parade, a sort of preliminary for the public, one item after another of the first part of our programme followed with model precision, giving one almost the impression that the Lipizzaner too were surpassing themselves. Everything was perfect, a state rarely achieved by riders, and was unstintingly praised by the critics. The papers stressed that this performance was of a far higher standard than the riding at Helsinki.

When I ended the first part of the programme with my solo on Pluto

Theodorosta the organizer asked me in the interval to ride alone into the arena for a special honour. I was so happy that I agreed, with serious consequences. I entered in a dignified collected canter, was picked up by the spotlight and waited, standing quite still in the only circle of light in the pitch-dark stadium for whatever was to happen. Suddenly I saw above me a helicopter with brightly illuminated cockpit sinking slowly to the ground. Unfortunately Pluto Theodorosta also saw the falling, shining, and noisy body in the night sky and made a move to flee from the arena. I knew him much too well not to realize that with his temperament nothing would stop him and already pictured myself on a wild chase completely at the mercy of the horse's panic, rushing about the spacious stadium to the accompaniment of laughter of more than 22,000, and felt more lonely and abandoned than ever before, for I thought I was about to experience the worst disgrace of my life. As a last resort I tightened the rein on the excited horse and increased the pressure of my legs even more. And it worked! Obedience had driven out his terror. He stood as still as a statue while this shining monster approached us with ever-increasing noise and the draught from the propellers actually whistled round our ears, and it was only through my tightly gripping legs that I could feel how violently he was trembling. About twenty yards from us the helicopter stopped and two children in Swedish costume stepped out. Pluto Theodorosta obeyed when I commanded him to approach them and the helicopter in the *passage.* There the girl presented me with a huge bouquet and the boy with one of the famous Swedish 'lucky' horses, but as big as a full-grown poodle. I had hardly recovered from my astonishment at the enormous weight of the gift than I realized that everyone had once more disappeared in the darkness and I stood alone again in the arena, not counting the reins I held in my hands, my hat and switch, the bouquet, and the heavy horse. How on earth was I to get out of the stadium? That was what worried me. I could not jettison my ballast, but I had to make my escape, so I put Pluto Theodorosta into a short gallop and made for the door. The rousing cheers, however, did not lighten the weight of the 'lucky' horse, which I could hardly hold, and so I put it down in front of me, hoping to bring it to safety in one piece. But the legs of this wooden counterpart stuck at every step into the stallion's neck, and, upset, he reacted with a noticeable quickening of tempo, so I once more tucked the red horse under my arm and finally arrived at the saddling enclosure. There Pluto Theodorosta was surrounded by many cavalry officers and other experts and praised as the most perfect dressage horse.

The second half of the performance concluded fittingly with the quadrille to the cheers of the vast crowd. There was no doubt that it was in the Stockholm stadium that the Spanish Riding School reached the zenith of its foreign successes.

My dressage contests on Lipizzaner stallions also reached their climax in Stockholm with the triumph of Pluto Theodorosta in the Kür, where the rider chooses his own programme. The horse was in particularly good form that year and had already been such a decisive winner when he took part in the International Horse Show in Salzburg at the beginning of July that he was acclaimed by the critics as being "in a class of his own" compared with the other contestants. In Stockholm in the Kür he left seven of the best riders behind, including the winner of the Gold Medal in the big dressage event at Helsinki, the Swedish Major St Cyr, and this in his own country! It was a wonderful and important triumph for me!

The long and exhausting tour was to end with performances in Gmunden and Wels, so I was not too pleased to receive invitations to visit Paris and Brussels in October. But all my attempts to refuse them failed, for I was reminded that we had already visited nearly all the countries of Western Europe except France and Germany more than once. So this highly gratifying but at the same time somewhat difficult invitation was accepted.

That was the first time in its long history that the Spanish Riding School visited Paris, entering the domain of the French Cavalry School of Saumur. Apart from the fact that we must expect very critical judgment there are many points of difference between the two schools of riding. The Spanish Riding School has remained true to the teaching of the great master de la Guérinière, while the French Cavalry School rebelled against his methods more than a hundred and fifty years ago and abandoned them abruptly. We had thus to reckon with a very critical public, on the one hand the layman with his local patriotism, and on the other the experts, because of the difference in riding methods between Vienna and Saumur. Our reception in Paris was very friendly, horses and staff were taken to the École Militaire, which was a great honour, and the riders had their quarters in big hotels. My return to Paris, where I had last been during the World Exhibition of 1937, was not so much disappointing as astounding! I was not surprised to rediscover the gentle rhythm of the city on the Seine that helps to make all the problems of life much easier, but I was amazed at the friendliness of the French in spite of the shadow of the recent past, taking the trouble to speak German to the grooms. Indeed, many of them said they had been prisoners of war for several years in Austria or Germany, and remembered these days without bitterness.

When I drove to the Hôtel Napoléon, and the porters hurried to deal with our baggage, one of them saw our dachs Lumpi, and said that taking dogs into the hotel was strictly forbidden. I asked my wife, who is much more diplomatic than I, to straighten things out with the receptionist. He confirmed with regret the prohibition on dogs, and advised her to put Lumpi in with the horses. My wife rejected this idea and spoke of going somewhere else, but the receptionist said excitedly "You could not do that to us! The suite has been prepared for you, and is already filled with flowers.

I know nothing about your dog; please just smuggle him into the hotel as unobtrusively as possible, so the other guests and my colleagues don't see him."

I carried Lumpi hidden under my coat in and out of the hotel at the same time each day for twelve days! At first I only had to be careful about the eager page-boys who wanted to take my coat, but later there were reporters as well. They passed me in the foyer and I had to talk to them and answer their questions while the little creature—as if he knew what was happening—kept quite still in my arms. But this dog business became ridiculous when we came back to the hotel on one occasion at two in the morning and our friends Crown Prince, Prince, and Princess zu Oettingen-Wallerstein thought it silly to bother to hide him in the middle of the night, as they were sure nearly everybody knew of Lumpi's existence. So we took Lumpi on his lead to the lift, but the porter dashed after us and objected. Prince Oettingen replied, "The dog belongs to me, and I am only visiting my friends for a short time." So the porter answered, "But you must take the dog away with you, for in no circumstances can he stay here overnight." So I accompanied my friends to the hotel entrance with the dachs running behind us in full view, then picked the little creature up and carried him back under my coat, so everything was quite all right.

There were two covered schools and an open riding square in the École Militaire where we could exercise our horses. The disappearance of the horse from the Army was particularly noticeable here in the empty stables, but there were always plenty of onlookers while we worked. In accordance with the wishes of our hosts a kind of dress rehearsal was held on the open riding square, the so-called courtyard of honour, which was attended by the commandant of Paris. Before the General arrived in the square, where a small platform had been erected, two Spahis in their colourful uniform took up their positions with drawn sabres on either side of the great wrought-iron entrance gates and remained there until the eminent officer had left the École Militaire. In view of this formality I also had the riders line up before we began our rehearsal and doff their hats in welcome. This was obviously very well received.

All the daily papers gave detailed accounts of our first appearances in the French capital, and extracts from our programme were reproduced in full-page pictures under banner headlines. Then followed rave notices such as very rarely appear in the Paris Press, and even the left-wing papers struck the same note.

The reporters' reactions were always the same whether they lived in the far north, in the south, or even in the heart of Europe. Perhaps this was due to the clear recognition that the Spanish Riding School's performances were an art form that could move and enthral people everywhere, regardless of nationality and temperament. The impression our appearance made

*A Verena Podhajsky, dedico este
pequeño detalle, con toda amistad*
Pinohermoso
1954

44. *Corrida* on Horseback: The Duke of Pinohermoso as a Rejoneador in Jerez de la Frontera, 1954

45. Evening Ceremony: The Minister of Agriculture conferring the Order Isabel la Catolica on behalf of General Franco in Jerez de la Frontera, 1954

46. Going Home

47. Farewell to Wels, 1955

in Paris was so great that the illustrated papers showed countless pictures covering several pages, and the *Semaine de France* of October 18 published a series of pictures with the large headlines: "The only rivals of the Cadre Noir of Saumur are the riders of the school from Vienna who are setting Paris by its ears."

So we managed to survive even this severe test, and in our few days in Paris scored an incomparable triumph. When my thoughts turn back now to that time all these successes seem like a real dream—only the black-and-white evidence of the printed notices proves that it all actually happened.

Of all the many experiences and encounters of a personal nature my meeting with the son of Colonel Danloux made a particularly deep impression. His father was a very well-known French cavalry officer, Commandant of the Saumur Cavalry School from 1929 to 1934, and in 1937 he had congratulated me in person quite spontaneously at the International Horse Show in Berlin for my performance on Nero. Fifteen years later in the Palais de Sports a somewhat shy young man addressed me, and told me that his father had so often raved about me that I had become a symbol to the son as well, although in Paris he had seen me ride for the first time. He told me that his father during the liberation of France, just before the Americans marched in, had been captured by the Maquis and murdered because he had greeted Germans during the War who had once been his riding companions. Here in Paris the son gave me the good wishes of his dead father, whom I had always remembered kindly as a true cavalier. I held Danloux's hand for a long time, accepting in spirit the last greeting of my good French riding comrade.

Of all our experiences, some of them very amusing, I remember one specially. On the last evening of the "Five Nights of the Horse" Prince Bernhard of the Netherlands was one of the most important people present. As each group of performers came in the military band played different marches: for Major St Cyr, who showed his Olympic horse, a Swedish military march; for Colonel Jousseaume, a French one; and our appearance was always greeted with the Prince Eugène March. On this gala evening at the first notes of this old Austrian cavalry march Prince Bernhard stood up in his box, whereupon the crowd of over 13,000 simultaneously rose and stood quite still with bared heads until the band stopped playing and our performance began. The Austrian Press made a good deal of the unappreciated anthem of the republic.

It had been obvious for a long time that the chief event of 1953, and of special significance for the Spanish Riding School, would be its participation in the Coronation Horse Show in London. This invitation, which in itself was a great honour for Austrian horsemanship and our country, naturally pushed all other plans into the background, including an extensive tour of Spain. The performances to be given at the Coronation Show involved particularly careful preparation, the more so because our part in this representative and professionally very important event had been already decided a year earlier. Everything else must give place to this task, so I had only half-heartedly agreed to a festival visit to Dortmund, and firmly declined an invitation to the International Horse Show at Aachen. Yielding to pressure from the Aachen–Laurensberger Rennverein and the intervention of various influential people in Germany, I then decided I would after all break the journey to London in Aachen, to arrange a few performances there. The main target remained London, where we must not arrive with tired horses.

Entrants from nine nations showed clearly that the International Horse Show in Aachen was in process of regaining the position that it had held in international riding between the wars. For me personally Aachen was a shining milestone on the long road of my equestrian career, for here I had won my first great foreign victory, and here on each appearance I had dominated every dressage competition. It is not difficult to understand why this success, and the friendly reception and incomparable atmosphere of Aachen, I had always retained such happy memories of it, and often longed to make a pilgrimage to the city of my triumphs. The Aachen meeting seemed in retrospect one of the big manifestations of peace, and I still remember what the captain of a foreign team said before the Second World War in a speech made in an atmosphere of rising tension: "If we as officers and most of all as riders were deciding our countries' policies, the question of war and peace would certainly not arise, for the horse binds us into one community regardless of what language we may use to make ourselves understood." And this vivacious speaker was cheered by us all!

The Spanish Riding School had also been fêted here in 1927, so we all went to Aachen with great expectation.

We had our first disappointment when the horses arrived. Nobody was at the station, and it was hours before we finally unloaded the Lipizzaner and reached the showground after a long walk. Here too there was nobody to receive us, so we had to go in search of the stables intended for the Spanish Riding School. What a contrast to the reception we had recently had in Hanover and Dortmund, and had enjoyed at festivals elsewhere!

At the stadium itself and in the near-by stable buildings not a trace remained of the War, although this city had also suffered damage. And on the level green of the Soer there seemed in fact to be an extension of the layout as it had been before the War.

The second disappointment was the arrangement of the ground for our performances, the view of the spectators from the cheapest places being spoilt by the permanent obstacles; nor were the movable obstacles taken right away during the performances, and even the people in the best seats could not follow the movements of the Lipizzaner without interference. When I protested I was merely told that there was no question of clearing the ring, as our appearance came in the middle of the jumping events. So there it was, and many spectators got only a glimpse of our performance! This was important also from a financial angle. The expenses incurred by our visit were very high, and because so little understanding had been shown over creating a suitable setting for us, even in this well-patronized stadium the attendances did not go up at all on our account.

We gave altogether four performances, lasting about fifty minutes, and were always asked to keep exactly to the prescribed time, although the individual jumping events often ended late. Altogether not a very stimulating atmosphere. The hundred thousand and more visitors who visited the Horse Show applauded us generously and amazed me by remaining so good-tempered in spite of the poor view.

With the Prix des Nations there was a parade and welcome for those taking part. With full pomp and ceremony the riders of each nation were individually introduced and welcomed as they passed the guests of honour by the playing of their national anthems. It was quite a long affair, which most of the competition horses endured with many signs of disobedience and friskiness, but the Lipizzaner stood for nearly an hour as motionless as statues in the vast arena, unmoved by anthems and applause. This was appreciated by all the knowledgeable spectators, so it is small wonder the Lipizzaner got an extra clap as they entered and left at the head of the competitors. This was, moreover, the only time that many of the spectators saw the riders of the Spanish Riding School properly as they rode past the stands.

In point of fact the problem of national anthems since the end of the First World War had been a strange one. The constant change of anthem has often given rise to situations some comic, some embarrassing, and some downright grotesque. So when in Aachen the Spanish team was being thus honoured a gentleman in the V.I.P. box leapt to his feet as the music started—it was the Spanish Ambassador—and gestured in surprise, the saluting Spanish cavalry officers dropped their hands, and, ignoring the music, rode back to their places. What had happened was that the band had played the Spanish Communist hymn for General Franco's officers, and this naturally caused a certain amount of excitement. One of the officials dashed up to my wife and asked whether the Spanish Riding School could not help out with the proper anthem. But the Spanish Riding School and Spain lie poles apart, and certainly have no affinity in the matter of anthems, so a messenger dashed off in a car to Bonn to get the music of the proper anthem from the Spanish military attaché. As the Spanish team then won the Prix des Nations, its victorious riders were able when the national anthem of their homeland was played to hold their heads proudly erect and raise their hands to their caps in salute. All's well that ends well!

We too ended our performance, rode once more with the rest of those taking part past the many thousands of people, who waved farewell to us with their handkerchiefs—a particularly attractive sight, this movement of tens of thousands of pieces of white cloth in time to the music of *Muss i' denn zum Städtle hinaus*.

While the Lipizzaner and those in charge of them moved towards the climax of the year, news of our festival appearances followed us in the many press reports. Meanwhile the riders of the Spanish Riding School had another but not less informed public to conquer, and did it so successfully that there too the critics searching endlessly for the right methods were silent.

CHAPTER 15

The Lipizzaner charm Queen Elizabeth II

While the riders and horses were approaching the Channel coast to cross via the Hook of Holland and Harwich on their way to London I flew in with my wife from Düsseldorf. As the plane flew across the Channel on this fine summer's day I could not help remembering my flight in similar circumstances four years earlier. Then too the International Horse Show was the object of my journey, but this time success depended not on me alone, but on the efforts of my companions. Above all, the meeting of the past with the present awaited me. It was with such thoughts that we landed at London Airport, were met and given a warm welcome by the President of the British Horse Society, Colonel Williams, and his wife. What a wonderful feeling of true friendship! We had not seen each other for a long time, but they both greeted us as kindly and affectionately as if we had been away only a few days. Of course we must go with them to their glorious place, East Burnham Park, and we found everything just the same as four years earlier, including Simon, who leapt joyfully up at us, and the exotic giant ducks waddling peacefully over the superb English grass.

The next day with Colonel Williams I inspected the White City stadium and the arrangements made for the Lipizzaner. Roomy boxes for the sixteen stallions had been prepared in tented stabling right next to the ring, covered with peat-litter, as the use of straw was prohibited by the fire-prevention authorities. When I said I was afraid that my white horses might turn canary colour after a night on this 'bed,' sawdust was immediately substituted for the peat, and I was told with a smile that hay was allowed for fodder. My Lipizzaner would be so plentifully supplied with roughage that this too might be useful for bedding, so the noble stallions were virtually bedded down in hay.

245

In the White City I found a clean turf square prepared for our performances just opposite the Royal Box and surrounded with flowering shrubs.
Colonel Williams informed me that this space would be kept permanently
free of obstacles, so that the grass would not be too badly worn by the jumping. Above all care would be taken that the effect of our performances should
not be marred by obstacles being too close, and the Lipizzaner would be
clearly visible from all sides. This thoughtfulness after our recent experiences did me as much good as the reception of the horses on their arrival
on July 15 by members of the British Horse Society, who had appeared
with the journalists and supervised the immediate transfer of the Lipizzaner
by horse-box to their stabling. This was typical of the Spanish Riding
School's welcome in England. The picture on the cover of the programme
was a full-page coloured photograph of me on Neapolitano Africa in the
passage. In other ways, too, I was constantly made aware that this horse and
his earlier efforts here in London had not been forgotten.

Unfortunately, Neapolitano Africa could not come this time, and his
substitute Maestoso Alea, was still far from following in the footsteps of his
gallant predecessor. He was a handsome and unusually nimble Lipizzaner,
but very difficult. An important factor in giving him such a complex nature
was his use when young for stud. He could make a convincing picture of a
riding horse—when he wanted to—and he could, if something did not
please him, be so unco-operative as to be barely recognizable. In London
the ponies affected him particularly and drove him mad. I usually had to
warm him up for a long time and give him a great deal of exercise, and often
thought with longing of my faithful Neapolitano Africa as I carried out this
exhausting work.

On the second day we met the Press photographers in the stadium. The
excellent shots taken on this occasion, including some perfect *caprioles*,
were then published as half- or full pages in the English papers and magazines, but they went abroad too, and the same pictures appeared in German,
American, French, Dutch, Spanish, and even Moroccan publications.

On July 19 we showed excerpts from our programme in a live television
broadcast that was to last ten minutes. I compiled a programme ending
with the quadrille, and, as this was the easiest to adapt to the time limit, we
arranged for a signal when time was nearly up, as I wanted to line up and
finish the broadcast with a salute. As arranged, I began the shortened programme, knowing that it was too late to make alterations now, for we were
already appearing on many hundreds of thousands of screens. Everything
went without a hitch, we were approaching the quadrille, and I was just
waiting for the prearranged warning signal. It seemed a great deal longer
than ten minutes, but when no sign came and the variations of the quadrille
were finished I decided on the spot to line up, salute, and thus wind up the
broadcast. Then the television staff rushed towards me, overwhelmed me

with praise and congratulations, and explained that the programme had been so marvellous that they had not had the heart to give the signal after nine minutes. The broadcast had lasted seventeen.

The next day saw the opening of the thirty-fourth International Horse Show. There were afternoon and evening performances on all six days; at each one we showed different parts of our programme for half an hour. The musical accompaniment was once more provided—as for my exhibition rides in 1949—by a Royal Marine band under the direction of the head of the Royal Marine Music School, Major V. Dunn, but this time the bandsmen had to play concert pieces unfamiliar to them, the Austrian compositions that always accompanied the Lipizzaner. The music of Mozart's Symphony in G minor, the accompaniment for the *Pas de Trois*, was missing, and the substitute of Haydn chosen by Major Dunn did not quite fit in with the horses' movements. Afterwards he listened to the symphony we wanted on our tape-recorder, and left the arena deep in thought.

I could scarcely believe my ears when on the opening day the strains of Mozart instead of Haydn greeted our entry for the *Pas de Trois*—so perfectly played that at first I thought it was the tape-recorder, until I traced it to Major Dunn's full band; an achievement showing not only goodwill but also great musical ability.

Signs of the Spanish Riding School's success began to be evident after its very first appearance. The Lipizzaner appealed to the crowds—the papers said later that the Horse Show had had the largest attendance ever, more than a hundred thousand spectators—and soon became the accepted idols of the English.

On the evening of July 22 the young Queen Elizabeth II came to the White City, and at the express wish of the organizers was shown two items from our programme: all the gaits and turns of the *haute école* demonstrated by Pluto Theodorosta, and the school quadrille. There was a heavy shower just before the evening performance, and it almost seemed as if we should have to perform for the Queen in the rain, but it cleared up just as we rode in, and there was a happy feeling of excitement and expectancy in the packed stadium.

I rode Pluto Theodorosta on a curb in a difficult programme of *pirouettes*, changes of leg, *piaffes*, the *passage*, and other movements, holding the reins in my left hand only, which was sometimes difficult as the surface was rough and covered with large puddles. However, Pluto Theodorosta went magnificently, although I had not been able to ride him much since Aachen because of an injury, and was enthusiastically applauded. The quadrille was very well received too. When we finally reached the saddling enclosure the horses and their riders were spattered with mud from head to foot as if they had just come in from hunting over heavy ground.

After the performance I was summoned to the Royal Box and presented to the Queen, and was very struck by her appearance. In all her disciplined movements and speech she revealed her queenliness in spite of her youth. Holding out her hand she said, "I have not seen anything for a long time that has impressed me as much as this performance by the Spanish Riding School."

After the presentation Colonel Williams asked me to go on to a reception at Kensington Palace arranged by the Duke of Beaufort. When we got there he told me that the Queen must have arrived already as her car was also waiting outside, and in fact she and her Consort, Prince Philip, were there with members of the aristocracy. She shook hands and remarked that she had already spoken to me at the White City. While my wife was being presented the Duke of Edinburgh, standing beside the Queen, congratulated me on the performance. Then the Duke of Beaufort took me by the arm, led me into the next room, and gave me a glass of champagne.

"You have worked hard to-day; you must be very thirsty."

The Duchess of Beaufort came up to me with a plate full of cakes, saying, "You have given me such pleasure with your horses, and I hear that you like sweet things."

As I stood holding the plate and my glass a man spoke to me, and, looking up, I recognized the Duke of Edinburgh, who had followed me. I had barely answered his first question when I heard a woman's voice on the other side of me, and, turning round, saw the Queen, and the three of us had a long conversation. The Queen, still lovelier than all her pictures with her wonderful English colouring, looked straight at me with her large shining eyes as she spoke. It seemed as if she combined in a rare harmony the naturalness of a charming woman with the dignity of a monarch. The Duke of Edinburgh too, tall and good-looking, looked intently at me as we talked, so that I was often in some doubt in answering the many questions which of the pairs of eyes I should meet.

The comparatively long talk with Queen Elizabeth II was for me a special experience. Although she was very fully occupied during the Coronation festivities with the countless banquets, parades, receptions, and presentations, she showed an incredible interest even in unimportant matters in those days, and in everything to do with horses. She inquired where the Lipizzaner had been during the War, what had happened to them afterwards, and how it had been possible for this once imperial riding-school to survive at all to the present day in spite of the collapse of the Austro-Hungarian Empire and all that had followed afterwards. I replied, "Because the Spanish Riding School is a cultural institution which even after 1918 carried on an old and venerable tradition. But a tradition can survive only if it remains in its entirety and is saved from gradual decay. Even leaving off a glove is a sign of decay."

At this the Queen turned to her husband and said emphatically, "He's right, isn't he?"

I was more than a little astonished when she mentioned the behaviour of Maestoso Borina, who carried his rider magnificently in the *passage*, but only gave a sketch of this step with pupils. I had written about it in my book *The Vienna Spanish Riding School*, which the Queen had borrowed from the Duke of Beaufort because at that time it was out of print. And I was specially struck by her keen observation when she said of Pluto Theodorosta, who particularly attracted her, "I was amazed that your horse, although he was only ridden with one hand on a curb, performed all those difficult exercises absolutely smoothly. What impressed me most, though, was that in the *passage*, although he trod in a puddle and splashed himself, he did not break his rhythm at all. Most horses would have tried to avoid the puddles."

She asked me whether I always rode Pluto Theodorosta in this way or whether he could be ridden on a snaffle, and asked for information on many other points of schooling. In this connexion she inquired whether she too would be able to ride him, or whether the direction he was accustomed to was any different from that of riding in general. So I answered, "Your Majesty, I should be greatly honoured if you would ride Pluto Theodorosta."

The Queen hesitated a moment and did not give a definite answer, although the Duke of Edinburgh said, "Go on, ride him, now that you have the chance."

In the meantime the rest of the company had formed a semicircle round us and were listening in silence to the conversation. The Queen thanked me for my explanation and left the party. The Duke of Beaufort, who had escorted her to the door, came up to me at once and said, "Her Majesty has asked me to find out whether the invitation to ride your horse was given merely out of politeness, or whether you really meant it. We are good friends you and I, so please tell me the truth." When I replied that I had offered my horse in all seriousness, the Duke said he would inform the Queen.

Pluto Theodorosta's solo had impressed one man particularly: the landowner who had described me as far back as 1949 as the "dressage rider with a soul." He came next day to the saddling enclosure and was most insistent that I should ride Pluto Theodorosta once more in the show. This was not included in the programme, so I said that the prearranged order of events ought not to be changed, for in no circumstances did I want to create the impression that I was anxious to push myself forward with my solos. He begged my permission to put his request to the organizers, and the next day Colonel Ansell asked me to ride Pluto Theodorosta once more in place of the *Pas de Trois*. When I rode back to the saddling enclosure, cheered by the audience, the landowner came to me, shook my hand vigorously, and, looking at me with shining eyes, said simply, "Thank you."

After our penultimate performance I was bidden with the riders to the

Royal box. There the Duchess of Beaufort presented each *Bereiter* with a souvenir medal of the Horse Show, and me with the Medal of Honour. This medal, awarded by the British Horse Society for outstanding services to riding in England, had only been given five times before, and I was the first foreigner to receive it.

At the close of this little ceremony the Duchess invited me into the Royal Box, where I had a very pleasant surprise. As I stepped in I at once noticed the former Governor-General of Canada, Lord Alexander, who stood up, held out his hand, and said, "You probably will not remember me, but I am Lord Alexander, and met you in Toronto and had a talk with you." What greatness and modesty for a man in his high position! How often I had met smaller people who made no secret of their resentment that I had not at once recognized them.

The intention of Queen Elizabeth to ride a Lipizzaner stallion had caught the imagination of the ordinary citizens of London more than I could have believed possible. The pros and cons were argued right up to the time when the horses were actually on their way to Buckingham Palace. The opponents of this "riding experiment" argued that it was irresponsible for the Queen in the middle of the Coronation festivities and just before her world tour to be exposed to the possible danger of injury from a foreign horse from a foreign country.

Pluto Theodorosta and four other Lipizzaner were taken with their riders by horse-box to the Palace, but the Duke of Beaufort warned me not to be disappointed if the Queen did not in the end actually ride as the objections had not completely died down. However, she would certainly come at 10.30 A.M. into the covered school to watch the handling and the "Airs Above the Ground," as she had not yet seen these items. Just the same I made complete preparations for the Queen's ride. Luckily, among the many details, I thought that my stirrup leathers might not have enough reserve holes to shorten them sufficiently, which would naturally have been rather an unfortunate discovery to make in the Queen's presence. The Duke of Beaufort, to whom I confessed my anxiety, sent for the stirrups from one of the Queen's own saddles.

The covered school at Buckingham Palace is unusually long and quite simply equipped. The iron girders across the roof were decorated with the various flags of the Commonwealth.

Punctually at 10.30 Queen Elizabeth, followed by the Duke of Edinburgh, their two children, and Princess Margaret, entered the room outside the school where the Duke and Duchess of Beaufort, the Crown Equerry, Sir Dermot McMorrough Kavanagh, and Colonel Williams with their wives and my wife had assembled. I noticed at once that the Queen was in riding clothes and therefore intended to ride Pluto Theodorosta. She greeted us individually, beginning with the Duchess of Beaufort. I shall never forget how the two women met. First they embraced and kissed each other on the cheek, then the white-haired Duchess, an aunt of the Queen, took one step backward, made a deep curtsy and kissed the young Queen's hand—the first greeting was for near relatives, the curtsy or bow and kissing of Her Majesty's hand for every one regardless of age or relationship.

I now asked the Queen whether I might show her the stallions trained for "Airs Above the Ground," and explained that the horses learnt these exercises first on the rein without their riders, and then with them. I showed *levades*, *caprioles*, and *courbettes* with three unmounted Lipizzaner, and then had the same movements repeated with their riders. Everybody followed this demonstration with obvious interest, and all were amazed at the exceptional willingness of the horses. After this short introduction I asked the Queen, remembering what I had said at Kensington Palace, whether she wanted to ride Pluto Theodorosta on a curb or a snaffle. She replied, "I prefer the snaffle," so I decided to ride him first on a snaffle, as he had become accustomed during our tours to being ridden only on a curb, so that I could make certain how this rather temperamental horse would behave under these conditions. When I had taken him through every step and the hardest movements I galloped up to the Queen and begged her to take my place. My groom quickly changed the stirrups, the Queen stepped forward and mounted.

When she was in the saddle and had taken the reins she asked me who besides myself rode Pluto Theodorosta, and when I replied that he was only led when I was away said, "Shall I really be the first strange rider he has carried?"

When the Queen began her ride I went into the middle of the school, keeping level with her, ready to jump forward if necessary, for I was very conscious of my heavy responsibility, but walking and trotting went fine, the Queen followed my suggestions promptly and finally broke into a gallop. During a breather she said, "How supple this horse is and how willing he is to gallop in either direction. My horse is not so easy in the gallop; he always wants to go to the right."

When the Queen had tried out some more basic steps, delighted with her success so far, I asked her if she would like to try the *piaffe* and *passage*. She said, "Oh, yes, I should love to, but I don't know what I have to do."

I gave her a few instructions and helped a little with my switch, and Pluto Theodorosta changed into the two steps of the *haute école*. Her Majesty's cheeks grew rosy, and when she finally stopped she called out excitedly, "I am thrilled!" And I, too, was pleasantly stimulated and happy. She dismounted and asked, "Might my husband also ride him? Then he can see how lovely it is to sit on a well-trained horse!" So the Duke of Edinburgh mounted Pluto Theodorosta, and rode him for a long time, but not so sensitively and quietly as the Queen, rather more in polo style. After the first quick parade I was horrified to see the increasing resistance of the stallion, and was glad when the Duke dismounted before there was any serious difference between horse and rider.

Then at the Duke's request I put Prince Charles on Pluto Theodorosta and led him round walking and trotting. Then seeing how longingly she watched her elder brother, I finally lifted Princess Anne on to the Lipizzaner's back.

When I had set her down the Royal Family crowded admiringly round Pluto Theodorosta, inspecting him closely, while the children, quite unafraid, offered him carrots and sugar. These he took eagerly, but carefully and gently out of the little hands.

Then something delightful happened. When I had heard that the Queen had had to borrow my book from the Duke of Beaufort I asked if I might present her with a copy. He said that she did not generally accept gifts, but if I did not mind I could give him a signed copy and he would try to find out whether I should be permitted to present it to the Queen. While we were exchanging a few words after the ride he suddenly pushed the book under my arm from behind, so I knew that I might offer it to the Queen and did so. The effect was magical. She took the book in both hands, looked at the title, and clasped it to her, saying, "I am absolutely delighted to have a copy of my own of your book about the beautiful horses. I was sorry to have to give back the one I borrowed."

She turned to Princess Margaret and said, "Look, now I have one of my own!" And, bending her knees to make herself smaller, she showed the open book to her children.

"See! This lovely book belongs to Mummy."

This little episode will always remain with me: the fêted Queen of England, cheered by millions of people during the Coronation festivities, had lost none of her warm, feminine charm!

When I came later to the White City and was asked for my impressions by Colonel Llewellyn I described the incident with enthusiasm. He smiled and said, "One more conquest! This Coronation is really nothing more than the adoration of millions of people for a Queen!"

The same afternoon some journalists asked for a few of my impressions of England, and especially for my experiences in London. I naturally omitted completely the morning at Buckingham Palace, and talked of many other things, but not a word about the Queen's ride, so I was very astonished to read next day an account of the visit of the Lipizzaner to the Palace, ending with my expressed comment that "The Queen impressed me by her remarkably light hands and her sensitive and intelligent riding. The Duke of Edinburgh, on the other hand, rode like a polo player."

Later it was discovered that these remarks had been made by some one present, and had been picked up by a reporter and attributed to me to make the story better. Somehow it must have got out that the Queen had ridden a Lipizzaner, for that same afternoon a sizeable crowd came to the stables, and everybody wanted to see Pluto Theodorosta, whose name became so well known that some months later I received a letter intended for me addressed to "Mr Pluto Theodorosta, Wels." The writer explained that he had not remembered my name, so he had used that of my horse, and the postal officials in Wels knew—full marks to them!—that it could only be intended for a member of the school. When we returned to Vienna one of the many reporters and photographers from all over the world was Mr Armstrong Jones, later to marry Princess Margaret. He said he did not want to take the usual pictures of the performance, but the portraits of Pluto Theodorosta and me.

Queen Elizabeth II's ride seemed to me to set the crown on my work as a rider. The purpose of any dressage work must be so to train a horse that it is agreeable to ride at any time for any rider, without his having to discover any special secrets about it.

The Horse Show closed its doors on July 25 after our quadrille. Once again I watched with emotion the closing ceremony displaying all the pomp of a world Power, with the fascinating musical exercises of the Royal Marine Band, the extinguishing of the lights, the slow lowering of the flag, and the sound of "God Save the Queen," which everybody heard with moist eyes and bared heads. As I stood there feeling a little sad I thought gratefully of the series of wonderful successes there had been for the Spanish Riding School and myself. I thanked God that I had been permitted to ride once again for Austria here in London, and I was happy that this time I could return from my triumphs in good health.

The success of the Spanish Riding School was more enduring than ever before. *The Times* said that "the last quadrille by the Spanish Riding School only made everyone still greedier for more," and when in 1958 we were invited to another festival the official letter said that our performances had been so impressive that the British Horse Society had abandoned all other exhibition items, as they had only proved disappointing. Without a doubt, therefore, 1953 brought our greatest success, and the subsequent visits to Salzburg and Passau were quite overshadowed by our English appearances, in spite of the presence of illustrious visitors from all over the world.

As the year drew to its close I looked back with satisfaction that the white horses of Austria had maintained their high standards and added many new friends to the crowds of old ones. Alongside the actual events and experiences certain disadvantages of these long tours were becoming increasingly obvious. I grew still more reluctant to accept the many invitations from abroad, and managed to get the Ministry to refuse a tremendous number of official ones: a visit to Belgrade and Athens; a tour of the four Scandinavian countries; a repeat of the performances in Hamburg and Rotterdam, and a tour planned several years before to San Francisco and Los Angeles. These measures were unavoidable because the Spaniards, after agitating for years, had at last obtained permission for a festival tour of the Vienna Riding School in 1954.

On the same grounds I at first stood firm in my refusal of an invitation to a second Horse Show in the new Westphalia Hall in Dortmund, although this was proof of the great success of the white horses' previous appearance, but when the President of the Dortmunder Reitverein protested that any other exhibition number at the resuscitated Westphalian Horse Show would be an anticlimax I relented. I realized that a repetition of our previous programmes might easily prove disappointing, so I suggested modifying and shortening them, and this worked out very well.

Seven nations took part in the International Horse Show in March, and the rebuilding had progressed enormously. This time the Lipizzaner were able to go direct to the stables erected close to the hall, which was completely sold out for the last three days. The papers spoke of a total of 64,000, and the Lipizzaner did not prove in any way disappointing, delighting thousands of spectators and inspiring the Press to give extensive coverage, and using such phrases as "æsthetic calming of the nerves"—as a matter of interest, the same remark that the London papers had used—and "creatures like statues that awoke at the sound of Mozart's music and became ballet-dancers on four legs."

My wife and I were invited to an intimate lunch at the house of the President of the Deutscher Sportbund, Herr Daume, at which the President of the Republic, Dr Theodor Heuss, also appeared. I found the German Head of State a jovial scholar with a pronounced sense of humour, a clever man with a penetrating eye for the tasks of the present day. I was struck by his directness and simplicity in all that he did and said. When my wife looked round for her place card the President said with a smile, "It's all right, Frau Podhajsky, just come up to me. To-day your place is here on my right." With these few words and a simple gesture he announced what was in fact a great honour.

When the Spanish Riding School ended the programme that day, performing before 14,000 people, the riders lined up after the big school quadrille in front of the German President's box for a small ceremony. Herr Wörneke, who was responsible for providing the musical accompaniment for us, recorded this event on tape and gave it to me as a present. Through his quick thinking, an example of German efficiency and a warm heart, I have preserved for me in sound one of the memorable moments of my life.

I saluted, and then the President made a speech outlining my career and bestowed on me, amid thunderous applause, the Grand Service Cross of the Service Order of the German Republic. Then he shook my hand warmly and congratulated me, while Herr Daume put the ribbon of the order round my neck.

After a few choked words of thanks I climbed back into the saddle and left the arena at the head of my riders in the *passage*, cheered by the audience, which clapped in time to the horses' steps. Our visit to Dortmund, where we had once again been received with great kindness, thus ended in honourable and triumphant splendour.

CHAPTER 16
━━━━━◆◆◆◆▶━━━━━

The Land of their Forefathers—Spain

For years the Real Jockey Club in Jerez de la Frontera had been agitating for the Lipizzaner to make a festival visit to Spain, and declaring in their invitation that it was quite incomprehensible that the Spanish Riding School should have made tours throughout the world but had not yet been to the country whose name it bore. They were most insistent that the Vienna Riding School should go to the Coronation Show in London via Spain and exhibit its horses at long last in the country of its origin. After a long exchange of letters I declined, as I knew too little of the conditions there, and in any case we obviously could not arrive in the British capital with overworked horses, so the Real Jockey Club asked me to pay a personal visit to make all the necessary arrangements on the spot for a festival tour.

In September 1953 I set off with my wife for Jerez de la Frontera by car. Our journey took us through France to the border at Irun, where we entered the Iberian peninsula, but though we could at first detect no differences compared with the rest of Europe, we changed our minds on the way from San Sebastian to Madrid. Once we left the coast the landscape gave us the impression of being in a completely different part of the world beyond the Pyrenees; we might have been in Africa already. Instead of the lush green vegetation of France and the border there was an endless stony desert scorched by a merciless sun. Wherever we looked we saw nothing but the red rock on either side of the winding road, which was good here and there but not much frequented.

Spain is a country whose inhabitants must be easily satisfied and tough, for the contrasts one meets are great. Bitter poverty reigns on the one hand and definite luxury on the other, particularly in the south. A stranger also notices the difference in temperament, from noticeably proud self-control

48. Back in Vienna, 1955

49. The Press is always Present

50. The Lipizzaner in the Historic Riding Hall in the Josefsplatz

to unrestrained outbreaks of fiery passion. As one gets to know the people and the country one understands the stormy history of the civil war waged for years with the greatest bitterness.

Our journey was unforgettably beautiful and romantic when, missing the way near Bilbao, we took a quite incomparable road along a high ridge and drank in the unusual landscape. The conditions of the roads and the great heat threw out all our calculations, and we arrived two days late at our destination. We did not like this at all—we had not yet become familiar with the meaning of the word *mañana*. In Jerez we were given a princely reception with true Spanish grandeur. As the vintage feast, for which we had been expected, was already at its height, we had to take part in the crowning of the Queen of the Grape Harvest, a somewhat wearisome pleasure with so many speeches in an unknown tongue. In spite of the big national holiday we were well looked after. I was shown the horses at the national stallion depot, and a preliminary riding lesson, all most formally carried out. Even the grooms leading the stallions wore white gloves with their spotless uniforms; it was not so much the dress and bearing of these people as the care of the horses and the well-polished saddlery that impressed me. We were always most punctilious about this in Austria, but what I saw in Jerez was of a still higher standard than our stable work, which had become quite famous.

Here in Jerez, the centre of Andalusian horse-breeding, I realized also the fallacy of the idea held throughout Central Europe that the old Spanish strain, in which the whole Continent takes such delight, survives only in the Lipizzaner. Although the horses in Spain have developed somewhat too fine bones through the frequent introduction of Arab blood, I still found several very beautiful creatures whose great similarity to our Lipizzaner showed that the original characteristics still survived. Only the correctness of their gait, in our view, left something to be desired—the Spaniards have quite a different ideal of beauty, rejoicing if the horses thrust out their forelegs, thus showing their movements to greater effect.

Of course, we also had to pay a long visit to the wine-cellars, the Bodega of Gonzales-Guerreros, and taste the various kinds of the famous sherry. In the heat of the day this was not very enjoyable, for some varieties were very heavy, but we did not want to spoil the pleasure of our friendly host.

When the visit was over I had to sign an old cask, standing next to one signed by the last King of Spain.

Andalusia is justly called the land of the best wines and the noblest horses. So this visit was followed by a reception at the Real Jockey Club, whose Vice-President was Ramon Guerrero. After a polo match arranged in my honour, winding up with a lunch, I was ceremonially elected an honorary member of the club and received from the hand of the President, Rico Cortés, an artistically inscribed certificate in a hand-carved frame.

The Mayor of Jerez, Alvaro de Domecq, one of the most popular amateur toreadors, invited us into his beautiful home and showed me the model stables, built in the Moorish style, in which each horse is kept in a princely box with the walls covered with sayings from the Koran in praise of the horse.

On this occasion we had our first discussion about the proposed tour, after I had closely inspected the bullring in which our performances were to be given. I did not let the honours bestowed on me influence me as to the candidates, and made frank comments to Señor Alvaro de Domecq and Ramon Guerrero. The place, with a capacity of over 15,000, was in itself frightening. How could enough spectators with appreciation for the performances of the old riding academy be found to fill such a huge arena from among a passionate people whose mentality was quite different from ours in Central Europe and who had a preference for noisy scenes? Apart from this the ground was far too hard and would have to be covered with a layer of sand. I visualized some unpleasant moments and I said so point-blank, for I could not involve the Spanish Riding School in any risky adventures, but both men tried to overcome all my misgivings with the remark that I did not know the Spanish well enough. They were tremendously interested in a visit from the Vienna Riding School.

With every conceivable honour and many flowers we said good bye to Jerez, and on our way home visited Granada, which made the greatest impression of our entire Spanish trip. The Moorish stronghold, the Alhambra, had resisted all attacks for centuries, and preserved in its design and the wonderful gardens of the Generalife a glimpse of the highly developed culture of these 'heathens,' a building so vast that anyone living in an era of technical marvels can only fold his hands in silent admiration before so much beauty. And here too, at the opposite end of the scale, is the Christian cathedral, the Cartuja, with an unbelievable wealth of gold and precious stones, providing a shining symbol of the newly awakened power of the spirit. Filled with the breath of a great past, we set off for home, spiritually strengthened.

The sun continued to shine from an azure sky, the ground reflecting a heat unusual for this time of year. On the way to Valencia I had to learn to console myself with the Spanish *mañana*. A sudden noise, the car skidded; there was obviously something wrong with the tyres. I got out and saw flames shooting out of a flat back tyre. My efforts to put out the fire with rugs were in vain, and very worried I began to pull out the luggage at top speed, while my wife tried to stop oncoming cars. Two buses halted at once and put out the fire with extinguishers, while other drivers and passengers helped to change the badly burnt tyre and repack the luggage in the car. In the confusion and understandable excitement everything was done rapidly and I hardly had a chance to thank my helpers. And not a single one of our many bits and pieces was missing!

As after this the back wheel was locking, we could only drive on to the next garage, leave the car there, and go by taxi to a hotel in Valencia. Getting the trouble fixed—it was a broken ball-bearing and there were no spares to be had—was magnificently handled by the Commandant of the cavalry depot, Colonel Angel Somalo Paricio. He even found a mechanic who had been his N.C.O. during the civil war and said he would make a new bearing himself. It was touching to see the joyful greeting of these two old comrades and the willingness of the former subordinate to help his colonel. We were thus held up in Valencia for several days, but the time did not hang at all heavy on our hands, for I had a telephone call from Jerez inviting me to go to Madrid by the express, which with its modern air-conditioning provided a welcome contrast to the often primitive trains. Alvaro de Domecq and Ramon Guerrero met me, and introduced me to the Chief of the General Staff and the Inspector of Cavalry in the War Ministry. Both generals expressed the great interest of the Army in a festival by the Spanish Riding School and assured me that it was ready to be responsible for smooth transport through Spain. So that was the last detail settled, and our Spanish journey fixed for 1954.

In Madrid we were invited to visit the cavalry school, where the Commandant and his officers and their wives awaited us and showed us everything. I was once more amazed to hear how much these officers knew about what had happened to the Spanish Riding School, and I even shook hands with an officer of the "Blue Division" who had visited the school in Vienna during the war.

There was an amusing incident on our return flight to Valencia. As always on our travels, we had our dachshund with us, and after our breakdown I had kept him in our compartment on the way to Madrid in a bag. When we flew back I would not relinquish the bag in which our trusty companion was quietly resting, but the porter became suspicious and insisted on stowing this small piece of luggage on the trolley. As he did so the bag began to move, and the man, gesticulating wildly and pouring forth a torrent of words, took me to the captain of the plane, who advised me to get a permit from the airport authorities to take the dog with me. When an official asked me where the dog was I showed him the bag; like a true Spanish Cavalier he smiled and gave me permission to take Lumpi into the plane with me.

After an enriching and adventurous journey we returned to Wels, and shortly afterwards the official invitation from the Real Jockey Club of Jerez to appear in several Spanish cities arrived. The festival tour was fixed for the spring of 1954.

So, only a few days after our return from Dortmund, we had to pack our bags once more, and the horses left their headquarters in Wels in late March. I was still not entirely happy about this undertaking, but felt better when the boxes were met after a six-day journey in Port Bou, on the Spanish border, by the Vice-President of the Jockey Club in person and a German-speaking staff officer. The latter saw to it that Customs formalities and unloading were quickly completed, and in a relatively short time the horses were able to continue their journey to Barcelona as a military transport.

When they arrived in the early morning an officer with twenty soldiers was waiting to take the horses and luggage into the cavalry barracks. The white horses from Vienna walking through the streets provided an unusual sight in the brilliant Spanish sunshine, watched and accompanied by a vast crowd of curious spectators and photographed for the newspapers and news-reels. It certainly caused a sensation: the Lipizzaner for the first time on Spanish soil!

The arrangements at the barracks bore the stamp of Spanish hospitality. The best stalls were vacated, disinfected, and freshly whitewashed; soldiers were detailed to help the grooms and stable-lads; and a covered and an open school were made available for exercising the horses. There was always a large groups of officers watching the Lipizzaner training, after the C.O. of the regiment had got my permission. The days preceding the first perfor-mance were packed with discussions of the final details, Press interviews, and radio talks, and these in particular occupied a great deal of time. My wife too had to face the reporters at the microphone and answer questions that were then translated by an interpreter. One woman asked which I managed better, my horses or my wife. She replied, "Both equally well. He has a very light hand with his horses, and he leads me too without my realizing it."

After an official visit to the Mayor and the Army commanders accom-panied by the German-speaking officer attached to me I was invited as guest of honour to the bullfight that took place a few days before our ap-pearance in the same arena. I must say that this visit reawakened all my old misgivings.

The contrasts in this land of contrasts are particularly marked in bull-fights. The seats, arranged in a vast circle like an amphitheatre, are filled with people in their best clothes, looking completely peaceful until their passions are roused as the struggle develops, and they indicate their approval or displeasure with noisy gestures.

The parade provides a marvellously colourful picture, sharply contrasting with the nature of the spectacle. Even at the beginning of the fight the beautiful picture is still in juxtaposition with the unleashed wild strength of bull and the elegant movements of the toreros, but with the entrance picadors, with the use of lances and banderillas, beauty gives place to For the objective observer the bullfight loses at this point any fair-wakens nothing but distaste in the majority of people who see the spectacle for the first time. But the crowds scream with joy—or with displeasure if the torero's efforts do not please them. In one corrida this spectacle of uncontrolled passion is repeated six times. Incidentally, it struck me that here were the only examples of punctuality in Spain: the commencement of the performances and the twenty minutes allotted to each bull for his dramatic death.

I was especially honoured in nearly every fight, when usually one of the matadors threw me his hat. But that also meant having the attention of the spectators focused on me, so I had to exercise strong self-control not to show my dislike of this bloody sport, for that would have been taken by the public as an insult to their national pastime.

When I returned to my hotel in the evening after the first bullfight I looked as pale and exhausted as one of the toreros to whom the public had denied its favour. I was so deeply upset that I was in no condition to go into the dining-room.

Apart from my personal feelings I now had the great worry as to how the white horses from Vienna would manage by their movements alone, without any kind of sensation, to win the approval of the public in this bloody place. A certain anxiety about his success is in any case a constant companion of a rider in the limelight, for only the harmonious co-operation of two creatures can conjure up the brilliance that ensures success. But here the public was merciless in demonstrating its feelings. During the bullfight I had seen more than once that the same torero whose appearance was greeted with noisy cheers because of his reputation would have to endure disapproving whistles and catcalls if any of his movements did not please, or were considered signs of failing courage; indeed, the accepted hero and idol of the masses left the arena at the end of the fight a beaten man jeered at by his former admirers.

By April 3 things were sufficiently advanced for the Spanish Riding School to make its first public appearance. More than ten thousand temperamental and expectant visitors had gathered in the Monumentale Arena. Following the custom of the country our performance was preceded by a ceremonial parade: at the head a detachment of the Barcelona police in their picturesque dress uniforms, followed by the eight Austrian white horses. The police horses shied at the pale sand spread over the square marked out in the circular arena for our performances, and this amused the crowd, but the first part of our complete programme obviously met with approval, for the spectators applauded thunderously the "Airs Above the Ground" and the quadrille. There was no longer any doubt that the magic of the Lipizzaner had not failed with the Spaniards. I realized the tremendous enthusiasm of the riding experts the next day at the lunch given in honour of the Spanish Riding School by the Barcelona Polo Club, where I heard nothing but praise and admiration both in the official speeches of welcome and in talk with club members, including many public figures. My formal election as an honorary member of this club must be taken as a particular expression of its delight in the white horses from Vienna.

This Sunday afternoon there was the second performance in the great arena, again before more than ten thousand spectators, and it almost seemed that we were being received even more enthusiastically than on the previous day, but I was touched when after the closing march of the quadrille an elderly man came to me and presented me with a large bouquet of flowers in the Austrian colours, tied with ribbon in the Spanish colours. He introduced himself as a former matador who had been so impressed by our performance, which he had already seen on the Saturday, that he felt he must express his admiration to me with flowers on the very spot where he had celebrated his own triumphs. The feelings of this grey-haired torero who had himself so often anxiously sought the favour of the crowd in this scorching ground must have been very profound indeed.

With our success in Barcelona widely reported in the Press, a great stone fell from my heart, and already we were preparing for our next appearance in Valencia, whither the horses were again to be taken by the military authorities. I must admit that the organization of the transport worked splendidly on each occasion, and the general punctuality was a pleasant surprise, for we simply could not get accustomed to the otherwise chronic unpunctuality of Spain.

The preparations for transporting the horses to Valencia were under the personal supervision of a general, who objected to the grooms travelling— as they had always done hitherto—in the same trucks as their horses, and ordered a First Class passenger coach to be set aside for them. This continued to form part of our transport train until we left Spanish territory.

The stallions were magnificently housed in the Artillery barracks in Valencia, and each groom was given two soldiers as assistants. The timing of our appearances showed clearly how little thorough organization there had been. In Valencia the last performance was arranged for Sunday, April 11, at noon, because in the afternoon there was to be a big international football match in the stadium, which had room for sixty thousand spectators. There could therefore not have been a less convenient time for our show, as all the informed authorities assured me. It was also the religious festival of Palm Sunday, which in Spain is of great importance, and the services lasted long after twelve o'clock. To make matters worse, the weather, quite unlike the sunny days in Barcelona, was grey and cool.

I was therefore quite astounded that, in spite of everything, some fifteen thousand spectators appeared in the stadium and followed the programme with great understanding. Even the local people were amazed at the large audience at such an unpropitious time. On this occasion the mounted trumpet corps of an artillery regiment escorted us into the arena and played some introductory marches until we were ready to begin. When I appeared at the entrance commands rang out, and the Commandant announced me while his men stood motionless, their heads turned towards me. My companion whispered an explanation, and I with rather odd feelings, walked once again after fifteen years past the ranks of soldiers, not in uniform this time, but for the first time in my life in civilian clothes.

The performance went exceptionally well and was as well received as in Barcelona. The papers reported fully and in superlatives on the "glorious school from Vienna, the embodiment of European culture." Then we were once more faced with a vacuum, for in the week before Easter there were no public performances. Murcia was next on our list, but the date was not yet decided. For the time being we stayed on in Valencia, although farewell had already been officially said by the Mayor at a reception in the Town Hall the day after the performances, and we spent Holy Week there. The city seemed dead, but towards the end of it splendid ceremonial processions were held in the late evening, often not ending before midnight.

As well as flags and pictures, relics from the church are carried in procession, and there are numerous tableaux depicting scenes from the Bible. Courtesans attach themselves to Roman nobles in splendid clothes and persecuted believers of early Christianity. Cloaked figures in mystical costumes recall the days of the Inquisition. For hours on end the colourful, sometimes strangely melancholy, procession moves past thousands of spectators, including many foreigners, stressing the national propensity for contrast: strict belief in and respect for the religious rites on the one hand and a fondness for pageantry on the other.

On Easter Eve we went on to Murcia. Our departure—as so often on this tour—came suddenly after days of fruitless waiting. Murcia presented a very different picture from the two cities we had visited. There were few foreigners to be seen, and the streets were crowded with native Spaniards. The bullfight on Easter Sunday showed me clearly what a temperamental, even uncontrollable and wild, public we must expect, for the arena seemed at times to be swamped in turbulent noise.

Here in Murcia I saw for the first time a bullfighter on horseback, the rejoneador Angel Peralta. The six bulls of the usual corrida were increased to seven, for the mounted matador to fight. If one can come to terms with the bloodshed in this form the spectacle presents a much more balanced picture because it is a genuine duel.

By way of introduction Peralta, who wore the simple but elegant dress of the Andalusian rider, rode two of his three saddled horses in steps of the *haute école*. He showed side-steps in the trot and extensive galloping with half and completed *pirouettes*, jump changes, and above all transition into an extended gallop, then suddenly pulling up and making his horse do *courbettes* and the *piaffe* and the *passage*.

Some captious critics of the demonstration of these difficult exercises could not lessen my admiration for Peralta's equestrian skill, for with the same horses he fought the bull and demanded complete obedience, showing that even training in the *haute école* is only a means to an end.

In a bullfight on horseback the rider must first sit motionless and let his raging opponent come closer, galloping away at the very last moment and shaking off his pursuer again and again with short turns. In the second part the rejoneador gallops towards the attacking bull, holding a kind of lance in his right hand, then just before the collision he pulls his horse slightly to the side and sticks the banderilla fixed in the point of his lance into the neck of his opponent as it thunders by. When the enraged animal, having missed its tormentor, halts, irresolute and panting, the rider tries through the *piaffe* and other such conspicuous movements to attract its attention again: a thrilling and beautiful sight. Most impressive of all is when the rejoneador, the bridle fastened to his belt and a banderilla still in his upraised hand, gallops towards the bull, directing his horse only by the pressure of legs and his weight, which is certainly one of the greatest tests of obedience for a riding horse. Even the killing of the bull with a dagger is carried out on the horse's back in a frontal attack, but if the rejoneador does not carry out this last act of the fight he must dismount and finish off the bull, to the often positively hostile shouts of the crowd.

Through talking to several rejoneadors I learned details that interested me specially as a rider. The main thing in this fight is that the horse must never show the bull its flanks, but always approach it from the front and only turn at the very last moment. This demands a well-schooled horse that goes absolutely straight and obeys the slightest direction, and never hesitates for a second to attack the bull fearlessly. The rejoneador, who must change his horse two or three times in a single fight, needs really spirited horses, and I was told that only Andalusian horses, near relatives of the Lipizzaner, are chosen for this fight; no thoroughbred could be persuaded to gallop straight at the bull rushing forward with head down and horns waiting to strike.

This unusual bullfight on horseback was followed by the customary fights and I witnessed something very remarkable. The rather excited crowd screamed and yelled when a bull did not seem wild and aggressive enough, until the President of the Arena disqualified the animal—but this is only allowed if no blood has flowed. At a sign from him four oxen came into the arena to drive out the bull. This happened several times in Murcia, thus watching the public on the eve of our appearance was not at all encouraging. The whole night the shouts of the people rang in my ears.

On Easter Monday we appeared in the same arena before 19,000 spectators, and I was astounded that this wild and passionate public could really find pleasure in the controlled movements of the Lipizzaner. One of the spectators even said afterwards that one could see that the ancestors of the Lipizzaner had left Spain many hundreds of years before, for they had quite lost their temperament, obeying their riders so quietly and without resistance.

From Murcia we went on to Seville for our next performance the following week. I went via Granada to enjoy once more the beauties of this city, and again we were captivated and spiritually refreshed by the treasures housed there, but in Seville came a rude awakening.

The Real Jockey Club had appointed as marshal an Austrian who had lived for many years in Spain, to be responsible for the propaganda and the musical accompaniments, and to act also as interpreter. But this man, in addition to his inherent Austrian easygoing nature—one might often call it slovenliness—had acquired in full measure the Spanish habit of unpunctuality, and this combination often stretched my nerves to breaking-point. As soon as I arrived I had to listen to grumbles about the inadequacies of the riders' and horses' accommodation, but the marshal was nowhere to be found, and kept me waiting for hours. Added to this annoyance was the intolerable weather, which badly upset my ideas of permanently blue Spanish skies.

On the Sunday before our appearance there was a bullfight in the same arena, and I had to attend as guest of honour. At once I grasped the difference between this crowd and the one in Murcia. The charming women in picturesque and beautiful national costumes retained their elegant manners in spite of all the passionate excitement that this nerve-racking fight awakened. However, I noticed something rather less gratifying: when it began to rain during the fight the crowded terraces emptied so fast that we were soon the only spectators. A Spaniard explained that his compatriots were so spoilt with sunshine that they really did not have to watch a spectacle in the rain and get wet.

The next day the white horses from Vienna performed in the most beautiful bull-fighting arena in the whole of Spain, belonging to the feudal Order of Real Maestranza de Caballeria de Sevilla, at one time the owners of the flourishing southern city. The biggest daily paper welcomed us in German: "We offer a hearty welcome in Seville to the Austrian Classic Spanish Riding School from Vienna." The Order gave a lunch in our honour in the reception rooms of the arena, adorned with a splendid picture gallery of its members, including several kings of Spain. In the afternoon the arena was sold out and filled with 20,000 spectators. Everybody of importance was there: the cream of the aristocracy, including several deposed European sovereigns living in Spain, and a particularly critical public full of expectation. A trumpet corps of a cavalry regiment on white horses escorted us into the ring, and we were given an enthusiastic reception.

But the sky grew darker and darker during the performance, and at last it began to rain during my solo, and, remembering at once what I had seen the day before, I was certain of disaster. I anxiously completed my programme, glancing repeatedly towards the terraces, but not a soul left the arena until we had finished, and the second half lasted thirty minutes, in the rain, a phenomenon that was hailed by the Press as showing the measure of success that had already been proved by the applause. Obviously Seville was the climax of our Spanish tour.

As our appearance took place on the first day of the Feria, I had an opportunity to see this annual spring festival. During these days all work seemed to stop, and everything was given over to the geniune southern gaiety and joy in music, rhythm and colourful spectacle. On every corner Spanish dances were played by musicians or came through loudspeakers, and children and grown-ups alike in full white skirts moved gracefully to the sound. In the cafés, alone or accompanied by the usual monotonous-tuneful voices of the singers, dancers of both sexes entertained a politely attentive audience that gradually became enthusiastic. The Moorish influence is discernible in the rhythms of the songs and dances—alternating continually between the deep melancholy and lively passion, rising almost to wildness. For me the highlight of the Feria was the *Corso* for groups of riders and teams. Glorious horses in teams of two and four drew carriages occupied by exquisite Spanish ladies, who accepted the homage offered to them with great self-possession. I admired especially the pairs who rode together: he slender in a close-fitting black suit sitting in the saddle, and she in a bright, tight-waisted costume on the horse's crupper, her legs to the left hidden by a full white skirt. Her right hand grasped her cavalier's hips, and with her left she supported herself on the horse's croup, both riders seeming at one with their horses walking and cantering. This was all so bewitching and colourful that it took me many decades back into the past to the *Blumenkorso* in Vienna in the Hauptallee of the Prater, which as a young man I had experienced before the dawn of the new era in Austria.

So far our tour had at least followed the general plan from Barcelona to Jerez, but here in Seville the poor organization became fully apparent. Our next appearance was originally to have been in Jerez de la Frontera, only sixty miles away, but not until twelve days after our performance in Seville. Instead of this we now travelled in the opposite direction some four hundred miles to the north to give a performance in between in Valladolid. The journey there was very interesting. After the joyous landscape of the south, here in Castile we found the mood serious, sometimes melancholy, for the various protracted struggles through the centuries have left their mark. The many fortresses and strongholds still surviving date from an unsettled past, and a wealth of very varied works of art recalls the ancient, long-vanished culture that once conquered half the world from here.

The accommodation of the horses in the cavalry barracks in Valladolid was again splendid, the interest taken in our training exceptional, and the joyful anticipation of our appearance tremendous. The three days before the performances were needed for other preparations, various interviews and working the horses, always watched by a large crowd. We had arrived in sunshine, but on the second day it began to rain without a break and ruined our plans. On the Sunday morning the performance had to be finally cancelled, as a postponement to the Monday was categorically re- fused by the Jockey Club in Jerez because of other arrangements there. This was regrettable considering all the interest we had aroused, but it be- came positively embarrassing when in the afternoon Valladolid was bathed in sunshine, but because of the complicated organization it was no longer possible to arrange for a performance after all.

We worked the horses on Sunday morning in the covered school, watched by nearly the whole corps of officers and the final year of the cadet school. When we had finished the riders of the Spanish Riding School were invited by the C.O. into the Officers' Mess. He was a chivalrous host, saying in a short speech that he and his officers were not blessed with this world's goods, but felt they must make the riders from Austria welcome in their midst. And the Commandant of the Army School gave a reception for us on the Monday, and so the next day I was really sorry to leave this city, where we had been received with such kindness, without being able to repay it in any way.

The Lipizzaner travelled back via Seville to Jerez de la Frontera after their unsuccessful sally to the north. The only result was the addition to the train of two trucks of hay, as this fodder was available only in small quantities in the south, and this went with the transport to its last stop in Lisbon.

Jerez was celebrating that year a special festival, the Horses' Week. Apart from our performance, a Horse Show, a parade of stallions and show horses, a carriage race, and other items, had been planned. The whole town was given over to the horse, music, and enjoyment.

The Lipizzaner were splendidly housed in spacious boxes at the Army Depot, and a large outdoor school surrounded by stands was at our disposal. We performed before more than ten thousand in the packed arena. As a symbolic overture the Duke of Pinohermoso met me to present me to the spectators. He galloped up to me on an Andalusian-bred white stallion as I waited by the entrance. Wearing the elaborate dress of a rejoneador, he doffed his hat, and requested me to follow him into the arena. We rode in a collected canter side by side, saluted the President and the spectators, and then left the arena once more in the *passage*. Then came our perfor- mance, which was very well received, and was followed by a bullfight on horseback, led by the Duke, who dedicated the fight to me, and at the end threw me from among the trophies awarded to him a bloody ear from the dead bull as a token of his esteem. It was the first time that a presentation by the Spanish Riding School had ever been coupled with a bullfight, a combination that struck me as risky, but pleased the many thousands of spectators uncommonly.

With this single performance our riding duties in Jerez were really at an end, but various celebrations had been planned, and on May 11 a splendid banquet was given in a beautiful park.

The tables for the invited guests were grouped round a square of sand in which gleamed a large P with a crown—the device of the Lipizzaner. On a raised daïs facing it, the Minister of Agriculture, Rafael Cavestany, who had come from Madrid, the Mayor of Jerez, the President of the Real Jockey Club, and the other dignitaries of the city took their place under a canopy in the colours of Spain and Austria, my wife on the right and myself on the left of the Minister. The riders too were present in traditional uniform. Before us in the park twinkling with coloured lights were gaily chattering people in full evening dress, and above us the clear starry heavens of a wonderful May night.

The banquet, arranged for eleven, had with the normal national procrastination begun late, so it was long after midnight when the Mayor, the Minister, and the President of the Jockey Club made their official after-dinner speeches, in which the importance of the Spanish Riding School and the skill of its riders was often mentioned. Then the leading judge of Spain, José Maria Peman, described the school in a passionate speech as the symbol of Europe, a shining signal that Europe with its flourishing culture still lived in spite of all the storms of the recent past. The applause that greeted these words mingled with the distant neighing of the two horses that had been saddled outside the park for the conclusion of the festivities. Then the Mayor, dressed as a rejoneador, and I mounted our horses, both white and both of Andalusian breed, even if the ancestors of my stallion had gone to Austria centuries before, and galloped side by side out of the darkness into the brightly lighted square, reining in after a ceremonial round in front of the daïs on which the Minister and the President of the Jockey Club awaited us. The Minister placed the Cross of a Commander of the Order of Isabel la Catolica round my neck in the name of Generalissimo Franco, I rode another round of honour with the Mayor in the *passage*, and then by myself showed Pluto Theodorosta in the square in a chosen programme. It was half-past one before this impressive and festive day drew to a close. I dismounted, and in the same place and before the same audience I made a presentation to my elderly groom and faithful companion on his completion of twenty-five years of service.

Two days later I organized as a sort of return hospitality a special performance before invited guests on the riding square in the depot, which included a parade of the winning horses and teams in the various competi-

tions. Here I had admired the many impeccably turned out vehicles drawn
by from one to six horses, and the very high standard of driving, and noticed
that of some 280 horses assembled in Jerez many of the Andalusians not
only still bore traces of their distant connexion with the Lipizzaner, but
some even surpassed the latter in quality, primarily in their proportions.
All the experts admired the Lipizzaner for their riding possibilities, but
did not like their long backs, which certainly do often lead to difficulties
during schooling.

The trials of the one-year-old steers to decide if they were suitable for
bullfighting were very interesting. They were released singly on the airfield,
chased by riders and brought down with a sort of lance. If the young steer
stayed down, or leapt up and ran away, then his fate for the stewpot was
sealed. If, however, he stood up again and faced the rider he was then given
the 'honour' of ending his earthly life after careful training in a welter of
blood in the sand of the arena before the eyes of thousands of spectators.

On May 26 a special performance was given for General Franco on the
wonderful Madrid racecourse. A carefully tended piece of grass in front of
the stands was set aside and bordered with a riot of flowers. Facing this, a
small platform was erected for the General and the few guests of honour,
and also decorated with flags and flowers. On one side of our square a
section of mounted police in dress uniform was drawn up, an unusually fine
sight, which seemed to have been conjured up from a long-departed era.
Away beyond the helmets, gleaming in the first of the lights, one could see
the silhouette of Madrid gradually disappearing as the twilight deepened.

Punctually at eight o'clock General Franco arrived at the racecourse with
his wife, escorted by his Moroccan bodyguard, in their picturesque uniforms,
and a long convoy of cars. He was welcomed by the Mayor of Madrid and
a host of high-ranking officers, including the famous defender of Toledo,
General Moscourdó, and myself; the performance began in the fading light
and was continued by floodlight. This successful piece of organization was
much praised, and General Franco received me afterwards to congratulate
me, and said how much he had enjoyed the performance, which he had
watched with an appreciative eye because of the beauty of motion, and with
a moist eye at the thought that the age of the horse has passed.

The Generalissimo did not seem at all like the imperious dictator he is
so often called, but had a simple, straightforward manner that was without
affectation. And without any show of emotion the cleverness of this man,
who had controlled the fate of Spain in the most critical period of its history
with extraordinary skill, was very apparent. The reception in the Racing
Club lasted till midnight as everybody present was enjoying himself so
much.

The next day the Mayor of Madrid gave a lunch in my honour for a few
people in a club room outside the city. The Vice-President of the Jockey

Club of Jerez was to pick me up half an hour before this two o'clock meeting at my hotel, as I did not know my way. We waited at the arranged time in the hotel lobby—in vain, as so often in that country—and finally arrived an hour late. When we got there all the other guests, obviously important people, had arrived, and the situation was so embarrassing that I began to stammer a few words of apology. The Mayor interrupted me most cordially: "Please say no more. You have come in the company of an Andalusian, and that is quite enough to explain your late arrival!"

During the lunch the tremendous success of our performance was the main topic, and the conversation lingered for a long time on the Lipizzaner; then the President of the Racing Club said, "I can tell you now that I did all I could to prevent your appearing on the racecourse turf, which I have cherished for years, as I did not want the grass to be ruined by horses' hoofs. I finally gave in with a heavy heart because the show was being put on for the Generalissimo. But I have inspected the square thoroughly and find that the turf is untouched. Your horses truly must have floated over it on wings."

The climax of our successful Spanish tour having been reached in Seville and here in Madrid, I should have welcomed the end of our festival at that time, and had agreed that only one more performance would be given in Saragossa on our way home. But now the chaotic planning of the whole journey came fully to light for the first time: instead of going home we were to be in Lisbon in a fortnight—this conclusion was only arranged during our stay in Madrid—and the interval was to be filled with performances in Córdoba and Antequera, so within a week the horses set off once more back on the route to Córdoba.

I had a mishap on the way there that held me up for many hours and upset me tremendously. In the tropical heat around midday I was driving through completely deserted villages, as the streets do not come to life before the evening. In a village outside Madrid a cyclist dashed out of a small side-road into my car, fell off, and lay motionless in the road. In a few minutes the street was filled with shouting and gesticulating people, whom I could not understand. To my great relief, the man finally got to his feet, and I was able to take him to a doctor, who sewed up a wound in his head. The hostile attitude of the excited inhabitants was only somewhat mitigated by a local official, a very intelligent and prudent man, who went into the question of blame at once with the police, and then explained that I could continue my journey as the investigation, unlike public opinion, proved clearly that the cyclist was at fault. As he said good bye he added that he was delighted that General Franco had so greatly enjoyed the performances of the Spanish Riding School, for he had realized from my number-plate that I must be the man with the General in the newspaper photographs.

By now it was six o'clock in the evening, and I had still 250 miles to put behind me, as we were to appear in Córdoba the next day. To make matters worse I had yet another puncture that night, so we did not reach our destination until five in the morning, absolutely exhausted. However, this puncture brought me once more in contact with Spanish chivalry, innate even in the 'little' man, for when we were stranded, completely alone on the dark road, the first truck stopped and three men helped me to change the wheel, although they were in their Sunday clothes and would not let me lift a finger, even offering their wine-bottles by way of refreshment. When they had completed this really dirty job they had to be pressed to accept a tip. In Córdoba we went straight to our hotel and asked not to be disturbed before noon, so that we could get a little rest. But our delay had caused such consternation—the police had already been looking for us—that by nine o'clock the Mayor and Commandant of the stud, where the horses were quartered, appeared to make sure we had arrived, so we had to be satisfied with three hours' sleep. Ahead of me lay an exhausting performance, and in addition I had to ride my horses beforehand because of our three-day break.

We gave our performance at six o'clock in the bullring in a temperature of 35 centigrade in the shade. The place was crowded, but the spectators were quite different from those in Madrid: they conformed in character to the southern Spaniard. By way of introduction several horse-drawn carriages appeared, and elegant society ladies in national dress stepped out, then a group of five horses from the Naional Stud gave a very smart and spirited display. These supple horses, very like the Lipizzaner, preceded our performance, which was well received. The strain of the heat after so little sleep was so great, however, that I thought at one point in the performance that I could not go on.

From here we went the 420-odd miles back to Lisbon. As we crossed the border into Portugal the character both of the landscape and of the people changed noticeably. The huge cultivated stretches of green indicated fertile land and an intensive agricultural use of it. Of the Moorish influence revealed in the inhabitants of Spain, particularly in the south, there was here no trace. One had the feeling of being in a younger country where the contrasts were much less marked than in neighbouring Spain. The horses were put into temporary but well-appointed stalls in the Campo Pequeno arena, and could be actually exercised in the bullring, which was doubly welcome, for the horses had had no training for twelve days, and the school put at our disposal was smaller than usual, which necessitated a rearrangement of the quadrille. The music was technically much simpler, but so well prepared that for the first time on our long tour we enjoyed faultless accompaniments.

Our performance at ten in the evening looked like being an outstanding social occasion. In spite of the enormously high cost of the tickets, the proceeds of which were to go towards the reconstruction of the Colégio de S. João de Prito, run by priests, they were sold out several days before our appearance in the arena, which held about ten thousand a night.

A starry sky stretched over the Campo Pequeno, and people in their party clothes, in high summer mood, began to fill the seats, among them a great many cavalry officers.

A military band played a gay overture and accompanied the ceremonial event of the evening, the parade of the performers after the style of the big bullfights on horseback. I came into the illuminated arena first in a collected canter flanked by the two bullfighters Rosa Rodriques and Ribeiro Teles, and reined in before the State box. Then the seven riders appeared in the brilliant circle of light and took up their places behind us, followed by the grooms who led in the rest of the horses and stood behind them with the rest of the corrida bringing up the rear. I and the two bullfighters saluted, sideways on to the stands, and galloped past the spectators; then we gave the first half of our performance, the same as in Spain. Next there was a bull-fight on horseback by Ribeiro Teles, but this conflict of apparent opposites was not particularly upsetting here, for the bull may not be killed in Portugal—any matador who is unlucky enough to let this happen can expect a fairly long prison sentence. Moreover, the riders had trained their horses to a much higher standard than the rejoneadors in Spain, and they wear clothes of the style worn in France at the time of the Guérinières, similar to the brown tail-coats worn by the riders from Vienna.

Before the bullfight the rider puts his horse through all the movements of the *haute école*, including the *piaffe*, *passage*, *pirouette*, and changes in the air. Then the bull is released and there begins the same sort of play between the two opponents as in Spain. It is an interesting spectacle when the rider, changing speed, gallops towards the attacking bull, turns with a half-*pirouette* just before the collision, and rides away at full gallop. Without a doubt this stressed the beauty of a highly trained motion combined with elegant dexterity, and makes one forget the cruelty of the game with an unarmed animal. When the bull appears sufficiently exhausted the rider leaves the arena, while eleven men dressed like Portuguese peasants with tasselled caps turn the attention of the animal on to themselves. When the bull rushes towards this group of men the first man advances, his head held high and his arms folded behind his back, allows himself to be picked up on the stunted horns, and clings on to the bull's body. The other men surrounding it grab it wherever they can get hold, until it submits to its fate, and the fight is over.

After this introduction came the second part of the programme, which once more ended with the quadrille. The loud applause during our performance welled to a roar at the end, and went on so long after we left the arena that I had to make a second appearance to thank the people for their ovation.

51. The Classic Style of Riding in a Baroque Setting

52. Siglavy Monterosa on Long Reins: Vienna, 1957

53. The Begum visits the Saddle-room, 1959

54. Tributes from all over the World

The long tour through Spain and Portugal, ending splendidly with our successful appearance in Lisbon, was to be our last foreign festival for a long time. When I look back on the seven years of the old Vienna Riding School wandering through Europe and America after the Second World War I realize with great satisfaction that wherever they appeared the Lipizzaner scored success after success, a triumphal procession unequalled in their long history, and the Spanish Riding School was everywhere accepted as the epitome of riding culture. I had led the white horses from Austria out into the wide world, and have to thank my charges for the chance to see and get to know the world from a high vantage-point. Because of them I was received like a king wherever I appeared with my beloved horses, and encountered sincerity and warmth from people of very different nations, so I think with gratitude of the efforts of my brave and faithful stallions, who opened up the world to me and showed me that the love of men for animals, particularly horses, cannot be driven out by the thrill of any technical discovery or the progress of the internal-combustion engine.

CHAPTER 17

The Spanish Riding School comes Home

In a unique series of victories the Lipizzaner and their riders had celebrated triumphs throughout the world: they had been admired and acclaimed like prima donnas, and spoilt like princes in a fairy-tale, away from the monotony of daily life. They had stolen the hearts of the whole world and given the Spanish Riding School an exalted reputation, but they still had not won back their home in Vienna, though it was years since their 'liberation.' This time we went quietly back to our humble quarters in Wels, which, in striking contrast to the general improvement throughout Austria since 1946, had not changed at all. They had, in fact, grown shabbier than ever, and only the brilliance of our successful trips shone for a while through the general gloom.

Neither the enthusiastic reports from every quarter nor the ever-increasing visits of foreigners to the Spanish Riding School in Wels did anything to improve this unhappy situation, and visitors only too often expressed their astonishment and disappointment at the setting in which the fêted white horses lived in their own country. We were in fact in exile, our accommodation was regarded as temporary, although it had served for almost a decade, and nobody would consider even the possibility of putting an end to this regrettable state of affairs. Finally the many criticisms were voiced in 1952 in an article in the Viennese *Presse* under the title "A Precious Stone in a Rusty Setting."

This revelation by an unknown friend of the Spanish Riding School evoked some discussion in high places for a time, but did nothing to alter the conditions themselves. Even the efforts of the Landeshauptmann of Salzburg to get a transfer of the school into the Festival city had no success. It continued to suffer the bitter lot of the refugee, highly respected, of course, but materially an embarrassment at that time.

274

We had reached 1954—thus nine and a half years since that day on which we thought we were only leaving Vienna for a few months—when in July I tried to end this hopeless situation by putting in a request for the return of the Spanish Riding School to Vienna, considering that the time had come when this could be carried out without danger. My application was sympathetically received by the Minister of Agriculture and Forestry, but negotiations had to be particularly delicately handled and the ground carefully prepared, so it took more than another year before the great moment arrived.

After Government approval in principle, given at a Cabinet Council on January 11, 1955, the rooms in Vienna, which never need have been occupied, had first to be vacated. After preliminary difficulties this was achieved more quickly than expected, thanks to the reputation that the Spanish Riding School had won through its great success abroad, so now we could begin restoring the rooms, which had suffered very badly indeed.

The school's great international triumphs began to have their effect even in Austria, for the redecoration of the home of the Lipizzaner was most splendidly carried out with a lavishness that would not have been forthcoming if the Spanish Riding School had stayed in Wels the whole time, leading a shadowy existence.

A great deal of structural restoration had to be done, beginning with new outbuildings at the Stallburg, the rebuilding of the stables, and complete redecoration of the riding-hall. This was, in fact, restored in its old style, and was more resplendent than for centuries. While all this was going on I had one very pleasant moment. The question of lighting for the hall was being discussed, and an official from the Ministry of Trade and Reconstruction declared that his Ministry was to carry out the work.

"I am told that there were once crown chandeliers here. Some say they were taken down by the Germans, others by the Russians. In any case they aren't here."

I was delighted to be able to say with pride, "It was neither the Germans nor the Russians; I took down the chandeliers myself before we had to leave Vienna, and they are quite safe in my care."

Everybody was so pleased that, striking while the iron was hot, I managed to get both galleries fitted up with smaller chandeliers, thereby improving the appearance of the wonderful riding-hall.

Obviously a propitious star hovered over the last act of the Odyssey of the White Horses, for a few months before our return Austria achieved her long-desired agreement with the other nations, and as a symbol of liberty there opened almost simultaneously in the heart of Vienna the doors of the two rebuilt national theatres, the Opera and the Burg, and the riding-hall in the Josefsplatz, which had stood empty for so long, giving the signal for the start of an incredible boom in my fatherland.

At the last moment our return was very nearly delayed, as the rebuilding in the Stallburg would not be finished in time, but I settled for provisional quarters for personnel and horses, as the arrival of the Spanish Riding School at the same time as the opening of the Opera and Burgtheater seemed to me very important. The rightness of this decision was later proved by the fact that the Stallburg, looking like a builder's yard, had to remain for years in its original state awaiting restoration.

The statement in the Cabinet Council by the Minister of Agriculture about the preparations for the return of the school to Vienna caused a public sensation. Press, radio, and newsreels gave the school the sort of publicity that we had previously only experienced abroad. I was really delighted to see that the Spanish Riding School had such a place in the hearts of the Austrian people, for I had thus achieved one of my most cherished ambitions from the day I took it over. Even the foreign papers considered its return an important event, so popular had the old academy become everywhere.

Before our return we gave what had now become traditional performances at the Salzburg Festival, our last for a long time. We were not sorry to say good bye to Salzburg, for torrential rain prevented our appearing on the first day and we had to give two performances the following day, which was very trying. This everlasting anxiety over the weather, on which we were dependent with open-air appearances, had in recent years become a great strain on the nerves, and all of us were glad to be free of it.

In the autumn of 1955 everything was ready for the return to Vienna. Just after the last occupation troops had left Austria the white stallions went home, a piece of staging by Fate that no director could have handled better. Even our departure from Upper Austria, as far as circumstances permitted, turned into a celebration, for ten years represent quite a big slice even in the history of an institution that can look so far back into the past.

On October 1 there assembled for the last time in the riding-school of the dragoon barracks in Wels a large number of Government officials, many representatives of Upper Austria, headed by the Landeshauptmann, Dr Gleissner (who had always shown great affection for the Lipizzaner), heads of local affairs, and public dignitaries. For the first time here the performance of the world-famous Spanish Riding School was not attended by any of the occupying Powers, who had now left Austria.

Preceding the actual performances there was a ceremonial parade of horses and riders before the guests of honour. On this day I rode in at the head of my riders, who had played their part in various phases of my life, with very mixed feelings. The tinge of sorrow that attends every parting was overlaid with the joy of going home at last to Vienna, and thus being able to leave behind many unhappy memories of the often all too grey workaday world. In this mood I greeted the assembled guests:

"We are returning to our original home in Vienna, but we leave Wels, and Upper Austria, with a feeling of gratitude. We can give no greater living expression of this than in the performance we are about to give. If in this riding-hall, where once the sons of Upper Austria received their military training, the snorting of horses is heard once more, and if they, acclaimed throughout the world as the wonderful dancing white stallions, can show you their skill, then we are offering with full hearts our thanks to our host, Upper Austria, for we are riding for you."

Then we worked through the traditional programme, beginning with the young stallions and ending with the school quadrille, to the accompaniment of constant applause from the festive crowd, who made every effort to store up as a lasting memory the enchanting picture of the gallant Lipizzaner. When the quadrille finished the riders formed a line in front of the guests, and Dr Gleissner made a heart-warming farewell speech.

The transfer to Vienna was carried out in stages, ending with the entraining of the white horses on October 10. When the Lipizzaner left their stalls that day and gathered in the barrack square, this time not only the great artists who had gone out into the world for the glory of Austria, but also a great number of young stallions still with their dark coats, there were large crowds to say good bye. With a vast escort of faithful admirers the noble animals from Lipizza walked to the station through a double line of curious onlookers.

If our departure from Wels was sad, our reception in Vienna was a day of joy in the truest sense of the word. At eight o'clock the next morning the white horses were unloaded and taken to the Stallburg in trucks, but by six o'clock enthusiasts were already waiting at the station for this historic moment, so at the appointed time I was confronted with a huge crowd of newsreel and television cameramen as well as radio and Press reporters. The Spanish Riding School had left Vienna quietly and in secret, but it returned in triumph. An excited and ecstatic crowd greeted the Lipizzaner at the gates of the Stallburg, and in the sea of smiling faces there was many a cheek wet with tears of joy. Filled with emotion, some people shyly touched their darling's bodies, as if they feared the whole thing was only an illusion, for they had no longer dared to hope that they would ever see the white stallions again. They stroked the silky coats and rejoiced that this was not merely a happy dream; the Lipizzaner were really back in Vienna.

I felt much the same myself, though I was too busy to give much attention to my emotions. For me the return to Vienna represented the fulfilment of my life's work. It is a rare feeling to know that you have reached your zenith, and of this I was quite certain on the day of the festival performance in the Winter Riding School.

The year 1955 will be remembered as a special milestone both in the history of Austria and in her capital. Politically it brought us the treaty at last, and with it independence. Hand in hand with this exciting event, and symbolic of the structure of our country, there were also memorable cultural events: the reopening of the Opera, the Burgtheater, and the Spanish Riding School. I may be permitted without arrogance to mention the return of the school in the same breath as the restoration of the national theatre, for the reaction throughout the world to the return of the Lipizzaner gives me that right. The Burgtheater began the round of festivities, and a few days afterwards, on October 2, the doors of the Winter Riding School opened.

After weeks of the most exhausting preparations the riding-hall was seen on the opening evening in all its splendour. The creation of Fischer von Erlach glistened like a lacy web after its tasteful restoration: the edging to the balustrades between the pillars contrasted well with the shining whiteness of the stucco, stressing once again the reputation this hall has enjoyed ever since it was built of being the most beautiful riding-hall in the world. The words from Goethe's *Annals* seemed to be embodied in a splendid setting:

> A well-appointed riding-hall is always imposing . . . it has such a beneficial effect on the intelligent man, for here, as perhaps nowhere else in the world, he sees with his eyes and appreciates in his mind the proper restraint of action, the rejection of anything arbitrary or even fortuitous.

Two dates stretching almost over the entire floor, picked out in pale yellow sawdust on the light brown surface, commemorated outstanding historic events: 1735 on the half by the doors, when on September 14 of that year the newly built hall was opened, and 1955 in front of the State Box, marking the return exactly two hundred and twenty years later of the Spanish Riding School. Nearly all the members of the Government of the Austrian Republic, many national, provincial, and local dignitaries, the entire Diplomatic Corps, and representatives of every important walk of life gathered in the discreetly illuminated riding-hall with its new lighting.

Punctually at eight o'clock the President, General Theodor Körner, entered the historic hall to the sound of the national anthem and took his place in the State Box, where for hundreds of years countless crowned heads of mighty states had enjoyed the riders' and horses' play of controlled power. The celebration began.

During a musical overture in the hall I sat with my riders in the Josefsplatz, surrounded by a tremendous crowd wanting to get at least a peep at the white horses with their gold trappings, and to stare at the guests arriving. But, oddly enough, I was miles away, filled with the thought that this was the greatest moment of my life. I did not even hear the murmur of the people round me, nor the excited, joyful shouts, but seemed to be listening to a sweet distant melody, a song of praise, a thankful, rapturous prize-song; like a medieval knight after a victorious tourney about to receive his laurel crown, certainly not from the delicate hand of a great lady, but from the powerful fist of Fate. Immersed in my dreams, I awaited the great moment, the symbolic entry of the Lipizzaner into the Riding Hall.

Fanfares rang out, the three great chandeliers gleamed in all their splendour, flooding the hall with brilliant light. The great glass doors opened slowly, and twelve snow-white horses entered the virginal arena and walked behind me up to the State Box. The riders bared their heads, and, deeply moved, I began to speak.

"Mr President, the Spanish Riding School is back in Vienna after an absence of more than ten years. In this historic moment, so significant for the school, when the doors of this magnificent hall open once more for the riders of the oldest riding-school in the world, to carry on through the merciful hand of Providence a remarkable art form in this traditional setting, one cannot help thinking back to the time when last the muffled hoof-beats of the Lipizzaner died away. In those dark days, oppressed by an anxious present, and looking forward into an unknown future, the members of the Spanish Riding School left their traditional home with heavy hearts.

"Their joy is all the greater to-day because the Spanish Riding School has managed to survive without loss the chaos of the final months of the War and those that followed, and they can at last celebrate their return.

"Two hundred and twenty years ago school horses entered this Riding Hall for the first time, having finally repulsed the Turkish threats after many years, and then Austria found itself on the threshold of a Golden Age. God grant that our re-entry to-day into this noble building may be a symbol of the happy advance of our liberated fatherland into an epoch of peace. The joy of our return is mixed with a strong feeling of gratitude— gratitude over our good fortune and towards all those people and authorities who have restored our traditional home to its old incomparable splendour. It falls to me to give expression to our thanks on this festive occasion, and in the name of the riders of the Spanish Riding School I formally pledge that we will devote all our strength, all our skill, and all our thoughts to the care of this rare and ancient Austrian treasure, to the honour and glory of our beloved fatherland."

After the Minister of Agriculture and Forestry had made a speech of welcome the riders left the hall and the real performance began.

The traditional programme was watched appreciatively by the attentive spectators, who hardly dared to disturb the stillness round the "dancing horses." But when the riders saluted after their individual numbers before riding away there was no controlling the thunderous applause of the excited guests. The noble hall in the Josefsplatz had once more witnessed a brilliant festivity worthy of its heritage.

The impact of this occasion throughout the world surpassed all former publicity, though this had been generous during our festival tours. Never had the Spanish Riding School evoked so much interest in the world Press as in those days of its return to Vienna. Papers and magazines everywhere stressed in every language that the Spanish Riding School in the years after 1945 had become an exalted example of European culture. How greatly it had succeeded in exciting the journalists was indicated in such headlines as: "The Great Equestrian Opera," "The Première of the White Ballet", "The Return of the White Dream Horses," "The Fairy-tale Horses Dance again in the Venerable Hall."

The Viennese had their Lipizzaner back, and I had the great good fortune to be chosen by Destiny to lead them home after an adventurous odyssey. Acclaimed in print and picture, sung in countless good and well-intentioned songs, praised in passionate letters, the white dancers attracted as much general interest as the newly reopened State Opera.

The great event to celebrate the homecoming of the Spanish Riding School was over. It was back to everyday existence, no longer grey and hopeless as in the years we were forced to spend in exile, but charged with the pulsating life of a people to whom joy over their newly regained liberty had given an unsuspected strength. Vienna in those days of 1955 enjoyed a boom, and consequently a programme of restoration not limited merely to the removal of the last traces of war damage.

As the festivities in the Winter Riding School after the defeat of Napoleon, at the time of the Congress of Vienna, became the centre of interest of nearly the whole of Europe, so now the performances of the Spanish Riding School attracted visitors from all over the world. The white stallions had performed on many tours in the preceding years, and now foreigners came to Vienna to see and admire these horses in their own palace.

The importance of the Spanish Riding School grew far beyond the rôle assigned to it in the First Austrian Republic, for it always featured in the programme of representative spectacles for the various State visits; but to see this once exclusively royal institution was also the ambition of all the congresses sitting in Vienna, so the many Sunday performances were always sold out after our return to Vienna, and a record number of visitors watched morning rehearsals. What a wonderful feeling for each of us to be able to give pleasure to people of the most varied nations and distinctive races! The school's significance for our country was stressed by the Minister of Education in a speech in which he said that Austria was a great power on cultural grounds, and was served by three outstanding *avant-gardes*: the Spanish Riding School, the Opera, and the Boy's Choir.

Its success was not, however, merely one of ideals, but produced practical financial results; the takings from the performances and morning rehearsals brought in more than the total cost of the school's upkeep, so for the first time since its inception it was self-supporting—the first time also that any cultural institution in Austria had ever shown a profit. Many who had known the Spanish Riding School from the old days received this news with scepticism, but were amazed to see the morning practices, which in the years after the collapse of the Austro-Hungarian Empire had never attracted more than twenty or thirty spectators, attended by hundreds of people who packed the galleries.

The return to Vienna also resulted in some fundamental changes, including the necessity of limiting foreign tours—or, rather, cutting them out altogether. In 1955 we received more invitations than ever, so it seemed wisest to refuse them all, which would be the best way to avoid any hurt feelings. I was never in doubt as to the rightness of this decision, which not only met with Austrian approval, but was fully understood by the majority of foreigners, though I personally particularly regretted not being able to follow up the invitation to take the Lipizzaner to the 1956 Olympic Games in Stockholm and show them in the same stadium where we had scored such a triumph four years earlier.

The many performances throughout the year, and the daily attendances at the morning rehearsals, tremendously increased the burden of each one of us, for whereas before there had always been pauses with less work between the various tours, now the horses had to be kept in peak condition practically all the year round. Every rider will know what a strain this entails. Above all I myself had many new problems to face, and many had their comic side. Thus after our return the stables were literally overrun by strangers during visiting hours, displaying their delight at the return of the "prodigal sons" with great emotion and enormous quantities of sugar. For obvious reasons I did not want to damp their enthusiasm by prohibiting the sugar altogether, and for some time watched this overfeeding of the horses with silent disapproval. The stallions concentrated their whole attention, as it were, on the visiting hour from two to three, but when people arrived with great packets of sugar, and at the same time I was criticized for doing nothing about this stupid feeding, I resolved to put a stop to it. Then I was positively bombarded with letters over my heartlessness towards the gallant horses, but the health of my charges was more important than this well-meant pampering.

Compared with what we had left behind, however, our everyday cares and needs were infinitesimal, and were quite transformed by a host of interesting encounters and pleasant experiences, which kept alive my great joy at our happy homecoming. Nobody of any note has left Vienna since 1955 without having seen the white horses.

The first special performance on November 18, 1955, for the State visit of the West German Foreign Minister, Dr Heinrich von Brentano, was symbolic of the political development of our country: the reconciliation of the two German-speaking nations and the removal of all unfriendly memories

of the recent past. Could there be a more fitting setting for the ceremonial strengthening of this intention than the ancient riding-hall? Dr
von Brentano came to the Spanish Riding School that evening obviously
in the best of spirits, accompanied by the Austrian Foreign Minister, Dr
Leopold Figl, and enjoyed the spectacle of the Lipizzaner so much that he
asked to inspect the stables afterwards. Here I showed him the various
horses, with suitable comments, and pointed out that Neapolitano Santuzza,
although he had been taught *caprioles* on the rein, never thought of lashing
out in his stall, and was as gentle as a lamb if one went into his stall. Dr
Figl thought this was the result of good training, but I replied that this
alone cannot produce such perfect behaviour. Dr von Brentano agreed with
me.

"You are quite right! We too always try to bring up people properly, and
they always lash out at the wrong moment!"

A week later the Dutch Foreign Minister, Dr Johan Beyen, attended a
special performance given in his honour, and said at the reception afterwards in the rooms of the school that Metternich must truly have been a
great diplomat, and known what he was doing when he invited his guests
to festivities in the Winter Riding School. After such a beginning negotiations could not help but be conducted in a more friendly and better atmosphere. In point of fact during later conferences and congresses I often
heard that after seeing the white horses all problems seemed easier to
solve, as these artists had a soothing effect on those who watched them.

Mr, now Sir Robert Menzies of Australia was particularly impressed,
and after one performance spent a long time in the stables. Before he got
into his car he wagged a finger at me, saying, "I have been looking forward
to this visit with pleasure and interest for the last six months, and have not
been disappointed. Everything is even lovelier than I expected."

Thus the Spanish Riding School became the focal point of interest for a
procession of visitors to the hallowed hall in the Josefsplatz, all regardless
of their position and immediate calling, rejoicing as ordinary people in the
cult of the poetry of motion. My personal encounters brought me a host of
observations, striking memories, and delightful experiences, for everybody
who came to gaze at the white horses spoke easily and with extraordinary
spontaneity, which only happens when people are deeply moved. I saw
before me a bright reflection of the structure of the new Europe—indeed,
of the whole world—which was beginning to alter its appearance so remarkably in our time.

Whether the visitors to the Riding School were crowned heads, and these
are gradually getting fewer, or the elected or otherwise established representatives of their people, all had retained their enjoyment of animals and
respect for an established tradition.

King Paul and Queen Frederika of Greece watched the Lipizzaner at work with great interest and saw them in their stalls. The Queen told me proudly of the two Lipizzaner that Marshal Tito of Yugoslavia had presented to her. Although these horses naturally had not the skill of the Vienna White stallions, they were simply wonderful. She said too that even Tito was very interested in Lipizzaner and rode a black one himself.

Prince Bernhard of the Netherlands and two of his daughters, Princess Beatrix and Princess Irene, keen riders themselves, followed all the various items of our performances with great understanding and enjoyed it all thoroughly. I was struck by the affection of the two princesses for their father, and watched with pleasure the close attention he paid his daughters.

How tremendously Vienna, once the centre of the powerful Danube empire, had become the meeting-point between East and West was most clearly demonstrated by two successive State visits within two months: that of the first representative of the Council of Ministers of the Soviet Union, Mr A. I. Mikoyan, and that of the Chancellor of the German Federal Republic, Dr Konrad Adenauer.

As soon as his programme of visits was drawn up Mr Mikoyan asked to visit the Spanish Riding School. He came into the Winter Riding School with a serious, almost grim, face, but left obviously contented, having expressed his admiration for the old traditions and the skilful performance, which, as he said, he could appreciate, being a rider himself.

The meeting with Chancellor Adenauer was quite an experience for me. I had the definite impression of meeting one of the greatest Europeans, who had completely freed himself from the conception of a Europe of small states, and saw in a united Europe the only solution to all the problems of the Western World. With almost youthful physical and mental vitality this eighty-two-year-old head of the West German Republic came towards me at our first meeting during a reception at the Chancellory and asked at once, "Why will you not come to West Berlin with the Spanish Riding School, Colonel?" I had already refused the invitation to go there several times.

He waved away my reply that the Spanish Riding School, since its return to Vienna, was no longer undertaking foreign tours.

"This old riding academy has already appeared all over Europe, but the most easterly outpost of the culture of Western Europe has so far been denied a visit."

When I realized that the German Chancellor was pressing for a decision I threw an inquiring look at the Austrian Chancellor, Mr Julius Raab, and he jumped in at once.

"Well, then, we must certainly take the Spanish Riding School to Berlin." And that was how the visit during the "Grüne Woche" came to be arranged.

Dr Adenauer watched the performance given in his honour with obvious interest, asking my wife to explain all the finer details. Once he turned to the Minister of Agriculture and Forestry and said, "The ballet company at the State Opera yesterday ought to pay a visit here and learn suppleness and precision from these riders." This remark the Minister repeated proudly at various gatherings!

In the long procession of Heads of State who have visited the Spanish Riding School the Prime Minister of Afghanistan, Prince Sadar Mohammed Davoud, stands out because of his exceptional interest in everything. He knew the French Cavalry School, the Cadre Noir, very well, and was most enthusiastic over what he had just seen. He shook my hand and thanked me, making me once more conscious of the strong bonds forged by the true spirit of horsemanship.

Many famous politicians expressed a wish to see the Spanish Riding School, and it was not only interesting but often very enjoyable to talk with these men: the shy former French Premier, Robert Schumann, the Italian Foreign Minister, Guiseppe Pella, or the jovial and witty Dr Ludwig Erhard, who watched the Lipizzaner as intently with his intelligent eyes as he did the various problems of his own Ministry. Professor Carlo Schmid was just as interested, and many others enjoyed the white horses and were warm in their praise.

Once I was showing the horses in their stalls when the wife of the French Secretary of State, M. Maurice Faure, whispered to her neighbour as she caught sight of the one bay Lipizzaner stallion, Neapolitano Ancona, "Evidence of a *mésalliance!*" Of course I sprang at once to defend the reputation of this differently coloured horse, announcing that in his veins too ran the purest Lipizzaner blood.

The Ambassador of Nationalist China, Paonan Cheng, followed a performance in the Winter School with obvious admiration, saying to me as he left, "Death will not be difficult for me, for in my lifetime I have seen so many beautiful things, and what I have just witnessed surpasses them all!"

The wife of the Indian Ambassador to Warsaw, Mr Krishna Menon, said with great feeling, "I am quite convinced that these animals were ballet-dancers in a previous existence," whereupon Mrs Velodi, wife of the Indian Ambassador, interposed, "Oh, no! These horses will appear as ballet-dancers in their next life."

This gave me a glimpse of the hidden psyche of Asia.

Soldiers now, as during the War, came to the *alma mater* of horsemanship, in spite of the complete mechanization of the Army. Not only did every general staying in Vienna, from the United States, France, and England, take the opportunity of inspecting the Spanish Riding School, but the Soviet War Minister, Marshal Rodion Malinovsky, came to a performance with several generals, and was so enthusiastic that before he left he smilingly presented me with a large bronze figure of a rearing horse, saying, "As you only have white horses, I have brought you a black one from the Urals, and hope that it will bring you great happiness."

The Swedish Minister of Defence, Sven Andersson, said with deep sincerity after one performance, "I have heard a great deal about your school, and expected still more, but what I have seen has surpassed all my expectations. I congratulate you!"

The Bulgarian General Vladimir Stoytchev, a nephew of my much-respected General Pongràcz, and an old rival, wrote in the guest book after his first post-war visit to the Spanish Riding School: "After forty years found the same tradition, but in much greater perfection."

Most of the artists too visited the white horses, whether they had any connexion with these creatures or not. Professor Paul Hindemith wrote in the guest book: "Although I know nothing of horses, I surrendered in admiration and with keen enjoyment to this almost incomprehensible art-form."

The British conductor Sir Malcolm Sargent, after seeing the Lipizzaner at work, remarked, "I always thought I could ride, but now I see how little I really can." When I replied that in riding the recognition of one's limitations is a sure sign of ability, he went on: "You are quite right. It is just the same in music. Only the amateurs think they have mastered it thoroughly."

So they all came, the charming Vivien Leigh, who overwhelmed me with her excited superlatives of praise, the public idols Tyrone Power, Gary Cooper, Charles Laughton, Willy Birgel, and the rest—always with the same result; they flocked there for the pleasure of watching two creatures moving as one. The *Stuttgarter Zeitung* of July 18, 1956, reported:

> It is the same act as for more than two hundred years, the same *piaffes*, leaps, and figures as in the famous engravings. They are—or so it seems— the same horses and the same riders. The perfect form of a completely formal age is preserved here in the action of man and animal, just as enduringly as in music and architecture. Only the gallery changes. The farther the spectators stray from that form themselves, the greater is their stillness in its presence.

From the great bouquet of blossoming memories I shall pluck out several small flowers too, which gave me great pleasure in spite of their modesty, since they showed the popularity of the institution I directed.

In 1957 Baroness Maria Augusta Trapp told me that an assistant in a shop in the Stephensplatz had advised her to visit the Spanish Riding School, and added, "I go once a week to watch the morning rehearsal, and to a performance nearly every Sunday, for, you see, what others feel about concerts and the Opera I feel about the white horses of the Spanish Riding School."

Late one evening I was crossing the Josefsplatz with a friend from

England when a simply dressed man broke into our meditations saying, "Excuse me, but have you seen the Spanish Riding School yet?" and gave us detailed information about what was to be seen. My friend offered him a cigarette, which he refused.

"No, thank you, I only wanted to tell you about our Spanish Riding School, for we Austrians are very proud of it."

Recently I found two women in a crowded surgery at my doctor's grumbling about the long wait. When I was put at the head of the queue one of the women spoke to me after the receptionist had gone. I expected some unfriendly remark, but all she said was, "Excuse me, but are you the gentleman with the beautiful horses?" When I nodded she went on, "May I, as an ordinary Austrian woman, thank you from my heart in the name of your silent admirers for what you have done for our homeland. We are really very proud of you and your work."

The year 1960 brought along with its increasing number of visitors many personalities from all over the world, and a positive throng to the performances and morning rehearsals. A special red-letter day for the former Hofreitschule was the first performance before a sovereign during a State visit since the foundation of the Republic. The Shah of Persia, welcomed by the Federal President, Dr Schärf, came with a large retinue and sat in the first gallery of the Winter School, a place occupied only by prominent people specially invited, and followed the show, lasting nearly an hour, with obvious interest. At the party afterwards in the reception-rooms, and during his inspection of the stables, the Shah laid aside his customary reserve, and listened with smiling attention to some stories about the Lipizzaner, stroking a horse here and there, and asking me questions about schooling character, and customs. According to remarks made later by his entourage, the Spanish Riding School was the highlight of his full and splendid programme.

Sometimes I look up from reading the book of memories in which each page brings before my inner eye events from the most stimulating period of my life—pictures of indescribable joy and great success after hours of worry, and experiences that were often of far-reaching importance. I see around me the reception and work rooms that I have created, and my glance falls on Hamilton's colourful picture of the foundation of the Imperial Lipizza Stud in 1717 opposite my writing desk. Then I can almost imagine I am waking from a long and disturbing dream, for everything seems just as it was twenty years ago. The present fades; all storms that have raged round it with such destructive fury sink into oblivion and there is a feeling of timelessness: this can be felt by visitors too, as Baroness Trapp proved to me.

"Please do not take offence at what I am about to say. It is meant as a compliment. When you move about this Riding Hall or through these heavenly rooms I get a strong feeling that you have been working here for two hundred years, because you have kept the tradition and everything else about this old riding-hall so very much alive. One might almost think here that a time that was devoted to the mastering of every movement, to the symbol of controlled power in the highest degree, and the preservation of pure beauty, had stood still for centuries."

My most earnest wish and prayer is that in the future too this atmosphere may be preserved. If it is I shall have no anxiety about the survival of the oldest riding-school in the world.

CHAPTER 18

—◆◆◆◆—

The Great American Venture

The great interest shown throughout the world in the Spanish Riding School during the early years after their return from exile was by no means a flash in the pan. It increased year by year, until the school became one of Vienna's—one could say Europe's—most valuable treasures, for many tourists planned their trip to Vienna round this artistic institution, often their whole tour of Europe. Walt Disney, creator of wonderful nature films, also used the Lipizzaner as his subject, and his picture *The Miracle of the White Stallions* was a memorial to them and their miraculous rescue from the turmoil of the Second World War.

For some years the Austrian Government declined all invitations to foreign festivals on the grounds that the Spanish Riding School was one of the most important attractions for the tourist trade. However, when the Columbia Artists Management succeeded in planning a tour at such a high level—Mrs Kennedy undertook to be a patron, and kept her word even after the assassination of the President—and of such tremendous significance for Austria as the assembly of nations at the World Fair in New York the Austrian Government agreed to make an exception. After all, every country was making an effort to send its best to the gigantic exhibition.

The preparations for this grand tour were difficult and tedious, and there were innumerable problems never encountered before. The Spanish Riding School was to give its performances in eight eastern cities in the United States in vast halls, the smallest of which can accommodate 6000 spectators, and these two-hour performances were to be individual items, not part of a horse show, as had been the case on the school's earlier visits. The transport for our valuable Lipizzaner and all their equipment, their care and accommodation, also caused us many headaches. Columbia, one

288

of the best-known American agencies, had wide experience with international philharmonic orchestras, ballet companies, temperamental prima ballerinas, and hypersensitive tenors, but the requirements of the four-legged dancers were something quite new. Never before had they had to deal with artists who could not be accommodated simply by booking hotel rooms, but had to have hay, straw, and earth provided and boxes built.

Since a sea voyage would be too long and exhausting for the stallions I decided to have them sent by air. Friends of the American national team gave me some very valuable advice about this, for American show horses are almost invariably sent by air on long journeys. I was strongly advised to give the horses sedatives before the flight, but decided to trust to the intelligence and good training of my white stallions and only consented to their having one influenza injection, which my friend Cecil Ferguson had sent.

All these preparations, the checking of a thousand details, the many questions from Columbia that had to be answered in writing, made the months preceding our departure truly hectic. The work mounted up impossibly, and the difficulties seemed insurmountable. On March 24, 1964, with a sigh of relief, we climbed at last into the Pan Am plane bound for New York, to complete there the final preparations before the twenty-one horses and fifteen riders and grooms followed us on March 26. Friends and relatives, the American Military Attaché, and officials of Pan Am stood waving at the airport. The great venture had begun.

We touched down in Frankfurt and London, and then the wonderfully calm flight over the Atlantic gave us breathing-space to think over what was behind us and prepare for what lay ahead. All the same we were not prepared for the quite wonderful reception awaiting us at Kennedy Airport. A stewardess of Pan Am stood waiting at the gangway with a Customs officer, and led us straight past all the people waiting and took us through passport and Customs. Our friends waved a red-and-white flag vigorously from the balcony while we waited for our numerous pieces of luggage. One case after another appeared, but not the small red one, the most important of all, containing all the papers, correspondence, and plans for our tour. We waited and waited, our friends waved and waved, but no red case appeared. At last we gave up waiting, our friends stopped waving, and the long-delayed welcome took place.

Mr Judd, President of Columbia, presented my wife with a huge bouquet of red and white carnations, and Mr Jones and Mr Miles, who were to accompany us on our tour, were also there. After the photographers had finished and there had been a great deal of activity over the missing case we were able to take a well-earned rest, for we had been on the go for twenty-five hours since getting up in Vienna. We were still rather disturbed over the fate of our most vital piece of luggage, but next morning we heard that our red case had been traced to London, where it had been unloaded in error. The stone that fell from our hearts must have been at least the size of a skyscraper.

Even now we could not breathe quite freely until our Lipizzaner were actually on American soil. At 8 A.M. on March 27 we stood with beating hearts at Friendship Airport, Baltimore, where the first K.L.M. machine with twelve stallions on board was expected at 8.10. With us waited the Columbia people, including the head man, Mr Weinhold, friends from Washington, and a large crowd of horse-lovers, some of whom had come miles to see the arrival of the white stallions. We had not slept well the night before, for this was the first time in the long history of the Lipizzaner that, like Pegasus, they had flown in the skies. The hours passed, filled with discussion, interviews, and reports.

"My heart is with my horses," I excused myself to the many reporters who besieged me with a thousand questions.

And then it was over. At last, at 2 P.M., the first plane taxied in, came to a halt at the appointed place, and I was allowed to go to my charges.

"They have been absolutely quiet," the captain of the K.L.M. machine assured me. He had long since piloted his thousandth horse transport. "With such passengers I would be quite happy to fly round the world."

All the same we were relieved that the horses had arrived safely, but before they could be brought out there were tedious official medical examinations to be gone through, blood tests to be made, and the horses' hooves disinfected. Before the first stallion finally set foot on American soil my poor darlings had been cooped up in their narrow boxes for fully twenty-two hours. Siglavy Morella came down the ramp first, let out a mighty neigh of greeting, and the reporters hastily switched on their tape recorders.

After prolonged negotiations the veterinary surgeon gave grudging permission for the horses to be walked round the airfield to stretch their legs after the long flight. He had once had an unfortunate experience when a steer had broken loose and made the entire airport unsafe. No planes had been able to land for the next two hours, until finally a man arrived and raised the siege by shooting the freedom-loving animal. My gallant horses, on the other hand, demonstrated their good upbringing when, three hours after the first plane, the second landed safely with nine horses on board and taxied with roaring engines up to the half-unloaded plane. They took no notice at all, as if an airfield were the most familiar place in the world.

All of them had stood up very well to the great adventure of flying for the first time except the youngest, a four-year-old and still coal-black. He stood apathetically in his box with a raging temperature and hanging head. "Shipping fever," said the vet, prescribed the necessary medicines, and ordered him to be taken out and isolated from the others.

When the Customs official walked up to examine the brands on the horses I discovered that he had been a Customs sergeant in General Patton's army. He asked whether there was a single horse left of those that he had led back in 1945 on General Patton's orders. Now the formalities were completed in an incredibly short time, and as we parted he handed me a four-leaved clover carefully wrapped in Cellophane.

"I carry it for luck," he said. "Now let it work for the Lipizzaner."

It was a brilliant day with an icy wind whipping across the airfield, but our friends and the crowds of horse-lovers stuck it out with us until the very last horse had been loaded into the waiting horse-vans. It was 9 in the evening by the time the procession moved off in the direction of Potomac and we had a chance to warm ourselves up with a hot meal.

The white horses' first destination was Potomac Horse Center, a private riding-school near Washington. Here the horses were to rest after the journey and become acclimatized, for they had the same difficulties as the humans in getting used to the difference in time, and the weather was particularly bad. It snowed and rained, and the cold made the animals listless and tired, so that it was four days before we could start work at all.

The news of the white stallions' arrival spread like wildfire, and the horse-lovers began to stream in. There were colossal traffic jams on the narrow roads, and every day literally thousands of people had to turn back, unable to get in. Although training did not begin until 8 A.M., by 6 o'clock or even earlier there were a good many spectators sitting on the roof covering the stands. Not only did these visitors show a great love of horses, but a remarkable understanding and keen observation. They noticed the smallest trifle, soon recognizing the individual horses and riders. They were also very considerate and fair, for when the owner of the school, Mr Harting, urged over a loudspeaker that those who had been watching for a long time should make room for other horse-lovers, a good many well-trained visitors actually got up, reluctantly of course, to let later arrivals enjoy a glimpse of the white stallions.

After a week of rest and training we set off once more—for Philadelphia. Twenty-two horses—two American Morgan horses had joined our white Lipizzaner, loaned by my friend Cecil Ferguson to open the performance—the extensive equipment, saddles and tack, clothes and uniforms, as well as fifteen riders and grooms, were put into one truck, three horse transporters, and a station wagon. The State Police escorted the motorcade safely over the main highways and then handed over at the city boundary to the City Police, who, to the great delight of the passengers, piloted it with screaming sirens through the red lights to the Stadium, waving the city traffic to one side.

Our first performances were to be given in Philadelphia, and the stadium had been sold out for weeks beforehand. But the problems seemed insoluble, the biggest of all being the floor. The cement surface had to be covered with six inches of earth with sawdust on top to give the necessary spring for the horses' movements. The weeks of rain had made the earth wet and muddy, and the ground was heavy and rutted like a field. Ploughs, harrows, and rollers rendered it more or less usable, but it was appallingly tiring for the horses throughout our stay. Another worry was the floodlighting, which was quite new to the stallions. They snorted with fear at their own sharply defined shadows, at the movements of the public (unfortunately seated much too close), which suddenly showed up in the ring of light. Our darlings needed all their patience to conquer their fear even partially. In the end they grew accustomed to these things and looked even more beautiful than usual in the stream of light. The delicate blue and brilliant yellow looked even clearer, and the gold borders and metal-work sparkled in the limelight.

Training the horses was particularly difficult, as we had only a very limited space at our disposal. Still worse, the horses had to enter the arena through a public door, and in the regrettably small stalls the air was close and oppressive, in spite of the rain. During our entire stay in Philadelphia our good angel was Miss Maudie Warfel of *Mon ami le cheval*. She supported us untiringly with advice and practical help, procured ventilation for the stalls, and worked far into the night opening bales of straw, and set to work wherever we were short-handed. She took an even greater interest in our fortunes, and when she came to one of our performances in New York we were really sorry to say good-bye to this true friend of the white horses.

Even before I left Vienna I had been worried about the huge halls built for hockey and big spectacles, where the skill of our stallions must surely look strange and unreal. In Vienna the performance takes place against the background of the unique riding-hall with its own feeling and atmosphere. To create this atmosphere and to bring home to the public an art often strange to them, I had built up a programme in which the history of riding in general, and of the Spanish Riding School in particular, was portrayed in living pictures. Introduced and announced by loudspeaker, Prince Eugène in purple silk and princely armour appeared in a ring of light, his horse executing the *levade*. The philosopher and Commander-in-Chief Xenophon, ancient Greek author of the first known book on riding, made a circuit in the *passage*, a brilliant red drapery fastened to his golden breast-plate fluttering round him. From his golden helm waved a long red plume. Next, in green and brown, came Grisone, master of the Renaissance, riding one of the Morgan horses; this always caused a great stir. The great French riding-masters of the seventeenth and eighteenth centuries, Pluvinel and Guérinière—the latter also on a Morgan horse, with a white plume in his large hat and wearing a full-bottomed wig—showed their horses in the *piaffe*, in the pillars, and in 'shoulder in.' Last of all came the *Bereiter* of the Spanish Riding School, where for the last four hundred years the noble art of horsemanship has been cultivated and preserved.

The storm of the revolution tore away the Habsburg flags, and to loud applause the microphone described the salvation of the Lipizzaner by General Patton. As a mark of gratitude the white stallions then paraded, thus introducing themselves to the public before the real performance began. "That's a proper history lesson," a young American lady said to me later with shining eyes. The performance itself followed its usual course, but, in place of the item given by the young stallions, two four-year-olds demonstrated exercises on the lunging rein to show the very beginning of the lengthy training. Then followed the *Pas de Trois*, handling work, work on long reins, my solo with Maestoso Mercurio, the "Airs above the Ground," and the traditional finale: the big school quadrille in red gala uniform.

Columbia had brightened up the hall with Austrian flags and flowers, and two delicate glittering white lustres recalled the costly crystal chandeliers in the Spanish Riding School in Vienna.

In the interval of this memorable first performance of our grand tour the white horses were officially welcomed by the Austrian Consul, Hubert Earle, who presented me with a commendation on behalf of the Mayor of Philadelphia. Then some of General Patton's officers who had brought back the stud were formally greeted, and Colonel Reed, who had commanded this operation, stood before me once more after nineteen years. It was a supreme moment to see the man who in the fateful days of spring 1945 had shown me such friendship. He too was deeply moved, and the enthusiasm of the crowd knew no bounds when we forgot all about protocol and hugged each other.

This first performance broke the spell. The stallions had found their spiritual balance once more and carried out their tasks with dash and pleasure, fired by all the applause. All those responsible for the success of the show carried out their duties faithfully. The spotlights followed with precision the movements of the four-legged dancers, and Maestro Popper kept the orchestra to their rhythm. With each evening the performances became more brilliant, and public enthusiasm grew in proportion; there were telephone calls of thanks and congratulation from unknown people, who all begged me to come back again. After every performance crowds of spectators waited by the exit for up to an hour to have their programmes, books, and pictures autographed. After the Sunday afternoon performance a little girl was brought to me. Her large, dark, rather melancholy eyes shining, she offered me a little porcelain horse from her precious collection. A great weight now fell from me, for I knew that our tour would be a success.

Our première in Washington was a great social occasion, attended by

Mrs Johnson, members of the Government, and almost the entire Diplomatic Corps. Many old friends were good enough to make long journeys to be present. Mrs Kennedy came to the afternoon performance with her small daughter, and afterwards visited the stalls, where little Caroline made a fuss of the horses and gave them carrots and sugar without a trace of fear. Mrs Kennedy recalled with pleasure details of the programme she had seen in Vienna in 1961 when the late President had a meeting with Khrushchev, and for a moment or two her large dark eyes lit up. The Press devoted a great deal of space to us, and one leading Washington paper published a front-page article on the white stallions—an unprecedented honour for an artistic show.

A shadow was cast over our happiness when the young stallion that had arrived at Friendship Airport with a temperature, and had been left behind under medical care in Potomac Horse Center, died of pneumonia. Although this was not discovered until the post-mortem, the poor fellow had been suffering from abscesses on the lung. It said much for the understanding of my American friends that they did not tell me this sad news until after the performance, so as not to upset me or spoil my pleasure in our success.

A flood of letters began to break over my head, swelling more and more from city to city, and with all the will in the world I could not stem it. I found one note from an eight-year-old pushed under my door in the Boston hotel, saying, "I came specially to Boston to see your horses. By the way—my room is not far from yours!"

Boston proved a specially big surprise. "Don't be disappointed by Boston after your reception in Philadelphia and Washington," Bill Judd had been careful to warn me. "The Bostonians are very reserved, and anyway this is not horse country like Maryland and Virginia." But the Boston Garden, packed every evening, proved that the dancing white horses from Vienna could whip up the cool people of Boston too. There was, indeed, a particularly warm and happy atmosphere in the vast hall, which seats 14,000. The first evening many of the tickets were bought on behalf of the International Friendship League, whose aim is to bring the youth of the different nations closer together. A really beautiful "Paul Revere" bowl will always remind me of this friendly association.

It was an unforgettable day, and of great spiritual significance to me, when I laid a wreath in the American and Austrian colours at the statue of General Patton, and Miss Totten, his enchanting young granddaughter, took us through the magnificent country house in Hamilton where trophies and mementoes in every room bore witness to the life and work of this great army commander, to whose sympathy and prompt action the Spanish Riding School has such cause to be eternally grateful.

The best indication of the wide appeal of our performances was that I could barely set foot in the street without being addressed. Society ladies came up to me and expressed their thanks for the unique experience of an evening with the white stallions; a passing car stopped suddenly and a whole family surrounded me, begging for autographs; and a car-park attendant waved away a tip most emphatically.

"No, thanks. I saw you ride yesterday, and you gave me such pleasure it's a great honour to help you!"

Our next stop was Chicago, which back in 1961 had approached the Spanish Riding School to make a festival tour and expressed great disappointment at being refused. The horse transporter, however, could not make the thousand-mile trip in less than two days, so we broke the journey in Buffalo. Here a riding-school put up the stallions, and when we arrived, there was already a crowd awaiting the white princes, intently watching the unloading and the final departure of the animals into the school. The next day—or, rather, the next evening—brought us the most anxious hours of the whole tour. Because transport trucks move more slowly than private cars we had, as usual, gone ahead of our procession, and now waited in Chicago for the horses to arrive. The hours passed, we grew more and more worried, especially when we heard that two of the reserve drivers had gone back to New Jersey, and the quite considerable distance had to be driven by only one man per transporter. There was no information from the Chicago City Police, and our motorcade was missing. It was a long and anxious night, until the three transporters finally arrived at half-past four in the morning. Not only had the escort of State Police considered their day's work finished and abandoned the column, but the lights of one of the heavy trucks had failed. This meant driving close behind one of the others, which had naturally slowed things up considerably. Then came the dreaded traffic cops, who wanted to arrest the driver on the spot. There was a good deal of argument, and it was not until the men protested about their valuable freight that they were let off with a forty-dollar fine. The horses had stood up to the adventure amazingly well, but Mr Miles resolved after that fearful night that in future he would follow the transporters himself and not let them out of his sight, and the reserve drivers were promptly ordered back.

Despite this unfortunate beginning our appearance in Chicago was a colossal success. The vast stadium, seating 18,000 and the biggest in the United States, filled us with astonishment. None the less the white dancers managed to fill it with their magic and skill. Here too the performances were big social occasions, and countless receptions, gala dinners, and cocktail parties were given in our honour. Before nearly three hundred guests of the Town and Country Equestrian Association, State Auditor Michael J. Howlett presented me, in the name of the Governor of Illinois, with a scroll giving me the freedom of this State, and I was made a Kentucky

Colonel, my wife receiving a vast bouquet of red roses with the words, "Behind every important man there is an important woman."

In spite of his over-full programme the Mayor received me to present officially the huge medal of the Freedom of the City of Chicago. As a thank-offering that the wish of the second largest city of the U.S.A.—to see the Lipizzaner there—had been fulfilled, the four days of our stay were declared Vienna and the Spanish Riding School Days.

Never before, we were assured by our envoy Dr Platzer, had an Austrian cultural or sporting event had such a resounding success in Chicago, or in any other city of North America, and this was borne out by the Press. The feared and famous Claudia Cassidy praised the Lipizzaner to the skies, and the other reviewers were unanimous in their enthusiasm for the unique skill of the dancing white stallions. The horses' fame spread far beyond Chicago through all the States, and there were notices in even the most remote town newspapers.

When we went back one afternoon to our hotel we found two small children, who had been waiting for a long time outside our door. While they were getting their autographs their father appeared, delighted that his children's greatest wish had been realized. He gave us his own impressions of the unforgettable evening until a quite distracted mother rang up to find out where the family could be, as the plane for New Orleans was due to leave in half an hour!

Many letters spoke of the long journeys and trouble visitors had taken to see the dancing white horses. One young secretary mentioned her nine-hour trip in a letter she wrote on her way home only an hour after the performance. One party had come from Colorado—a thousand miles—and there were devotees of the noble art of horsemanship from St Louis and San Francisco. But the longest journey of all was by charter flight from Hawaii to Chicago. The postman who brought in our enormous postbag every morning was Hungarian, and he spoke of the Lipizzaner with tears in his eyes.

Our success was so wonderful and so stimulating, the receptions and gala suppers were so interesting, that, although I was greatly honoured, I found it a great strain. After the performances, in which I rode four horses and for which I was entirely responsible, I often had to stand for hours in the receiving line shaking literally hundreds of hands. The enthusiasts talked to me, asking me for details of the horses' training, the history of the Spanish Riding School, and of our tour. Often there was a reunion after many years with friends who had waited patiently for this moment, but in the hubbub I could not give them as much attention as I should have liked. There were endless photographs, so I did not manage to get a meal, and the waiter often took away my plate with the food on it hardly touched.

Inevitably all this strain took its toll. The first morning in Detroit I woke with swollen cheeks and an abscess on my upper lip. Bill Judd was deeply concerned, and his friend Nick Londes, the manager of the Olympia Stadium, drove us at once to the Henry Ford Hospital. The doctors there are not only distinguished and exceedingly friendly, but very thorough as well, so I spent several hours daily at the hospital, and although I felt wretched, with their help I was able to appear at the première, watched by the doctors treating me and by the President of the hospital. As soon as I was better they told me that things had looked pretty serious at first. Unfortunately this meant that I saw no more of Detroit than the Henry Ford Hospital, but, anyway, it was well worth seeing!

The big surprise in Detroit was the green sawdust. Nick Londes had seen us in Philadelphia and had come home full of the idea that the horses would look beautiful on green sawdust, but it was not so easy to realize his dream. The sawdust had to be spread by the sackful and then sprayed with edible colouring to prevent any risk to the horses. The results were stunning; against the illuminated green background the white stallions looked like precious porcelain figures that had suddenly sprung to life at a magician's command. Every leg movement was clearly visible, and the horses moved spiritedly as if the green floor under them reminded them of their youth in the mountain pastures.

Nick Londes took a very personal interest in the Spanish Riding School and everything connected with it. In addition to taking me to hospital himself every day with the devotion of a guardian angel, he saw to it that the stallions were marvellously housed in the perfectly maintained and well-run stadium. They had air and space, and their roomy boxes had been given a special coat of white paint.

The Press carried daily news, interviews, and pictures; there was a feature on the care and saddling of horses, while a hard-bitten sports editor waxed lyrical describing the love which alone achieved the complete harmony between horse and rider that he had seen in my solo with Maestoso Mercurio. And even in Toronto there were articles filling several columns, one actually in the form of a poem describing in flowery language the dance of the white horses.

The Mayor of Toronto with all his City Council welcomed us, and the Austrian Ambassador, Dr Leitner, made a sincere speech of thanks for our friendly reception. As the stadium was called Maple Leaf Garden, the manager gave my wife a farewell present of a gold brooch shaped like a maple leaf; it was engraved with the dates of our performances.

We were astonished at the enormous number of Europeans, Austrians in particular, who sat with tears in their eyes enjoying this glimpse of the native land they had never forgotten, and taking the memory home with them to treasure. A Swiss girl who had already written to me in Vienna was very disappointed not to be able to get through the crowd to my dressing-room, and called me at my hotel late that night to say that she had made a thousand-mile flight to speak to me, and her only chance had now gone for ever.

Finally my wife promised to let her know what time we were leaving next morning, and there she was, punctually at seven, in front of our hotel waiting to shake hands, thank us extravagantly, and wave good-bye. We heard from some spectators that they had already tried to see us in Philadelphia, Boston, and Chicago, and only managed to get tickets in Toronto.

In the middle of May we arrived in New York, sweltering in a sudden heatwave. After our exciting and steadily mounting success, reports preceding us to every fresh city, I entered Madison Square Garden wondering whether the magic of the dancing white horses would be enough for the critical New Yorkers, and whether our performance would attract the same attentive audiences as in 1950.

Without any doubt at all, New York proved to be the zenith of our tour. The World Fair had brought people from every country to this gigantic city. Moreover, our première was to take place on Austria Day, and there was to be an official presentation.

A crowd of people in evening dress packed the vast stadium to the roof. Never, so experts assured me, had Madison Square Garden been sold out for any sporting event connected with horses. But on this evening, as also on the following one, every single seat was taken, even those with a very restricted view.

"You looked very small," one young girl wrote, "and I could not see more than a third of what was going on in the ring, but I loved every minute of it."

This first evening was more than usually brilliant, for there was a formal presentation of a five-year-old stallion to the American Army in recognition of its invaluable help in making possible the continuance of the Spanish Riding School at the end of the Second World War. High officials, the Austrian Ambassador, and the Austrian Military Attaché attended the ceremony, at which the national anthems of both countries were played. I had ridden the young stallion into the ring, and, to symbolize the handing over, an American officer then mounted and rode him out to a standing ovation. A representative of the Mayor of New York presented me with an award that my friends told me was a very great honour and very seldom bestowed. The evening festivities ended with a gala supper, at which I could not appear until an hour after it had started because of the crowd of autograph-hunters outside the exit of Madison Square Garden. Small children gave me touching drawings of white horses, with woolly tails stuck on, executing their *levades* in a meadow made of tufts of green woollen grass.

Many distinguished visitors attended the performances. The Duke and Duchess of Windsor were at the first night, as was Elizabeth Arden, who later gave a small and enjoyable lunch party for my wife and myself. Although he is allergic to horses, and tears poured down his cheeks, the former Vice-President Richard Nixon waited for me with good-humoured patience to thank the riding-school, congratulate me, and ask in slightly injured tones why the western side of the United States was being so neglected.

"The people of San Francisco and Los Angeles are crazy to see the white stallions," he assured me. "The West is the real horse country. . . ."

The members of the Columbia staff, with whom our long business relationship had blossomed into a most agreeable friendship, once again spared no expense in the matter of decoration, or in spoiling us and the horses, who had roomy, airy stalls, fresh red and white carnations every day, and bouquets of flowers in the space between the boxes.

One evening the man whose job it was to pull up the curtain at the end of the performance happened to be talking to someone. Mr Miles, who was responsible for giving the signal, was also chatting, so at the end of my solo I rode towards the closed exit. At the last moment Mr Miles saw me, snatched back the red and white curtain, but it fell back over Maestoso Mercurio's head, then rose again to let us through. I was really annoyed, and the remorseful Mr Miles kept out of my way for the rest of the evening, but the next day, when I had completely forgotten the incident, I found a white orchid in my dressing-room.

"To Mercurio—for performing heroically beyond duty and beyond that d——d red curtain."

All who had had a hand in the success of our tour, including the grooms and lighting men, were invited to a huge farewell party given for us by Columbia. It was a wonderful end to our New York visit, a fitting celebration of our weeks of collaboration, shared troubles and joys, stage-fright, and the ever-growing success that had brought us all so close. Each was aware of his individual responsibility and spoke proudly of the triumphs of "our riding-school."

"Collaboration has turned into friendship," I said in thanking the Presidents of Columbia. "You were not only our managers, you were our friends."

Our last days in New York would have been marvellous, especially as at the final performance the New York Philharmonic Orchestra, 106 strong, accompanied the dance of the white stallions in perfect harmony, if only I had not felt so ill. An abscess in my ear, fever and leaden weariness, and a painful dry cough made riding painful on that final evening. Instead of going on to Montreal after a day's rest I had to stay in bed, worrying all the time as to whether I should be fit to take part in the last four performances of our tour. George Jacobson kept telephoning desperately from Montreal. For the day of the première he had invited two hundred and fifty eminent people, including the Governor-General, and at least twenty-seven ambassadors and envoys to a gala lunch. So I dragged myself out of bed and flew there in the morning. It was a hectic day, involving five changes of clothes for me. During the meal George Jacobson, as President of the Canadian Horse Shows Association, presented me with a gold medal decorated with a maple leaf for outstanding services to riding. This ceremony was transmitted to Europe by Telstar.

Before the opening I had to ride my horses, which had been led for the last four days, and throughout the evening I was aware of looks of concern from my wife and Bill Judd as they followed every movement. Although fortunately I felt better, I was sincerely thankful when the kindly Mayor of Montreal whispered to me at the reception afterwards that he would give me time to greet all my friends and then take me back before the supper began.

The Soviet Ambassador, one of the twenty-seven who had attended the première, listened smiling as his wife congratulated me fervently and added, "You and your Lipizzaner are really the best Austrian envoys!"

There was a feeling of melancholy about our time in Montreal, for the moment of departure was approaching inexorably. It was therefore all the more gratifying that the Spanish Riding School succeeded in charming the public here as well. The manager of the Forum, which was sold out for every performance, ruefully admitted his mistake.

"Montreal is a hockey city," he had explained months earlier. "The white stallions of Vienna will get one good audience at the most, and then the stadium will be only half full!"

His conversion was so complete that he would have liked to extend the performances to the end of the week. Columbia spoiled us all, showing their friendship in a hundred ingenious ways. The stallions had the best boxes of the entire tour, painted white and very roomy, in a huge light room. A big party was given for the riders in one of the club houses, and the young ladies of Montreal were invited. Our friend Bill kept on saying how wonderfully smooth and without unpleasantness our collaboration had been.

"The artists we engage will have a hard time from now on," he wrote me later in Vienna. "The Spanish Riding School has spoiled us thoroughly with its punctuality and reliability, not to mention its devotion to work and determination to succeed."

On June 5, 1964, we once again spent the whole day at the airport, loading the stallions into the same K.L.M. planes that had brought them ten weeks earlier to Friendship Airport in Baltimore. But how many excitements, problems, and triumphs we had experienced in the interval!

As usual, there was a huge crowd, planes taking off and landing incessantly, jets and four-engined monsters, and strange-looking water-planes and little private machines. Our splendid Lipizzaner took not the slightest notice of the deafening din, but walked on board as if they had been travelling by air all their lives. They found a bundle of hay in their boxes, intended for the same purpose as sweets or gum for the human passengers: to reduce the pressure on the eardrums by chewing.

Before the planes took off I had a chance to read to the riders and grooms the telegram that our Federal Minister, Dr Schleinzer, had sent to all of us: "My heartiest congratulations on the wonderful success of the Spanish Riding School. . . . Austria will be delighted to see its white ambassadors back in Vienna. . . ."

Our farewell was an emotional one. We shook hands again and again with Bill Judd and Mr Miles, saying repeatedly how wonderful these weeks together had been, and how sad it was that it was all over. As the plane rose into the air my wife and I looked down with the feeling that we had left some true friends on the American continent.

We had an interesting experience on the way home. In Zurich we were invited into the cockpit to complete the flight to Vienna in the narrow compartment filled with complicated instruments. Radio contact was made with one of the two K.L.M. planes which, although it had started hours earlier, was only due to land one hour after our own arrival in Vienna. I was relieved to hear from Oberbereiter Irbinger that everything was fine, and that my charges were quite quiet and well-behaved. I was very much struck by the tremendous contrast between the roaring jets, this conversation high in the air—indeed, the whole flight—and the centuries-old art that the Spanish Riding School represents!

Our arrival in Vienna was sensational. Officials from my own ministry, radio reporters, television and newsreel men, and relatives awaited us, not forgetting my dachshund Strolchi, who greeted me with joyous whimpers and yaps and would not stop licking me. The Viennese gave "their Lipizzaner" a joyful greeting when the latter landed in good order and started to graze eagerly on a stretch of meadow at the edge of the airfield. We were home again.

Reviewing the tour, I was able to give the assurance at a large Press conference that the stallions had stood up not only to the flight, but to the many long journeys between cities, the changes of climate and surroundings, and, above all, the daily performances, without any ill-effects. One stallion had fallen out for two days, and another for three with slight colds; otherwise, in spite of all the prophecies, the horses had kept in excellent health. Yet another proof of the strength and sturdiness of this ancient race.

I was glad to have an opportunity of paying tribute to the keen co-operation of all the riders. Just before our grand tour the Spanish Riding

School had been in serious difficulties. One young and very talented rider had been killed in a motor accident, and another seriously injured. Only by each man's determination to do his utmost had it been possible to bring the school up to the necessary standard.

But there was little time for recuperation, for a few days after our return the public performances recommenced with a special show (like the many charity evenings in the U.S.A.) for physically handicapped children, who followed the dancing white horses with shining eyes.

The *Christian Science Monitor* in its issue of April 30 had said:

> Pegasus in all his glory had only two things the Lipizzaners don't have. Wings . . . And even without them these magnificent steeds of the Spanish Riding School are almost airborne. . . .
>
> The Lipizzaners put on neither a circus nor a rodeo. . . . The horses take an obvious pride and joy in their accomplishments. Here is a heartwarming display of courage, patience, care, rhythm, poise, balance and especially love. . . .
>
> Perhaps the most impressive display of dressage was turned in by Colonel Podhajsky astride Maestoso Mercurio. Since the signals from rider to horse were imperceptible, one had the sensation that the Colonel and Mercurio had achieved a mental union. There was a touching sense of mutual respect. The result was incredibly beautiful. . . .

It was a great relief to me that the big gamble had paid off better and better as the tour progressed, the countless fan letters assuring me of the pleasure given by the artistry and magic of the dancing white horses, and the close attention paid to them.

The letter I treasure most came from a lady in Chicago:

> The Lipizzaners have given me back my faith in mankind. They have proved that the masses are not interested only in boxing and singers with waggling hips and uncut hair, but that humanity yearns for the genuine, the noble and the beautiful and is still capable of recognising true art.